The Prehistory of Gold Butte

NUMBER 127 • 2013

The Prehistory of Gold Butte

A Virgin River Hinterland, Clark County, Nevada

Kelly McGuire, William Hildebrandt,
Amy Gilreath, Jerome King, and John Berg

THE UNIVERSITY OF UTAH ANTHROPOLOGICAL PAPERS
THE UNIVERSITY OF UTAH PRESS
Salt Lake City

The Defiance House Man colophon is a registered trademark of
the University of Utah Press. It is based on a four-foot-tall Ancient
Puebloan pictograph (late PIII) near Glen Canyon, Utah.

18 17 16 15 14   1 2 3 4 5

LIBRARY OF CONGRESS CATALOGING-IN-PUBLICATION DATA

McGuire, Kelly R.
    The prehistory of Gold Butte : a virgin river hinterland, Clark County, Nevada / Kelly
McGuire, William Hildebrandt, Amy Gilreath, Jerome King, and John Berg.
        pages cm.—(The University of Utah anthropological papers ; number 127)
    Includes bibliographical references and index.
    ISBN 978-1-60781-305-7 (pbk. : alk. paper)—ISBN 978-1-60781-306-4 (ebook)
1. Indians of North America—Nevada—Clark County—Antiquities. 2. Excavations
(Archaeology)—Nevada—Clark County. 3. Clark County (Nev.)—Antiquities. I. Title.
    E78.N4M35 2013
    979.3'13—dc23
                                                        2013021893

Contents

Figures

Tables

Preface

This book represents the final research report for prehistoric cultural resource investigations within the Gold Butte study area. The study area encompasses 364,116 acres in the northeast corner of Clark County, Nevada, abutting the state of Arizona, south of Mesquite, Nevada. Bounded by the Virgin River to the north and west and the Colorado River to the south, this region manifests at least 12,000 years of continuous human use, including the westernmost expansion of the ancestral Puebloans from their core southwestern territories at about AD 800 to 1250. The study area itself, however, is located in a desert hinterland to the east of Puebloan settlements situated along the Virgin and Muddy river corridors. The role of this hinterland with regard to the land-use practices of these agriculturally oriented communities is a major research theme throughout this book. The study area also appears to have been a crossroads for later-dating populations, including the Patayan and ultimately the Southern Paiute, after the regional collapse of Puebloan settlements at approximately AD 1250.

Not surprisingly, the study area exhibits a heterogeneous archaeological record replete with multiple ceramic wares, spectacular examples of both Great Basin and Southwestern rock art traditions, higher-elevation pinyon camps, river-oriented pithouses, massive agave-roasting features, and the ever-ubiquitous flaked and ground stone scatter. These resources, however, are not spread evenly across this landscape but are concentrated in a few select localities. In fact, much of the study area appears to have either been neglected or at least underutilized for most of prehistory.

To unravel this story, we implemented a combined program of statistically representative (Class II) sample survey followed by nonrandom survey and, finally, limited test excavation at selected sites. The purpose of the first phase was to determine the density and distribution of key site, feature, and artifact classes with respect to a series of major landforms and habitat types. Nonrandom survey was primarily directed at expanding our sample of sites in the resource-rich areas. The goals of the limited excavation were to facilitate chronological ordering and the recovery of artifact and dietary remains from controlled contexts. This work was conducted by Far Western Anthropological Research Group over a two-year period between 2006 and 2008. All told, 31,196 acres were surveyed, resulting in the documentation of 341 sites with only a prehistoric component, another 36 sites with both prehistoric and historic components, and 387 isolated prehistoric finds. In addition, nearly 26 m^3 was hand-excavated at nine prehistoric sites.

This study was undertaken at the request of the Bureau of Land Management (BLM), Las Vegas Field Office, which manages Gold Butte. Gold Butte is a complex of management units that include Areas of Critical Environmental Concern (ACECs), existing Wilderness Areas, and Wilderness Study Areas. The investigation was prompted by growing concern on the part of the BLM, Native American tribal groups, and the local environmental community about an increase in recreational use at Gold Butte and the accelerating disturbance and destruction of cultural resources. The pages herein have their genesis in the BLM technical reports produced for this project; however, they have undergone substantial revision as part of the editorial review process. In addition, site location information, to the extent possible, has been either modified or redacted.

Acknowledgments

No project of this scale comes to successful completion without the dedicated work of dozens of individuals. We especially express our appreciation to those who served as field directors, crew chiefs, and technicians. Among the field supervisory staff were Mike Darcangelo, Tod Hildebrandt, Allen McCabe, Dustin McKenzie, Allika Ruby, Greg Seymour, and Amy Getanbee. Technicians included Will Barrick, Mark Darrow, Kish LaPierre, Mike Lenzi, Ed Mike, Ian Milliken, Melinda Pacheco Patrick, Ian Patrick, Brandon Patterson, Gene Romanski, Reese Abell, Herschel Beail, Kim Brineagar, Kate Clark, Jamie Dotey, Julie Garibaldi, Lindsay Hartman, Regina Nalton, Andrea (Coco) Nardin, Epie Pius, Naomi Scher, Mark Kile, Neil Puckett, Kyle Ross, Doug Smit, Devin Snyder, G. James West, Bob Whalley, and John Yelding-Sloan.

Organizations and individuals from southern Nevada volunteered their help with recording rock art and providing valuable information about this unique archaeological resource. We are grateful to members of the Cultural Resources Committee of the Moapa Band of Paiutes, Friends of Gold Butte (especially Nancy Hall), the Nevada Rock Art Foundation (especially Elaine Holmes, Anne McConnell, and George Phillips), and Nevada State Site Stewards (especially Roy and Betsy Miller).

Post–field data organization and analysis benefited mightily from the efforts of Tod Hildebrandt, Mike Lenzi, Allen McCabe, Melinda Pacheco Patrick, Ian Patrick, Brandon Patterson, Denise Ruzicka, and Sharlyn Street, as well as our lab director, Liz Honeysett, supported by Darren Andolina, Adelina Asan, Laura Brink, Aaron Buehring, Nora Cary, Kaely (Romney) Colligan, Julie Garibaldi, and Angela Tingey. Also critical to this effort was our GIS staff, headed by Paul Brandy and assisted by Melissa Cascella, Ryan Mitchell, Darla Rice, and Daniel Troglin.

Report production was under the supervision of Heather Baron and Tammara Norton, assisted by Larry Chiea, Wendy Masarweh, Kathleen Montgomery, Peter Mundwiller, Dave Nicholson, and Mike Pardee. We are particularly indebted to Heather Baron, who coordinated the editorial review process with the University of Utah Press. We also thank Rebecca Rauch, University of Utah Anthropological Papers series editor, for her patience and her steadfast support of this effort.

A number of individuals and consultants assisted us in technical studies, including Eric Wohlgemuth, Jamie Doety, and Bill Stillman (archaeobotanical analysis); Eva Jensen and Greg Seymour (ceramic studies); D. Craig Young (geomorphology); Tim Carpenter (ArcheoMetrics, Inc., obsidian hydration and faunal analyses); Richard Hughes (Geochemical Research Laboratory, XRF obsidian source analysis); Linda Scott Cummings (PaleoResearch Institute, pollen studies); and Ginny Bengsten (ethnographic studies).

We are grateful for our research collaboration with the Kimmel Center at the Weizmann Institute of Science, in Rehovot, Israel. Infrared spectroscopic analysis of materials from sites 26CK1991 and 26CK8047 was conducted by Steve Weiner, director, Kimmel Center for Archaeological Science; and analysis of radiocarbon samples from the overlapping agave ovens at 26CK1991 was provided by Elisabetta Boaretto, director, Radiocarbon Dating and Cosmogenic Isotopes Laboratory.

This work was sponsored by the Bureau of Land Management (BLM), Las Vegas Field Office, which manages the public lands that comprise most of Gold Butte. We thank current and former BLM archaeologists Susanne Rowe, Tom Burke, Stan Rolf, and Pat Barker for making this project possible and for allowing us the opportunity to be a part of this important study.

1 Introduction

Gold Butte lies at the crossroads of the Mojave Desert, Great Basin, and Colorado Plateau in southern Nevada, and its 12,000-year record of human occupation contains archaeological elements that can be traced to all three of these culture zones (Figure 1.1). This region is perhaps best known as the westernmost point of expansion of the ancestral Puebloans from their core territories in the Southwest from about AD 800 to 1250. Iconic sites such as Lost City, Main Ridge, and Mesa House, found along the bottomlands of the Virgin and Muddy Rivers, are emblematic of this Puebloan occupation. Gold Butte itself, however, is a desert hinterland situated immediately east of these more famous Puebloan settlements. The role of this hinterland with regard to the land-use practices of these riverine, agriculturally oriented communities, as well as to the lifeways of those peoples who occupied this region before and after the Basketmaker and Puebloan periods, is the central research theme of this book.

Noteworthy is the scale of this study, incorporating more than 31,000 acres of systematic survey crosscutting a variety of environmental zones—mostly barren hills, eroded fans, and narrow valleys, but also including the pinyon-cloaked Virgin Mountains as well as a series of spectacular red rock sandstone formations that served as a magnet for human occupation throughout the prehistoric sequence. Complementing this effort were archaeological excavations at nine prehistoric sites, including several rock shelters.

A total of 377 sites containing prehistoric components were recorded, including complex and simple habitations, flaked stone scatters, pottery and milling gear concentrations, agave ovens, pithouses, quarries and single reduction locations, and rock art sites—the latter including elements representative of Great Basin, Southwestern, and Lower Colorado River stylistic traditions. The survey and excavation programs also yielded nearly 300 projectile points, hydration and source data on 325 obsidian artifacts, 32 radiocarbon assays from mostly discrete feature contexts, more than 4,500 pottery sherds, and a variety of archaeobotancial and faunal remains.

These data are used to assemble a trans-Holocene picture of prehistoric land use and culture change in an area subject to at least four markedly different cultural occupations—Archaic, Basketmaker/Puebloan, Patayan, and Southern Paiute—in just the last several thousand years. A theoretical perspective rooted in human behavioral ecology and other foraging models is used to explain many of these changes.

We begin with a brief overview of the natural and cultural context of Gold Butte (Chapter 2). The former pays close attention to the geological, topographical, hydrological, and habitat communities that may have conditioned prehistoric lifeways and that form the basis of the environmental stratification used in our survey sample design. The cultural context includes a brief summary of regional prehistoric assemblages, lifeways, and land-use patterns organized by major time periods, as well as a review of the Numic-speaking Southern Paiute and the Yuman-speaking Hualapai, whose legacies are most relevant for the study area. Chapter 3 then provides a discussion of research issues, while Chapter 4 includes a review of the survey sample design and the

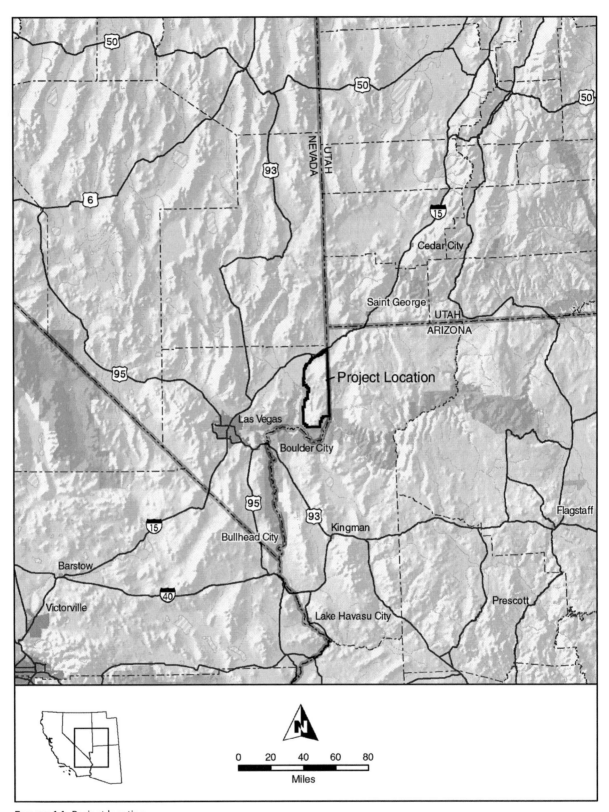

FIGURE 1.1. Project location.

results of the field inventory effort. These results are used to model the atemporal distribution of prehistoric cultural resources across major environmental zones; at this stage of the analysis, we do not attempt to delineate changes in land use over time.

In Chapter 5 we establish project-wide chronological controls. We review the results of the analyses for all chronological data sets recovered during survey and test excavation, including radiocarbon assays; time-sensitive projectile points; shell and glass beads; pottery wares associated with Basketmaker/Puebloan, Patayan, and Southern Paiute; and source-specific obsidian hydration.

With a basic understanding of the spatial distribution of prehistoric cultural resources and temporal parameters established, we present the results of the excavation program in Chapter 6. As previously indicated, this effort was directed at sites having good potential for datable materials, intact stratigraphy, and robust assemblages. According to the project's multiphased plan,

these in turn assist in the chronological ordering of site components documented during survey. This chapter is divided into a series of nine site reports and concludes with a synthetic discussion of the features and assemblages associated with each temporal period. In Chapter 7 our attention turns to the 42 rock art sites and the nearly 400 panels that represent perhaps Gold Butte's most spectacular prehistoric resource.

Chapter 8 integrates data derived from both the inventory and excavation programs in an attempt to place Gold Butte's archaeological record within a broader regional and interregional research context. This context, promulgated in the project research design, emphasizes shifts in technology, demography, land use, and symbolic expression that are observable across the Holocene but are most apparent in the last two millennia with the rise of agriculturally based food production. Finally, Chapter 9 summarizes our results and offers a concluding statement.

2 | Natural and Cultural Context

We begin this chapter with a review of the broad environmental characteristics of the Gold Butte study area, followed by a more expanded discussion of the developments throughout prehistory. The chapter concludes with a consideration of the Native American groups in the surrounding area and their ethnographic past.

ENVIRONMENTAL CONTEXT

The Gold Butte study area lies at the interface between the Mojave Desert and the Great Basin, and just west of the stair-stepped Colorado Plateau that constitutes the Arizona Strip. It is bounded on three sides by rivers, the Virgin River to the north and west and the Colorado River to the south, both now overlain by the Lake Mead (LAME) National Recreation Area (NRA). The north half of the study area is dominated by the Virgin Mountains, rising from 1,650 feet along the Virgin River floodplain to 7,700 feet at Virgin Peak. In contrast, the southern half of the study area is made up of a series of eroded, north-south-trending ridges, each two to three miles wide, which rise from about 2,500 feet on the narrow valley floors up to anywhere from 4,200 to 4,900 feet. Of the multiple springs that exist in the area, the handful with dependable flows tend to be on the slopes of the Virgin Mountains. Most of these have been improved either as livestock troughs and tanks or as guzzlers for large game and birds. Most springs, however, run only intermittently and wither quickly into the ground.

Climate

Temperature and precipitation records from selected weather stations in the region provide baseline data for the area's modern climate (Table 2.1). For a far more comprehensive consideration of microvariations in modern temperatures and a review of past climatic data sets, the reader should consult Rose's (1989) overview for the Arizona Strip.

As Figure 2.1a indicates, a strong unimodal pattern characterizes the region's temperature, regardless of elevation. December and January see the coolest average high temperatures, on the order of 60°F at the lower elevations (e.g., Beaver Dam and Temple Bar, AZ, and Mesquite and Overton, NV), and 50°F at high elevations (e.g., Tuweep, AZ). Temperatures gradually climb until July, when they top out at around 105–110°F (95°F at high elevations). They then begin a gradual descent through autumn and into winter.

In comparison to temperature, precipitation patterns are much more varied, with a bimodal annual pattern that is greatly influenced by elevation (Figure 2.1b). May and June are the driest months throughout the region. At high elevations (e.g., Mt. Trumbull and Tuweep, AZ) the late summer monsoonal weather pattern causes July and August to be the wettest months of the year. The monsoonal influence is much reduced at lower elevations, where it breaks the summer drought with a short-lived, secondary pulse that tapers off into September. Precipitation then slowly increases from fall into winter, with January through March being the wettest at low elevations, which receive roughly three-quarters to an inch of rainfall per month.

These climatic patterns underpin the growing season for the region (Figure 2.2). Now, as in the prehistoric past, agriculture is viable in the Saint George Basin, northeast of the Gold Butte study area, and in the Virgin River Basin adjacent to the west. If the summer monsoonal rains could be relied on year after year, dry-land

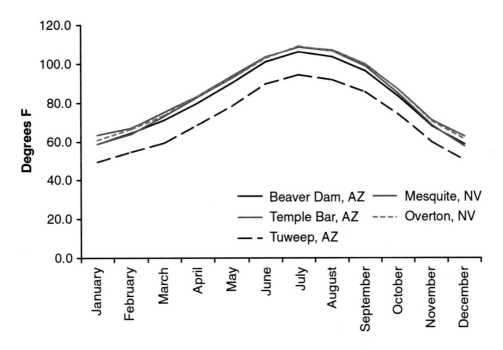

a. Average Maximum Temperatures in the Region.

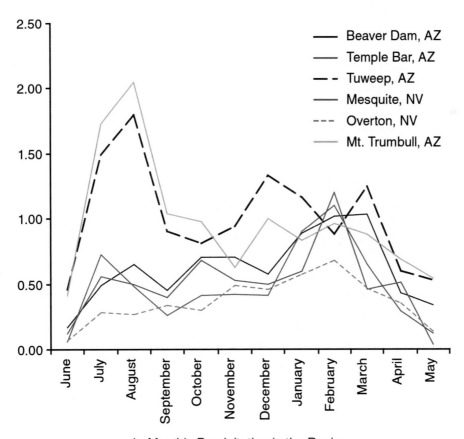

b. Monthly Precipitation in the Region.

FIGURE 2.1. Climatic information for the Gold Butte area.

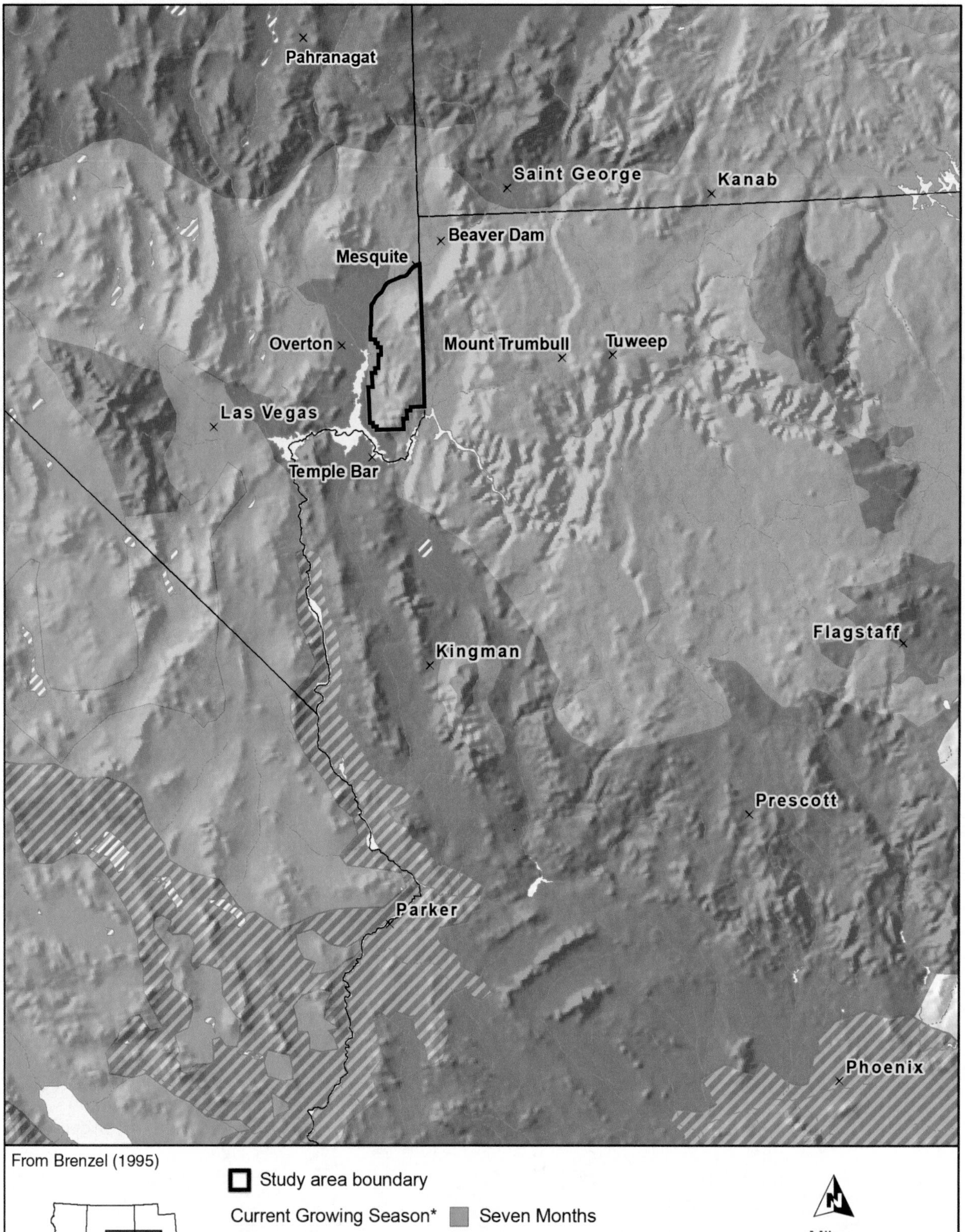
Pahranagat
Saint George
Kanab
Beaver Dam
Mesquite
Overton
Mount Trumbull
Tuweep
Las Vegas
Temple Bar
Kingman
Flagstaff
Prescott
Parker
Phoenix
From Brenzel (1995)
Study area boundary
Current Growing Season*
Four Months
Six Months
Seven Months
Eight Months
Eight Months (non-continuous)
* Sunset Western Garden Zones. Zones are based on winter minimum temperatures, summer maximum temperatures, length of growing season, humidity and rainfall patterns.
Miles
0 25 50
0 50 100
Kilometers

FIGURE 2.2. Current growing seasons in the Gold Butte region.

TABLE 2.1. Summary Temperature and Precipitation Data for the Gold Butte Area.

Location	Beaver Dam, AZ	Temple Bar, AZ	Tuweep, AZ	Mesquite, NV	Overton, NV	Mt. Trumbull, AZ
Data Set Interval	8/1/1956 12/31/2005	12/1/1987 12/30/2005	7/1/1948 12/9/1985	3/1/1956 12/31/2005	7/1/1948 12/31/2005	10/1/1919 12/31/1977
Temperature (°F)						
Jan	58.7	58.6	49.4	63.1	60.9	n.d.
Feb	64.4	63.7	54.7	66.8	66.2	n.d.
Mar	71.0	73.2	59.0	75.1	73.9	n.d.
Apr	79.6	82.7	68.5	83.3	83.2	n.d.
May	90.3	92.7	78.5	93.5	92.7	n.d.
Jun	100.7	103.4	89.5	103.3	103.1	n.d.
Jul	106.0	108.6	94.4	108.5	109.1	n.d.
Aug	103.5	106.7	91.5	107.1	106.8	n.d.
Sep	96.2	98.8	85.4	99.7	100.1	n.d.
Oct	83.4	85.2	74.3	87.2	87.0	n.d.
Nov	68.2	68.5	59.6	71.2	70.6	n.d.
Dec	58.9	57.6	50.5	62.9	61.3	n.d.
Average	81.7	83.3	71.3	85.1	84.6	n.d.
Precipitation (inches)						
Jan	0.89	0.90	1.16	0.60	0.57	0.83
Feb	1.02	1.10	0.88	1.20	0.68	0.96
Mar	1.03	0.65	1.25	0.46	0.47	0.88
Apr	0.43	0.29	0.60	0.51	0.35	0.69
May	0.34	0.12	0.53	0.04	0.14	0.54
Jun	0.17	0.06	0.46	0.12	0.07	0.41
Jul	0.49	0.73	1.49	0.56	0.28	1.73
Aug	0.65	0.48	1.80	0.50	0.27	2.05
Sep	0.45	0.26	0.90	0.40	0.34	1.04
Oct	0.70	0.41	0.81	0.68	0.30	0.98
Nov	0.70	0.42	0.94	0.53	0.49	0.63
Dec	0.57	0.41	1.33	0.50	0.46	1.00
Annual Average	7.44	5.81	12.13	6.09	4.42	11.73

Note: Data obtained from Western Regional Climate Center, http://www.wrcc.dri.edu.

farming on higher elevations across the Colorado Plateau would be a worthwhile practice. Prehistoric archaeological and environmental records provide ample evidence, however, of the fickle nature of the summer monsoon.

Geology and Landforms

The geologic foundation of the study area is a complex of uplifted ridges, eroded plutons, and broad alluvial fans. Bounded by the Grand Wash of northwestern Arizona and the Virgin River Valley, the study area extends from its Precambrian highpoint in the Virgin Mountains southward, through the tilted limestone, conglomerate, and sandstone beds that characterize the South Virgin Mountains (Longwell et al. 1965). The southern half of the study area falls within the South Virgin Mountains,

and the southern half of that unit rises as an uplifted and eroded pluton, reaching a highpoint at Jumbo Peak. These Precambrian, plutonic rocks, the oldest in Nevada, are evident as bulbous granitic outcrops. At Azure Ridge, on the eastern margin of the southern range, the granitic rocks are submerged by the sedimentary sequence that dominates the northern portion of the range. The South Virgin Mountains are split by the Gold Butte fault, overlain today by Cataract and Catclaw washes and shifting over to Spring Wash as one continues northeast. North of this fault, a series of intersecting, north-south-trending faults form the Tramp and Lime ridges, and near the north end of those ridges we find the colorful, uplifted Aztec sandstone monoliths.

The sedimentary sequence includes sandstones and limestone breccias and has members of the late

Permian beds in the Kaibab and Toroweap formations, the Triassic Moenkopi and Chinle formations, and the Jurassic Aztec sandstone (Longwell et al. 1965). Local structure and faulting expose gray limestone cliffs in the Kaibab/Toroweap formation, gray to yellow limestone and breccia in the Moenkopi and Chinle formations, and bright orange bluffs, canyons, hoodoos, and badlands in the red Aztec sandstone. Many rock shelters, rock art panels, and tanks or tenajas are associated with the Aztec outcrops. Opportunistic chert-nodule quarries are associated with eroded gravels in the Kaibab/Toroweap formation.

The topographic relief of faulted sedimentary rocks and ancient uplifted plutons provides ubiquitous erosional material for conglomerate deposits and alluvial aprons. Tertiary-age rocks of the Horse Spring and Muddy Creek formations, separated by erosional unconformities, are made of limestone breccias (broken and weathered rocks eroded from older units), siltstones and clays of internal basins, and occasional volcanic deposits of flows and tuffs (Longwell et al. 1965). The Horse Spring formation is faulted, like the older units it rests upon. The younger Muddy Creek formation is flat-lying and forms prominent valley-margin mesas of caliche-capped sandstones and limestone breccia. The only Tertiary-age volcanic rocks in the study area outcrop along the head of Quail Spring Wash along the Gold Butte fault.

Quaternary-age fans emanate from the uplifted mountain fronts to form broad pediments and bajadas. Most of the fan deposits are Pleistocene in age, the oldest fans fronting the north-facing uplift of the Virgin Mountains. These older, early Pleistocene fans are heavily dissected and tend to have well-developed soils and pavements on their interdrainage ridges. South of the Virgin Mountains the late Pleistocene fans are only moderately dissected but also show prominent pavement development along with strong carbonate cementation. On all flanks of Virgin Peak, though, the fans are occasionally cut by prominent dry washes that preserve Holocene depositional terraces. Prominent Holocene-age washes include Mud, Lime, Quail Spring, Horse Spring, and Garden, in addition to numerous minor ones that drain both sides of the study area. Though extensive, the Quaternary fans have not completely buried the mesas and high ridges of the Muddy Creek formation.

Aeolian deposits do not make up a significant part of the recent geological record. Quaternary-age processes were predominantly headward erosion and basin extension of alluvial deposits. However, the chemical and physical breakdown of the limestone breccias and sandstones, along with the sediments stored in the terraces of the dry washes, provided large amounts of material for aeolian reworking. Although rarely mapped, shallow dunes, typically stabilized by sparse vegetation, are common at the transitions between Mesozoic sedimentary rocks and more recent alluvial fans. These transitions form the upper boundary between valley-margin faulted outcrops and ridges.

Common landforms in the Gold Butte study area follow topographic transitions in a predictable downward sequence: from mountain ridges to colluvial slopes to faulted outcrops to alluvial fans and washes to fluvial drainages. In leeward or enclosed areas, aeolian deposits may cap landform transitions with shallow dunes and sand sheets. Although many other variables are undoubtedly involved (e.g., water, exposure), landforms play an important role in the prediction and understanding of archaeological site type, structure, chronology, and preservation.

Vegetation

The following review of the common plants and plant communities that blanket the study area relies heavily on Ellis et al. (1982). They identify and characterize eight plant communities, drawing from the classification of Bradley and Deacon (1967).

Desert Riparian Community

The desert riparian community is confined to narrow corridors along usually dry arroyos. Common trees are desert willow (*Chilopsis linearis*), catclaw (*Acacia greggii*), and mesquite (*Prosopis glandulosa* var. *torreyana*), and frequent understory shrubs include desert tomato (*Lycium andersonii*), cheeseweed (*Hymenoclea salsola*), pygmy-cedar (*Peucephyllum schottii*), ball sage (*Salvia dorrii*), and desert almond (*Prunus fasciculata*).

Stream Riparian Community

The stream riparian community is restricted to a narrow corridor along year-round flowing waterways. It covers the banks of the Virgin River, and in the Virgin Mountains this habitat exists at Cabin, Juanita, Whitney, and Big Springs. Associated trees include the introduced salt cedar (*Tamarix parviflora*) and indigenous mesquite, cottonwood (*Populus fremontii*), Arizona ash (*Fraxinus velutina*), willow (*Salix gooddingii*), and hackberry (*Celtis reticulata*), in addition to isolated stands of fan palm (*Washingtonia filifera*). Whether the latter were comparatively recently brought into the region or are remnant, ancient stands is hotly debated (Anderson 2005:162–165; Spencer 2005). Particularly noteworthy understory plants that were used by Native groups include arrow weed (*Pluchea sericea*), watercress (*Rorippa nasturtium-aquaticum*), rush (*Juncus* spp.), curly dock (*Rumex crispus*), and Arizona grape (*Vitis arizonica*).

Creosote Community

Like the Mojave Desert in general, huge tracts of the study area are blanketed by the monotonous creosote community. Growing primarily between 1,200 and 3,800 feet (370 and 1,158 m), the signature co-dominant desert shrubs of this community are creosote (*Larrea tridentata*) and bursage (*Ambrosia dumosa*), often found accompanied by dispersed Mojave yucca (*Yucca schidigera*). Associated shrubs and perennials include Mormon tea (*Ephedra nevadensis*), California buckwheat (*Eriogonum fasciculatum*), indigo bush (*Psorothamnus fremontii*), peppergrass (*Lepidium fremontii*), ratany (*Krameria erecta*), brittlebush (*Encelia virginensis*), and boxthorn (*Lycium cooperi*).

Blackbrush Community

Flora shifts to the blackbrush community at mid-elevations, ranging from 3,800 to 5,200 feet (1,158 to 1,585 m). For the Gold Butte area, it is described as a "dense, uniform, low, shrub-dominated association" of *Coleogyne ramosissima* growing "almost to the exclusion of other species" (Ellis et al. 1982). Associated perennials include Joshua tree and banana yucca (*Yucca brevifolia* and *Y. baccata*), Mormon tea, boxthorn, winterfat (*Krascheninnikovia lanata*), agave (*Agave utahensis*), horsebrush (*Tetradymia* sp.), galleta grass (*Pleuraphis rigida*), and rabbitbrush (*Chrysothamnus* sp.).

Springs and Marsh Community

Small seeps result in isolated mesic alkaline patches that have a distinctive vegetation community. Common trees in these damp spots may include fan palm, cottonwood, willow, hackberry, and Siberian elm (*Ulmus pumila*). The most common shrubs and understory species are currant (*Ribes cereum*), rose (*Rosa woodsii*), arrow weed (*Yerba mansa*), quail bush (*Atriplex lentiformis*), thistle (*Cirsium neomexicanum*), and horehound (*Marrubium vulgare*).

Rocky Cliffs and Talus Slope Associations

The vegetation on rocky cliffs and talus slopes is highly varied from one spot to the next, dictated by local conditions such as elevation, rock type, and exposure. Depending on local context, one might find big sagebrush (*Artemisia tridentata*), cliff rose (*Purshia mexicana* var. *stansburiana*), rock spirea (*Petrophytum caespitosum*), snowberry (*Symphoricarpos longiflorus*), agave, redbud (*Cercis occidentalis*), biscuitroot (*Lomatium* spp.), vari-

ous barrel or ball cacti, Gambel oak (*Quercus gambelii*), and mountain mahogany (*Cercocarpus ledifolius*).

Chaparral Community

The chaparral community, or fire climax community, occurs on burned-over areas in the higher elevations of the Virgin Mountains, from 5,000 feet (1,524 m) to the summit. If not for repeated burns from lightning strikes, a pinyon-juniper woodland would cover these settings. The main species in the chaparral community are mountain mahogany, silk-tassel bush (*Garrya flavescens*), serviceberry (*Amelanchier utahensis*), scrub oak (*Quercus turbinella*), mountain lilac (*Ceanothus greggii*), barberry (*Berberis fremontii*), manzanita (*Arctostaphylos pungens*), yerba santa (*Eriodictyon angustifolium*), and currant.

Pinyon-Juniper Woodland

The pinyon-juniper woodland grows between 3,600 and 7,400 feet (1,100 and 2,275 m) and is dominated by Utah juniper (*Juniperus osteosperma*) and single-needle pinyon (*Pinus monophylla*). Understory shrubs are similar to those in the chaparral community, with the addition of Gambel oak, big sagebrush, agave, and banana yucca.

Fauna

Many of the animal species present in the Gold Butte area are found in both the Mojave Desert and the Great Basin. The greatest variety occurs in reptile species, with sundry small lizards, including horned-toads; large lizards, including Gila monster (*Heloderma suspectum*), desert iguana (*Dipsosaurus dorsalis*), and chuckwalla (*Sauromalus obesus*); snakes, including several kinds of rattlesnake (*Crotalus* spp.); and desert tortoise (*Gopherus agassizii*). The latter is a listed endangered species.

Small mammals are well represented, primarily by rodents, including kangaroo rats (*Dipodomys* spp.), woodrats (*Neotoma* spp.), several species of pocket and other mice (*Perognathus* spp., *Onychomys* spp., *Peromyscus* spp.), pocket gophers (*Thomomys* spp.), and the white-tailed antelope squirrel (*Ammospermophilus leucurus*). Various small bats (*Macrotis* spp. and *Pipistrellus* spp.) appear at twilight and work through the night. Black-tailed jackrabbits (*Lepus californicus*) and desert cottontails (*Sylvilagus audubonii*) are especially abundant in the area. Carnivorous mammals common here include coyote (*Canis latrans*), kit fox (*Vulpes macrotis*), mountain lion (*Felis concolor*), and bobcat (*Felis rufus*). Large mammals include desert bighorn sheep (*Ovis canadensis*) and mule deer (*Odocoileus hemionus*); both are successfully hunted in the Virgin Mountains today.

Cattle have roamed throughout the study area since the 1870s, contributing to the reduced amount of native big game now found throughout the uplands.

Small birds are seasonally numerous, particularly in the lower elevations and at water sources (e.g., in the desert riparian, stream riparian, and creosote communities), and include any number of songbirds, sparrows, and perching birds, particularly horned lark (*Eremophila alpestris*), black-throated sparrow (*Amphispiza bilineata*), and cactus wren (*Campylorhynchus brunneicapillus*). Medium to large birds common to the area include roadrunners (*Geococcyx californianus*), mourning dove (*Zenaida macroura*), Gambel's quail (*Callipepla gambelii*), and raven (*Corvus corax*). Raptors include red-tailed hawk (*Buteo jamaicensis*), American kestrel (*Falco sparverius*), and the occasional golden eagle (*Aquila chrysaetos*). The large and common carrion-eating turkey vulture (*Cathartes aura*) completes the list of commonly sighted avifauna.

PREHISTORIC CONTEXT

Chronological schemes for the southern Great Basin, particularly for the earlier periods, generally follow the lead of Warren (1984; Warren and Crabtree 1986) in maintaining a strong focus on environmental changes and their concomitant effects on the archaeological record. For our purposes, when discussing desert-adapted hunter-gatherer cultures, we have collapsed the Warren scheme into three broad temporal intervals, which we refer to as Paleo-Archaic, Early Archaic, and Late Archaic. When moving to the more recent end of the chronology, we follow the Pecos Classification for Basketmaker II through Pueblo III period nomenclature, using the most recent local application proposed by Allison (2000). Earlier iterations of the local Puebloan chronology include Shutler (1961) and Altschul and Fairley (1989). We refer to all post-Puebloan (i.e., post–AD 1250) prehistoric archaeological manifestations as the Late Prehistoric period. Table 2.2 presents our chronological scheme; unless otherwise noted, period dates are expressed throughout this presentation in calibrated radiocarbon years.

Paleo-Archaic (pre–5900 BC)

The earliest Paleo-Archaic occupation in the region is reflected in certain fluted, Clovis-like projectile points found in generally isolated contexts in southern Nevada (Jones and Edwards 1994; Perkins 1967, 1968; Roberts and Ahlstrom 2000), southern Utah (Copeland and Fike 1988), and the Arizona Strip (Altschul and Fairley 1989). Elsewhere in western North America and the Southwest, Clovis points have been found in association

TABLE 2.2. Cultural Sequence.

Period	Dates
Late Prehistoric	AD 1250–Contact
Pueblo III	AD 1175–1250
Pueblo II	AD 950–1175
Pueblo I	AD 800–950
Basketmaker III	AD 400–800
Basketmaker II	350 BC–AD 400
Late Archaic	2500–350 BC
Early Archaic	5900–2500 BC
Paleo-Archaic	Pre–5900 BC

with the bones of extinct megafauna (e.g., mammoth and large bison), and it seems clear this occupation was primarily focused on the taking of large game (most Clovis sites in the Great Basin generally do not occur with milling equipment [Willig and Aikens 1988]). These earliest populations were no doubt highly mobile, traveling in small groups and settling around lakes and along rivers, where game also tended to aggregate. No direct associations of extinct fauna and Clovis materials have been substantiated in southern Nevada or Utah, although several large-scale attempts to do so were made at Tule Springs near Las Vegas (Harrington and Simpson 1961; see also Fowler and Jennings 1982; Shutler 1967).

Prehistoric occupation in the Mojave Desert and southern Nevada at the recent end of this period is documented by various large lanceolate and stemmed projectile points (Great Basin Stemmed, Silver Lake) that typically occur with a variety of heavy core tools, bifaces, patterned and unpatterned flake tools, and chipped-stone crescents around the former shores of extinct pluvial lakes and other ancient landforms. Milling gear is rare in these assemblages. Warren and Crabtree (1986) argue that this complex is a regional reflection of the Western Pluvial Lakes tradition (Bedwell 1973), characterized by a settlement focus on lake- and stream-margin habitats and a hunting focus on large game.

By contrast, Basgall and Hall (1992, 1994a, 1994b; see also Basgall 2000) argue that environmental conditions in the Mojave Desert were relatively stable and that essentially modern flora and fauna were in place 10,000 years ago. They conclude that the apparent focus on lake-margin habitats resulted from archaeological sampling biases. Further, they note that milling gear is a "constant, if minor, constituent of assemblages of such age" (Hall 1992:19) and point out that Lake Mohave faunal assemblages show a variety of small and medium-sized mammals, suggesting a more generalized pattern of hunting and gathering. The variety of materials used in flaked stone tools and the high degree of curation and maintenance of these tools suggest a widely ranging, highly mobile settlement pattern. Further evidence for this is provided at sites throughout the southern Great Basin where obsidian source profiles of projectile points and other tools dating to this time consistently exhibit the highest source variation observed for any prehistoric period (Basgall and McGuire 1988; McGuire 2002).

More regional evidence of this occupation is indicated by work at Tule Springs in the 1960s, which recovered a small assemblage of artifacts from strata dating to at least 10,000 radiocarbon years BP (Fitzwater 1967; Shutler 1967; Stein 1967). Furthermore, Great Basin Stemmed points and Lake Mohave components have been found in the Las Vegas Valley (Ahlstrom 2005:Figure 2; Rafferty 1984), along the Kern River Pipeline corridor in southern Nevada and southern Utah (Reed et al. 2005), and around the margins of desert playas at Nellis Air Force Base (Kolvet et al. 2000), and are ubiquitous on a variety of old landforms and playa margins in more western areas of the Mojave Desert (Basgall 2000). Great Basin Stemmed points, however, do not appear to be as strongly represented in similar dated components to the east and south, that is, in areas traditionally identified as the Southwest. At Ventana Cave, for example, Pinto series projectile points appear to have a greater antiquity and represent the primary time marker for this period. This indicates perhaps a higher degree of cultural diversity for these early-dating populations than previously thought.

Early Archaic (5900–2500 BC)

While recognizing changes in certain tool forms, particularly projectile points, some investigators have a tendency to view the Archaic period in the Southwest as somewhat static, leading to the appearance of Formative lifeways by at least 2,000 years ago (Plog 1997; Vierra 2005). The divisions that are recognized appear more related to large-scale changes in climate and resource productivity than to fundamental changes in lifeways or land use (Geib 1996:15–35). A more variable picture emerges from the Mojave Desert, where a number of researchers see important shifts in assemblages, lifeways, and settlement structure roughly corresponding to the middle/late Holocene transition at about 2500 BC (Byrd et al. 2005; McGuire and Hildebrandt 2005; Warren 1986). The latter of these two frameworks seems more promising with respect to the Gold Butte area, and thus we divide this discussion between the Early and the Late Archaic periods.

Early Archaic period assemblages in the Mojave Desert are generally similar to Paleo-Archaic assemblages, distinguished primarily by the introduction of the Pinto series projectile point. Basgall (2000:130), however, notes that upward of 63 percent of sites at Fort Irwin that contained Pinto points also produced Great Basin Stemmed points, suggesting some level of temporal overlap of these point forms—an issue noted by other researchers as well (Gilreath and Hildebrandt 1997; Schroth 1994; Vaughan and Warren 1987). Similarly, many of the sites typically cited as Pinto occupations may date to the earliest part of the Early Archaic period (cf. Schroth 1994), and the dearth of later-dating Pinto components is cited as evidence for the possible abandonment of the southern Great Basin during the middle Holocene warm period (Seymour 2001:70; Warren and Crabtree 1986:187).

Early Archaic milling gear is generally more abundant than in early Holocene assemblages, which both Warren (1986) and Basgall and Hall (1992, 1994a, 1994b) take to indicate a greater reliance on small seeds. Warren (1986) notes a correlation between Pinto sites and perennial springs, and therefore proposes a middle Holocene settlement shift toward these locations in response to environmental desiccation. In contrast, and as indicated above, Basgall (2000) argues that Pinto sites are found in many of the same contexts as earlier-dating Paleo-Archaic assemblages and retain many of the same tool categories. Thus, with some variation on the theme, the residentially mobile, wide-ranging, and generalized land-use pattern of the early Holocene is also held to continue through this period, as evidenced by the continuing high level of curation of flaked stone tool kits and diverse obsidian source profiles.

Pinto series points are reasonably ubiquitous throughout the region and are not an uncommon occurrence in many large-scale inventories conducted on land surfaces of appropriate age. Ahlstrom (2005:Figure 2) lists more than 23 Early Archaic/Pinto manifestations in Las Vegas Valley alone. There is, however, little documentation of components dating to this period in intact, stratified contexts—an exception being O'Malley Shelter (Fowler et al. 1973), located north of the study area, which contains diffuse evidence of Early Archaic/Pinto occupation in its lower strata.

Late Archaic (2500–350 BC)

There are two competing perspectives regarding Late Archaic settlement patterns. Basgall and Hall (1992) find that Gypsum-period deposits in the Mojave Desert continue to indicate a generalized pattern of land use, with a full complement of flaked, ground, and battered stone tools, as well as diverse faunal assemblages. They argue that this reflects a wide-ranging settlement system similar to that of earlier intervals, geared to recurrent, short-term occupation of generalized areas rather than specific locations. The increasing use of a formalized biface technology typical of this period is thought to reflect a mobile but highly structured settlement pattern in which access to raw lithic material could be scheduled in the context of a seasonal round (Bleed 1986; Kelly 1988).

By contrast, McGuire and Hildebrandt (2005; see also Byrd et al. 2005; Hildebrandt and McGuire 2002) argue that the Late Archaic/Gypsum period, far from representing mobile, wide-ranging foragers, may actually represent the "trans-Holocene highpoint" of residential stability in the nonagricultural areas of the Great Basin. They point to an emerging village pattern that appears at this time in such varied locations as the Carson Desert (Kelly 2001; Zeanah 2004), the northwestern Great Basin (Elston et al. 1994; McGuire 1997, 2002; Riddell 1960), Owens Valley (Delacorte 1999:17), and the eastern Great Basin (Madsen and Simms 1998). A similar village pattern has been indicated for the Mojave Desert (Byrd et al. 2005).

Warren (1984) also posits major, as opposed to incremental, changes in subsistence and settlement, arguing, as McGuire and Hildebrandt (2005) do, that large-game hunting escalated during this interval while the use of plant resources continued to intensify, the latter reflected by increases in the frequency of milling equipment. Along with these changes in subsistence focus, Warren and Crabtree (1986) hypothesize a shift from family-based organization to larger, multifamily bands akin to the village pattern described above. The greater use of milling equipment, along with an apparent increase in storage and artifact caching, suggest a pattern of resource intensification based on hard seeds and other plant resources and an increasingly structured seasonal round.

In essence, then, the Late Archaic represented a settlement shift from the band-level, mobile foragers of the preceding periods to a somewhat more residentially stable pattern that included increased levels of logistical procurement emanating from base camps. Thus it is no surprise that this is when we begin to see the emergence of true settlement hierarchies, including base camps, hunting camps, processing stations, and other specialized sites. For example, it is during the Late Archaic when specialized ritual sites related to hunting magic appear at such sites as Gypsum Cave (Gilreath 2009; Harrington 1933), Newberry Cave (Davis and Smith 1981), and Firebrand Cave (Blair 2004). Some

(but clearly not all) rock art sites identified in the study area also probably date to the Late Archaic.

As defined by Warren (1984; Warren and Crabtree 1986), the Late Archaic period is characterized by several medium-sized dart types, including Elko, Humboldt, and Gypsum series. It is important to note, however, that time spans generally associated with these types extend beyond the Late Archaic as defined here and encompass the subsequent Basketmaker II period (see below). With regard to the Gypsum series type, Carpenter et al. (2005:30–31; see also Berry and Berry 1986; Mabry 1998; Marmaduke 1978) suggest that this form reflects a new technology that used adhesives to attach the point to the haft, a technology that diffused northward, along with maize cultivation, from central Mexico at the end of the middle Holocene warm period (ca. 2000 BC). This technological complex, which has also been tied to the Uto-Aztecan expansion into the Southwest and southern California at this time (Hill 2003), may have cultural and ethnolinguistic significance as well.

Basketmaker II and III (350 BC–AD 800)

The seemingly abrupt appearance in the lowland Moapa and Virgin Valleys of what Lyneis (1995:210–215) identifies as pit structures, which generally occur in groups of one to five with fire hearths, clay floors, and other architectural details (see also Harrington 1937; Larson 1987; Larson and Michaelsen 1990; Schroeder 1953a, b; Shutler 1961; Winslow 2006), marks a clear departure from earlier Archaic manifestations and places the study area squarely within the influence of the greater Southwest. Winslow's (2006; Winslow et al. 2003a, b) preliminary descriptions of the Basketmaker II–III components (Black Dog Mesa complex) overlooking the Muddy River—the best local example of Basketmaker culture—are particularly effusive as she compares the internal structure of the multiple pithouses documented at this site with classic Basketmaker II communities in the Kayenta Branch heartland.

The dating of this transition remains difficult to pinpoint in the two-rivers area but seems to have begun by around 2,300 years ago (Lyneis 1995; Shutler 1961; Winslow 2006). The local importance of agriculture during Basketmaker times is also in some dispute, and direct archaeobotanical evidence for Basketmaker II maize cultivation is drawn mostly from the Colorado Plateau and more eastern reaches of the Virgin River (Billat et al. 1992; Janetski and Wilde 1989; McFadden 1994; Nussbaum 1922). Both Larson (1987) and Winslow (2006; see also Winslow et al. 2003b) report maize cobs in pithouses associated with the Black Dog

Mesa complex, and most researchers argue that some level of agricultural production began during Basketmaker II times. Along these lines, radiocarbon assays from domesticated plant residues (i.e., corn, gourd) are also associated with the Black Dog Mesa complex, as well as Firebrand Cave and a shelter in our study area (26CK8047).

The transition from Basketmaker II to III times (referred to as the Moapa and Muddy River phases by Shutler [1961]) is generally placed around 1,600 years ago. The two main traits that distinguish these periods are the appearance of pottery and, in Basketmaker III, arrow-sized points. Notwithstanding its importance for trade, exchange, and social relationships, the significance of pottery looms large because of its ability to increase reliable food storage and to create incentives to invest more time in cultivating domesticates. Pottery dating to this time, however, is often found in open campsites, suggesting continued exploitation of wild resources. The other technological change, the replacement of the atlatl and dart with the bow and arrow, is recognized in the archaeological record by the replacement of larger projectile points (e.g., Elko and Gypsum forms) with more gracile forms (e.g., Rose Spring).

On the face of it, the emphatic break in Archaic lifeways, coupled with the sudden appearance of Basketmaker sites in the two-rivers lowlands, suggests a site unit intrusion (i.e., migration) into the area, and recent research in the greater Southwest supports this general notion. Matson (2005) points out several major developments over the last several decades that fundamentally alter our understanding of the Southwest at the Archaic/Formative interface. The first is the shrinking age estimates associated with the domestication of maize in central Mexico (from 5000 BC to 1400 BC), and the second is the expanding age estimates for full-blown agricultural settlements (from ca. 900 BC to AD 1) in the Southwest. Matson (2005:279–281) believes that this compressed timeframe argues against agriculture evolving in situ from indigenous hunter and gatherers and strengthens a faster transfer (migration) between Mexico and the Southwest.

The Moapa and Virgin River Valleys, however, certainly are a geographic outlier from developments in the ancestral Puebloan heartland, and it may be that—notwithstanding Black Dog Mesa—the acceptance of agriculture was much more gradual (Cordell 1997; Diehl and Waters 2005). Larson and Michaelsen's (1990; see also Larson 1987) demographic reconstruction of Basketmaker and Puebloan occupation of the Virgin River lowlands would seem to fit this model. Estimated population densities rise only slowly through their periods

I and II (roughly Basketmaker II and III [AD 100–800]). Sites dating to this time contain from one to four pithouse structures and are widely dispersed on the Virgin and Muddy Rivers. Larson and Michaelsen (1990) view these sites as the remains of dispersed nuclear families primarily dependent on hunting and gathering. Basketmaker pithouses, as opposed to later-dating Puebloan settlements, were not positioned in areas conducive to intensive agriculture (see also Clark 1984), although maize and squash may have been grown in small gardens to supplement wild resources. Lyneis (1995:221), however, disputes what she sees as an overemphasis on hunting and gathering, arguing instead that maize was an important food by Basketmaker II times.

As mentioned, Basketmaker II and III settlements focused on the major river drainages—Larson and Michaelsen (1990) report that sites dating to this time average about one for every two miles of river corridor. A record search for the Gold Butte area and surroundings confirms this pattern: 20 previously recorded sites with pithouse depressions were identified (though some of them may date to later Puebloan occupations; see below).

Puebloan Period (AD 800–1250)

Of course the most dramatic manifestations of southwestern-influenced prehistoric culture in southern Nevada are found in the Lower Moapa Valley at above-ground site complexes such as Main Ridge at Lost City de Nevada and Mesa House (Harrington 1930; Hayden 1930; Lyneis 1992; Shutler 1961). These classic, later-dating sites emerged from developing Basketmaker and Puebloan occupations that are described both above and below. Based primarily on house and storage facility configuration, community layout, and ceramic styles and technology, the Puebloan period has been traditionally broken into subperiods following the Pecos Classification. The most recent local chronology (Allison 2000) places Pueblo I from AD 800 to 950, Early Pueblo II from AD 950 to 1050, Middle Pueblo II from AD 1050 to 1100, Late Pueblo II from AD 1100 to 1175, and Pueblo III from AD 1175 to 1250. Pueblo I through Middle Pueblo II generally correspond to Shutler's Lost City phase, and Late Pueblo II and Pueblo III generally correspond to his terminal Mesa House phase.

Pueblo I

Pithouse structures continued to be used, although they are somewhat more formalized, containing benches and occasionally ventilators. Storage cists become more oval and are arrayed end to end in arcs. Lyneis (1995:211) sees this arrangement of pithouses and storage cists as an attempt to define outdoor space, anticipating the more formal courtyards of Pueblo II times. Larson and Michaelsen's (1990:Figure 5) demographic reconstructions for their Period I (Pueblo I) occupation of the lowland Virgin River and Moapa Valley areas show a sharply increasing population at this time, as well as increasing levels of storage capacity (see also Larson 1987). Coupled with settlement shifts to areas more favorable for irrigation agriculture, Larson and Michaelsen argue that by AD 1000 the transition to intensive farming was mostly complete.

While a welter of pottery attributes and types suggest trade, exchange, and other social relationships with populations to the east, an unambiguous indicator is the olivine temper in gray wares from Basketmaker III to Pueblo III times in local sites (Colton 1952; Lyneis 1992; Rowe 2002a). The source of the olivine is Mt. Trumbull, 100 km to the east. As reported by Rowe (2002a), olivine-tempered pottery is found well west of Moapa Valley, extending into Las Vegas Valley and beyond. The frequency of olivine-tempered gray ware in relation to other wares has also been used as a chronological marker to date archaeological components (Larson and Michaelsen 1990; Lyneis 1992). Expanding relationships with areas to the west, including California, are also indicated by the increase in Pacific marine shell (e.g., *Haliotis* and *Olivella*) in Basketmaker III and Pueblo II components.

Pueblo II

As exemplified by the Main Ridge site in Moapa Valley (Lyneis 1992), room blocks in this period tend to have been set on or near the surface and fashioned from adobe and cobble footings (Lyneis 2000). Rooms are circular to square with clay-coated or slab-lined walls, deflector slabs for fire pits, ash pits, and clay ridges on floors adjacent to fire pits (Fowler and Madsen 1986). Settlements remain small, and habitations are often arranged in an arc, forming a courtyard. Each "courtyard unit" contains about 4–5 m² of storage space per habitation room; these units were generally not clustered into large villages. Lyneis has argued that the large quantities of sherds in Pueblo II structures, the amount of above-ground storage, and the consistent location of sites dating to this period on terrace margins close to rivers indicate that these were year-round residences. It is also during Late Pueblo II times that there was a population explosion and expansion of settlements (Aikens 1966:55; Fowler and Madsen 1986) and Larson and Michaelsen's (1990) population estimate quickly reaches its apex. Although no water diversion facilities have been locally documented, Pueblo II populations

were sustained by intensive, irrigation-based farming that, along with maize, now included squash, beans, and cotton.

But just as during Basketmaker III and Pueblo I, Pueblo II type sherds continue to be found in a variety of nonagricultural sites some distance from riverine settlements. For example, Puebloan ceramics often are present in the upper veneer of remote rock shelters in the region (Duke et al. 2004; Fowler et al. 1973). Lyneis (2000:261) believes that "it is possible, even likely, that task groups or families went to upland resource areas for short stays to hunt and forage," an idea that has important implications for upland hinterlands such as Gold Butte. She identifies mesquite beans, pine nuts, cactus fruit, and yucca as the most likely wild plant resources, and deer, bighorn sheep, rabbit, and tortoise as important animal foods. On the Shivwits Plateau, for example, it is not uncommon for campsites in the pinyon-juniper zone to contain both Puebloan I and II ceramics (Altschul and Fairley 1989:143).

It is during Middle Pueblo II times that corrugated gray and traces of red and orange wares appear in regional assemblages, and these mark the most intense period of ceramic importation from the Colorado Plateau (Allison 2000). Lyneis (2000:261) characterizes this movement of goods as "extraordinary" and as "the most visible marker of a complex and intense interaction between plateaus and lowlands." It should be noted that the Gold Butte study area is between the eastern plateaus and western lowlands, and the larger east/west-trending drainages and low passes through our area are considered prime corridors for this trade.

Pueblo III

At sites such as Main Ridge (Lyneis 1992), toward the end of Pueblo II times and during the short-lived Early Pueblo III period, the Puebloan lifeway locally came to an abrupt end. The best-studied local Pueblo III settlements are Mesa House and Three Mile Ruin. Lyneis (1995) notes a distinguishing feature at these sites: their courtyards are almost completely enclosed by a curve of habitation and storage rooms. Still, they remain comparatively small settlements, and at least in the case of Mesa House, the site has far more storage than habitation rooms.

Larson and Michaelsen (1990) tie the collapse of Puebloan lifeways to the combined effects of expanding population and extreme drought between AD 1050 and 1100, the latter causing severely reduced stream flows on the Virgin River and thus much reduced agricultural productivity. Lyneis (1995) critiques certain aspects of this hypothesis but still concludes that it is likely some combination of climate change and population-to-resource imbalance brought an end to resident Puebloan occupation (see also Euler et al. 1979). Increasing economic and social strains between the Moapa-Virgin valley area and Puebloan centers to the east is indicated by the fall-off of olivine-tempered pottery in Late Pueblo II and Early Pueblo III assemblages (Lyneis 1992).

Lower Colorado Buff wares also appear at this time and perhaps signal an increasing presence of non-Puebloan foragers. It is also about this time when ancestral Southern Paiute groups become recognizable in the archaeological record. They are thought by some to have originated from the west and made their way into this region (Madsen and Rhode 1994). There is a wide range of opinion as to whether there was such an intrusion, let alone whether it was benign or fraught with conflict (Ambler and Sutton 1989; Euler 1964; Huffman 1993; Janetski 1993; LeBlanc 1999; Lyneis 1995; Sutton 1987). The defensive character of Mesa House, positioned on a steep-sided terrace point, is taken as proxy evidence of its defensive stance to protect agricultural stores from raids (Ambler and Sutton 1989; Hayden 1930). Similar defensively oriented settlements have been observed in Pueblo II sites elsewhere on the Virgin River (Jenkins 1981).

Late Prehistoric Period (post–AD 1250)

The Late Prehistoric period begins with the abandonment of Puebloan settlements along the rivers at about AD 1250 and continues until the Spanish intrusions into the Southwest at AD 1600 or somewhat later along this western frontier. This period is coterminous with the arrival of Numic-speaking (Southern Paiute) desert foragers into the region, and thus several researchers have dubbed this period the Neo-Archaic (Altschul and Fairley 1989:147).

Certainly the return of hunter-gather populations into an area after nearly a 1,500-year tradition of agriculture would seem to signal a major cultural upheaval, but the character, timing, and outcome associated with Southern Paiute interactions with their predecessors at Gold Butte are poorly understood. Earlier we reviewed the evidence from Mesa House and the argument for direct conflict between these two populations. The timing at least appears to be supported by linguistic evidence that puts the arrival of Numic-speakers in the area at or slightly before the collapse of Pueblo lifeways (Miller 1986; Rhode and Madsen 1994). On the Arizona Strip, however, Altschul and Fairley (1989:141–142) argue that there are stratigraphic breaks separating Puebloan and Paiute occupations at several sites. These gaps are thought to represent up to a 150-year hiatus between the Puebloan retraction ca. AD 1250 and the Paiute expansion at about AD 1300–1350. This suggests that the Southern Paiute may have simply walked into a largely abandoned cultural landscape (see also McGuire and Hildebrandt 2005:708).

Based in part on what she believes are contemporaneous assemblages of gray (Pueblo) and brown (Paiute) wares at certain sites, Lyneis (1994) offers a third alternative, suggesting that the Paiute and Virgin Puebloans lived in a comparatively benign, mutualistic relationship. The former were more mobile hunter-gatherers living in the hinterlands whereas the latter occupied farming hamlets; Lyneis proposes that they interacted in mutually beneficially ways. In contrast to those who advocate a militaristic expansion, she sees little evidence for defensive positioning of either Pueblo II or early Pueblo III settlements in the area. Given this interaction, Lyneis (1995:232–233) speculates that the Paiute may have assimilated the vestiges of the Virgin Puebloans, but she acknowledges that this viewpoint necessarily requires that the Puebloans were flexible in their subsistence pursuits rather than single-minded agriculturalists.

This flexibility may have cut both ways, for there is evidence (Fowler 1995; Kelly and Fowler 1986) that the Southern Paiute adopted certain horticulture practices during this period. Although this adoption is assumed to have occurred toward the recent end of this period (but before Euro-American contact), Lyneis (1994:148 after Fowler et al. 1969 and Fowler and Fowler 1981:133) suggests the possibility that agriculture/horticulture was learned from the Virgin Puebloans and so possibly dates to that time. There is, however, no archaeological support for this hypothesis, and we concede that recognizing Southern Paiute archaeological occupations remains problematic.

As Lyneis (1994:144) points out, brown ware ceramics and Desert Side-notched projectile points are usually cited as the most unambiguous signatures of the Southern Paiute presence, but these items are often absent or underrepresented in local components that date to this time. Elsewhere in the Great Basin, Numa settlements tend to have almost a stand-alone domestic quality about them, as might be expected from a series of much dispersed, short-term occupations by small but demographically inclusive family units. Artifact assemblages therefore often are minimal but have a gender-balanced profile (McGuire 2002).

Based on the substantial amount of paddle and anvil ceramics documented in the study area during the current investigation, it now is clear that the area also experienced a substantial Patayan (ancestral Yuman) occupation. This is perhaps not surprising given the proximity of ethnographic Yuman-speakers such as the Hualapai. The Patayan are represented by archaeological assemblages, found mostly along the lower Colorado River, which contain paddle and anvil pottery variously classified as Tizon Brown Ware, Prescott Gray Ware, or Lower Colorado Buff Ware (Lyneis 2004). Patayan pottery is thought to have been introduced into the region sometime around AD 900 to 1100 (Lyneis 2004; Jensen et al. 2006; Seymour 1997). Plain (undecorated) Patayan ceramics are thought to have persisted until at least AD 1500 in this region (Seymour 1997). This dating scheme raises the possibility of interactions between Southern Paiute and Patayan groups, and perhaps even Puebloans in the area. This subject is explored further later in this book.

Notwithstanding interactions between prehistoric Patayan and Southern Paiute, the latter occupied the study area at the time of historic contact and continue to have a local presence to this day. This contact commenced with the Spanish/Mexican Exploration period (1540–1848) of the greater Southwest and continued through the Early (1826–1840) and Late (1840–1865) American Exploration periods. In the study area almost all this initial activity centered on the Old Spanish Trail along the Virgin River corridor. In this sense, it is likely that the study area and its Native American inhabitants were subject to at least some Euro-American influences relatively early on. More permanent Euro-American settlements were established with the arrival of Mormon settlers in 1865. It is at this time that the effects of disease, raiding, and the destruction of Native habitat by livestock combined to devastate the Southern Paiute, whose population declined an estimated 50 to 80 percent (Stoffle and Evans 1976).

Previously Documented Prehistoric Resources in the Study Area

The Gold Butte area contains a variety of site types and archaeological manifestations from residents and their diverse land-use practices in the foregoing periods. Of the 215 sites previously recorded in the Gold Butte study area, 179 are prehistoric and 10 contain both prehistoric and historic components. A complete accounting of the records search for the study area is contained in the Research and Class II Sample Design (Gilreath et al. 2006).

The 189 sites with prehistoric components contain a wide variety of constituents, including flaked stone; ground stone; ceramics; habitation debris such as fire-cracked rock, animal bone, and midden soil; agave roasting pits; hearths; rock art; and architectural features such as Basketmaker/Puebloan ruins and storage pits. Although the quality of information provided in the site records varies widely, some general observations can be made as to the character and distribution of various kinds of sites.

Nineteen sites contain rock art, all of which are located on the distinctive Aztec sandstone substrate in the central part of the study area. Very few of the records documenting these sites make any mention of associated artifacts or habitation debris; most were recorded in the context of rock-art-specific documentation efforts by the vanguard of the Nevada Rock Art Foundation (NRAF). Stylistic and other aspects of the rock art are discussed in detail in Chapter 7.

The record search highlighted 37 sites with pithouses, architectural remains, and/or storage features. Each is along the banks of the Virgin River. A few additional records refer to Pueblo-affiliated materials (i.e., specific pottery types) in the interior of the study area, where structural remains are lacking.

Thirty-five sites are described as rock shelters or caves, most with habitation debris such as fire-cracked rock, dietary bone, and/or midden soil. Flaked stone and sherds are also common. Most notable among these sites is 26CK5434, a large limestone-solution cavern containing a variety of perishable artifacts, including dart shafts, basketry, and cordage (Blair 2004). A total of 20 radiocarbon dates was obtained on artifacts from the cave, most dating to the initial part of the Late Archaic period and some 3,000 to 4,000 years old. It is a singular site; the others are small shelters mostly located in the Aztec sandstone exposed in the central part of the study area.

Twenty-two sites contain agave roasting pits, either as isolated features or associated with a range of artifacts and other features. Presumably their distribution relates to that of agave on the landscape. Most are in the uplands on the south flank of Virgin Peak, in the northern part of the Virgin Range. Almost all the recorded features were identified during a survey by Ellis et al. (1982) that was specifically directed at recording these features.

Most of the remaining prehistoric sites identified in the record search are open-air scatters consisting of various combinations of flaked stone tools and chipping debris, ground stone tools, and ceramics. Six flaked stone scatters in the central and northern parts of the study area are specifically identified as quarry areas for cryptocrystalline stone. Seven "sites" are isolated artifacts.

ETHNOGRAPHIC CONTEXT

Two major Native American groups occupy lands in and adjacent to the study area today, and did so reaching back into the comparatively recent past.

Southern Paiute Lifeways

Gold Butte was occupied by the Southern Paiute just before Euro-American contact. Their traditional territories extended across southern Utah, Nevada, and northern Arizona and down along the western side of the Colorado River into California (Figure 2.3). Kelly and Fowler (1986) list at least 16 Southern Paiute groups or bands in the region, each with its own territory. The Moapa band lived along the Muddy and Virgin Rivers and controlled the Gold Butte area. They shared a boundary with the Shivwits band of Southern Paiute along the Nevada-Arizona border (Kelly 1934), roughly corresponding to the eastern boundary of the study area. The Colorado River separated them from their southern neighbors, the Yuman-speaking Hualapai (Kelly and Fowler 1986; Kroeber 1935; McGuire 1983).

Like other Numa groups, most Southern Paiute bands were mobile hunter-gatherers who followed a seasonal round within their territory. Small game, including rabbits, various rodents, and tortoise, was the primary source of protein. Individual and small-group hunting was commonplace, but communal rabbit drives were organized periodically and generated substantial amounts of meat and pelts. Large game was less important and was mostly limited to mountain sheep in the Gold Butte area (Kelly and Fowler 1986). These were stalked by small groups or individuals but (like rabbits) sometimes were the subject of group drives. Larger parties also ran sheep into the clefts of canyons, onto inescapable promontories, or off cliffs, sometimes using fire as an aid (Kelly 1976; Kelly and Fowler 1986).

A great variety of plant foods were used and made a much larger contribution to the diet than game. Pinyon nuts, a staple among the Moapa, were available on the flanks of Virgin Peak and to the south in Cedar Basin. They were harvested and eaten in the fall, and were stored for later use in the winter and spring. Agave could be harvested all year but was best taken in the spring when the stalk was just beginning to form. The root crown and stalks were roasted in large stone-lined ovens for two to three days, and the carbohydrate-rich food was either eaten right away or dried and stored for later. During the summer the stalks left intact would produce flowers and seed clusters; these could also be eaten immediately or stored for later use (Bean and Siva Saubel 1972). Agave is relatively abundant at Gold Butte,

particularly along the 4,000-foot contour within the limestone formations that exist along the lower reaches of the Virgin Mountains. The record search identified a number of agave ovens in this zone.

Today mesquite is quite rare in the Gold Butte study area, but in times past it was an important resource in the lowlands below 3,000 feet along alluvial fans and washes, where its deep roots could penetrate the water table. Although flowers and green seed pods were collected and consumed in the spring and early summer, the naturally dried pods presented the best nutritional returns in early fall. Dried pods could be stored, broken into pieces and immediately eaten, or ground into a meal that was processed and served in a variety of ways. Small seeds were also critical resources, especially goosefoot (*Chenopodium* sp.), rice grass (*Achnatherum hymenoides*), and chia (*Salvia columbariae*). Most were knocked into a conical basket with a basketry seed beater and then winnowed, parched, and ground into meal or flour on a milling slab before being turned into mush or bread (Bean and Siva Saubel 1972; Kelly and Fowler 1986).

The Southern Paiute's basic economic unit was the nuclear family, but other related individuals could join the group and form a larger extended family. Because of the dispersed nature of subsistence resources, with regard to both seasonal availability and distribution across the landscape, the Southern Paiute moved across the land with regularity. Their annual cycles differed from place to place based on local environmental conditions. Some groups preferred to spend the winter at high elevations close to pinyon groves and their pine-nut caches, while others wintered at the base of the hills or in protected canyons. Winter houses were conical structures composed of wooden supports covered with brush and loosely woven matting. Rock shelters and caves also served as winter homes in certain areas. People dispersed during the warm seasons, moving across resource patches as the productivity of these locations fluctuated through the year. Formal houses were not built during the warm times, due to the limited stays at most camps. Short-term domiciles consisted of a simple shade structure built against a tree, and many camps had no structures at all (Kelly and Fowler 1986).

This subsistence-settlement pattern was altered a few decades before the arrival of Euro-Americans when a few bands began to practice low-level agricultural production (Desert Research Institute 1996; Kelly and Fowler 1986; Lockwood 1872; Lyle 1872; Steward 1938; but see Stoffle and Zedeño 2001). The Moapa people cultivated gardens on the bottomlands of the Muddy

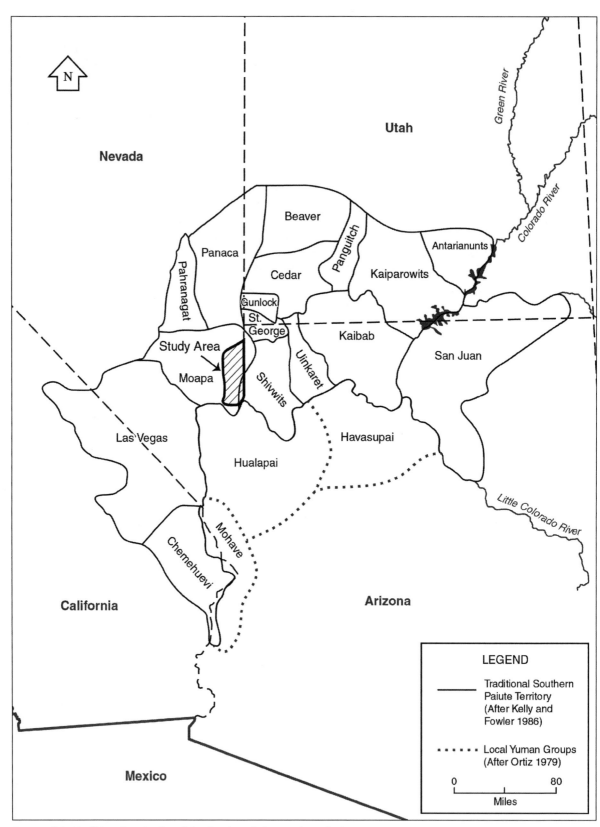

FIGURE 2.3. Traditional territories of the Southern Paiute and nearby Yuman groups.

and Virgin Rivers, where they grew corn, squash, pumpkins, cantaloupes, muskmelons, watermelons, gourds, beans, sunflower, winter wheat, and devil's claw.

The Southern Paiute practiced shamanism, and shamans received their power through dreams. During these dreams the prospective shaman was visited by one or more tutelaries, usually in animal form. The tutelaries bestowed the shaman with power and provided instructions and songs (Kelly and Fowler 1986). For some Southern Paiute people, dreams could sometimes be obtained by spending a night alone in one of several caves (Kelly 1936). Kelly states (1936:129): "If shamanistic power did not come unsolicited, it could be acquired by visiting Gypsum Cave (Pua'rïnkan, doctor-cave), in Vegas territory, or a cave on Kwi'nava mountain, across the Colorado, in Yavapai country. Neither offering nor fasting was required. The person went 'alone, at night, and talked to the cave, telling it what kind of a doctor he wanted to be.' He stayed the night and by daybreak had received a dream, that is, a spirit visitation." Also of importance to the Southern Paiute were songs that were given to singers through dreams, including the Funereal, Deer and Mountain Sheep, Bird, Salt, Quail, and Coyote songs. These songs were based on "themes centered on travels, with the naming of places, natural phenomena, and animals, and with no action save the journey itself" (Kelly and Fowler 1986:385). It was common for singers to receive their songs in much the same manner as shamans received their power, such as by spending time alone in certain caves.

The Southern Paiute utilized relatively few ceremonies and dances. These included the Mourning Ceremony or Cry (yakappi), the Ghost Dance of the 1890s, the Round Dance (nikkappi or kiyappi), and a dance involving the Deer or Mountain Sheep Song (Kelly and Fowler 1986). The annual fall festival was an important occasion for the Southern Paiutes of southern Nevada, and people traveled great distances to participate in it (Steward 1938).

Southern Paiute mortuary practices varied among the different bands. The deceased was sometimes cremated or buried in a rock crevice, rock shelter, rock slide, or shallow wash (Desert Research Institute 1996; Kelly 1976; Kelly and Fowler 1986). Personal property was often destroyed, including eagles, horses, dogs, and, sometimes, a relative "to keep them company." About a year after a person's death, people in Las Vegas, Chemehuevi, and Moapa held a Mourning Ceremony, or Cry. This ceremony, held in the fall, included a night of songs, along with the burning of baskets, blankets, nets, and other offerings. Guests were invited to attend from long distances as well as locally. Relatives were expected to bring offerings to be burned (Desert Research Institute 1996:3–42).

The Hualapai

The Hualapai lived south of the Colorado River, separated from the Southern Paiute by the rugged canyon that marks this country. They practiced a subsistence economy that relied on wild foods but also carried out some amount of agricultural production. According to McGuire (1983), they focused on agave during the spring, constructing earth ovens along the foothills and canyons where the plants could be found. After the agave harvest they moved down into the lowlands to gather small seeds using techniques similar to those of the Southern Paiutes. By midsummer the fruits of several cacti had ripened and the Hualapai moved back up into the canyons and foothills. Late summer and fall was dedicated to gathering pinyon nuts, as well as juniper and sumac berries. Camps in winter were larger and more sedentary than during other times of the year, and the populations subsisted largely by hunting game and using stored plant foods.

It is unknown how much the Hualapai relied on agricultural foods. Although Kroeber (1935) felt that farming was intermittent at best, Dobyns and Euler (1976) argue that agricultural production was much more important in precontact times and that the Hualapai's Native subsistence system was essentially destroyed by the time early historians and ethnographers visited them in the late 1800s and early 1900s. Despite this uncertainty, postcontact groups were observed cultivating corn, pumpkins, beans, and sunflowers in low, well-watered valleys. Gardens were taken care of by men, but women helped with irrigation, cultivation, and harvesting, particularly when men were out foraging for other resources (Kroeber 1935).

Southern Paiute–Hualapai Interactions

A review of both the Southern Paiute and Hualapai ethnographies shows no evidence that Hualapai ever used the Gold Butte area, as it was controlled by the Moapa band of Southern Paiute. Kelly and Fowler's (1986:370) discussion of "external relations" mentions the Hualapai only once: "The Moapa, Shivwits, and Saint George sometimes crossed the Colorado and encountered Hualapai hostility." McGuire's (1983) review of the Hualapai is similar, stating that their northern boundary was the steep Colorado River canyon, and his only mention of the Southern Paiute refers to the historic period, when there were some trade relations involving guns, and the north-to-south spread of the Ghost Dance occurred.

As outlined above, the abundant presence of paddle and anvil (Patayan) pottery at Gold Butte indicates that this ethnographic boundary did not extend into the prehistoric past. Patayan ceramics in Gold Butte reflect at least subsistence forays by the Hualapai or their Yuman relatives, but they more likely represent control over the land for some unknown length of time. The latter scenario seems probable because the primary subsistence resources found at Gold Butte (pinyon groves, tracts of agave, small-seeded plants, and small and large game) are the same as those in the Hualapai homelands, ruling out the likelihood that they came here to obtain a special

class of food. So while the Late Prehistoric expansion of the Numa (Southern Paiute) and their displacement or replacement of Virgin Puebloan peoples has been a major research issue for several years, we now must add the potential displacement/replacement of Yuman (Hualapai) populations at Gold Butte as a new topic of archaeological investigation (see Chapter 3).

The 36 isolates from these units comprise a variety of flaked and ground stone tools, as well as seven isolated rock rings (see Table 4.7). The latter may be related to Basketmaker/Puebloan occupation since they are also present at several of the Basketmaker/Puebloan sites.

3 Research Issues

As the natural and cultural contexts have indicated, Gold Butte is situated at the interface of several physiographic provinces and on the periphery of multiple culture areas. In terms of physiographic provinces, it is at the extreme eastern edge of the Mojave Desert, at the southeastern extent of the Great Basin, and on the western margin of the Colorado Plateau. In terms of broad cultures zones, influences from the Great Basin, Southwest, and Yuman-speaking areas of lower Colorado River were all operable to varying degrees, depending on the prehistoric time frame.

In addition to having a rich and varied culture history, Gold Butte served as a hinterland to the prehistoric farming communities established in the bottomlands of the Virgin River Basin and Colorado River. The proximity and co-associations of prehistoric farmers and hunter-gatherers is potentially fertile theoretical ground for the study of foragers, low-level food production, and full-blown agriculture—and the events and forces that guided the transition between them. In our view, human behavioral ecology, particularly its optimization assumptions and conception of opportunity cost, provides the preferred theoretical framework for addressing such issues and is validated by some recent treatments of this same subject (Kennett and Winterhalder 2005; see also Barlow 2005). Through this theoretical lens, our analytical approach views changes in settlement-subsistence and lifeways at core settlements along the riverine corridor as having corresponding, measurable effects on the character and intensity of hinterland land use.

Of course, a wide array of other research issues are associated with Gold Butte, some either not or only tangentially related to food production. In this chapter, along with a discussion of agricultural production and hinterland use, we identify a variety other research topics, including those related to local chronology, archaic settlement systems, interregional exchange, rock art, and Puebloan abandonment.

LOCAL CHRONOLOGY

Reliably dating different types of cultural remains, from specific artifacts to broader cultural-historical assemblages, is a consistent problem in western archaeology. This problem is of particular concern since the temporal ordering of archaeological materials is an essential prerequisite for investigating all "higher order" research issues dealing with diachronic changes in human behavior. Most of our sites and components within sites are dated based on radiocarbon assays, ceramic styles, projectile points, and source-specific obsidian hydration data.

Three ceramic traditions are represented in the area, those associated with the Virgin Branch Basketmaker/Puebloans, with the Patayan groups from the Colorado River, and with the Southern Paiute. The timing of these separate traditions is critical for evaluating models of subsistence-settlement change (e.g., is there a hiatus between the periods of use for Virgin Branch and Southern Paiute pottery?) and for determining the economic and sociopolitical relationships between resident and neighboring groups. And on closer inspection, the timing of various styles and wares within the suite of pottery found on sites is critical for charting the local culture history and for better understanding when and to what degree populations along the river valleys traded with people in the uplands to the east, such as the Shivwits and Uinkaret Plateaus. Analysis of the Gold Butte sample relies on the physical attributes and chronological assignments developed by Lyneis (1986), Larson and Michaelsen (1990), Allison (2000), and Jensen (2002) to accomplish these goals.

Projectile points have proven to be effective horizon markers over much of the Great Basin, and the basic time and space parameters for a number of projectile point types have been well established for some time (Bettinger and Taylor 1974; Holmer 1986; Thomas 1981). Some researchers, however, have struggled with the chronological accuracy of certain types. Haarklau et al. (2005), for example, have essentially given up, simply classifying thousands of projectile points from southern Nevada as either pre- or post-Mazama in age (before or after ca. 5800 cal BC). A more positive result has been achieved by Seddon (2005), who analyzed source-specific obsidian hydration data from a large sample of projectile points from southern Utah classified according to the standard Great Basin sequence (i.e., Desert Side-notched, Rosegate, Elko, Gatecliff, Humboldt, Pinto). He found that the mean rim values for each point series arrayed themselves in the expected sequence, demonstrating their basic utility as temporal indicators. Based on this finding, as well as projectile point assemblages recovered from single-component rock shelter deposits (e.g., Gypsum Cave) and well-dated room blocks (e.g., Lost City) in the surrounding area, we use the standard Great Basin temporal types and cross-check them with obsidian hydration, associated radiocarbon dates, and other time-sensitive artifacts found in associated contexts (e.g., sherds).

Obsidian hydration is often the only available means of dating the open-air lithic scatters that are ubiquitous in the region. Early attempts to use this dating technique are fraught with misgivings about its analytical veracity (e.g., Elston and Juell 1987); others were faced with data sets so small that they defied pattern recognition (e.g., Hull 1994; Lyneis et al. 1989; Myhrer and Lyneis 1985). The technique's analytical utility is best demonstrated in the western Great Basin, where large obsidian quarries are common: relatively accurate rates have been developed for major sources such as Coso and Casa Diablo based on association with radiocarbon-dated contexts and rim values from time-sensitive projectile points (e.g., Basgall 1990; Gilreath and Hildebrandt 1997; Hall

and Jackson 1989). Although obsidian is relatively rare at Gold Butte, rough age estimates are made for three primary sources (Delamar Mountains, Kane Springs, and Modena/Panaca Summit) using the methods outlined above.

ARCHAIC SETTLEMENT SYSTEMS

As exemplified by Jennings's concept of the Desert Culture and Steward's characterization of the family band, there is a long tradition of viewing Archaic lifeways in the arid West as the domain of small-group, residentially mobile foragers. The environment is seen as much too harsh to allow any sort of settlement elaboration beyond this basic pattern.

While most researchers would generally agree that this profile of mobile foragers describes Early Archaic lifeways (roughly 6000 to 2500 BC), there is an emerging, alternative framework for the subsistence-settlement after 2500 BC, the Late Archaic period. McGuire and Hildebrandt (2005; see also Hildebrandt and McGuire 2002) have argued that the Late Archaic, far from representing mobile, wide-ranging foragers, may actually represent the "trans-Holocene highpoint" of residential stability in the Great Basin. They point to an emerging village pattern that appears at this time in such varied locations as the Carson Desert (Kelly 2001; Zeanah 2004), the northwestern Great Basin (Elston et al. 1994; McGuire 1997, 2002; Riddell 1960); Owens Valley (Delacorte 1999:17); and the eastern Great Basin (Madsen and Simms 1998). To this list we might add the appearance of pithouse residential sites dating to Basketmaker II, with the earliest on Black Dog Mesa radiocarbon dated as early as AD 260 (Winslow 2006).

Most of these larger settlements were critically positioned to take advantage of a wide range of generally lower-ranked but abundant resources, often in lowland settings. This settlement configuration is conditioned by the activities and goals of women, children, and older males (Zeanah 2004). Prime-age males, in contrast, became more focused on high levels of long-distance, logistically based, large-game hunting and hunting-related activities (e.g., toolstone resupply), as well as an expansion of interregional exchange.

Given these characterizations of the Archaic periods, we expect to see an Early Archaic settlement pattern represented by a series of small foraging camps containing a limited but eclectic range of artifacts reflecting small-family-group, residential behavior. After 2500 BC there may have been a settlement transformation in the latter part of the Late Archaic and into Basketmaker times, when more centralized base camps were established in lowland areas, associated with evidence of greater long-range logistical activity. In a hinterland such as Gold Butte, we expect less evidence of residential activity, since it has now shifted to the Virgin River corridor, and a greater abundance of the specialized hunting camps and lithic procurement/reduction areas that supported long-range hunting forays. Ceremonial sites reflecting the escalated importance of hunting (e.g., Firebrand Cave) and many specialized rock art locations may also reflect this settlement shift.

AGRICULTURAL PRODUCTION AND THE USE OF HINTERLAND AREAS

Cultivation of maize began in the Gold Butte area with the initiation of Basketmaker II adaptations sometime around 350 BC. The importance of maize versus wild plants during this early time has been the subject of lively debate, but all researchers agree that by Puebloan times the agricultural diet had broadened to include beans and squash and that the role of wild plants had been reduced (Larson and Michaelsen 1990; Lyneis 1995; see also Diehl and Waters 2005; Huckell et al. 2002). Larson and Michaelsen (1990) argue that more intensified use of domesticates was accompanied by major population increases along the Virgin and Muddy Rivers, with densities staying relatively low through Basketmaker II and most of Basketmaker III times but exploding in the Puebloan phases, reaching a fourfold increase in Pueblo II just before the catastrophic crash at about AD 1200.

If this scenario is correct, it has major implications for the use of the Gold Butte hinterland. During Basketmaker II and III times, when population densities were rather low and local peoples were using a broad mix of both domesticated and wild plants, Gold Butte would have been regularly visited on subsistence forays that focused on a variety of wild plant and animal resources. With greater dependence on the production and storage of agricultural products, visits to Gold Butte would have been reduced, perhaps restricted to obtaining large game and other high-ranked resources such as pinyon. By the Late Prehistoric period, after the Puebloan collapse, we should see an increase in activity at Gold Butte, with Paiute populations intensively using all available subsistence resources.

Measuring the intensity of land use is not a simple task, but it can be achieved through calculating the frequency of radiocarbon dates, projectile points, and obsidian hydration readings per time period; tracking the distribution of dated sites across different environmental zones; and assessing changes in artifact assemblages

over time. Following the lead of Barlow (2005), we also model the caloric return rates of wild foods versus domesticated plants and indirectly assess the success of Puebloan food production by analyzing the composition of floral and faunal remains through the Gold Butte occupational sequence (i.e., did the Virgin Puebloans exploit low-ranked wild foods at Gold Butte or not?).

INTERREGIONAL EXCHANGE

Some items that commonly occur in archaeological assemblages come from distant areas seemingly beyond the reach of local peoples, and obtaining them may have incurred high costs. Exchange of these items can be a means for groups to mediate their socioeconomic interactions and manage real or perceived long- and short-term risks (Allison 2000). The intensity and nature of cultural contacts and socioeconomic interactions, and the interregional solutions for equalizing local resource imbalances, can be monitored through trade-ware pottery, nonlocal toolstone (e.g., obsidian from several distinctive source areas), and precious minerals and marine shell used for currency, decoration, and/or funerary offerings.

Physiographically and culturally, the Gold Butte area is a western extension of the Arizona Strip and the Shivwits Plateau, and so can rightfully be perceived as part of the corridor along which commodities moved between the Kayenta Branch populations centered in the upland plateaus to the east and the Virgin Branch populations centered on the Muddy and Virgin Rivers to the west. One of the most common nonlocal items that occurs regularly and in appreciable frequency in Gold Butte sites is gray ware pottery manufactured in the uplands to the east, such as Moapa and Shivwits wares. A persistent but small amount of San Juan Red and Tsegi Orange wares, also produced east of the Uinkaret Plateau, find their way into sites in our vicinity as well.

There are a variety of reasons why pottery exchange occurred in the local area. One of the most compelling has been proposed by Jensen (2002:44), who argues that farming in the uplands to the east was a high-risk endeavor compared with farming along the lowland floodplains to the west, watered by the reliable spring-fed Muddy River. The eastern upland populations could have provided pots in exchange for corn from the western lowland populations, allowing upland people to buffer subsistence risks and lowland people to maintain social ties and/or to obtain valued items.

For the pottery in the Gold Butte study area to reveal something about the development, timing, and intensity of trade relations between eastern and western populations, we must determine the age placement of the pottery encountered and, by extension, when sites were occupied or used. We anticipate two alternative distributional patterns that can be used to identify the intensity of exchange through the Gold Butte study area. If Gold Butte was simply a transport zone lying between more important central places, then trade wares (e.g., Moapa) and local wares (e.g., Tusayan) should be tightly clustered along a narrow trade corridor and their distribution would suggest that the surrounding area was an unoccupied hinterland during Puebloan times. If Puebloan pottery is scattered throughout our study area and the ratios of different wares mimic trends documented at Puebloan sites along the rivers, we may conclude that this hinterland was used for a wide range of purposes by Puebloan peoples.

There are numerous obsidian sources throughout the tri-corners area, the most important being Kane Springs, Delamar Mountains, and Modena/Panaca Summit as we move north. We expect that most obsidian will come from these sources, with the addition of small amounts of diverse glasses from more distant quarries throughout northern Utah, southern Nevada, and eastern California. The relative frequencies of these commodities may change through time and, if so, would reflect shifts in interregional exchange that could be related to population replacements at Gold Butte (e.g., an increase in obsidians from Arizona may indicate greater Patayan use of the area).

Whereas pottery establishes the upland-lowland, east-west exchange pattern across moderate distances—something on the order of 100 km (Gold Butte to Mt. Trumbull)—certain ornaments represent trade in different and more distant directions. Imported shells, for example, reflect interactions with people on the Pacific Coast and the Gulf of California (Lyneis 1992:69–71). The frequency of these materials, however, is quite low in the local area, even in major Basketmaker and Puebloan settlements (Allison 2000:187–189).

Salt was widely traded throughout the desert West, and the Virgin Branch served as an important production center for this important commodity. Large salt caves were mined near Lost City, and the mineral is thought to have been distributed east and southeast into the core Puebloan and Hohokam areas (Lyneis 1982). Copper ore also appears to have been an important local commodity. The blue-green material, which was ground up and used as paint, has been found in burials at Lost City. Lyneis (1992) suspects there was a local source for this mineral and refers to copper-bearing deposits near Overton and Bunkerville. Ethnographic accounts note

that the Southern Paiute obtained it from copper deposits along the Arizona Strip, from what is now known as the Grand Gulch Mine, and used it for body paint.

Rock Art

The rock art in Gold Butte has long been one of the main attractions drawing the public to this area. Surprisingly little is known, however, about its age, its relationship to the styles of rock art in the surrounding regions, and its cultural affiliation. From its broader archaeological context, some proportion of the art may be expected to be the markings of Virgin Branch ancestral Puebloans and/or their northern Fremont relatives; the Archaic desert people who preceded them; Patayan groups commonly associated with lands to the south, along the lower Colorado River and extending into the Colorado Desert; and ancestral and ethnographic Paiute. The approach we used to gain insight into who made this rock art, and by extension, when and why it was fabricated, relies primarily on inter- and intraregional stylistic comparisons.

A general stylistic chronology founded on the work of Heizer and Baumhoff (1962) and Heizer and Clewlow (1973) has been applied to rock art throughout the Great Basin and formed the basis for a sequence that White (2002) has proposed for Clark County. That scheme, however, is woefully inadequate for our purposes since it underplays the Southwestern influences strongly represented in the county and does not recognize Patayan as a distinct rock art style. To supplement that scheme, we turn primarily to Schaafsma (1971, 1980) for the defining stylistic characteristics of Basketmaker/Puebloan rock art in what is now Arizona and Utah; and to Christensen and Dickey (2001) and Hedges (2003) for the defining characteristics of Patayan rock art. With these augmentations, we recognize four broad categories with temporal significance: abstract Desert Archaic, representational, Protohistoric, and Early Historic. The rock art in Gold Butte might reasonably date to a wide range of time and be associated with various known styles. The major styles defined for the eastern Great Basin, Mojave Desert, and northwestern Southwest are presented in Chapter 7; they provide the context for interpreting the age, function, and cultural affiliation of Gold Butte's rock art.

Puebloan Abandonment

Identifying reasons for the collapse of Puebloan culture throughout the Southwest has been the subject of debate for many decades. This is certainly the case for the Virgin Branch, where a variety of scenarios have been proposed, including abandonment due to devastating droughts, withdrawal due to violent conflict with the Southern Paiute, and assimilation with the Paiute and a return to a foraging way of life.

Larson and Michaelsen (1990) are the primary proponents for a drought-induced abandonment by the Virgin Branch Puebloans. Two periods of severe drought were identified. The first occurred between AD 966 and 1020, followed by increasing rainfall between AD 1020 and 1120, with a return to drought conditions beginning in the early 1120s and persisting for the next 30 years.

The first drought is thought to have put extreme pressure on the availability of wild foods, forcing local Puebloan occupants to intensify agricultural production. After AD 1020, population growth accelerated rapidly due to favorable conditions, reaching four times the density found in Basketmaker times. The second drought (AD 1120–1150s) was much more difficult to cope with than the first, as human population levels were too high for traditional responses to adverse climatic conditions (e.g., going back to the use of wild foods), leading to the abandonment of the area.

Although Lyneis (1995) agrees that climatic stresses may have contributed to the fall of Puebloan populations, she argues that this may not have been the primary factor behind the Virgin Branch Puebloan collapse. One of the major problems with the climatic model proposed by Larson and Michaelsen (1990) is that many Virgin Branch settlements persisted into the early AD 1200s, which postdates the AD 1120–1150 drought event (Lyneis 1995:232). As a result of this discrepancy, she suggests that multiple factors may have been involved, including complex interactions with Numic-speaking peoples from the west (i.e., the Southern Paiute).

It is clear that the Southern Paiute ultimately replaced the Puebloans in the Gold Butte region, but it is unclear whether they moved into an abandoned area, actively displaced the farming population, or assimi-lated the remnant Puebloans into their hunter-gatherer culture. Advocates for the active displacement hypothesis note that conflicts along the Numa frontier were a common occurrence during the historic period and probably occurred on a regular basis in prehistory as well (Ambler and Sutton 1989; Hayden 1930; see also Altschul and Fairley 1989). Lyneis (1994), in contrast, argues that Pueblo and Paiute peoples lived side by side free of major conflict and probably had mutualistic interactions (e.g., the exchange of useful commodities). Janetski (1993) and Huffman (1993) agree, and suggest that the Virgin Puebloans were less committed to agricultural production than many of their eastern relatives, creating flexible interactions with their neighbors and thus raising the likelihood that they were assimilated by the Paiutes.

Given the hinterland nature of this study area, we are not able to develop detailed tests for all the issues outlined above. We should be able, however, to distinguish between an abrupt Puebloan collapse and abandonment (Larson and Michaelsen 1990) and a more gradual process of de-intensification and assimilation with the adjacent Southern Paiute population (Huffman 1993; Janetski 1993; Lyneis 1995). If, for example, Pueblo II populations were largely dependent on agricultural products and abandoned the area quickly, we should see little change in the spatial distribution of sherds over the entire period of Puebloan occupation of the region (e.g., use of pinyon and agave areas should be relatively low throughout). If, in contrast, the Puebloans were more flexible and able to adopt the Paiute way of life, the tail end of the Puebloan sequence should look different from its earlier phases of occupation and should mimic the Paiute land-use pattern marked by brown ware pottery and Desert Side-notched projectile points. The latter pattern should be quite generalized, making use of a wide range of habitats.

4 Survey Methods and Results

In this chapter we describe the overall structure of the random and nonrandom survey. For statistical reasons, the kinds of sites and features encountered in these separate phases are reported separately.

SURVEY METHODS

The survey included both random-sample and nonrandom elements. The random-sample survey was intended to allow quantitative estimates of site densities within the larger study area, while the nonrandom survey was intended to allow focused investigation on specific areas or site types.

Both phases of survey employed the grid of 500-×-500-m units established at the outset of the study. This grid was laid out on UTM NAD 83 Zone 11 coordinates, and each unit was given a unique identifier according to its row-column position in a grid anchored at the southwest corner of the study area (e.g., unit 101-34 is in the 101st row up from the bottom and the 34th column to the right). Each unit totaled 25 ha (61.775 ac). Excluding units falling within private inholdings or lands managed by other agencies (e.g., the Lake Mead National Recreation Area, National Park Service lands in the southern and western edges of the study area), there were a total of 5,442 units available for selection in the sample survey.

FIELD METHODS

Both the random-sample and nonrandom surveys consisted of complete pedestrian coverage of these sample units. All cultural resources, both prehistoric and historic, were recorded in each unit regardless of the purpose for a given unit's selection; methods were kept consistent through all phases of the survey to ensure comparability of results.

Field personnel were organized into four-person crews, each led by a crew chief. Survey units were traversed using two pairs of down-and-back sweeps; crew members were placed at 30-m intervals, and four sweeps thus provided complete coverage of each sample unit. Where the terrain was too rugged to safely traverse, crew members broke from their transects but attempted to provide coverage by following contours or by specifically targeting small flats, overhangs, or rock shelters for inspection. Accurate navigation within the survey unit was maintained with handheld GPS units. Detailed information on survey coverage, ground visibility, and cultural resources encountered, as well as general observations on vegetation, fauna, and terrain, were noted on a 1:5,000 scale map of each survey unit and an accompanying form filled out by the crew chief.

The recording of cultural resources adhered largely to BLM standards but deviated in the following ways in response to the nature of the local archaeology. Sites were defined as four or more spatially dispersed items, and/or one feature or more (hearth, rock art panel, agave oven, etc.). Other remains (including segregated reduction locations [SRLs] and pot drops) were recorded as isolates. Both of these items are analogous to a broken bottle. Additional characteristics of an SRL are provided later in the chapter.

With the exception of a few very large historic-period sites, all sites were recorded in their entirety, irrespective of survey unit boundaries. All sites were recorded on standard IMACS forms, using either the long or the short form as appropriate to the complexity of the resource. Site mapping data points and isolate locations were recorded using handheld GPS units, and individual artifact and feature locations were recorded on sketch maps. For some larger sites, internal details were also mapped with GPS. Overview photos, as well as photos of individual features (e.g., rock art panels), were taken.

A program of enhanced recordation was employed at prehistoric sites in order to provide additional information on site structure and function, lithic technologies, and site age:

- An in-field analysis of flaked stone debitage was undertaken to assess technological variability as well as to characterize toolstone types and natural attributes. At smaller sites the entire surface assemblage was analyzed, while at larger sites one surface analysis unit (SAU) or more was laid out in the area of highest density. The dimensions of these SAUs were adjusted to provide a minimum of 50 pieces of debitage in the analysis.
- One 25-×-25-cm test probe or more was excavated as necessary to determine whether subsurface deposits were present. These were excavated in 10-cm levels until sterile soil or bedrock/hardpan was reached, and the soils were passed through ⅛-inch screen. All cultural materials from these units were retained and catalogued.
- All formed flaked and ground stone tools evident on the surface were provenienced and described using a standard set of morphological/functional criteria (e.g., projectile points, bifaces, flake tools) and technological classifications (e.g., biface stage, ground stone wear type).
- Temporally diagnostic items were collected, including projectile points, obsidian items for sourcing and obsidian hydration analysis, and selected sherds. Although the original plan was to restrict sherd collection to rims and obvious exotic pieces like red ware, review of the initial results showed that in-field identification of pottery was problematic, and larger samples of pottery were collected from nearly every site (n = 24) with an appreciable quantity. Finally, samples of charcoal or charcoal-rich sediment suitable for radiocarbon dating were collected from shallow probes (<30 cm deep) in agave ovens.

Random-Sample Survey

For the random-sample survey, the universe of sample units was stratified into a series of five domains in order to ensure adequate sampling in each of the various environmental zones making up the study area (Figure 4.1). These five strata were lowlands, the Virgin River floodplain/riparian zone, the Red Rock zone, uplands, and pinyon-supporting uplands.

Uplands and lowlands were distinguished using digital elevation data from the U.S. Geological Survey's National Elevation Dataset (http://ned.usgs.gov). We derived the average slope value for each sample unit and divided uplands versus lowlands on the arbitrary value of 15 degrees.

Uplands were subsequently subdivided into pinyon-supporting and general upland units, based on data on existing land cover from the Southwest Regional Gap Analysis Project (http://fws-nmcfw ru.nmsu.edu/swregap/default.htm). Sample units with more than 50 percent coverage of the pinyon-juniper woodland community were defined as pinyon-supporting. Most of these units are in the Virgin Range, but a few are in the Cedar Basin area in the southeastern part of the study area.

Lowlands were also subsequently subdivided into three areas: the Red Rock zone, the Virgin River floodplain, and general lowlands. The Red Rock zone was defined by the occurrence of Aztec sandstone, as depicted on 1:24,000 scale geologic maps of the central part of the study area (Beard 1991, 1992, 1993), as well as a more generalized geologic map of the Gold Butte area (Longwell et al. 1965). All lowland units within 100 m of a mapped sandstone outcrop were defined as the Red Rock zone. The Virgin River floodplain/riparian zone was defined by selecting lowland units within one kilometer of the Virgin River floodplain, as defined by floodplain soil units from published soil surveys (http://soildatamart.nrcs.usda.gov /State.aspx).

An initial 5 percent random sample of the study area was selected, drawn evenly from each of these five domains, resulting in a total of 273 units (6,825 ha/ 16,865 ac) throughout the study area. These units were surveyed over the course of five nine-day field rotations between October 11 and December 16, 2006.

After the completion of this initial random-sample survey, and concurrently with parts of the nonrandom survey, a second round of random-sample units was selected from two of the more productive domains. Twenty-eight units in the Red Rock zone and ten units in the pinyon-upland zone were selected, bringing the total to 17.2 percent and 7.4 percent of these domains respectively, and the total amount of random-sample survey coverage up to 311 units (7,775 ha/19,212 ac; Table 4.1). These units were surveyed between March 27 and June 10, 2007.

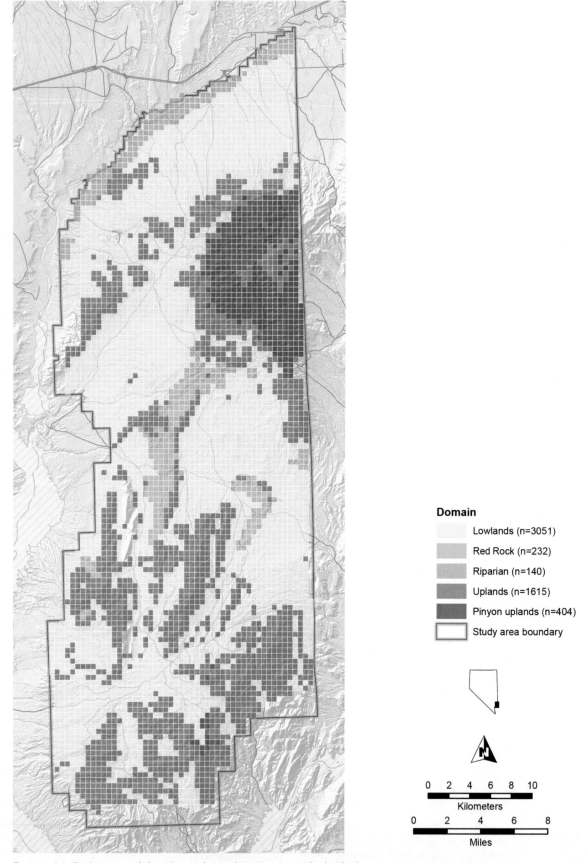

FIGURE 4.1. Environmental domains and sample unit universe (individual survey units not depicted).

TABLE 4.1. Survey Acreage.

Domain	Total Units	Random		Nonrandom		Total	
		Units	% of Units	Units	% of Units	Units	% of Units
Lowlands	3,051	153	5.0	81	2.7	234	7.7
Lowlands, Red Rock Zone	232	40[a]	17.2	47	20.3	87	37.5
Virgin River Riparian Zone	140	7	5.0	25	17.9	32	22.9
Uplands	1,615	81	5.0	33[b]	2.0	114	7.1
Uplands, Pinyon Zone	404	30	7.4	8	2.0	38	9.4
Total	5,442	311	5.7	194	3.6	505	9.3

[a] Includes nine units initially selected for nonrandom survey.
[b] Includes one unit outside sample universe.

Nonrandom Survey

After the completion of the initial phase of the random-sample survey, nonrandom survey coverage was chosen in consultation with BLM archaeologists and project historians in order to target specific areas of interest for both prehistoric and historic sites. For prehistoric sites, eight separate groups of survey units were selected, as detailed below, totaling 164 units; an additional 30 units were selected to target locations of historic interest (Figures 4.1, 4.2; Table 4.1). These 194 nonrandom units, totaling 4,850 ha (11,984 ac), were surveyed between January 23 and June 13, 2007.

South Virgin Range

Fifteen units were chosen on the flanks of the Virgin Mountains, in an area where a previous study (Ellis et al. 1982) had documented agave roasting pits and associated habitation debris.

Red Rock Zone, North

Fifty-two nonrandom units were selected in the northern and central parts of the Red Rock zone because of the very high density and diversity of sites observed in this area during the random-sample survey. (Eight additional units in this area were originally selected and surveyed as part of this nonrandom coverage but later were randomly selected and counted with the second phase of random-sample coverage.) Together with the other units in the Red Rock zone, these units were selected so as to encompass all but three of the previously recorded rock art sites in the study area.

Red Rock Zone, South

Three units in the southern part of the main Red Rock zone were selected because avocational rock art recording efforts had identified several sites in the area that were thought likely to contain additional, unrecorded habitation debris. (A fourth surveyed unit in this area was later selected and counted with the random-sample coverage.)

Mud Hills

Random-sample survey results, as well as information from Friends of Gold Butte (FOGB) and other local interested groups, indicated the possibility of habitation debris, ovens, and/or rock art in the Mud Hills. Seven units were selected in this area.

26CK5434 Area

Five units in the vicinity of site 26CK5434 were selected for survey to assess whether it is an isolated phenomenon or whether habitation sites exist that may be associated with the use of this important site.

Cedar Basin Pinyon Zone

Avocational survey by John Lear and colleagues indicated that habitation and other sites exist in Cedar Basin. While both Cedar Basin and the Virgin Mountains support pinyon, the gentler terrain of the former suggested a potentially much higher density of pinyon-related sites. The initial round of survey indicated that the pinyon-upland domain was defined too conservatively in this area and that the actual distribution of pinyon is much wider. A block of 14 units was selected.

Springs

Forty-three units surrounding named springs not previously covered by random-sample coverage, lying primarily in the southern part of the study area, were selected for survey on the premise that the springs should support a generally higher density and diversity of prehistoric sites than surrounding country.

Virgin River Riparian Zone

Twenty-five units were selected along the Virgin River to document the Basketmaker/Puebloan occupations along the river corridor. Results from the random-sample survey indicated that the domain was drawn too widely, and thus the units selected for nonrandom survey were limited to those immediately adjacent to the river floodplain.

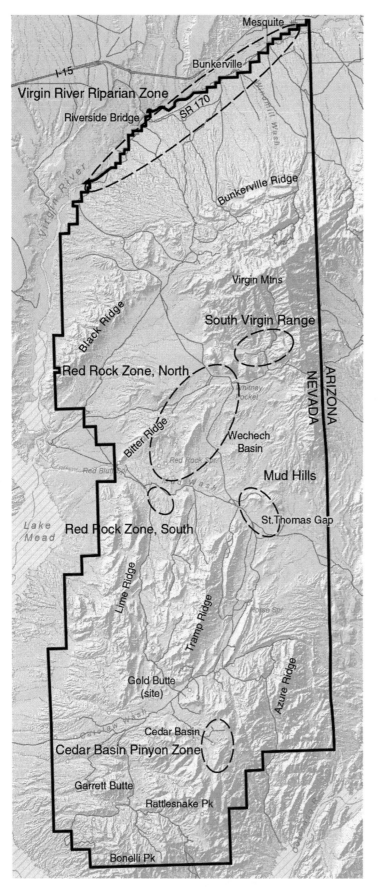

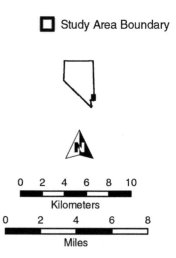

Study Area Boundary

| 0 | 2 | 4 | 6 | 8 | 10 |
Kilometers

| 0 | 2 | 4 | 6 | 8 |
Miles

FIGURE 4.2. Areas of interest selected for nonrandom survey coverage.

Historic Units

Thirty units were selected in areas of interest for historic-period sites. These units were surveyed by specialist teams led by Ron Reno and Charles Zeier. Although the primary focus of this phase of work was historic remains, prehistoric sites encountered in these units were recorded using the same methods employed during other phases of survey. The historic team also conducted additional reconnaissance and site-recording work (not systematic survey) along historic roads and at complex or extensive historic-period sites identified by other survey crews.

Prehistoric Site Types

Prehistoric sites were assigned to type using the typology presented below. As detailed below, the Habitation, Limited Habitation, Simple Nonflaked Stone, and Simple Flaked Stone types are mutually exclusive but are combined with Rock Art, Agave Oven, and/or Quarry types as appropriate. Neither the overall size of the assemblage nor the presence of subsurface remains is a defining element of the typology.

- *Habitations.* The distinguishing feature of this type is the presence of structural remains, thermal features, and/or midden soil, typically but not always in combination with a range of flaked stone tools, milling equipment, and pottery. Outside the Virgin Range riparian corridor, most habitation sites are found in and surrounding rock shelters, though not all sites with rock shelters are defined as habitations. Habitation sites in the Virgin River corridor tend to comprise housepit depressions and storage cists with a very limited range of associated artifacts, perhaps due in large part to a long history of informal collection.
- *Limited Habitations.* This type includes sites with appreciable quantities of flaked stone tools and/or debitage in association with milling equipment and/or pottery but lacking residential features or middens that indicate extended habitation activities.
- *Simple Nonflaked Stone Sites.* This type includes sites with milling gear and/or pottery but with few or no flaked stone items. (Individual pot-drop features were recorded as isolates.)
- *Simple Flaked Stone Sites.* These sites contain only flaked stone tools and/or debitage. This is by far the most common prehistoric site type in the Gold Butte area; typically, these sites are small and lack an associated subsurface deposit.
- *Rock Art.* As the name implies, this type includes sites containing rock art, whether alone or in combination with other remains.
- *Agave Ovens.* Again, as the name indicates, the type

implies the presence of agave ovens (roasting pits), with or without associated artifacts.
- *Quarries/Segregated reduction locations (SRLs).* These are areas where locally available raw toolstone has been reduced, leaving a narrow range of artifacts, such as cobble cores and early-stage bifaces, in association with debitage. (Single SRLs were recorded as isolates.) In contrast to a site, an isolated SRL contains pieces of a single artifact (reduction of a single nodule, single core, or single biface). They are analogous to a broken bottle. They are confined to a pavement surface or on the surface of a residual lag deposit that contains a low density of broadly dispersed nodules of toolstone-quality cryptocrystalline silicate (CCS) and basalt as part of a lithic landscape.

A few of the smaller sites remained untyped because they contained unusual associations of features and/or tools or were so ephemeral as to resist meaningful classification (e.g., two flakes and one sherd); these were typed simply as Other.

Analytical Methods and Special Studies

As discussed above, limited collections were made at prehistoric sites during the survey phase, including diagnostic or datable surface artifacts (projectile points, selected sherds, obsidian items, beads, perishables), cultural materials from shovel probes, and charcoal-rich sediment samples from feature contexts. All collected materials were processed and catalogued at the Far Western Anthropological Research Group laboratory in Davis, California. The temporal significance of the projectile points, pottery, and beads is discussed below (see also Chapter 5).

Radiocarbon Dating

Apart from the radiocarbon-dating assays on samples from sites investigated during test excavation (see Chapter 6), ten additional dates were obtained from survey samples from selected agave roasting ovens. Nearly all radiocarbon measurements were made by BetaAnalytic of Miami, Florida. Two additional samples were processed by Elisabetta Boaretto, director of the Radiocarbon Dating and Cosmogenic Isotopes Laboratory, Weizmann Institute of Science, Rehovot, Israel. A review of all results is presented in Chapter 5.

Obsidian Hydration and Sourcing

As a general rule, only a trace amount of obsidian was encountered at any location. Consequently, the pieces were provenienced and collected for special analysis. In nearly every instance, five or fewer obsidian items were

TABLE 4.2. Summary Distribution of Sites and Isolates.

	Random (311 units)	Nonrandom (194 units)	Nonrandom/ Non-unit	Total
Sites				
Prehistoric	104	237	—	341
Historic	45	79	38	162
Multicomponent	8	26	2	36
Total	157	342	40	539
Isolates				
Prehistoric	171	214	2	387
Historic	339	361	—	700
Noncultural/Indeterminate	5	6	—	11
Total	515	581	2	1,098

noted and collected. No more than ten pieces were collected from the rare context where obsidian was more abundant. In total, 179 of the 191 pieces of obsidian collected during survey were sent for geochemical sourcing via x-ray fluorescence (XRF) and obsidian hydration measurement. The XRF sourcing was conducted by Richard Hughes, Geochemical Research Laboratory, Portola Valley, California; obsidian hydration was measured by Tim Carpenter of Archaometrics, Woodland, California. Results of these analyses are reviewed in the Chapter 5.

SURVEY RESULTS

Table 4.2 summarizes the results of both phases of survey. A total of 539 sites was recorded, of which 341 are prehistoric in age, 162 date to the historic period, and 36 contain both historic and prehistoric components; Table 4.3 lists those with prehistoric components. Of these, 40 sites (primarily historic roads) were recorded outside the context of systematic survey. Fifty-nine sites were updates of previously recorded sites, while the remaining 480 were newly recorded. An additional 39 previously recorded sites originally mapped within the survey areas were not re-recorded, typically because they were not relocated.

A total of 1,098 isolates was recorded from all phases of survey (Table 4.2): 387 of prehistoric age, 700 dating to the historic period, and 11 items of uncertain age or unassociated with human occupation (pack rat middens, empty shelters). The remainder of this discussion focuses on prehistoric resources exclusively.

Random-Sample Survey

In the 311 units selected for the random-sample survey, 112 sites containing prehistoric components and 171 prehistoric isolates were recorded (Table 4.2). Fifteen of the random-sample units lie in extremely precipitous terrain that could not be systematically surveyed; however, these units are assumed to have been similarly inaccessible to prehistoric people and thus to lack prehistoric sites.

Table 4.4 shows the distribution of the 112 prehistoric components with respect to the five survey domains defined at the outset of the study. Because this is a random-sample survey, the site totals and densities for each domain can serve as quantitative estimates of overall totals and densities in those domains; it is also possible to calculate the standard error in these estimates. As the table shows, site density figures vary widely among the domains, ranging from a low of 0.07 ± 0.03 sites per survey unit in the uplands domain (one site per 883 acres), to a high of 1.80 ± 0.31 sites per unit in the Red Rock domain (one site per 34 acres). Note, however, that the standard error in the density estimates for some of the domains is rather high relative to the averages. This is because site counts do not follow a statistically normal distribution (i.e., most of the sample units contain no sites while a few contain as many as five or six). This affects only the size of the standard error figure, however, not the accuracy of the density estimate.

The overall density of prehistoric sites from the random-sample survey is 0.36 sites per sample unit; however, this figure is not a valid density estimate over the sampling universe because of the different sampling proportions in each of the domains. In particular, the rock art domain is much more heavily sampled than other domains and also contains a much higher average density of sites, skewing the figure upward. After we correct for the differences in sampling proportions, the figure is indeed quite a bit lower, at 0.21 ± 0.03 sites per survey unit. Notwithstanding the many impressive prehistoric sites found in the study area, this is a very low

TABLE 4.3. Sites with Prehistoric Component(s).

Site (26CK)	Agency No. (CrNV-53-)	Is Update	Type	Domain(s)	Phase	Area (m²)
6666	—	Yes	Limited habitation/Rock art	Red Rock zone	2nd random	2,017
6666	—	Yes	Limited habitation/Rock art	Red Rock zone	2nd random	320
6672	—	Yes	Limited habitation/Rock art	Red Rock zone	Nonrandom	11,711
6698	—	Yes	Limited habitation	Red Rock zone	Nonrandom	20,301
6699	—	Yes	Other (hunting blind)	Red Rock zone	Nonrandom	<75
7029	—	Yes	Habitation/Rock art	Red Rock zone	Nonrandom	17,184
7574	—	Yes	Habitation	Lowlands; Uplands	Nonrandom	715,641
7874	7666	No	Habitation	Lowlands	1st random	914
7876	7668	No	Simple flaked stone	Lowlands	1st random	825
7877	7669	No	Simple flaked stone	Lowlands	1st random	773
7878	7670	No	Limited habitation	Lowlands	Nonrandom	<75
7879	7671	No	Simple flaked stone	Lowlands	Nonrandom	92
7880	7672	No	Other (Simple nonflaked stone/ hunting blind)	Lowlands	Nonrandom	1,909
7882	7674	No	Limited habitation	Lowlands	Nonrandom	277
7883	7675	No	Limited habitation	Uplands	1st random	1,989
7884	7676	No	Simple flaked stone	Lowlands	Nonrandom	796
7885	7677	No	Limited habitation	Lowlands	Nonrandom	5,533
7886	7678	No	Limited habitation	Lowlands	Nonrandom	1,734
7887	7679	No	Limited habitation	Lowlands	Nonrandom	1,346
7889	7681	No	Limited habitation	Lowlands	Nonrandom	520
7890	7682	No	Habitation	Lowlands	Nonrandom	3,194
7891	7683	No	Simple nonflaked stone	Lowlands	Nonrandom	<75
7892	7684	No	Limited habitation	Lowlands; Pinyon zone	Nonrandom	7,920
7893	7685	No	Simple nonflaked stone	Pinyon zone	1st random	227
7895	7687	No	Simple flaked stone	Lowlands	Nonrandom	<75
7896	7688	No	Simple flaked stone	Lowlands	Nonrandom	370
7897	7689	No	Simple flaked stone	Lowlands	Nonrandom	583
7898	7690	No	Simple flaked stone	Lowlands	Nonrandom	234
7899	7691	No	Simple flaked stone	Lowlands	Nonrandom	338
7900	7692	No	Simple flaked stone	Lowlands	Nonrandom	<75
7901	7693	No	Other (point, pot drop)	Lowlands	Nonrandom	970
7903	7695	No	Limited habitation	Lowlands	Nonrandom	1,190
7904	7696	No	Limited habitation	Lowlands	Nonrandom	2,170
7905	7697	No	Habitation	Lowlands	Nonrandom	8,343
7906	7698	No	Limited habitation	Lowlands	Nonrandom	993
7907	7699	No	Habitation	Lowlands	Nonrandom	1,613
7908	7700	No	Limited habitation	Lowlands	Nonrandom	265
7909	7701	No	Limited habitation	Lowlands	Nonrandom	179
7910	7702	No	Limited habitation	Lowlands	Nonrandom	99
7911	7703	No	Other (2 flakes, 1 pottery)	Lowlands	Nonrandom	<75
7912	7704	No	Other (2 flakes, 1 pottery)	Lowlands	Nonrandom	<75
7913	7705	No	Limited habitation	Lowlands	Nonrandom	8,347
7914	7706	No	Limited habitation	Lowlands	Nonrandom	532
7915	7707	No	Limited habitation	Lowlands	Nonrandom	3,305
7916	7708	No	Simple nonflaked stone	Lowlands	Nonrandom	156
7917	7709	No	Habitation	Lowlands	Nonrandom	2,730
7918	7710	No	Other (2 flakes, 2 pottery)	Lowlands	Nonrandom	<75

TABLE 4.3. (cont'd.) Sites with Prehistoric Component(s).

Site (26CK)	Agency No. (CrNV-53-)	Is Update	Type	Domain(s)	Phase	Area (m²)
7919	7711	No	Limited habitation	Lowlands	Nonrandom	1,301
7920	7712	No	Limited habitation	Lowlands	Nonrandom	525
7921	7713	No	Limited habitation	Lowlands	Nonrandom	1,929
7922	7714	No	Limited habitation	Lowlands	Nonrandom	<75
7923	7715	No	Limited habitation	Lowlands	Nonrandom	688
7924	7716	No	Limited habitation	Lowlands	Nonrandom	283
7925	7717	No	Simple flaked stone	Lowlands	Nonrandom	124
7926	7718	No	Simple flaked stone	Lowlands	Nonrandom	<75
7927	7719	No	Simple flaked stone	Lowlands	Nonrandom	<75
7930	7722	No	Other (stained soil)	Uplands	1st random	209
7932	7724	No	Simple flaked stone/Oven	Lowlands	1st random	1,214
7935	7727	No	Limited habitation	Lowlands	1st random	4,266
7936	7728	No	Limited habitation/Oven	Lowlands	1st random	1,334
7937	7729	No	Limited habitation	Lowlands	1st random	1,191
7940	7732	No	Simple flaked stone	Lowlands	Nonrandom	139
7941	7733	No	Simple flaked stone	Lowlands	Nonrandom	207
7945	7737	No	Limited habitation	Lowlands	Nonrandom	1,505
7946	7738	No	Simple flaked stone	Lowlands	Nonrandom	883
7947	7739	No	Simple flaked stone	Lowlands	Nonrandom	611
7948	7740	No	Quarry	Red Rock zone	1st random	3,181
7949	7741	No	Quarry	Red Rock zone	1st random	84
7950	7742	No	Quarry	Red Rock zone	1st random	4,564
7951	7743	No	Limited habitation/Oven	Uplands	1st random	419
7954	7746	No	Simple flaked stone	Red Rock zone	2nd random	2,705
7955	7747	No	Simple flaked stone	Red Rock zone	1st random	<75
7956	7748	No	Quarry	Red Rock zone	1st random	684
7957	7749	No	Simple flaked stone	Red Rock zone	1st random	<75
7958	7750	No	Quarry	Red Rock zone	1st random	2,444
7959	7751	No	Simple flaked stone	Red Rock zone	2nd random	819
7960	7752	No	Simple flaked stone	Uplands	1st random	614
7961	7753	No	Quarry	Lowlands	1st random	205
7963	7755	No	Simple flaked stone	Red Rock zone	2nd random	2,210
7964	7756	No	Simple flaked stone	Red Rock zone	2nd random	237
7965	7757	No	Other (slab, hearth)	Red Rock zone	2nd random	332
7966	7758	No	Habitation	Red Rock zone	2nd random	21,912
7967	7759	No	Simple flaked stone	Red Rock zone	2nd random	246
7968	7760	No	Limited habitation	Red Rock zone	2nd random	2,361
7969	7761	No	Simple flaked stone	Red Rock zone	2nd random	133
7970	7762	No	Simple flaked stone	Red Rock zone	2nd random	159
7971	7763	No	Simple flaked stone	Lowlands	Nonrandom	572
7972	7764	No	Limited habitation/Quarry	Lowlands	Nonrandom	14,316
7973	7765	No	Limited habitation	Lowlands	Nonrandom	9,869
7974	7766	No	Simple flaked stone	Lowlands	Nonrandom	437
7975	7767	No	Habitation	Lowlands	Nonrandom	3,001
7976	7768	No	Limited habitation	Lowlands	Nonrandom	1,963
7977	7769	No	Other (Simple flaked stone/ Hearth)	Lowlands; Red Rock zone	Nonrandom	1,042
7978	7770	No	Simple flaked stone	Red Rock zone	Nonrandom	<75

TABLE 4.3. (cont'd.) Sites with Prehistoric Component(s).

Site (26CK)	Agency No. (CrNV-53-)	Is Update	Type	Domain(s)	Phase	Area (m²)
7979	7771	No	Simple flaked stone	Red Rock zone	Nonrandom	2,298
7980	7772	No	Simple flaked stone	Red Rock zone	Nonrandom	<75
7981	7773	No	Habitation	Red Rock zone	Nonrandom	444
7982	7774	No	Simple flaked stone	Red Rock zone	1st random	1,026
7983	7775	No	Limited habitation	Red Rock zone	1st random	2,641
7984	7776	No	Limited habitation	Red Rock zone	1st random	885
7985	7777	No	Limited habitation	Red Rock zone	1st random	12,333
7986	7778	No	Limited habitation/Quarry	Lowlands; Red Rock zone	1st random	15,947
7987	7779	No	Limited habitation	Red Rock zone	1st random	2,924
7988	7780	No	Other (Simple flaked stone/Hearth)	Red Rock zone	Nonrandom	2,956
7989	7781	No	Simple flaked stone	Red Rock zone	Nonrandom	376
7990	7782	No	Simple flaked stone	Red Rock zone	Nonrandom	3,633
7991	7783	No	Limited habitation	Lowlands	1st random	419
7992	7784	No	Habitation	Red Rock zone	2nd random	175
7993	7785	No	Simple flaked stone	Lowlands	Nonrandom	8,048
7994	7786	No	Habitation	Red Rock zone	Nonrandom	1,247
7995	7787	No	Simple flaked stone	Red Rock zone	Nonrandom	399
7996	7788	No	Limited habitation/Rock art	Red Rock zone	Nonrandom	2,412
7997	7789	No	Rock art	Red Rock zone	2nd random	<75
7998	7790	No	Habitation	Red Rock zone	2nd random	173
7999	7791	No	Simple flaked stone	Red Rock zone	2nd random	117
8001	7793	No	Habitation	Red Rock zone	2nd random	1,144
8002	7794	No	Simple flaked stone	Red Rock zone	2nd random	<75
8003	7795	No	Simple flaked stone	Red Rock zone	2nd random	220
8004	7796	No	Limited habitation	Red Rock zone	2nd random	3,798
8005	7797	No	Simple flaked stone	Red Rock zone	2nd random	<75
8006	7798	No	Simple flaked stone/Hunting blind	Lowlands	Nonrandom	6,987
8007	7799	No	Simple flaked stone/Hunting blind	Lowlands	Nonrandom	224
8008	7800	No	Simple flaked stone/Hunting blind	Lowlands	Nonrandom	<75
8009	7801	No	Simple flaked stone/Hunting blind	Lowlands	Nonrandom	10,559
8010	7802	No	Simple flaked stone/Hunting blind	Lowlands	Nonrandom	4,071
8011	7803	No	Limited habitation	Red Rock zone	Nonrandom	6,524
8012	7804	No	Limited habitation	Red Rock zone	Nonrandom	5,805
8013	7805	No	Limited habitation	Red Rock zone	Nonrandom	2,077
8014	7806	No	Simple flaked stone	Red Rock zone	Nonrandom	2,590
8015	7807	No	Limited habitation	Red Rock zone	Nonrandom	13,739
8016	7808	No	Simple flaked stone	Red Rock zone	Nonrandom	6,565
8017	7809	No	Simple flaked stone	Red Rock zone	Nonrandom	2,251
8018	7810	No	Limited habitation	Red Rock zone	Nonrandom	7,571
8019	7811	No	Limited habitation/Rock art	Red Rock zone	Nonrandom	246
8020	7812	No	Limited habitation	Red Rock zone	Nonrandom	1,401
8021	7813	No	Simple flaked stone	Red Rock zone	Nonrandom	248
8022	7814	No	Simple flaked stone	Red Rock zone	Nonrandom	<75
8023	7815	No	Simple flaked stone	Red Rock zone	Nonrandom	2,003
8024	7816	No	Habitation	Red Rock zone	Nonrandom	1,070
8025	7817	No	Quarry	Lowlands	1st random	275
8026	7818	No	Simple flaked stone	Lowlands	Nonrandom	364

TABLE 4.3. (cont'd.) Sites with Prehistoric Component(s).

Site (26CK)	Agency No. (CrNV-53-)	Is Update	Type	Domain(s)	Phase	Area (m²)
8028	7820	No	Limited habitation	Red Rock zone	Nonrandom	660
8029	7821	No	Simple flaked stone	Red Rock zone	Nonrandom	482
8030	7822	No	Simple flaked stone	Red Rock zone	Nonrandom	185
8031	7823	No	Habitation	Red Rock zone	Nonrandom	1,401
8032	7824	No	Limited habitation	Red Rock zone	Nonrandom	2,756
8033	7825	No	Simple flaked stone	Red Rock zone	Nonrandom	197
8034	7826	No	Quarry	Red Rock zone	1st random	2,997
8035	7827	No	Limited habitation	Red Rock zone	1st random	1,530
8036	7828	No	Limited habitation	Red Rock zone	1st random	2,341
8037	7829	No	Limited habitation	Red Rock zone	2nd random	677
8038	7830	No	Simple flaked stone	Red Rock zone	2nd random	<75
8039	7831	No	Simple flaked stone	Red Rock zone	2nd random	416
8040	7832	No	Simple flaked stone	Red Rock zone	2nd random	377
8041	7833	No	Simple flaked stone	Red Rock zone	2nd random	858
8042	7834	No	Simple flaked stone	Red Rock zone	2nd random	730
8043	7835	No	Simple flaked stone	Red Rock zone	Nonrandom	<75
8044	7836	No	Limited habitation	Red Rock zone	Nonrandom	<75
8045	7837	No	Other (hunting blind)	Red Rock zone	2nd random	<75
8046	7838	No	Simple flaked stone	Red Rock zone	2nd random	276
8047	7839	No	Habitation	Red Rock zone	2nd random	7,804
8048	7840	No	Other (5 pottery, 2 FFTs)	Red Rock zone	2nd random	124
8049	7841	No	Simple flaked stone	Red Rock zone	2nd random	<75
8050	7842	No	Simple flaked stone/Hunting blind	Red Rock zone	Nonrandom	427
8052	7844	No	Simple flaked stone	Red Rock zone	Nonrandom	2,434
8053	7845	No	Simple flaked stone/Hunting blind	Red Rock zone	Nonrandom	<75
8054	7846	No	Simple flaked stone	Red Rock zone	Nonrandom	1,856
8055	7847	No	Simple flaked stone	Red Rock zone	2nd random	2,621
8056	7848	No	Simple flaked stone	Red Rock zone	2nd random	244
8057	7849	No	Simple flaked stone	Red Rock zone	2nd random	501
8058	7850	No	Simple flaked stone	Red Rock zone	Nonrandom	15,845
8059	7851	No	Habitation	Red Rock zone	Nonrandom	4,416
8060	7852	No	Simple flaked stone	Red Rock zone	Nonrandom	1,220
8061	7853	No	Simple flaked stone	Red Rock zone	Nonrandom	174
8062	7854	No	Limited habitation/Rock art	Red Rock zone	Nonrandom	282
8063	7855	No	Simple flaked stone	Red Rock zone	Nonrandom	1,631
8064	7856	No	Habitation/Rock art	Red Rock zone	Nonrandom	5,207
8065	7857	No	Rock art	Red Rock zone	Nonrandom	<75
8066	7858	No	Simple flaked stone	Red Rock zone	Nonrandom	426
8067	7859	No	Limited habitation	Uplands	Nonrandom	4,612
8068	7860	No	Simple flaked stone	Uplands	Nonrandom	590
8069	7861	No	Simple flaked stone	Uplands	Nonrandom	208
8070	7862	No	Rock art	Uplands	Nonrandom	449
8071	7863	No	Rock art	Uplands	Nonrandom	<75
8072	7864	No	Simple flaked stone	Uplands	Nonrandom	<75
8074	7866	No	Simple flaked stone	Red Rock zone	Nonrandom	<75
8075	7867	No	Simple flaked stone	Red Rock zone	Nonrandom	<75
8076	7868	No	Limited habitation	Red Rock zone	Nonrandom	<75
8077	7869	No	Limited habitation	Red Rock zone	Nonrandom	8,606

TABLE 4.3. (cont'd.) Sites with Prehistoric Component(s).

Site (26CK)	Agency No. (CrNV-53-)	Is Update	Type	Domain(s)	Phase	Area (m²)
8078	7870	No	Simple flaked stone	Red Rock zone	Nonrandom	1,297
8079	7871	No	Simple flaked stone	Red Rock zone	Nonrandom	306
8080	7872	No	Simple flaked stone	Lowlands	1st random	<75
8081	7873	No	Simple flaked stone	Red Rock zone	Nonrandom	371
8083	7875	No	Simple flaked stone	Uplands	Nonrandom	394
8084	7876	No	Habitation/Rock art	Red Rock zone	Nonrandom	1,005
8085	7877	No	Simple flaked stone	Red Rock zone	Nonrandom	<75
8086	7878	No	Limited habitation/Rock art	Red Rock zone	Nonrandom	1,735
8087	7879	No	Rock art	Red Rock zone	Nonrandom	<75
8088	7880	No	Habitation	Red Rock zone	Nonrandom	1,664
8089	7881	No	Quarry	Lowlands	1st random	<75
8090	7882	No	Quarry	Lowlands	1st random	7,250
8091	7883	No	Simple flaked stone	Uplands	1st random	213
8092	7884	No	Limited habitation	Red Rock zone	Nonrandom	<75
8093	7885	No	Habitation/Rock art	Red Rock zone	Nonrandom	14,395
8094	7886	No	Limited habitation/Quarry	Red Rock zone	Nonrandom	1,330
8095	7887	No	Limited habitation	Red Rock zone	Nonrandom	<75
8096	7888	No	Rock art	Red Rock zone	1st random	<75
8097	7889	No	Limited habitation	Red Rock zone	1st random	299
8098	7890	No	Rock art	Red Rock zone	1st random	652
8099	7891	No	Simple flaked stone	Red Rock zone	2nd random	731
8100	7892	No	Simple flaked stone/Rock art	Red Rock zone	2nd random	287
8101	7893	No	Limited habitation	Red Rock zone	2nd random	6,830
8102	7894	No	Simple flaked stone	Red Rock zone	2nd random	341
8103	7895	No	Simple flaked stone	Red Rock zone	Nonrandom	7,751
8104	7896	No	Simple flaked stone	Red Rock zone	2nd random	6,235
8105	7897	No	Simple flaked stone	Red Rock zone	2nd random	11,638
8106	7898	No	Limited habitation	Red Rock zone	Nonrandom	150
8107	7899	No	Limited habitation	Red Rock zone	Nonrandom	3,812
8108	7900	No	Limited habitation	Red Rock zone	Nonrandom	393
8109	7901	No	Habitation	Red Rock zone	Nonrandom	12,279
8110	7902	No	Simple flaked stone	Red Rock zone	Nonrandom	1,613
8111	7903	No	Simple flaked stone	Lowlands	1st random	214
8112	7904	No	Quarry	Lowlands	1st random	144
8113	7905	No	Quarry	Lowlands	1st random	1,103
8114	7906	No	Simple flaked stone	Lowlands	1st random	84
8115	7907	No	Limited habitation	Red Rock zone	Nonrandom	3,445
8116	7908	No	Habitation	Red Rock zone	Nonrandom	138
8117	7909	No	Simple flaked stone	Red Rock zone	Nonrandom	814
8118	7910	No	Simple flaked stone	Red Rock zone	Nonrandom	335
8119	7911	No	Simple flaked stone	Red Rock zone	Nonrandom	243
8120	7912	No	Habitation	Red Rock zone	Nonrandom	10,638
8121	7913	No	Simple flaked stone	Red Rock zone	Nonrandom	<75
8122	7914	No	Simple flaked stone	Red Rock zone	Nonrandom	202
8123	7915	No	Habitation/Rock art	Red Rock zone	Nonrandom	3,638
8125	7917	No	Habitation	Red Rock zone	Nonrandom	101
8126	7918	No	Quarry	Red Rock zone	Nonrandom	3,978
8127	7919	No	Limited habitation	Red Rock zone	2nd random	3,489

TABLE 4.3. (cont'd.) Sites with Prehistoric Component(s).

Site (26CK)	Agency No. (CrNV-53-)	Is Update	Type	Domain(s)	Phase	Area (m²)
8128	7920	No	Limited habitation	Red Rock zone	2nd random	<75
8129	7921	No	Rock art	Red Rock zone	2nd random	<75
8130	7922	No	Limited habitation	Red Rock zone	2nd random	1,320
8131	7923	No	Simple flaked stone	Red Rock zone	Nonrandom	2,889
8132	7924	No	Simple flaked stone	Red Rock zone	Nonrandom	<75
8133	7925	No	Simple flaked stone	Lowlands	Nonrandom	336
8134	7926	No	Simple flaked stone	Red Rock zone	Nonrandom	420
8135	7927	No	Other (hunting blind)	Red Rock zone	Nonrandom	<75
8136	7928	No	Simple flaked stone/Rock art	Red Rock zone	Nonrandom	141
8137	7929	No	Limited habitation	Red Rock zone	Nonrandom	410
8138	7930	No	Simple flaked stone	Lowlands	1st random	<75
8139	7931	No	Quarry	Lowlands	1st random	169
8140	7932	No	Habitation/Rock art	Red Rock zone	Nonrandom	75,058
8141	7933	No	Simple flaked stone	Red Rock zone	Nonrandom	201
8144	7936	No	Simple flaked stone	Lowlands	1st random	114
8148	7940	No	Limited habitation/Oven	Red Rock zone	Nonrandom	3,286
8149	7941	No	Habitation	Red Rock zone	2nd random	2,161
8150	7942	No	Limited habitation	Red Rock zone	2nd random	<75
8152	7944	No	Simple flaked stone	Red Rock zone	Nonrandom	365
8153	7945	No	Simple nonflaked stone	Red Rock zone	Nonrandom	<75
8154	7946	No	Simple flaked stone	Lowlands	1st random	573
8155	7947	No	Habitation	Red Rock zone	1st random	309
8156	7948	No	Rock art	Red Rock zone	Nonrandom	<75
8157	7949	No	Simple flaked stone	Red Rock zone	Nonrandom	580
8159	7951	No	Simple flaked stone	Red Rock zone	2nd random	<75
8160	7952	No	Simple flaked stone	Lowlands	1st random	<75
8161	7953	No	Simple flaked stone	Uplands	Nonrandom	<75
8163	7955	No	Simple flaked stone/Oven	Lowlands; Uplands	Nonrandom	2,813
8164	7956	No	Simple flaked stone/Oven	Lowlands; Uplands	Nonrandom	801
8165	7957	No	Rock art	Uplands	Nonrandom	<75
8166	7958	No	Rock art	Uplands	Nonrandom	<75
8168	7960	No	Limited habitation	Uplands	Nonrandom	235
8169	7961	No	Simple flaked stone	Uplands	Nonrandom	769
8170	7962	No	Limited habitation/Oven	Lowlands; Uplands	Nonrandom	8,657
8171	7963	No	Simple flaked stone	Lowlands	Nonrandom	1,199
8172	7964	No	Limited habitation/Oven	Lowlands	Nonrandom	286
8173	7965	No	Habitation	Uplands	Nonrandom	574
8174	7966	No	Simple flaked stone	Lowlands	Nonrandom	<75
8175	7967	No	Simple flaked stone	Uplands	Nonrandom	<75
8176	7968	No	Limited habitation/Oven	Lowlands	Nonrandom	2,572
8177	7969	No	Limited habitation	Pinyon zone	1st random	698
8179	7971	No	Habitation/Oven	Pinyon zone	1st random	580
8182	7974	No	Limited habitation/Oven	Uplands	1st random	375
8192	7984	No	Habitation	Lowlands	1st random	8,594
8193	7985	No	Limited habitation	Lowlands	1st random	550
8197	7989	No	Quarry	Riparian	Nonrandom	<75
8198	7990	No	Habitation	Riparian	Nonrandom	1,132
8200	7992	No	Other (rock rings, BRMs)	Riparian	Nonrandom	127

TABLE 4.3. (cont'd.) Sites with Prehistoric Component(s).

Site (26CK)	Agency No. (CrNV-53-)	Is Update	Type	Domain(s)	Phase	Area (m²)
8206	7998	No	Habitation	Riparian	Nonrandom	95
8207	7999	No	Other (cists/rock rings only)	Riparian	Nonrandom	<75
8209	8001	No	Habitation	Riparian	Nonrandom	<75
8213	8005	No	Habitation	Riparian	Nonrandom	392
8215	8007	No	Simple flaked stone	Riparian	Nonrandom	<75
8217	8009	No	Habitation	Riparian	Nonrandom	1,326
8218	8010	No	Habitation	Riparian	Nonrandom	865
8219	8011	No	Limited habitation	Riparian	Nonrandom	669
8223	8015	No	Simple flaked stone	Riparian	1st random	<75
8224	8016	No	Simple flaked stone	Lowlands	1st random	<75
8230	8022	No	Simple flaked stone	Lowlands	1st random	100
8232	8024	No	Quarry	Riparian	Nonrandom	5,369
8233	8025	No	Simple flaked stone	Riparian	Nonrandom	<75
8234	8026	No	Quarry	Riparian	Nonrandom	1,832
8235	8027	No	Simple flaked stone	Riparian	Nonrandom	124
8236	8028	No	Quarry	Riparian	Nonrandom	626
8237	8029	No	Quarry	Riparian	Nonrandom	183
8238	8030	No	Quarry	Riparian	Nonrandom	2,661
8239	8031	No	Quarry	Riparian	Nonrandom	6,412
8240	8032	No	Habitation	Riparian	Nonrandom	<75
8241	8033	No	Quarry	Riparian	Nonrandom	1,931
8242	8034	No	Habitation/Quarry	Riparian	Nonrandom	7,979
8243	8035	No	Limited habitation/Quarry	Riparian	Nonrandom	2,029
8244	8036	No	Quarry	Riparian	Nonrandom	167
8245	8037	No	Quarry	Riparian	Nonrandom	<75
8246	8038	No	Quarry	Riparian	Nonrandom	4,929
8247	8039	No	Quarry	Riparian	Nonrandom	3,207
8248	8040	No	Quarry	Riparian	Nonrandom	3,843
8249	8041	No	Quarry	Riparian	Nonrandom	475
8250	8042	No	Quarry	Riparian	Nonrandom	1,166
8251	8043	No	Quarry	Riparian	Nonrandom	13,817
8549	8172	No	Simple flaked stone	Lowlands	Nonrandom	117
8554	8177	No	Habitation	Lowlands	Nonrandom	431
8556	8179	No	Habitation	Lowlands	Nonrandom	1,291
8561	8184	No	Simple nonflaked stone	Lowlands	Nonrandom	693
8562	8185	No	Simple nonflaked stone	Lowlands	Nonrandom	2,022
8563	8186	No	Simple nonflaked stone	Lowlands	Nonrandom	<75
8564	8187	No	Other (pinyon cache)	Lowlands	Nonrandom	<75
8569	8192	No	Limited habitation	Uplands	Nonrandom	649
8572	8195	No	Limited habitation/Oven	Lowlands	Nonrandom	14,618
8579	8202	No	Limited habitation	—	Nonsystematic/non-unit	15,362
8580	8203	No	Limited habitation	—	Nonsystematic/non-unit	2,134
8594	8217	No	Limited habitation	Lowlands	Nonrandom	343
8602	8225	No	Habitation	Riparian	Nonrandom	<75

Note: FFT=formed flake tool

TABLE 4.4. Distribution of Prehistoric Components by Sample Domain Based on Random Survey.

Domain	Lowlands	Lowlands, Red Rock	Uplands	Uplands, Pinyon	Riparian	Total
Surveyed Units	153	40	81	30	7	311
Prehistoric Sites	26	72	6	7	1	112
Sites/Unit	0.17	1.80	0.07	0.23	0.14	0.21
Standard Error	0.04	0.31	0.03	0.12	0.05	0.03
Site Types[a]						
Habitation	2	8	—	2	—	12
Limited Habitation	5	19	3	4	—	31
Simple Flaked Stone	12	30	2	—	1	45
Simple Nonflaked Stone	—	2	—	1	—	3
Other	—	3	1	—	—	4
Rock Art	—	9	—	—	—	9
Oven	2	—	2	2	—	6
Quarry	7	8	—	—	—	15

[a] Rows do not equal prehistoric site totals because rock art, oven, and quarry attributes are not mutually exclusive to other site types.

average density. Translated into area measures, the study area contains only one site per 294 acres (0.84 site/km²). The overall population estimate for the entire study area is 1,156 ± 161 prehistoric sites.

Table 4.4 also shows the distribution of the various site types among the five domains. There are a number of patterns apparent in these data that go beyond simple site densities; in order to explore these patterns further, we show counts of specific artifact and feature types in Table 4.5. The findings also suggest some potential refinements in the way these environmental zones are defined.

Lowlands

A total of 26 sites was recorded in the 153 random-sample units surveyed in this domain. The distribution of site types in the domain skews toward Simple Flaked Stone and Quarry sites at the expense of Habitations and Limited Habitations (Table 4.4). Of the seven sites typed as Habitations or Limited Habitations (26CK7874, -7935, -7936, -7937, -7991, -8192, and -8193), three are clustered in the southeastern part of the study area and another two are located near Juanita Springs. One of the latter (26CK8192) contains an apparent rock-lined structure foundation; this may be the only prehistoric architecture in the study area outside the immediate vicinity of the Virgin River. Additionally, two sites in this domain contain agave ovens (26CK7932 and -7936), both in the southeastern part of the study area. Finally, seven sites comprise CCS quarrying debris, all of them lacking habitation or other nonflaked stone items. These sites are scattered throughout the central part of the study area.

The 70 isolates recorded in this domain (Table 4.5) generally reflect the composition of the sites, being dominated by flakes, cores, and SRLs. Finished flaked stone tools are rare; only two projectile points were noted. The only ground stone items noted were a single handstone and three bedrock slicks.

Lowlands, Red Rock Zone

The Red Rock zone contains by far the highest density of sites of any of the domains, with 72 sites recorded in 40 units, for an average density of 1.80 sites per unit (Table 4.4). This domain contains all nine of the rock art sites recorded during this phase of the survey (26CK1978, -3206, -6666 Locus 1/2, -6666 Locus 3, -7997, -8096, -8098, -8100, and -8129) and all but three of the 30 sites with rock art recorded in the subsequent nonrandom survey. Four of these lack associated artifacts, while the remainder are associated with various types of assemblages. Most notable among the rock art sites recorded during this phase are 26CK1978, containing more than 180 individual elements; and 26CK6666 Locus 1/2, containing more than 50 elements.

The Red Rock zone, as originally defined by outcrops of Aztec sandstone, contains two major and one minor area. The former covers a band on the north side of Mud Wash, between Whitney Pocket on the northeast and Red Rock Springs to the south. The latter corresponds to the Mud Hills area, where no rock art sites were recorded during the course of survey. In reality, the sandstone does not form prominent cliffs or outcrops in this area. However, the Mud Hills area contains a high density of other types of sites, suggesting that the

TABLE 4.5. Random Survey Site and Isolate Constituents.

Domain	Sites					Isolates [a]					Total
	Lowlands	Lowlands, Red Rock	Uplands	Uplands, Pinyon	Riparian	Lowlands	Lowlands, Red Rock	Uplands	Uplands, Pinyon	Riparian	
Units	153	40	81	30	7	153	40	81	30	7	—
Resources	26	72	6	7	1	70	75	15	7	4	—
Artifact/Feature Counts											
Projectile Points	8	27	2	2	—	2	5	4	—	—	50
Bifaces	11	70	6	7	—	8	7	3	2	—	114
Other Flaked Stone Tools	12	66	2	—	—	1	3	—	—	—	84
Segregated Reduction Loci	14	1	—	—	—	15	7	2	—	—	39
Millingstones	6	43	3	10	—	—	2	—	3	—	67
Handstones	25	31	—	7	—	1	1	—	—	—	65
Misc. Ground Stone	4	—	—	1	—	—	—	—	—	—	5
Bedrock Milling	4	—	—	2	—	3	—	1	—	—	10
Battered Cobbles	10	26	—	1	1	—	—	—	—	—	38
Shelters	1	19	—	3	—	—	—	—	—	—	23
Hunting Blinds	—	3	—	—	—	—	—	—	—	—	3
Ovens	5	—	3	7	—	—	—	—	—	—	15
Hearths/Thermal Features	—	8	—	3	—	—	—	—	—	—	11
Pithouses	1	—	—	—	—	—	—	—	—	—	1
Other Rock Features	2	2	—	2	—	—	—	—	—	—	6
Rock Art Panels	—	34	—	—	—	—	—	—	—	—	34
Counts of Resources with…											
Pottery	5	20	3	3	—	—	4	—	1	—	36
Midden	2	6	—	2	—	—	—	—	—	—	10
Debitage/Cores	26	63	6	5	1	40	47	5	1	4	198

[a] Rows do not equal resource totals because of multiple-item isolates.

sandstone has some effect on overall attractiveness for habitation, regardless of its suitability as a palette for rock art.

Twenty-seven sites are typed as Habitations or Limited Habitations, a higher proportion than in lowlands generally (37 percent vs. 27 percent). Of these, eight sites are in the eastern Mud Hills area; this prompted additional nonrandom survey of the area, as discussed above. The remaining sites include 30 Simple Flaked Stone scatters, one of which also contains rock art; two Simple Nonflaked Stone sites (26CK1978 and -3210, both having milling gear associated with shelters, the former also associated with rock art); and three sites typed as Other. The latter are an isolated hunting blind, a milling slab and isolated hearth, and a small scatter of pottery with two flaked stone tools. Additionally, eight sites contain CCS quarrying debris, including two loci at the very extensive, multilocus site 26CK3206 in the Red Rock Springs area, another site nearby associated with Limited Habitation debris (26CK8034), and six additional sites that lack other types of remains. Most of these are in the Mud Hills vicinity.

Site types alone do not fully convey the comparative richness of the record in this domain, however. As Table 4.5 shows, the domain contains 19 of the 23 rock shelters recorded during the random-sample survey; 6 of the 10 sites containing midden soil; 8 of the 11 hearths/fire-cracked rock concentrations; and 20 of the 31 sites containing pottery. Additionally, the domain contains the only three hunting blinds noted during the random-sample phase and 32 of the 50 projectile points, suggesting that this zone was a major focus of hunting activity as well as habitation.

The 75 isolates recorded in this domain are dominated by flaked stone tools and debitage. Only three isolated pieces of milling gear and four pot drops or isolated sherds were recorded (Table 4.5).

Uplands

As expected, the uplands domain showed the lowest site density of any of the domains (one site per every 883 acres; Table 4.4). Only six sites were recorded in the 81 units surveyed. However, of these six, three are typed as Limited Habitations (26CK7883, -7951, and -8182), two of which (26CK7951 and -8182) also contain agave ovens. This may seem a surprising result given the overall paucity of findings; however, two of these are immediately adjacent to units in the pinyon-zone domain and thus likely reflect the same patterns observed there. Of the remaining sites, two (26CK7960 and -8091) are Simple Flaked Stone scatters while the one typed as

Other (26CK7930) is a patch of stained soil, possibly midden, but without associated artifacts.

Only 15 isolates were noted in this domain, all of which are flaked stone tools or debitage, except for a single bedrock slick (Table 4.5).

Uplands Pinyon Zone

While the density figure for the uplands pinyon domain is substantially higher than for uplands generally (one site per every 269 acres; Table 4.4), most of the units in this domain lie in the extremely precipitous terrain of the Virgin Range (Figure 4.1). The seven sites in this domain are clustered in only three survey units, which have areas of terrain suitably flat for habitation. Three of the sites are located in one of the two units in the gentler terrain of the Cedar Basin area, suggesting that this part of the southeast area likely supports a much higher density of sites than the Virgin Range. Survey also showed that the distribution of pinyon is wider in the Cedar Basin area than the bounds of the domain indicate, prompting additional survey in this area, as noted above.

Of the seven sites recorded in this domain, six are typed as Habitations or Limited Habitations (26CK 3090, -3091, -6082, -6088, -8177, and -8179), a much higher proportion than in other domains, including the Red Rock zone. Two of these contain agave ovens (26CK3091 and -8179), and both lie on the southern slope of the Virgin Range. Site 26CK8179 is unique in that it contains an agave oven inside a rock shelter. The one remaining site (26CK7893) is a Simple Nonflaked Stone site containing only milling gear and pottery.

The apparent emphasis on plant-food gathering and processing in this domain is borne out by the isolate totals as well (Table 4.5), which include three milling slabs (found as isolated artifacts only in this domain and in the Red Rock zone) but no projectile points.

Virgin River Riparian Zone

Only a single prehistoric site (26CK8223) was recorded in the seven units in the Virgin River riparian domain, and even this was a Simple Flaked Stone site, not a Basketmaker/Puebloan habitation site, as was expected to typify this area. The failure of this domain's sample to show elevated site densities relative to the other lowland units likely has to do both with the small sample size and with the fact that the domain was too broadly defined (i.e., the corridor was drawn too wide), so that most of the units selected were not representative of the riparian corridor. This prompted selection of additional units during the nonrandom phase from a narrow strip immediately adjacent to the Virgin floodplain, as noted above.

TABLE 4.6. Distribution of Prehistoric Components in Nonrandom Survey Areas.

	Surveyed Units	Prehistoric Sites	Sites/ Unit	Site Type[b]							
				H	LH	SFS	SNFS	Other	RA	O	Q
South Virgin Range	15	23	1.53	4	8	7	—	1	3	13	—
Red Rock Zone, North	52	101	1.94	17	25	46	1	2	19	2	2
Red Rock Zone, South	3	10	3.33	2	3	1	—	—	8	—	—
Mud Hills	7	14	2.00	2	3	7	—	2	—	—	1
26CK5434 Area	5	1	0.20	—	—	1	—	—	—	—	—
Cedar Basin Pinyon Zone	14	35	2.50	7	20	3	1	4	—	—	—
Springs	43	29	0.67	—	8	18	1	1	—	1	—
Virgin River Riparian Zone	25	39	1.56	16	2	3	—	2	—	—	18
Historic Units	30	14[a]	0.47	4	4	2	3	1	—	1	—
Nonsystematic/Non-unit	—	2	—	—	2	—	—	—	—	—	—
Total	194	268[a]		52	75	88	6	13	30	17	21

Note: H = Habitation; LH = Limited Habitation; SFS = Simple Flaked Stone; SNFS = Simple Nonflaked Stone; RA = Rock Art; O = Oven; Q = Quarry.
[a] Includes four components within 26CK7574 (two H, one LH, and one SFS). The actual site total is 265.
[b] Rows do not equal prehistoric site totals because rock art, oven, and quarry attributes are not mutually exclusive to other site types.

Only four isolates were noted in this domain (Table 4.5), all of which were debitage.

Nonrandom Survey

During the nonrandom survey phase, 263 sites were recorded during systematic survey of 194 survey units; an additional two sites were recorded during nonsystematic survey of a historic road (Table 4.2). Site totals are complicated somewhat by the fact that four noncontiguous prehistoric components are recorded as part of the very extensive historic-period site 26CK7574 at the Gold Butte town site; in the absence of the historic component, these would have been recorded as separate prehistoric sites.

Also during this phase, 214 prehistoric isolates were recorded. Table 4.6 summarizes the distribution of the prehistoric components in the nine areas selected for nonrandom survey. Table 4.7 summarizes site assemblage and isolate totals for these areas.

South Virgin Range

A total of 23 sites was recorded in the South Virgin Range, a block of 15 units. Thirteen sites contain roasting pits, most of them associated with Habitation or Limited Habitation assemblages. These units contain 56 of the 75 agave ovens recorded in the course of the entire project (Table 4.7). There are also three sites containing rock art, one associated with both habitation debris and roasting pits (26CK3093), and two that lack an associated assemblage (26CK8165 and -8166). These are the only rock art sites recorded outside the

Red Rock zone, but in fact they are on outcrops of Aztec sandstone. The outcrops were merely too small and isolated to merit inclusion on the geological maps of the area.

Like the nearby random-sample units in the Virgin Range pinyon zone, site assemblages in the South Virgin Range are disproportionately Habitations and Limited Habitations (12 sites) rather than Simple Flaked Stone (seven sites; Table 4.6), in comparison to surrounding lowlands. The single site typed as Other (26CK3092) is a rock wall in a shelter with only one tool, a handstone. Artifact totals further underscore the emphasis on plant processing, with a relatively high proportion of both portable milling gear and stationary bedrock slicks (Table 4.7).

Thirteen isolates were recorded in this area, all flaked stone tools or debitage except for a single milling slab (Table 4.7).

Red Rock Zone, North

The group of 52 units in the northern Red Rock zone yielded a total of 101 prehistoric sites, for an overall density of one site per every 32 acres, nearly identical to the random-sample result (Table 4.6). Nineteen of these sites contain rock art, nine lack an associated assemblage, and the remainder are mostly associated with Habitation or Limited Habitation assemblages. Most notable among the rock art sites are 26CK8140, which contains some 650 individual rock art elements on nearly 70 panels, interspersed with a series of shelters containing habitation debris; and 26CK5608/Site 3,

TABLE 4.7. Nonrandom Survey Site and Isolate Constituents.

	Units	Resources	Projectile Points	Bifaces	Other Flaked Stone Tools	SRLs	Millingstones	Handstones	Misc. Groundstone	Bedrock Milling	Battered Cobbles	Shelters	Hunting Blinds	Ovens	Hearths/Thermal Feats	Pithouses	Cists	Other Rock Features	Rock Art Panels	Pottery	Midden	Debitage/Cores
Sites																						
South Virgin Range	15	23	13	25	6	—	30	6	—	14	1	14	—	56	—	—	—	1	9	8	4	19
Red Rock Zone, North	52	101	58	120	65	5	83	54	1	—	44	43	5	2	16	—	—	2	70	17	10	90
Red Rock Zone, South	3	10	2	7	1	—	3	7	—	2	5	2	—	—	—	—	—	1	180	3	2	6
Mud Hills	7	14	3	16	12	—	8	1	—	—	1	—	—	—	8	—	—	—	—	3	—	14
Firebrand Cave Area	5	1	2	7	3	—	—	—	—	—	2	—	—	—	—	—	—	—	—	—	—	1
Cedar Basin Pinyon Zone	14	35	17	62	2	—	54	32	2	1	10	14	—	—	1	—	—	6	—	31	4	35
Springs	43	29	24	34	5	—	13	5	—	3	5	7	19	1	—	—	—	1	—	10	—	26
Virgin River Riparian Zone	25	39	—	18	43	21	3	2	1	25	10	—	—	—	2	51	38	8	—	6	2	33
Historic Units	30	14	2	7	2	—	23	7	—	—	—	4	—	1	—	—	—	3	—	7	3	7
Historic (Nonsystematic/Non-unit)		2	—	1	—	—	3	—	—	—	1	—	—	—	—	—	—	—	—	1	—	2
Isolates[a]																						
South Virgin Range	15	13	—	2	1	1	1	—	—	—	—	—	—	—	—	—	—	—	—	—	—	9
Red Rock Zone, North	52	72	10	10	2	5	1	2	—	—	—	—	—	—	—	—	—	—	—	1	—	41
Red Rock Zone, South	3	8	—	—	—	1	—	—	—	—	—	—	—	—	—	—	—	—	—	—	—	7
Mud Hills	7	15	—	1	1	6	—	—	—	—	—	—	—	—	—	—	—	—	—	—	—	7
Firebrand Cave Area	5	3	—	—	—	—	—	—	—	—	—	—	—	—	—	—	—	—	—	—	—	3
Cedar Basin Pinyon Zone	14	17	1	—	1	—	2	—	—	—	—	—	—	—	—	—	—	—	—	2	—	11
Springs	43	44	—	4	3	—	8	4	1	1	—	—	—	—	—	—	—	—	—	2	—	22
Virgin River Riparian Zone	25	36	—	2	5	4	1	1	1	—	1	—	—	—	—	—	—	7	—	—	—	15
Historic Units	30	6	2	—	1	—	2	—	—	—	—	—	—	—	—	—	—	—	—	—	—	1
Total	—	—	134	316	153	43	235	121	6	46	80	84	24	60	27	51	38	29	259	91	25	349

Note: SRL = Segregated reduction locus.
[a] Rows may not equal resource total because of multiple-item isolates.

which contains 225+ elements on two elaborate panels and which lacks associated habitation debris.

Among the 101 sites, 42 are typed as Habitations or Limited Habitations, a proportion similar to that observed in the random-sample survey of the Red Rock zone (Table 4.6). Of these, nine have associated rock art (26CK1984, -8019, -8062, -8064, -8084, -8086, -8093, -8123, and -8140). Forty-six sites are typed as Simple Flaked Stone scatters, two in association with hunting blinds (26CK8050 and -8053) and one with rock art (26CK8136). One small ground stone assemblage in a shelter (26CK8153) is typed as a Simple Nonflaked Stone assemblage. The two sites typed as Other (26CK6699 and -8135) are isolated hunting blinds.

Two sites (26CK1984 and -8148) contain agave ovens in association with either Habitation or Limited Habitation assemblages. Finally, two sites contain quarrying debris, one in association with a Limited Habitation (26CK8094) and another without other associated materials (26CK8126).

As was observed in the random-sample survey of this area, the Red Rock zone arguably shows the widest range of activities and most substantial occupations in the study area. While the Cedar Basin pinyon zone (see below) has a heavy concentration of Limited Habitations and associated milling gear and pottery, the Red Rock zone has a higher proportion of formal Habitations as opposed to Limited Habitations. This is reflected in much higher counts of thermal features (Table 4.7). And consistent with the random-sample findings, hunting appears to be a primary activity in this area, indicated by the presence of hunting blinds as well as high quantities of projectile points and bifaces.

A total of 72 isolates was recorded in the nonrandom units in this area, primarily debitage but also including 22 flaked stone tools of various types and a few ground stone tools (Table 4.7).

Red Rock Zone, South

Ten sites were recorded in the southern Red Rock zone, a group of three units that yielded the highest site density of any of the nonrandom survey areas (Table 4.6). As expected, rock art sites are common in this area; eight of the ten sites contain rock art. Additionally, the area contains the highest density of recorded rock art panels, with a total of 182 panels, as opposed to 111 in the entirety of the northern Red Rock zone (Table 4.7). Most of the recorded panels are at the extensive site 26CK7029, which has the highest concentration of rock art of any site in the study area, containing nearly 900 individual elements on more than 130 panels; other notable rock art sites are 26CK6672 and 26CK5179 Locus K, both associated with Limited Habitation assemblages. Four

of the rock art sites lack an associated assemblage. Of the six sites containing constituents other than (or in addition to) rock art, five are Habitations or Limited Habitations (26CK5179 Locus K, -6672, -7029, -7994, and -7996) and one (26CK7995) is a Simple Flaked Stone scatter.

Only eight isolates were recorded in these units, all individual pieces of debitage or SRLs (Table 4.7).

Mud Hills

Fourteen sites were recorded in the seven survey units of the Mud Hills, including five sites typed as Habitations or Limited Habitations (a proportion similar to that of the main Red Rock zone); seven Simple Flaked Stone sites; and two sites typed as Other. The two Other sites are Simple Flaked Stone scatters with associated hearths (all other hearths are found at Habitation sites). One of the Limited Habitation sites also contains CCS quarrying debris. The 15 isolates from this area are all flaked stone tools, debitage, or SRLs.

26CK5434

Only a single Simple Flaked Stone site (26CK7993) was identified in 26CK5434, a block of five survey units. However, the site is noteworthy in being located adjacent to a previously unmapped, flowing spring and in containing projectile points that indicate an early Holocene/Early Archaic occupation. Only three isolates, all debitage, were recorded.

Cedar Basin Pinyon Zone

The Cedar Basin pinyon zone, a block of 14 survey units, was extremely productive, yielding 35 sites and thus the second-highest density of any of the nonrandom areas (one site per every 25 acres; Table 4.6). These are heavily dominated by Limited Habitations (20 sites) and, to a lesser extent, Habitations (7 sites). Most are located in and around shelters formed by the granite boulders and outcrops strewn throughout the area. Only three Simple Flaked Stone scatters were recorded. An additional small scatter of ground stone is typed as Simple Nonflaked Stone (26CK7891). The remaining four sites, typed as Other, are all very small associations of flaked stone and pottery. Site assemblage artifact totals (Table 4.7) underscore the heavy emphasis on milling in this area; the overall density of milling tools is by far the highest of any of the survey areas. In addition, the proportion of sites with pottery is the highest of any of the survey areas (31 of the 35 sites, or 88 percent).

The 17 isolates recorded in these units comprise primarily flaked stone tools and debitage but also include two milling slabs and four pot drops or individual sherds (Table 4.7).

Springs

The group of 43 scattered survey units in the springs zone was relatively unproductive compared with other nonrandom survey areas, yielding only 29 sites. Only eight of these sites are classified as Limited Habitations; these units actually have among the lowest proportion of these types of sites among any of the nonrandom survey areas. Among the remaining sites, 18 are classified as Simple Flaked Stone scatters, 5 of which contain hunting blinds. All told, 19 blinds were recorded; the only other hunting blinds in the study area were all recorded in the Red Rock zone (Table 4.7). Among the remaining sites, one (26CK7916) is a milling station with associated pottery, typed as a Simple Nonflaked Stone site; another (26CK7880) is a hunting blind with associated milling gear and pottery; and the last (26CK3073) is an isolated agave oven.

While site densities in these units may be unimpressive, it is nonetheless clear that springs have a strong influence on the distribution of prehistoric sites in the study area. The density of sites in these units is far higher than in unwatered lowland areas (one site per every 92 acres vs. one site per every 363 acres for the general lowlands in the random-sample survey); additionally, many of the most productive springs in the study area had been previously surveyed and thus were not surveyed or counted with this group of units (e.g., Red Rock Springs). Additionally, the presence of hunting blinds, along with the general prevalence of hunting-related site types and artifacts, suggests that many of these springs were mainly used as hunting locations rather than as primary sources of water to support habitation sites.

A total of 44 isolates was recorded in these units, comprising a variety of flaked stone tools and debitage, ground stone tools, and pottery (Table 4.7).

Virgin River Riparian Zone

Survey of the 25 units of the Virgin River riparian zone yielded 39 prehistoric sites (Table 4.6). While the overall site density in these units is not particularly high, the survey documented a Basketmaker/Puebloan occupation, as anticipated. In total, 17 sites containing Basketmaker/Puebloan pithouses and/or storage cists were recorded (26CK1704, -3226, -3545, -4891, -4892, -4893, -4898, -8198, -8206, -8207, -8209, -8213, -8217, -8218, -8240, -8242, and -8602). Several sites also contain rock rings not readily identifiable as houses or cists. Many of these sites lack associated pottery or other surface artifacts, however, suggesting informal collection. All the sites containing prehistoric architectural remains are classified as Habitations except for one site with only cists that was typed as Other (26CK8207). An additional two sites lacking architecture (26CK8219 and -8243) are typed as Limited Habitations, and three (26CK8233, -8235, and -8215) as Simple Flaked Stone scatters. The additional site typed as Other (26CK8200) is a one-of-a-kind prehistoric site, with 25 bedrock mortars associated with rock rings and pottery, all lying on a prominent sandstone bluff overlooking the river floodplain. Also notable in this area is a group of 18 sites containing CCS and quartzite quarrying debris, all clustered in a few survey units in the northeasternmost part of the study area. One of these sites (26CK8242) also contains prehistoric architecture, but it is not clear that these components are related.

The 36 isolates from these units comprise a variety of flaked and ground stone tools, as well as seven isolated rock rings (Table 4.7). The latter are possibly related to Basketmaker/Puebloan occupation since they are also present at several of the Basketmaker/Puebloan sites.

Historic Units

Fourteen prehistoric components (counting separately the four noncontiguous prehistoric components at 26CK7574 [Gold Butte town site]) were recorded in the 30 historic survey units. These include eight sites typed as Habitations or Limited Habitations, two Simple Flaked Stone sites, and three Simple Nonflaked Stone sites. The latter three (26CK8561, -8562, and -8563) are all milling stations located in a single survey unit in the Cedar Basin area; two of these sites also contain rock rings that appear to be pinyon caches. The single site typed as Other (26CK8564) is also in the same survey unit and consists of an isolated pinyon cache. Aside from a possible pinyon cache recorded at site 26CK6078/6095 (in the Cedar Basin pinyon zone), these are the only documented pinyon caches in the study area.

Nonsystematic/Non-unit

Two prehistoric sites (26CK8579 and -8580) were recorded during nonsystematic survey of the historic Grand Gulch road. Both sites are typed as Limited Habitation; however, the assemblages from these sites were not fully characterized because they were incidental finds.

5 Chronological Controls

One of the unique aspects of this project was a program to select archaeological sites to test for the express purpose of providing additional chronological controls for improving the interpretation of inventory results. This chapter thus incorporates chronometric data from both inventory and site testing. Specific data sets include radiometric assays; time-sensitive projectile points; pottery encompassing the three major groups: Basketmaker/Puebloan, Patayan paddle and anvil, and Southern Paiute brown ware; shell and glass beads; and source-specific obsidian hydration.

The discussion below focuses on data presentation. More detailed inferences related to lifeways, land use, population movements, and other higher-order reconstructions are presented in Chapter 8.

RADIOCARBON

A total of 32 radiocarbon assays from 18 sites were run as part of this project, 20 from sites excavated during the evaluation program and 12 from rock oven features identified during the survey effort (Table 5.1). With the exception of a yucca fiber and a corncob fragment, all samples were of charcoal obtained from the light fraction of flotation samples. As can be seen in Table 5.1, calibrated dates range from 2870 BC to less than one hundred years ago; most (87 percent), however, date within the last 2,000 years.

In addition to the project samples, there are at least 26 previously obtained radiocarbon dates from Gold Butte (Table 5.2). Twenty of these are from one site, 26CK5434 (Blair 2006), and show a mostly Late Archaic

occupation dating to around 3,500 to 4,000 years ago. Also documented were subsequent Basketmaker II and Late Prehistoric period visits to the cave. Several additional dates have been obtained from large oven features (Ellis et al. 1982) and Basketmaker III pithouses (Larson 1987:88) in the study area.

The profile of radiocarbon dates has implications for land use in the Gold Butte hinterland, particularly during the later-dating Puebloan and Late Prehistoric periods. This issue is further explored in Chapter 8.

PROJECTILE POINTS

In total, 280 time-sensitive projectile points were recovered from the study area, 173 during the survey phases and 107 during excavation (Table 5.3). With the notable absence of Clovis-age variants, the array of point types spans the entire Holocene. Interestingly, especially given the sizable Puebloan occupation previously documented along the adjacent Virgin River, the dominant point form recovered is Elko series variants, a Late Archaic marker. Again, the land-use implications associated with the distribution and frequency of these artifacts is reviewed elsewhere in this report. What follows is a brief review of the stylistic and temporal implications of each point type.

Stemmed Series

Insofar as the study area yielded no evidence of Clovis occupation, the first indication of occupation—the Paleo-Archaic/Lake Mohave period—is marked by Great Basin Stemmed series projectile points

TABLE 5.1. Radiocarbon Dates from the Gold Butte Project.

Lab Number[a]	Sample Number	Flot #	Site (26CK)	Unit	Depth (cm)	Feature	Material	Intercept with calibration Curve[b]	Conventional ^{14}C BP Age	$^{13}C/^{12}C$	2-Sigma Range cal BP
Beta-241977	3201-F9	9	3201	N3/W1	20–30	—	charcoal	cal AD 1160 (cal BP 790)	900 ± 40	-19.4	730–920
Beta-241978	3201-F10	10	3201	N3/E0	30–40	—	charcoal	cal BC 300 (cal BP 2260)	2200 ± 40	-24.1	2120–2330
Beta-241979	3201-F11	11	3201	N3/W1	126–146	—	charcoal	cal BC 160 (cal BP 2110)	2110 ± 40	-23.6	1990–2290
Beta-241986	4891-9	—	4891	Unit 5, Post Hole 1	48–54	—	charcoal	cal AD 690 (cal BP 1260)	1280 ± 60	-25.1	1060–1300
Beta-241970	6078/6095-F4	4	6078/-6095	S5/E1	20–30	Upper Midden	charcoal	cal AD 1800 (cal BP 150)	170 ± 40	-24.3	0–300
Beta-241971	6078/6095-F5	5	6078/-6095	S5/E1	50–70	Lower Midden	charcoal	cal BC 870 (cal BP 2820)	2730 ± 40	-20.7	2760–2900
Beta-241967	6080/6081-F1	1	6080/-6081	S3/W3	35–45	1	charcoal	cal AD 340 (cal BP 1610)	1710 ± 50	-22.3	1520–1720
Beta-241968	6080/6081-F2	2	6080/-6081	S2/W4	5–10	3	charcoal	cal AD 1650 (cal BP 300)	250 ± 60	-22.8	0–470
Beta-241969	6080/6081-F3	3	6080/-6081	S3/W5	66–80	—	charcoal	cal BC 40 (cal BP 1990)	2030 ± 40	-22.2	1890–2110
Beta-241972	7994-F6	6	7994	N14/W28.5	35–50	—	charcoal	cal AD 580 (cal BP 1370)	1490 ± 40	-23.3	1300–1500
Beta-241973	7994-50	—	7994	Feature 1–Interior bottom	20–30	1	yucca fiber	cal AD 130 (cal BP 1820)	1860 ± 50	-25.3	1700–1900
Beta-241974	8013-F7	7	8013	S1/E49 and S1/E51	0–15	—	charcoal	cal AD 1650 (cal BP 300)	250 ± 40	-23.7	0–430
Beta-241975	8047-F8	8	8047	S1/W4, Rock Shelter 5	—	—	charcoal	cal AD 1910 (cal BP 40)	90 ± 40	-26.2	0–270
Beta-241976	8047-5	—	8047	Rock Shelter 5	Surface	Lower Midden	corn cob	cal AD 220 (cal BP 1730)	1820 ± 40	-9.5	1630–1860
Beta-241980	8179-F12	12	8179	N5/W5	40–70	—	charcoal	cal BC 2870 (cal BP 4820)	4190 ± 50	-21.0	4570–4850
Beta-241981	8179-F13	13	8179	S6.5/W1.5	100–115	—	charcoal	cal BC 1440 (cal BP 3390)	3170 ± 50	-22.4	3280–3470
Agave Ovens											
Beta-241982	1991-F25	25	1991	Pit 4	Stratum I	—	charcoal	cal AD 1580 (cal BP 370)	330 ± 50	-20.0	290–500
Beta-241983	1991-F26	26	1991	Pit 4	Stratum II	—	charcoal	cal AD 1800 (cal BP 150)	160 ± 40	-21.8	0–290
Beta-241984	1991-F27	27	1991	Pit 3	Stratum III	—	charcoal	cal AD 1800 (cal BP 150)	160 ± 40	-22.0	0–290
Beta-241985	1991-F28	28	1991	Pit 3	Stratum IV	—	charcoal	cal AD 810 (cal BP 1140)	1200 ± 60	-23.5	970–1280
RT-5900	1991-47	—	1991	Pit 4	Stratum IV	—	charcoal	cal AD 1101 (cal BP 850)	920 ± 30	-10.5	765–920
RT-5901	1991-48	—	1991	Pit 4	Stratum IV	—	charcoal	cal AD 1654 (cal BP 295)	250 ± 30	-21.1	0–430
Beta-241987	7932-1	14	7932	TU 1	0–10	—	charcoal	cal AD 1880 (cal BP 60)	100 ± 40	-22.7	0–280
Beta-241988	7951-5	15	7951	TU 1	0–10	—	charcoal	cal AD 900 (cal BP 1050)	1130 ± 40	-21.6	950–1160
Beta-241989	8163-3	16	8163	TU 1	20+	Roasting Pit 1	charcoal	cal AD 1440 (cal BP 510)	460 ± 40	-19.9	480–540
Beta-241990	8163-5	17	8163	TU 2	0–10	Roasting Pit 2	charcoal	cal AD 1450 (cal BP 500)	410 ± 40	-21.3	320–520
Beta-241991	8170-11	18	8170	TU 2	20+	—	charcoal	cal AD 1260 (cal BP 700)	790 ± 40	-23.3	670–780
Beta-241992	8172-2	19	8172	TU 1	20+	—	charcoal	cal AD 1660 (cal BP 290)	220 ± 40	-20.9	0–310
Beta-241993	1990-5	21	1990	TU Roasting Pit 3	20+	Roasting Pit 3	charcoal	cal AD 140 (cal BP 1810)	1850 ± 40	-21.9	1700–1880
Beta-241994	3091-1	22	3091	TU N0/E0	30–40	—	charcoal	cal AD 890 (cal BP 1060)	1140 ± 40	-21.3	960–1170
Beta-241995	3093-2	23	3093	TU 1	10–20	—	charcoal	cal AD 1560 (cal BP 390)	320 ± 50	-25.3	290–500
Beta-241996	3073-1	24	3073	TU 1	0–20	Isolate Roasting Pit	charcoal	cal AD 1490 (cal BP 460)	360 ± 40	-21.5	310–510

Note: References for the calibration data (INTCAL09) and the mathematics applied to the data are the following: Heaton et al. 2009; Reimer et al. 2009; Oeschger et al. 1975; Stuiver and Braziunas 1993; Talma and Vogel 1993.

[a] Radiocarbon labs: Beta Analytic, Miami, Florida; Radiocarbon Dating and Cosmogenic Isotopes Lab, Kimmel Center of Archaeological Science, Weizmann Institute of Science, Rehovot, Israel.

[b] Includes mean value for samples with multiple intercepts.

TABLE 5.2. Radiocarbon Dates Previously Obtained from Gold Butte Prehistoric Sites.

Site (26CK)	Calibrated Mean Probability	Conventional Age ^{14}C	Material	Reference
5434	1511 BC (cal BP 3461)	3230 ± 80 BP	dart shaft/wood	Blair 2006
5434	1684 BC (cal BP 3634)	3385 ± 88 BP	dart shaft/wood	Blair 2006
5434	1767 BC (cal BP 3717)	3449 ± 55 BP	dart shaft/wood	Blair 2006
5434	1840 BC (cal BP 3790)	3502 ± 154 BP	dart shaft/wood	Blair 2006
5434	2290 BC (cal BP 4240)	3834 ± 97 BP	dart shaft/wood	Blair 2006
5434	3101 BC (cal BP 5051)	4430 ± 70 BP	dart shaft/wood	Blair 2006
5434	1527 BC (cal BP 3477)	3242 ± 153 BP	basketry (coiled, 2 rod and bundle)	Blair 2006
5434	1628 BC (cal BP 3578)	3340 ± 76 BP	firebrand/torch	Blair 2006
5434	1946 BC (cal BP 3896)	3590 ± 78 BP	firebrand/torch	Blair 2006
5434	2068 BC (cal BP 4018)	3680 ± 50 BP	cordage (2 ply, Z twist)	Blair 2006
5434	2161 BC (cal BP 4111)	3750 ± 40 BP	cordage (single ply, S twist)	Blair 2006
5434	2161 BC (cal BP 4111)	3750 ± 40 BP	cordage (2 ply, Z twist)	Blair 2006
5434	2323 BC (cal BP 4273)	3850 ± 40 BP	butcher-marked deer bone	Blair 2006
5434	2681 BC (cal BP 4631)	4113 ± 123 BP	netting	Blair 2006
5434	AD 635 (cal BP 1315)	1400 ± 100 BP	basketry (coiled, 2 rod and bundle)	Blair 2006
5434	AD 629 (cal BP 1321)	1407 ± 55 BP	basketry (coiled, 2 rod and bundle)	Blair 2006
5434	AD 520 (cal BP 1430)	1523 ± 97 BP	basketry (coiled, 2 rod and bundle)	Blair 2006
5434	AD 339 (cal BP 1611)	1700 ± 60 BP	spirit stick/regalia	Blair 2006
5434	AD 312 (cal BP 1638)	1722 ± 88 BP	charcoal from probe associated with corn kernels	Blair 2006
5434	AD 1794 (cal BP 156)	152 ± 74 BP	wood	Blair 2006
1987	571 BC (cal BP 2521)	2450 ± 155 BP	—	Ellis et al. 1982
1992	528 BC (cal BP 2478)	2400 ± 80 BP	charcoal w/ burial	Ellis et al. 1982
3064	AD 676 (cal BP 1274)	1355 ± 70 BP	—	Ellis et al. 1982
4892	AD 717 (cal BP 1233)	1320 ± 80 BP	soil	Larson 1987:88
4893	AD 635 (cal BP 1315)	1400 ± 100 BP	soil	Larson 1987:88
4898	AD 684 (cal BP 1266)	1350 ± 80 BP	charcoal	Larson 1987:88

(Figure 5.1, n = 11). Great Basin Stemmed points are weakly shouldered, percussion-flaked projectiles with relatively long contracting stems and rounded bases; stem margins are often ground. The Silver Lake variant is more strongly shouldered and exhibits a wide, more squared-off stem (Figure 5.1). There is a general consensus that these point variants date from about 10,500 to 6000 BC (Basgall 1993, 2000; Gilreath and Hildebrandt 1997; Warren 1984; Willig and Aikens 1988).

Stemmed series points have been found in the Las Vegas Valley (Ahlstrom 2005:Figure 2; Rafferty 1984), along the Kern River Pipeline corridor in southern Nevada and southern Utah (Reed et al. 2005), and around the margins of desert playas at Nellis Air Force Base (Kolvet et al. 2000), and are ubiquitous on a variety of old landforms and playa margins in more western areas of the Mojave Desert (Basgall 2000). Stemmed series points, however, do not appear to be as strongly represented in similar dated components to the east and south, that is, in areas traditionally identified as

the Southwest. This may in part explain their relative dearth at Gold Butte.

Pinto

First recognized at Pinto Basin in the Mojave Desert (Amsden 1937; Campbell and Campbell 1935; Schroth 1994), the Pinto variants exhibit a large measure of morphological variation but can be generally characterized as large, thick, percussion-flaked, bifurcate-stemmed projectiles (Figure 5.2, n = 11). They have been distinguished from their more gracile and generally later-dating cousins, the Gatecliff series, in the northern and central Great Basin (Basgall and Hall 2000). Pinto series points are generally ascribed to a time frame of 6000 to 2000 BC.

Pinto series points are reasonably ubiquitous throughout the region and are not an uncommon occurrence in many large-scale inventories on land surfaces of appropriate age (see Ahlstrom (2005:Figure 2; Ruby and Gilreath 2006). There is, however, little documentation

TABLE 5.3. Projectile Point Frequencies by Type and Project Phase.

Point Type	Survey	Evaluation	Total
Desert Series			
Desert Side-Notched	3	17	20
Cottonwood	8	8	16
Rosegate	20	6	26
Small Stemmed	—	1	1
Arrow-Sized	4	8	12
Elko	56	41	97
Gypsum	7	2	9
Pinto	10	1	11
Humboldt	11	4	15
Stemmed Series			
Great Basin Stemmed	7	—	7
Silver Lake	4	—	4
Leaf-Shaped	2	2	4
Side-Notched Dart	5	1	6
Large Concave Base	—	1	1
Dart-Sized	35	13	48
Indeterminate	1	2	3
Total	173	107	280

Silver Lake Variants

26CK8100 -1   26CK8103 -3

0   5
cm

Great Basin Stemmed

26CK7993 -2   26CK8049 -1   26CK8077 -2   26CK8109 -3

FIGURE 5.1. Selected projectile points: Great Basin Stemmed and Silver Lake.

of these points in components dating to this period in intact, stratified contexts.

In establishing temporal parameters for this point form, however, it is worth noting that well over half the sites at Fort Irwin that contained Pinto points also produced Great Basin Stemmed points (Basgall 2000:130), suggesting some level of temporal overlap of these point forms—an issue noted by a number of other researchers (Gilreath and Hildebrandt 1997; Schroth 1994; Vaughan and Warren 1987). At Ventana Cave, for example, Pinto series projectile points appear to have a greater antiquity, perhaps supplanting Great Basin Stemmed time markers in this area. Similarly, many sites containing Pinto points may date to the earliest part of the Early Archaic/Pinto period (Schroth 1994), and the dearth of later-dating Pinto points and components is cited as

FIGURE 5.2. Selected projectile points: Pinto, Elko, and Gypsum.

evidence for the possible abandonment of the southern Great Basin during the middle Holocene warm period (Seymour 2001:70; Warren and Crabtree 1986:187).

Elko/Gypsum

Elko series points are large corner-notched points with proximal shoulder angles generally below 150 degrees, characterizing side-notched and other point forms

(Figure 5.2, n = 106). The series as recognized here includes corner-notched and eared forms (cf. Heizer and Baumhoff 1961; Heizer et al. 1968). Of similar size, but with a contracting stem, is the Gypsum variant first recognized at Gypsum Cave (Harrington 1933) and sometimes referred to as Elko contracting-stem in other contexts. Gypsum points tend to be more common in the southern Great Basin, Mojave Desert, and areas of the Southwest; in the study area, however, Elko outnumber Gypsum points by more than ten to one.

As summarized by Beck (1995) and others, Elko series points appear to have differing temporal expressions depending on location in the Great Basin. While acknowledging several hiatuses, Holmer (1986) sees evidence for their continuous use from about 6,000 to 1,000 years ago in the eastern Great Basin. By contrast, the western Great Basin manifestation is more narrowly dated to between about 1500 BC and AD 750 (Bettinger and Taylor 1974; Thomas 1981). As noted in Chapter 2, Carpenter et al. (2005:30–31; see also Berry and Berry 1986; Mabry 1998; Marmaduke 1978) suggest that Gypsum points reflect a new technology from central Mexico that used adhesive to attach projectiles to hafts and that diffused northward, along with maize cultivation, at the end of the middle Holocene warm period (ca. 3000 to 2000 BC). With regard to chronology building for this project, both Elko and Gypsum series points are perceived primarily as Late Archaic period implements and assumed to date to 2000 BC to AD 800. It is important to remember, however, that this point series dates to Basketmaker II and III in the local sequence.

Humboldt

First defined by Heizer and Baumhoff (1961) in west-central Nevada, Humboldt series points are typically unshouldered, lanceolate forms with slight basal concavities to deep basal notches (Figure 5.3, n = 15). A variety of subtypes and look-alike types have also been defined (e.g., Concave Base A, Concave Base B, Triple T, Basal-notched, Pinto shoulderless), but there remains a large measure of morphological and temporal confusion surrounding this type. Most examples are large enough to be considered dart forms, and some researchers have posited that they are roughly contemporaneous with Elko/Gypsum (Basgall and McGuire 1988; Gilreath and Hildebrandt 1997). Other investigators (Delacorte 1997: 78–80; McGuire et al. 2004:58–59) argue for a somewhat older use between 6,000 and 3,000 years ago. In the eastern Great Basin, Holmer (1986) sees two periods of use, one between 6000 and 4000 BC and the other between 3000 and 1000 BC. The project sample is probably not large enough to settle this matter, although hydration data from the several obsidian Humboldt points recovered is more in keeping with their manufacture during the Early Archaic period.

Other Large Projectiles and Dart-Sized Fragments

Dart-sized points that have broken and defy more exacting morphological classification are placed in this catchall category, which includes side-notched, leaf-shaped, and concave-based forms.

Side-Notched Darts

A total of six side-notched points was recovered. Although the majority were in fragmentary condition, most either are, or were at least originally, quite large (i.e., dart-sized), thus distinguishing them from the later-dating Desert Side-notched items. All have proximal shoulder angles in excess of 150 degrees, the threshold that separates them from corner-notched darts. This point style is typologically similar to what Thomas (1981) has referred to as "Elko Side-notched," but perhaps because of the confusion surrounding this type with the earlier-dating Northern Side-notched variant (geographically confined to the Plateau and northern Great Basin), this terminology has never been widely accepted. Still, it could very well be the case that side-notched darts are a Late Archaic/early Basketmaker marker—the one obsidian hydration rim value we have for this type is 10.5 microns, similar to the few obsidian Gypsum and Elko points found in the study area.

Leaf-Shaped Darts

A total of four leaf-shaped projectiles was recovered, all reasonably complete. Because all are relatively large (>5.7 g), they are considered darts (as opposed to arrow tips) and thus probably predate AD 750.

Large Concave Base

While smaller, concave-based specimens typical of the Humboldt series are well represented in the study area, an exception is a single large, concave-base specimen. The point is fragmentary but exhibits a complete base 27.8 mm wide; it is not, however, basally ground. Large concave-base points have been documented in low frequencies at a number of Great Basin localities and are thought to be Paleo-Archaic or Early Archaic time markers (Basgall 1988; Gilreath and Hildebrandt 1997).

Dart-Sized Fragments

The generic category of dart-sized fragments includes fragmentary, typologically ambiguous, or morphologically unique specimens (n = 48). All, however, were originally large (with weights reconstructed at 3.0 g or more) and thus are characterized as darts predating AD 750.

Rosegate

First described by Heizer and Baumhoff (1961) and Lanning (1963), and further refined by Thomas (1981), the Rosegate series consolidates Rose Spring and Eastgate forms. Rose Spring points are small triangular points with expanding stems, the bases of which vary from straight to moderately convex (Figure 5.3, n = 26). The Eastgate variant is similar, although the barbs formed

Humboldt

26CK6078/6095 -51   26CK7979 -1   26CK7994 -1

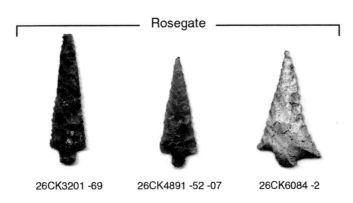

Rosegate

26CK3201 -69   26CK4891 -52 -07   26CK6084 -2

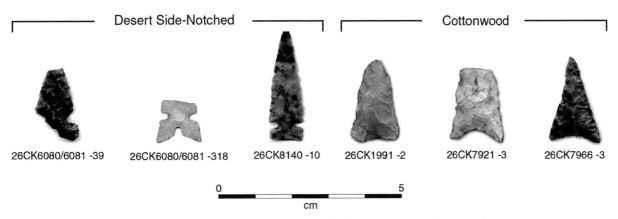

Desert Side-Notched

26CK6080/6081 -39   26CK6080/6081 -318   26CK8140 -10

Cottonwood

26CK1991 -2   26CK7921 -3   26CK7966 -3

0   5
cm

FIGURE 5.3. Selected projectile points: Humboldt, Rosegate, and Desert series.

by the notches often extend to the level of the base (see Bettinger 1989; Heizer and Baumhoff 1961). While Eastgate points may have cultural significance in some areas of the Great Basin, they are treated as contemporaneous with Rose Spring in the present study and subsumed under the Rosegate time marker.

Rosegate points, ubiquitous throughout the Great Basin, are generally understood to mark the introduction of bow and arrow technology. The most accepted time frame for this point series is from about AD 750 to 1250, at which time they were displaced by Desert series forms (Bettinger and Taylor 1974; Thomas 1981).

There is some evidence, however, that this series may have appeared somewhat earlier in this region, and therefore the introduction of the bow and arrow. A bow from Black Dog Cave returned a two-sigma calibrated radiocarbon date range of AD 410–600 (Winslow et al. 2003a, b). In the Las Vegas area, Rose Spring points have been found in association with calibrated radiocarbon dates ranging between AD 400 and 700 (see Ahlstrom 2005; Brooks et al. 1975). Similar earlier evidence for the bow and arrow has been documented in core zones of the Southwest located to the east (Geib and Spurr 2000).

An earlier regional introduction of the bow and arrow, and an expanded temporal range for Rosegate series points, would comport well with the Basketmaker II–III transition, variously dated to about AD 400. Indeed, the dominant point types at the Puebloan settlement at Lost City (Shutler 1961) are small-cornered notched variants equivalent to the Rosegate series. The series is thus a reasonable proxy for late Basketmaker/ Puebloan use of the study area. Interestingly, both Elko and Desert series points were recovered in higher frequencies than Rosegate points in the study area, perhaps indicating less intensive use of the desert hinterland located away from the Virgin River during Puebloan times.

Desert Series

As described by Baumhoff and Byrne (1959), Desert Side-notched points are small (<1.5 g), delicately flaked, triangular points with notches placed high on the sides (Figure 5.3, n = 36). They are ubiquitous throughout the Great Basin and are thought by some researchers to be Numa markers that were carried north and east by Numic-speaking peoples, beginning about one thousand years ago (Delacorte 1997; Holmer 1986; Janetski 1994). If that is true, they may mark Paiute occupation of the Gold Butte area. Cottonwood series points are small (<1.5 g), unnotched triangular points. Both types are thought to date to about AD 1250 and thereafter.

Other Arrow Tips and Arrow-Sized Fragments

Most of the 13 tools in the category of arrow tips and arrow-sized fragments are small, delicately flaked fragments of projectile points assumed to have originally weighed less than 3.0 g. As such, they are considered arrow tips, probably dating to after AD 750. The one complete item is a small (2.0 g), typologically unique, lanceolate specimen with slight corner notching and a square stem. It is most likely an arrow tip with a commensurate age estimate.

POTTERY

Although pottery was documented at 117 prehistoric sites and found in ten isolated contexts (Tables 4.5 and 4.7), actual collections were obtained from 81 sites and five of the isolates. This subset, however, includes pottery recovered during the survey phase, in which only

rim fragments, pieces of uncommon style or color, those with vestiges of a painted design, and those found in subsurface probes were collected. In recognition of this sampling bias, we returned to 29 project sites and isolates that had an appreciable quantity of pottery and collected all sherds within a delimited area at each context. Complete collections were also obtained from all sites formally tested as part of the evaluation program, bringing the total of systematically collected contexts to 33.

Notwithstanding sampling strategies, a total of 4,699 sherds was collected as part of this project; analytical results are summarized in Table 5.4 by series, ware, type, and surface treatment. Of this total, 4,466 specimens were systematically collected from the aforementioned 33 sites and sorted by series, ware, and type (Table 5.5). In the analysis presented here, interpretive emphasis is given to these representative samples.

Individual sherds were classified at the most general level into one of three groups: Puebloan, Paddle and Anvil, and Brown Ware. More exacting series, ware, and type assignments were made based on factors such as technology, temper, clay quality and color, and surface decoration and finish. As further detailed below, the analysis relies heavily on previous regional classifications by Allison (1996, 2000); Jensen (2002); Jensen et al. (2006); Larson and Michaelsen (1990); Lyneis (1986, 1988, 1992, 1995, 2004, 2007, 2008), Seymour (1997); Seymour and Perry (1998), and Walling et al. (1986). Typological assignments conducted as part of this analysis were performed by Amy J. Gilreath and Gregory Seymour.

Classification and Chronology

Age-range assignments applied here are offered as general approximations, with emphasis placed on a type's central tendency rather than the broader possible ranges that some offer (Figure 5.4). For Puebloan sherds, age assignments consider the Pecos scheme as well as macrotrends noted by pottery analysts familiar with Southwestern pottery in the Arizona Strip, in southwest Utah, and along the Virgin/Moapa drainage (especially Allison 2000; Larson 1987; Lyneis 2008; Walling et al. 1986). The time range for the various paddle and anvil sherds relies primarily on Seymour (1997:144–148), Seymour and Perry (1998), and Jensen et al. (2006). As has long been noted, because of an inadequate suite of local radiocarbon-dated sites and absent a tree-ring chronology, the pottery chronology for this area has developed with considerable reliance on cross-dating. For Puebloan pottery, this local sequence primarily references Kayenta Branch styles. For paddle and anvil sherds, the local sequence primarily references the

TABLE 5.4. Gold Butte Sherd Collection.

Type	Plain	Corrugated	Incised	Painted	Indeterminate	Total
Puebloan						
Fremont Gray	1	—	—	—	—	1
Logandale Gray	126	—	—	—	—	126
Moapa Gray/White	458	1	—	15	—	474
Shivwits Gray	115	18	—	—	—	133
Virgin Series—Tusayan Gray/White	1,252	33	—	91[a]	1	1,377
San Juan Red	2	—	—	—	—	2
Tsegi Orange	1	—	—	1	—	2
Subtotal	1,955	52		107	1	2,115
Paddle and Anvil						
Paddle and Anvil	1,074	1	2	—	—	1,077
Brown Ware						
Southern Paiute	679	104	52	—	1	836
All Identified Subtotal	3,708	157	54	107	2	4,028
Indeterminate	90	17	9	—	555	671
Total	3,798	174	63	107	557	4,699

[a] Two provisionally identified as Kayenta series

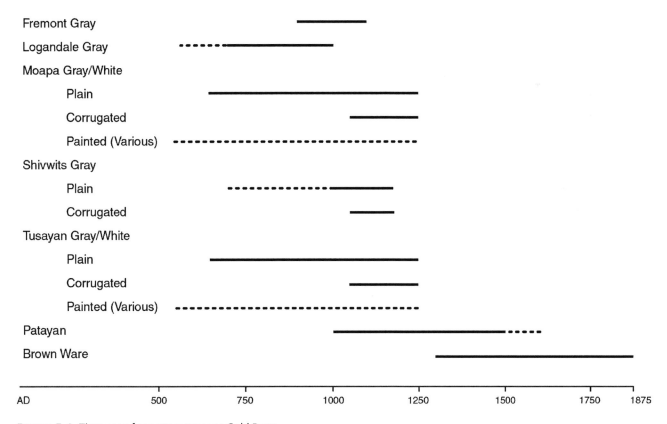

FIGURE 5.4. Time span for pottery types at Gold Butte.

TABLE 5.5. Pottery Types by Context—Representative Sample.

Site (26CK)	Puebloan Wares								Patayan Wares					Brown Ware	Indeterminate		Total
	FRE	MOA	SHI	LOG	SJR	TSE	TUS	Subtotal	BUF	P/A	PRE	TIZ	Subtotal		TSTA	UNK	
1988	—	3	2	—	—	—	9	14	—	—	—	—	0	—	—	—	14
1991	—	11	7	—	—	—	11	30	—	71	—	1	72	—	2	2	106
3201	—	20	19	1	1	—	120	160	—	8	—	—	8	16	19	9	212
3208	—	2	—	—	—	—	13	15	—	10	—	—	10	—	—	1	26
4891	—	6	—	76	—	—	214	296	—	3	—	—	3	—	33	2	334
6078/6095	—	25	4	10	—	—	83	122	—	79	—	4	83	18	11	9	243
6080/6081	—	54	3	17	—	—	166	240	1	410	12	61	484	138	183	12	1,057
6082	—	13	—	—	—	—	11	24	—	20	1	6	27	—	9	—	60
6084	—	1	—	1	—	—	8	10	—	39	—	—	39	1	—	—	50
6088	—	5	2	3	—	—	6	16	—	16	—	—	16	6	—	—	38
6672	—	43	6	1	—	—	32	82	—	38	—	—	38	—	4	—	124
7574	—	7	—	2	—	—	14	23	—	12	1	1	14	6	—	2	45
7892	—	13	4	—	—	—	5	22	—	34	—	2	36	1	—	2	61
7893	—	1	—	—	—	—	—	1	—	17	—	—	17	3	3	—	24
7901	—	—	—	—	—	—	—	0	1	112	5	—	118	—	22	—	140
7903	—	—	—	1	—	—	19	20	—	27	—	4	31	8	6	—	65
7921	—	33	—	—	—	—	1	34	—	11	2	13	26	—	6	—	66
7966	—	55	51	—	—	—	139	245	—	18	—	8	26	36	133	1	441
7983	—	1	—	—	—	—	2	3	—	—	—	—	0	151	21	—	175
7985	—	—	—	—	—	—	—	0	—	—	—	—	0	259	40	—	299
7992	—	7	—	—	—	—	8	15	—	3	—	—	3	6	—	—	24
8001	—	58	—	—	—	—	—	58	—	—	—	—	0	—	30	—	88
8013	—	—	—	—	—	—	—	0	—	—	—	—	0	83	17	—	100
8032	—	21	8	2	—	1	5	37	—	9	—	—	9	—	3	1	50
8035	—	19	—	—	—	—	2	21	—	—	—	—	0	—	—	—	21
8036	—	—	—	—	—	—	159	159	—	—	—	—	0	—	12	39	210
8037	—	—	—	—	—	—	155	155	—	—	—	—	0	—	9	—	164
8047	—	—	1	—	—	—	4	5	—	—	—	—	0	3	—	—	8
8168	—	4	—	—	—	—	4	8	—	—	—	—	0	—	—	—	8
8170	—	43	4	2	—	1	29	79	—	3	—	—	3	8	—	—	90
8172	—	—	—	—	—	—	—	0	—	—	—	—	0	—	2	16	18
8562	—	—	—	—	—	—	—	0	—	—	—	—	0	66	—	—	66
8580	1	5	22	—	—	2	2	30	—	—	—	—	0	—	9	—	39
Total	1	450	133	116	1	2	1,221	1,924	2	940	21	100	1,063	809	574	96	4,466

Note: FRE = Fremont Gray; MOA = Moapa Gray/White; SHI = Shivwits Gray; LOG = Logandale Gray; SJR = San Juan Red; TSE = Tsegi Orange; TUS = Tusayan Gray/White; BUF = Lower Colorado Buff; P/A = Paddle and Anvil; PRE = Prescott Gray; TIZ = Tizon Brown Ware; TSTA = Too small to analyze; UNK = Unknown.

chronology for the lower Colorado River. For both, though, "a time-lag for the interval needed for design styles to 'migrate'" (Walling et al. 1986:354) to this area is typically allowed. In assigning a date range to Brown Ware, we rely on Walling et al. (1986:369) and Lyneis (2004).

Puebloan Pottery

Gray Ware, White Ware, and Red/Orange Ware sherds are grouped as Puebloan pottery, using a ware/type classification modeled on Jensen (2002) and Walling et al. (1986) and informed by Lyneis (2008). Five types of gray/white ware sherds are present in the Gold Butte collection—Fremont Gray, Logandale Gray, Moapa Gray/White, Shivwits Gray, and Virgin Series–Tusayan Gray/White—in addition to two types of Red/Orange Ware, San Juan Red and Tsegi Orange. Collectively, Puebloan pottery accounts for 52.5 percent of the diagnostic sherds (Table 5.4).

Fremont Gray Ware

The one Fremont sherd from Gold Butte is a plain gray rim fragment. It is classified as Snake Valley Gray, a type that occurs throughout the Fremont sequence and has a regional distribution concentrated in southwestern Utah. This plain type can be assigned only a general age-range estimate of AD 900 to 1100. Madsen (1977) places this type in a coil-and-scrape ware and describes it as having plain surface treatment and fine to medium angular temper inclusive of quartz, feldspar, and biotite mica. Watkins (2006) retains Snake Valley Gray as a type within the Snake Valley series of Fremont Desert Gray Ware.

Logandale Gray Ware

Crushed limestone temper readily distinguishes Logandale Gray Ware from other sherd types (Figure 5.5a). In many instances the temper has leached out, leaving the sherd with a sponge-like pocked appearance. This ware occurs at Gold Butte only with a plain finish, with 126 sherds collected (Table 5.4). No painted types have been described, and elsewhere only a few corrugated examples have been reported (Seymour and Perry 1998:49). Logandale Gray may well be the earliest pottery in our area, and it appears to have been made locally. Lyneis (2008:6) points to the Upper Moapa Valley and south of the Virgin River Gorge as likely manufacturing centers. Logandale Gray is most prevalent toward the early end of the Puebloan pottery sequence, in Basketmaker III contexts, but its use appears to extend into early Pueblo II times. A start date of AD 700 applied here allows a 100-year lag for Basketmaker III from the Four

Corners area, and an end date of AD 1000 extends its use minimally into the Pueblo II interval. In the Moapa Valley, Winslow (2004, 2006) has recently reported dates for Basketmaker III pithouses consistent with a thermoluminescence date that indicates Logandale Gray may have been in use locally as early as AD 400.

Moapa Gray/White Ware

Olivine-tempered sherds (Figure 5.5a) were classed as Moapa Ware and, like Tusayan sherds (see below), separated further based on surface finish. Following recent convention (Lyneis 2008), plain and corrugated sherds are included under Moapa Gray Ware, and painted ones under Moapa White Ware. As summarized in Table 5.4, of the 474 Moapa Ware sherds, 96.6 percent are plain gray and only one is corrugated. Among the 15 painted pieces (Table 5.6), rarely was enough of a design present to allow for finer classification. The prevailing view is that Moapa Ware was manufactured in the vicinity of Mt. Trumbull and subsequently conveyed west, since it is the source of the olivine xenoliths used as temper (see Allison 2000).

Plain sherds, typed as Boulder Gray (which now subsumes Moapa Brown), date from Basketmaker III to Pueblo II, according to Lyneis (2008; see also Larson and Michaelsen 1990), which Walling et al. (1986:355) equated (for Moapa Brown + Boulder Gray) to AD 525–1250 in southwest Utah. Allowing for some lag, a range of AD 650 to 1250 is applied here. Moapa Corrugated appears comparatively late in the sequence, confined to the mid to late Pueblo II period, according to Lyneis (2008). This remains generally consistent with Walling et al.'s (1986:355) suggested time span of AD 1050–1250. In the Moapa Valley, Allison (2000) and Lyneis (2007) provide some indication that Moapa Ware (regardless of type) was at peak popularity in middle Pueblo II times, when it may account for 30 percent or more of the Puebloan pottery (Lyneis 2008:10).

Shivwits Gray Ware

Pottery tempered with a mixture of both olivine and crushed sherds (Figure 5.5a) was classed as Shivwits Ware (Lyneis 1988). Only plain and corrugated types are known; no painted examples have been recognized. Of the Shivwits Ware sherds from Gold Butte, 115 are plain and 18 are corrugated (Table 5.4). Lyneis (1992) and Allison (ongoing research cited in Lyneis 2008) suggest that this ware was produced on the Shivwits Plateau, perhaps chiefly in the southern portion of the plateau (but see Jensen 2002). In southern Nevada, Lyneis (2008:15) has noted that this ware has a restrictive temporal and spatial distribution, occurring "in

TABLE 5.6. Painted Sherds by Type.

Primary Pecos Association	Kayenta Series			Virgin Series			Moapa Ware			Tsegi Orange	Total
	Type	Walling et al. 1986:355	Count	Cognate	Walling et al. 1986:355	Count	Cognate	Walling et al. 1986:355	Count	Count	
BM-III	Lino	AD 610–800	—	Mesquite	AD 550–700[a]	2	Boulder	AD 550–760	1	—	3
P-I	Kana-a	AD 800–900	—	Washington	AD 700–900	11[b]	Boysage	AD 735–890	—	—	11
Early to Mid P-II	Black Mesa	AD 1025–1130	1	St. George	AD 900–1100	9	Trumbull	AD 900–1100	2	—	12
Late P-II/ Early P-III	Sosi & Dogoszhi[c]	AD 1075–1200	1	North Creek & Hildale	AD 1100–1225	9	Moapa & Slide Mtn.	AD 1110–1225	4	—	14
P-III	Flagstaff	AD 1060–1250	—	Glendale	AD 1125–1250	—	Poverty Mtn.	AD 1125–1250	—	—	—
Subtotal			2			31			7	—	40
Indeterminate			—			58			8	1	67
Total			2			89			15	1	107

[a] Timespan from Jensen et al. 2006:279, who shorten Walling et al.'s range of AD 525–750.
[b] Includes one typed as Washington/St. George.
[c] The appearance of Dogoszhi appears to slightly postdate Sosi

large quantities in middle Pueblo II time" in the Moapa Valley. As noted above, however, olivine temper can occur in Puebloan wares as early as Basketmaker III times. While the central temporal trend for Shivwits Gray appears to correspond to about AD 1000 to 1150, it may have some earlier expression (Lyneis 2008:14–15). On the other hand, Shivwits Corrugated appears much more restricted, coming into use at AD 1050 and continuing to AD 1150.

Virgin Series–Tusayan Gray/White Ware

Sand-tempered sherds of well-made pots, light to medium gray, sometimes grading into tan, were classified as Virgin Series–Tusayan Gray/White Ware. Unpainted plain and corrugated pieces were typed as North Creek Gray (n = 1,252) and North Creek Corrugated (n = 33), respectively. Of the 89 painted sherds, only 31 could be more specifically typed to the local cognates of Kayenta Branch design styles (Table 5.6). No painted corrugated Virgin Series–Tusayan sherds are present in the Gold Butte sample, though pieces of such bowls have infrequently been encountered elsewhere.

Much, perhaps most, of this pottery appears to have been manufactured locally, a practice that began in Basketmaker III times and continued into the early Pueblo III period, thus spanning nearly the entire duration of ancestral Puebloan occupation of the area. In the Lowland Virgin area Lyneis (1995:208, 217) has sug-

gested a date range for the series on the order of AD 650 to 1200/1250 (but see Allison [1996:Table 1], who extends Virgin Branch occupation of the region to AD 1300, based in part on radiocarbon dates from the St. George Basin and Arizona Strip). Manufacturing centers have not been isolated. Rather, this pottery appears to have been made throughout the Virgin Branch Puebloan area. Not surprisingly, variability in sherd color and quality has been noted, as well as variability in the quantity and characteristics of sand grains used for temper.

North Creek Gray appears to have been used throughout the sequence and is assigned a date range of AD 650–1200. North Creek Corrugated is presumed to have come into production synchronous with other corrugated wares, beginning around AD 1050 and lasting until Puebloan retraction, estimated at AD 1200. Though a relative sequence for the different painted styles is fairly well understood, their exact dating is not. Age ranges assigned to the various types of painted sherds at Gold Butte are charted in Table 5.6, cross-referenced to the Pecos scheme.

San Juan Red Ware and Tsegi Orange Ware

One or two sherds each of San Juan Red Ware and Tsegi Orange Ware were collected from Gold Butte sites (Table 5.5; Figure 5.6f). Temper is the main distinguishing characteristic for these imported pieces (Figure 5.5b): the former was tempered with crushed

26CK4891-44 Logandale
17× Magnification

26CK4891-57 Logandale
17× Magnification

26CK6672-7A Moapa
17× Magnification

26CK6672-7B Moapa
17× Magnification

26CK8580-2 Shivwits
17× Magnification

FIGURE 5.5a. Cross-section magnification of different pottery types.

26CK1991-16 San Juan
17× Magnification

26CK8032-5 Tsegi
17× Magnification

26CK6080/6081-220 Paddle/Anvil
17× Magnification

26CK3201-174 So Paiute
17× Magnification

FIGURE 5.5b. Cross-section magnification of different pottery types.

andesite while the latter was made by incorporating crushed sherds in the temper (Lyneis 1992). Where manufactured, San Juan Red Ware dates to ca. AD 700 to 1040 (Christenson 1994) while Tsegi Orange Ware dates to ca. AD 1040 to 1240. Low amounts of these exotic wares appear in southern Nevada after AD 1050 (Jensen et al. 2006:279). Lyneis (1992:55) and Jensen (2002:20) suggest that they occur in middle to late Pueblo II contexts, on the order of AD 1100.

Patayan Pottery (Paddle and Anvil)

In total, 1,076 sherds from 30 sites, and one isolated sherd, were made using paddle and anvil technology (Table 5.4 and Figure 5.5b). Aside from three pieces with either corrugation or fingernail incising, all are plain (Table 5.4). This pottery technology is associated with groups south of Gold Butte across the Colorado River,

with those west of the river across the Colorado Desert, and especially with groups concentrated along the lower Colorado River (Lyneis 1988). It is commonly referred to as Patayan-tradition pottery (Jensen et al. 2006:276). Various names, sorting schemes, and types have been proposed, resulting in a classification convention that remains "unsettled, to put it politely" (Lyneis 2004:9). Lyneis (2004:9) states succinctly: "The plain varieties of Tizon Brown Ware, Prescott Gray Ware, and Lower Colorado Buff Ware from the northern part of the lower Colorado River are both highly variable and show overlap in kind of temper and in fired clay colors. I know of no set of criteria for distinguishing them." As intimated by her statement, paddle and anvil pottery was locally made over a very large area.

A few Prescott Gray Ware and Lower Colorado Buff Ware sherds were initially identified in the Gold

FIGURE 5.6. Surface designs and decorations on selected sherds from Gold Butte.

Butte collection, but as the sample of project sherds increased, all semblance of within-group distinctiveness disappeared. Nonetheless, paddle and anvil pottery was easily distinguished from Puebloan and Paiute wares by the remnant paddle marks found on many pieces. Among those, the most distinctive tendencies noted were the following: a fairly high number had a high amount of small, size-sorted, crushed rock temper; some had a high amount of mica in the temper (silver as well as brassy yellow); a small percentage had distinct, small, garnet-like (hornblende?) mineral inclusions in the temper; a fairly high number had clay with a moist/ sticky appearance evocative of gingerbread in texture and color; and many were well fired, with a smooth, nicely burnished exterior. None was painted.

A date range of AD 1000 to 1500 was applied to the Patayan pottery at Gold Butte. One might quibble that AD 900 is a more appropriate beginning date, provided that some of this pottery is Prescott Gray Ware and allowing for a slight time lag from its core area. This ware is common in a zone that reaches 80 miles to the southeast of Gold Butte. Hayes-Gilpin (2001) describes Prescott Gray's core area as extending west into the Juniper Mountains and north roughly to U.S. 40, where a date range of AD 800 to 1400 is applied. However, Christenson (in Lyneis 2004:9) indicates that "there was some production of the type in the 900s, although it is not particularly frequent until ca. 1100." An equally appropriate start date of AD 1000 tracks the spread of Lower Colorado Buff Ware from the south to the northern part of the lower Colorado River valley. According to Jensen et al. (2006:276), "a Patayan ceramic tradition does not appear in the archaeological record in southern Nevada until about AD 900," and such sherds are not widespread across the desert until the Patayan II period, AD 1000 to 1500 (see also Seymour 1997:144–145). Though paddle and anvil pottery continued to be made after 1500 along the lower river and throughout southern California, the tradition underwent an elaboration of surface treatment during the Patayan III period (AD 1500 into the 1800s), when paint and appliqué became more common.

Based on the high incidence of Patayan II but general absence of Patayan III sherds in Las Vegas Valley sites, Seymour (1997) concluded that there was an extensive local Patayan presence between AD 1050 and 1500, when the Patayan largely abandoned the region. An end date of AD 1500 is applied here based on the absence of painted or appliquéd paddle and anvil sherds in Gold Butte and on the strength of the Las Vegas Valley pattern. Along these lines, Gold Butte was occupied by the Southern Paiute at the time of historic contact; this group manufactured the Brown Ware that is found throughout the study area (see below).

Brown Ware

Brown Ware is distinguished from other pottery types in the area by its non-size-sorted temper, often from granitic sources, and its thick walls of clay fired to dark hues of black to red. In general, the sherds readily crumble, due to the clay quality and a low firing temperature. In total, 836 Brown Ware sherds were collected from Gold Butte. Most (n = 679) are plain, 104 have a corrugated surface (most from a single pot in one site; Figure 5.6b, c), and 52 have fingernail incisions. All are considered locally made by the Southern Paiute.

Perry's (2003) summary of radiocarbon dates on contexts with Southern Paiute sherds in southwestern Utah suggests a time range from AD 1220 to modern times. Lyneis (2004) reports a comparable radiocarbon date from the Yamashita sites in Moapa Valley, with a two-sigma range spanning cal AD 1310 to 1360 and cal AD 1390 to 1660. Consequently, she places a date range of AD 1300 to the 1800s on Brown Ware. A range of AD 1300 to 1900 is applied here.

Indeterminate

A total of 671 sherds remain of indeterminate type. Most of them (n = 574) are simply too small (less than the size of one's small fingernail) to deserve consideration. Under magnification, the remaining 97 pieces (most of them also small bits) had temper of ambiguous or unusual composition.

Discussion

The quantities and types of Puebloan sherds found at Gold Butte suggest several broad trends. First, the recognition that corrugated surface treatment was most popular at the latter end of the Puebloan sequence (i.e., Late Pueblo II and III) has been demonstrated locally (Allison 2000; Larson and Michaelsen 1990; Lyneis 1986, 2008), as well as in other core areas of the Southwest (e.g., Plog and Hantman 1986). At Gold Butte, only 52, or 2.5 percent, of the 2,115 Puebloan series sherds identified exhibit corrugated surface treatment (Table 5.4), indicating minimal occupation during Late Pueblo II and III times. The lack of other Pueblo III pottery types (e.g., Dogoszhi- and Flagstaff-like sherds) supports this inference.

Larson and Michaelsen (1990:233) argue that olivine tempering, characteristic of Moapa and Shivwits wares, is relatively more common at the early end of the Puebloan period (Basketmaker III, Pueblo I), slightly less common during Pueblo II times, and virtually absent from Pueblo III contexts. Allison (2000:133) agrees with the latter end of this characterization but believes that olivine-tempered ceramics may have been most popular in middle Pueblo II times. Approximately 30 percent of all Puebloan ceramics at Gold Butte are olivine tempered (Table 5.4). As we detail in Chapter 8, where we review a seriation of corrugated and olivine-tempered ceramics, the evidence at hand would support Larson and Michaelsen's notion of significant use of olivine-tempered ceramics during Basketmaker III and Pueblo I times.

TABLE 5.7. Glass and Shell Beads from Excavations.

Site (26CK)	Catalog Number	Type	Color	Diameter (mm)	Thickness (mm)	Perforation Diameter (mm)
Glass						
6080/6081	144	DIIa	Blue	3.7	2.3	1.3
6080/6081	305	DIIa	White	4.2	3.4	1.4
6080/6081	306	DIIa	Teal	3.8	3.0	1.5
6080/6081	331a	DIVa	Red/White	4.1	2.2	1.0
6080/6081	331b	DIVa	Red/White	4.0	1.9	1.4
Shell						
6080/6081	330	Disk	n.a.	14.2	2.4	3.8
3201	209	G1	n.a.	4.6	1.3	1.2
7994	28	G2	n.a.	6.3	1.5	2.7
8179	153	*Dentalium*	n.a.	−0.3	20.3 long	n.a.

Note: DIIa = Drawn, monochrome, tumbled-oblate; DIVa = Drawn, polychrome, tumbled-oblate; Disk = Abalone epidermis disk; G1 = *Olivella* tiny saucer; G2 = *Olivella* normal saucer.

This early profile of Puebloan pottery at Gold Butte is supported by the recovery of Logandale Gray Ware, which strongly correlates with Basketmaker III use. These limestone-tempered sherds comprise about 6 percent of all Puebloan pottery and occur at 33 percent of all sites with Puebloan pottery (Table 5.5). In the absence of seriations with other Puebloan pottery types or other comparative data, it is difficult to know what this frequency representation means with respect to land use, other than some level of use of the study area by Basketmaker III peoples.

At a broader level, the documentation of nonlocal wares (Fremont Gray, Moapa Gray/White, Shivwits Gray, and Red/Orange wares) attests to the Lowland Virgin River area's involvement in interregional exchange. These nonlocal wares collectively amount to 30 percent of the Puebloan pottery and are present at more than 86 percent of the sites with Puebloan pottery (Table 5.5). Allison (2000:78) argues that this exchange may have peaked around AD 1050 to 1150, although, as we noted above, local populations may have made substantial use of olivine-tempered ceramics before this time.

Other analyses directed at regional ceramic assemblages dating to this time have documented shifts in vessel shape based on rim profile (e.g., Allison 2000) and in painted design styles based on measurement of line thickness, dots versus flags, and so on (e.g., Allison and Coleman 1998; Rowe 2002b). The number of substantial rim fragments and painted sherds from Gold Butte, however, were too low to permit productive application of the approaches.

Perhaps one of the more surprising aspects of the Gold Butte pottery assemblage is that the post-

Puebloan wares (Patayan and Brown Ware) are almost as common as Puebloan, notwithstanding the presence of adjacent Virgin Branch settlements (Table 5.4 and Table 5.5). Patayan ceramics, in particular, dominate the assemblage and indicate that the study area was occupied by Yuman-speakers whose traditional territory encompasses lands to the south and southwest, including the lower Colorado River Basin. The distribution of Patayan and Brown Ware ceramics across the study area has implications for Late Prehistoric land use and cultural geography that are further explored in Chapter 8.

SHELL AND GLASS BEADS

Five glass beads, three shell beads, and fragments of a *Dentalium* shell were discovered during the test excavations (Table 5.7). The glass beads were found at 26CK6080/6081 (Ian's Rock Shelter) and are classified according to the typology created by Kidd and Kidd (1970). They are all drawn specimens that were manufactured by drawing or stretching molten glass into long canes that were then cut and shaped. Three of the beads are drawn, monochrome, and tumbled-oblate (DIIa), and are white, blue, and teal in color. The other two are drawn, polychrome, and tumbled-oblate (DIVa), and are red with a white interior. All these bead types were manufactured in Venice, Italy, and used as trade goods by Euro-American colonists all over the world. They are common throughout California, the Great Basin, and the Southwest, and typically correspond to the earliest period of contact. All the beads were found in the shallow, Late Prehistoric component at the site.

The shell bead assemblage was classified following the lead of Bennyhoff and Hughes (1987) and King (1990), and includes a single abalone epidermis disk bead, an *Olivella* tiny saucer (G1), an *Olivella* normal saucer (G2), and a longitudinal fragment of a piece of *Dentalium*. The abalone epidermis disk bead is also from the Late Prehistoric component at 26CK6080/6081. It is relatively large (14 mm in diameter and 2.4 mm thick) and has a conical perforation measuring about 3.8 mm across. This bead type typically dates to the Late period in southern California (King 1990).

Olivella saucer beads are made from the wall of the main body whorl of the shell. Tiny saucer (G1) beads have diameters ranging between 2.0 and 5.0 mm. They are commonly found in post–AD 1500 contexts but can also occur in many other time periods throughout southern California (Bennyhoff and Hughes 1987). The current specimen was found in the Pueblo II component at 26CK3201 (Collapsed Rock Shelter). The normal saucer (G2) was found on the surface of 26CK7994. They have diameters ranging between 5.0 and 10.0 mm and date to the Middle period along the southern California coast (Bennyhoff and Hughes 1987), which probably corresponds to the major Basketmaker occupation of the site.

Dentalium shell is seldom found in Great Basin archaeological contexts. The shell originates from the Oregon-Washington coast and reflects long-distance trade through groups to the northwest. A few pieces have been recovered in what are usually Late Prehistoric contexts in northern Nevada (Lovelock Cave and Humboldt Lakebed in Churchill County; Bennyhoff and Hughes 1987). Two smaller slivers of one ornament were recovered from 26CK8179 (Sheep Shelter), deep in the shelter's midden deposit (S6.5/W1.5, 70–80 cm). Associated material and a radiocarbon date indicate that it is a Late Archaic period trade item.

OBSIDIAN HYDRATION AND SOURCE ANALYSES

In total, 324 project obsidian specimens were subjected to hydration and chemical source (x-ray fluorescence [XRF]) analyses, the former by Tim Carpenter of ArchaeoMetrics and the latter by Richard Hughes of the Geochemical Research Laboratory. These data include two basic analytical groups: those specimens collected as part of the sample survey (n = 179) and those recovered as part of the test evaluation program at select sites (n = 145). With respect to sampling procedures, the former included all obsidian specimens identified while the latter generally entailed drawing targeted samples from specific contexts (e.g., features, strata, radiocarbon-dated deposits; see applicable site reports in Chapter 6).

Although the value of obsidian hydration for chronology building is well known, with the addition of chemical source analysis it can become a powerful tool in elucidating broad adaptive shifts in land use, population replacements, the rise and fall of trade networks, and other aspects of prehistoric culture change (Basgall and McGuire 1988; Bettinger 1999; Gilreath and Hildebrandt 1997; Hughes 1986). Unfortunately, there has not been much systematic treatment of regional source-specific hydration rates, and what data are available appear to be at best highly variable and at worst contradictory. While source variation is a potential concern, much of this problem is likely related to issues surrounding the effective hydration temperature (EHT) of the hydration process. Basically, rates of hydration are accelerated in more extreme EHT contexts, such as the hot desert ground surfaces that characterize most of the Gold Butte study area. Finally, there is an increasing awareness that variable laboratory standards and techniques can limit the comparability of results between analysts.

The Dominant Sources: Kane Springs, Delamar Mountains, and Modena/Panaca Summit

As arrayed in Table 5.8, ten separate known source groups are represented in the Gold Butte obsidian database, as well as potentially five separate unknown sources. Of these, three sources constitute about 85 percent of the database: Kane Springs, Delamar Mountains, and Modena/Panaca. All are located about 50 to 60 km north to northwest of the study area and represent the closest known obsidian source locations (Figure 5.7).

The Kane Springs and Delamar Mountains sources are in close proximity, and both are part of a volcanic geological feature known as the Kane Springs caldera. Two trace-element signatures have been identified on glass that occurs as nodules in Kane Springs Wash and other secondary contexts in the surrounding area. Nomenclature associated with these two source groups is confusing, but Delamar Mountains and Kane Springs (referred to respectively as Kane Springs Wash Caldera Variety 1 and Variety 2) have been retained by Richard Hughes in this book. The Modena/Panaca Summit source straddles the Utah-Nevada border approximately 50 km due north of the study area. Variously referred to as Panaca Summit, Modena, and Dry Valley, the Modena/Panaca nomenclature is maintained here.

The analytical potential of obsidian studies from these source groups has only recently begun to receive attention in this region, best demonstrated by Haarklau et al. (2005) and Seddon (2005); see also Ruby et al. (2005). Thus, for example, data from the southern Utah segment of the Kern River 03 project (Seddon 2005)

TABLE 5.8. Obsidian Source Profiles by Project Phase.

Source	Survey #	Survey %	Test #	Test %	Total #	Total %
Modena/Panaca Summit, NV	61	34.1	46	31.7	107	33.0
Kane Springs, NV	62	34.6	40	27.6	102	31.5
Delamar Mountains, NV	37	20.7	29	20.0	66	20.4
Shoshone Mountain, NV	3	1.7	2	1.4	5	1.5
Timpahute Range, NV	2	1.1	1	0.7	3	0.9
Black Tank, AZ	1	0.6	2	1.4	3	0.9
Burro Creek, AZ	1	0.6	—	—	1	0.3
Government Mountain, AZ	—	—	1	0.7	1	0.3
Partridge Creek, AZ	2	1.1	13	9.0	15	4.6
Wild Horse Canyon, UT	4	2.2	5	3.4	9	2.8
Unknown						
Unknown Variety 1	—	—	4	2.7	4	1.3
Unknown Variety 2	1	0.6	—	—	1	0.3
Unknown Variety 3	1	0.6	—	—	1	0.3
Unknown X	2	1.1	1	0.7	3	0.9
Unknown	2	1.1	1	0.7	3	0.9
Unknown Total	6	3.4	6	4.1	12	3.7
Total	179	100.0	145	100.0	324	100.0

demonstrate that for this region, mean hydration values for the prevalent point types array themselves in the expected sequence, from old (wide bands) to young (narrow bands). The problem is that these mean values vary considerably between localities. Along the Kern River 03 project corridor in southern Utah, the entire sequence, from Pinto to Desert series, is compressed between 6.0 and 1.0 microns, whereas in hot desert areas near Las Vegas, hydration readings from Pinto and Elko points routinely fall between 15.0 and 10.0 microns (Ruby et al. 2005). As indicated above, such disparity suggests a strong EHT bias. Fortunately, the Gold Butte obsidian database includes a number of rim values obtained from time-sensitive projectile points, as well as from radiocarbon-dated contexts. This allows us to construct and evaluate an internally consistent hydration rate sensitive to the EHT regime(s) of the Gold Butte area.

Figure 5.8 arrays the project-wide hydration profiles for each of these sources obtained during survey. What becomes immediately clear is the wide range of micron values associated with each group, spanning from below 2.0 to almost 18 microns. Significantly, the distribution profile of all three groups is similar, suggesting that the hydration process is roughly equivalent and not substantially affected by the chemical differences associated with each. At least with regard to rate formulation, this allows us to group these sources together into a single analytical framework.

What remains is to identify the micron ranges that correspond to the temporal periods of the regional cultural sequence. One approach is to use the hydration values from independently dated projectile point types and calculate a correlation with the mean and maximum age ranges of the different point forms (Bettinger 1980; Hall 1983; Hockett 1995; McGuire et al. 2004). To accomplish this, we use the hydration means of projectile point types derived from the surface survey sample from the project (Table 5.9). These means are then used to plot a hydration curve (Figure 5.9). To provide a hydration bracket for each period, we then plot the means against the midpoint of the corresponding age range for a given point form (see projectile point discussion above). Thus, for example, the hydration mean for the Pinto series is 12.8 microns, corresponding to about 4200 BC, the midpoint of the time frame for Pinto points (i.e., 5900–2500 BP). Where the beginning and ending dates of this period intersect the hydration curve constitutes the hydration bracket for this time span. The brackets derived in Figure 5.9 are arrayed in Table 5.10.

For a variety of reasons, this attempt at hydration dating can be considered only provisional. First, its efficacy is only as good as our understanding of the time ranges associated with each projectile point type, which

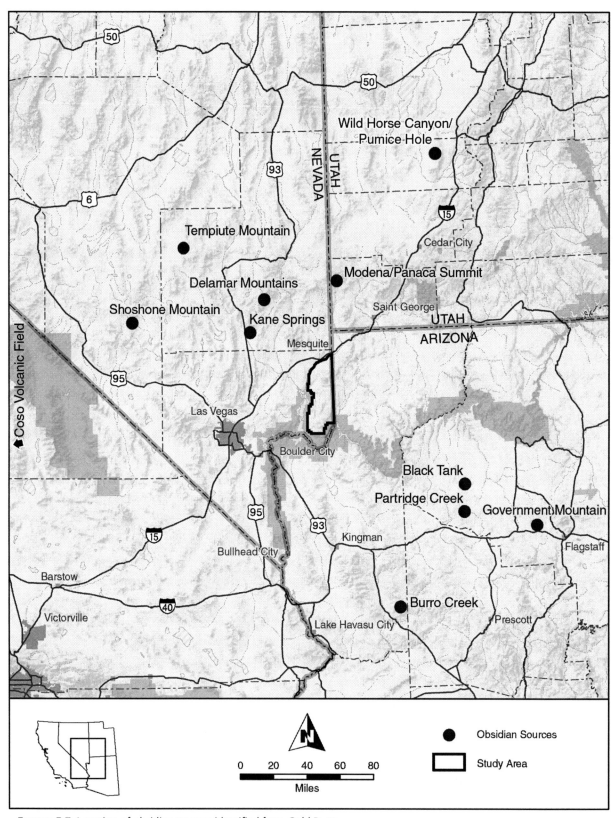

FIGURE 5.7. Location of obsidian sources identified from Gold Butte.

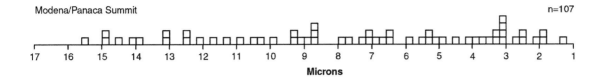

Modena/Panaca Summit   n=107

Microns

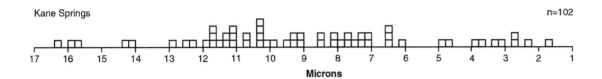

Kane Springs   n=102

Microns

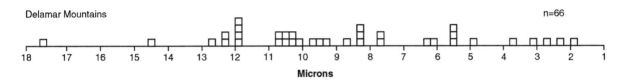

Delamar Mountains   n=66

Microns

FIGURE 5.8. Hydration profiles for the three primary source groups: Modena/Panaca Summit, Kane Springs, and Delamar Mountains.

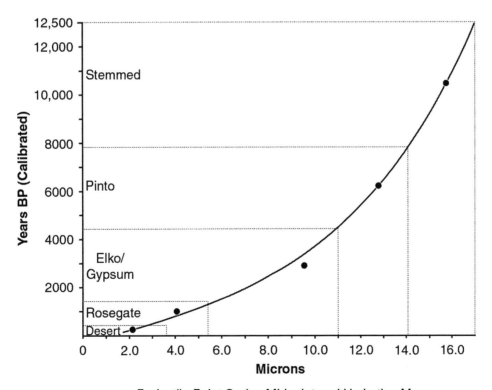

• Projectile Point Series Midpoint and Hydration Mean

FIGURE 5.9. Hydration curve plotted from mean rim value of time-sensitive projectile points (Modena/Panaca Summit, Kane Springs, and Delamar Mountains source groups).

TABLE 5.9. Hydration Means for Projectile Point Types (Kane Springs, Delamar Mountains, and Modena/Panaca Summit Sources): Survey Sample.

Point Type	Number	Mean	Values
Rose Spring/Rosegate	2	4.0	3.9, 4.0, (7.7)
Elko/Gypsum	3	9.5	8.0, 8.1, 12.4
Pinto	5	12.8	9.1, 11.4, 15.0, 15.8, 17.6
Humboldt	2	14.4	14.4, 14.5
Great Basin Stemmed	1	15.7	15.7
Dart-Sized	8	10.1	5.3, 8.6, 6.1, 10.8, 11.3, 11.9, 12.6, 14.1

TABLE 5.10. Hydration Brackets for Major Time Periods at Gold Butte.

Age	Period	Time Marker	Hydration Bracket (μ)
AD 1250–Contact	Late Prehistoric	Desert Series	1.0–3.8
AD 400–AD 1250	BM-III/P-I–III	Rosegate	3.8–5.4
2500 BC–AD 400	Late Archaic/ BM-II	Elko/ Gypsum	5.4–11.0
5900 BC–2500 BC	Early Archaic	Pinto	11.4–14.0
Pre–5900 BC	Early Holocene	Stemmed	>14.0

TABLE 5.11. Hydration Means for Projectile Point Types (Kane Springs, Delamar Mountains, and Modena/Panaca Summit Sources): Survey and Excavation Samples.

Point Type	Number	Mean	Values
Desert Side-notched	3	2.6	2.0,[a] 2.4,[b] 3.4
Rose Spring/Rosegate	4	4.2	3.9, 4.0, 4.7, (7.7)
Elko/Gypsum	4	8.8	6.8, 8.0, 8.1, 12.4
Pinto	5	12.8	9.1, 11.4, 15.0, 15.8, 17.6
Humboldt	3	14.1	13.6, 14.4, 14.5
Great Basin Stemmed	1	15.7	15.7
Dart-Sized	8	10.1	5.3, 8.6, 6.1, 10.8, 11.3, 11.9, 12.6, 14.1

Note: Parentheses represent outliers.
[a] Black Tank specimens.
[b] Partridge Creek specimens.

is often incomplete. Second, this sample of projectile points is very small, amounting to 13 rim values spread over five time periods. Still, the values are internally consistent with the hydration profiles for these source groups obtained from the study area, and with the generally accepted temporal sequence for this region.

Obsidian from Buried Components

The obsidian hydration and radiocarbon data from the study area also afford us a unique opportunity to further evaluate hydration rates for these primary source groups. This involves comparing hydration data from our three major source groups directly against radiometric assays obtained from the same or arguably associated depositional contexts. Such a comparison allows for an independent assessment of the provisional rate developed above from the hydration trends associated with time-sensitive projectile points.

Furthermore, and as we have previously noted, regional hydration rates associated with the major source groups (Kane Springs, Delamar Mountains, and Modena/Panaca) are highly variable, no doubt conditioned by local EHT regimes. Similar variations in EHT can be expected for the Gold Butte study area. We are also confronted with those materials collected from the ground surface (which have been subjected to much higher ambient temperatures through time) versus those obsidian items recovered from buried archaeological contexts (Table 5.11), where temperature extremes are presumably moderated to some extent. An assessment of hydration-radiocarbon pairs may also shed light on these issues.

The excavation program at Gold Butte resulted in the identification of four subsurface contexts suitable for the development of hydration-radiocarbon pairs (Table 5.12). All were generated from intact stratigraphic contexts at rock shelters, including 26CK3201, -6080/6081, and -8179. Details of these contexts are presented in the appropriate section of Chapter 6. These four pairs are then plotted along the slope line developed for the surface projectile point sample (Figure 5.10).

For those pairs associated with radiocarbon dates less than about 2,300 years old, the plots fall almost directly on the curve plotted from surface projectile points. This suggests that there does not seem to be much of a difference in the rate of hydration for surface as opposed to buried material. This tends to confirm what was previously noted regarding the mean hydration values for time-sensitive projectile points from surface versus buried contexts, namely, that there was little variation between the two (compare Tables 5.10 and 5.9).

TABLE 5.12. Hydration-Radiocarbon Pairs.

Provenience	Calibrated Intercept: Radiocarbon Date	¹⁴C Date (cal BP)	Mean	No.	S.D.	Range	C.V.	Outliers
N3/W1 0–20 cm; N3/W1 20–30 cm (¹⁴C)	cal AD 1160	790	4.3	11	0.8	2.2–5.1	0.19	7.3, 10.1
N3E0;N3/W1 30–50 cm (¹⁴C)	cal BC 300	2260	7.1	9	0.4	6.5–7.7	0.06	4.6, 13.4, 13.6
S3/W5, 5–10 cm (¹⁴C); S3/W5 0–30 cm	cal AD 1650	300	2.1	5	0.81	1.0–2.9	0.38	6.4
S4.5/W1.5 0–40 cm; S6.5/W1.5 50–120-cm; S6.5/W1.5 110–115 cm (¹⁴C)	cal BC 1440	3390	4.8	21	1.24	2.5–7.1	0.26	

Note: Kane Springs, Delamar Mountains, Modena/Panaca Summit specimens only; s.d. = standard deviation; c.v. = coefficient of variation; see Table 5.10.

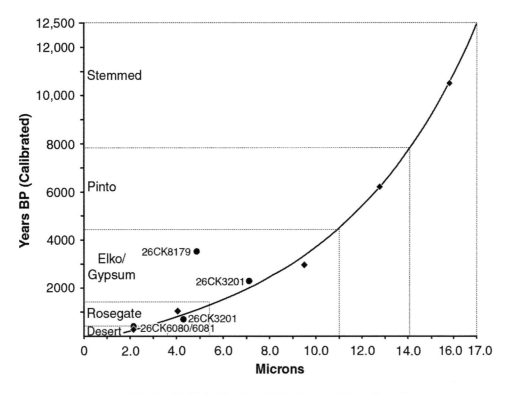

● Projectile Point Series Midpoint and Hydration Means
● Radiocarbon Date-Hydration Pairing

FIGURE 5.10. Radiocarbon date-hydration pairings plotted in reference to hydration curve derived from time-sensitive projectile point mean values.

The exception includes the pair from 26CK8179 (Sheep Shelter). Site 26CK8179 (at an elevation of 5,680 feet [1,730 m]) is unique because it is a north-facing rock shelter situated in the pinyon-juniper zone several thousand feet above the surrounding desert pediments and hills that make up most of the study area. The 1440 cal BC date is paired with a mean hydration value of 4.8 microns, very much lower than the midpoint value (9.5 microns) for the Elko-Gypsum surface

projectile point sample. This is a clear example of a less exposed, high-elevation, cool depositional context depressing the hydration rate (i.e., lowering the EHT).

In sum, and notwithstanding the important data limitations enumerated above, the hydration brackets for the three primary source groups established here are internally consistent and provide a provisional framework for the chronological positioning of project components. At least at the later, post–AD 1 end of the

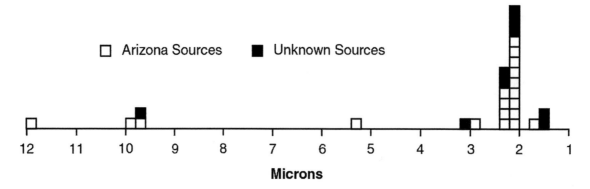

FIGURE 5.11. Hydration profile for Arizona and unknown obsidian source groups. (*Note:* Arizona source groups include Black Tank, Burro Creek, Government Mountain, and Partridge Creek. Unknown sources include at least four separate groups.)

sequence, there does not appear to be much difference in the hydration rate associated with surface material versus that from buried contexts. As with most hydration rate formulations, however, the efficacy of the rate deteriorates as one moves back in time, most likely the result of depositional disturbances, limited data, incomplete projectile point chronologies, or a poor understanding of the chemical and physical processes that affect hydration. There is evidence for a pronounced EHT effect at buried site components located at higher elevations (i.e., >5,000 feet) in the study area, but very few sites were identified in these settings.

Other Source Groups

In addition to the three primary source groups, there are seven identifiable sources represented in the project database, as well as at least five "unknown" chemical source groups (Table 5.8; Figure 5.7). They account for about 15 percent of the sample. The identifiable specimens fall into three broad geographic groups: (1) a series of four sources from Arizona to the southeast (Burro Creek, Black Tank, Government Mountain, and Partridge Creek; (2) two Great Basin sources to the northwest (Shoshone Mountain and Tempiute Range); and (3) Wild Horse Canyon material, located north of Cedar City, Utah.

When combined with hydration data, the most noteworthy of these minor groups include the Arizona and unknown sources; these data are plotted in Figure 5.11. Unlike the expansive hydration profile for the three primary sources, these two source classes cluster around two microns. The hydration characteristics of these glasses are not well understood within the EHT regime of the study area, but the few substantially larger rim values in this profile suggest at least a rough equivalence to the hydration process reported for the primary

obsidian sources. The conclusion, then, is that the representation of both the Arizona and unknown source groups reflect a decidedly later-dating, post-Puebloan phenomenon in the study area. These data point to perhaps more sustained, late interactions with Yuman populations to the south and southwest, although it is worth reiterating that the three major source groups (Modena/Panaca Summit, Kane Springs, and Delamar Mountains) remain in use.

The fact that the unknown source groups also show a very late-dating hydration profile has important implications for land use, perhaps indicating a more dispersed toolstone procurement strategy that incorporated visitations to very minor, previously unexploited glass outcrops and/or nodule deposits (minor in the sense that these sources have not yet been located and that their archaeological manifestations appear to be very limited). This pattern seems more in keeping with the desert foraging lifeways associated with late-arriving Numic-speaking groups.

The Great Basin obsidian sources represented in the project sample include five specimens from Shoshone Mountain and two from the Tempiute Range, both of which are located about 120 km to the northwest (Figure 5.7). In the former case, hydration values range from 11.0 to 8.1 microns, and in the latter, from 8.7 to 4.0 microns. Of perhaps greater interest is the complete lack of Coso obsidian, despite its dominance as an exchange commodity in central and southern California.

Toward the northeast, however, nine obsidian specimens from Wild Horse Canyon are documented at Gold Butte, even though this source lies some 160 km away in south-central Utah. Hydration values associated with this glass range from 9.9 to 2.5 microns, indicating its use over a substantial period of time.

6

Excavations
Site Reports

Nine prehistoric archaeological sites were selected for test excavation. The purpose of this work was to collect data that would help improve the dating of key artifact forms, develop obsidian hydration rates for the major sources used at Gold Butte, and improve our understanding of local subsistence economies through the discovery of chronologically discrete artifact assemblages and subsistence remains. We had originally hoped to discover one or two deep, stratified rock shelters that could produce these results, similar to the way Gatecliff Shelter contributed to the larger Monitor Valley project (Thomas 1983). Unfortunately, however, no sites of this character were found. Instead, all the midden deposits we encountered were relatively small and shallow, as was made clear by the small probes dug during survey. As a result of this finding, it was necessary to unravel the local chronological sequence by focusing on single-component deposits from multiple sites in the study area.

A multiphased selection process was used to identify the suite of optimal sites for excavation. We first selected all sites with well-developed midden deposits. We then segregated them into rough time periods based on temporally diagnostic projectile points and pottery types, giving the highest priority to single-component deposits (i.e., those producing time-sensitive artifacts from a single time period). Once this was accomplished, we classified the single-component deposits according to their geographic context, which gave us the opportunity to obtain information from a variety of environmental settings (Figure 6.1).

Eight of the nine sites selected for excavation are

habitation areas, and the other (26CK1991) is a concentration of agave ovens. The excavation effort produced 14 chronologically discrete component areas, as some of the sites had stratified deposits (Table 6.1). None of the components predates the Late Archaic (2500–350 BC), suggesting that Gold Butte was not the focus of intensive occupation for much of the early and middle Holocene (i.e., these early occupations did not produce midden). By the Late Archaic period, use of the area increased, and it is represented at four of the nine sites. Basketmaker occupations are also represented at four sites, and Puebloan components are found at three. Finally, the Late Prehistoric period is also represented at three sites.

Six geographic areas are covered by the nine sites (Table 6.1; Figure 6.1). These are the upland pinyon habitats in the Virgin Mountains (26CK8179) and Cedar Basin (26CK6078/6095 and -6080/6081), the Whitney Pockets area (26CK1991), the Virgin River (26CK4891), the Black Butte area (26CK3201), and the Red Rock Springs/Mud Wash area (26CK7994, -8013, and -8047).

METHODS

Detailed field methods are presented in the individual site reports that follow. Analytical methods for the artifacts and subsistence remains are provided here. All the recovered materials were catalogued under accession numbers obtained from the Nevada State Museum, where the collection will be curated in perpetuity. Cataloguing procedures followed a standardized format in which all materials were processed in sequential order (by site, unit, or feature; level from top to bottom). Each

TABLE 6.1. Excavated Locations and Temporal Components.

Site (26CK)	Location	Late Archaic	BM-II	BM-III	P-I	P-II	Late Prehistoric	Mixed
1991	Whitney Pockets	—	—	—	×	—	×	—
3201	Black Butte	×	×	—	—	×	—	—
4891	Virgin River	—	—	×	—	—	—	—
6078/6095	Cedar Basin	×	—	—	—	—	—	×
6080/6081	Cedar Basin	—	×	—	—	×	—	—
7994	Red Rock Springs/Mud Wash	×	×	—	—	—	—	×
8013	Red Rock Springs/Mud Wash	—	—	—	—	—	×	—
8047	Red Rock Springs/Mud Wash	—	—	—	—	—	—	×
8179	Virgin Mountains	×	—	—	—	—	—	—

tool received an individual catalog number; fauna, flora, debitage, and so on were assigned a group or lot number; and debitage was grouped by basic raw material type (e.g., obsidian, cryptocrystalline silicate, basalt).

Beyond cataloguing, a variety of special studies and analyses were carried out. Technical studies, such as those associated with radiocarbon, as well as obsidian hydration and XRF trace-element analysis, are reviewed in Chapter 5. Projectile points, pottery, and beads and their temporal classification have already been discussed (see Chapter 5). Analytical procedures associated with the few items that don't traditionally fall within the broad categories of flaked or ground stone (e.g., modified bone, ochre, palettes) are detailed in the site reports.

Provided below is a brief review of the analytical methods associated with the commonplace artifacts and subsistence remains that make up the overwhelming balance of the project collection.

Flaked Stone

Flaked stone artifacts recovered from project sites include projectile points, bifaces, formed flake tools, simple flake tools, cores, core tools, and debitage. Bifaces show percussion and/or pressure flaking on opposing sides of a continuous margin. Most are basically symmetrical in plan and cross section. In addition to the basic measurements, technological observations noted during analysis of the biface assemblage included reduction stage, presence of cortex, fracture type, presence of a flake detachment scar, and reason for rejection or discard (structural flaw, human error). Reduction stage is the primary attribute used throughout the book and hence warrants additional discussion. Stage 1 bifaces display rough bifacial edges and thick sinuous margins, and less than 60 percent of the perimeter edge is shaped. Stage 2 bifaces are percussion-shaped specimens with a rough outline. Stage 3 bifaces are percussion-thinned,

well-formed items. Evidence of intermittent pressure flaking is seen on Stage 4 bifaces, which are further-reduced, more-or-less symmetrical preforms. Stage 5 bifaces are fragments of extensively pressure-flaked implements and are considered (nondiagnostic) finished tools (e.g., projectile points, knives).

Formed flake tools are flakes that have been modified, usually unifacially, to the degree that the original edge shape has been highly altered. They typically show steep, intrusive flaking on one or more margins. Technological observations on formed flake tools include flake type, presence of cortex, flake termination angle, whether the item might have been intended as a flake blank (i.e., a biface formed by fairly minimal modification on the margins of a flake), striking platform type, number and shape of worked edges, working edge angle, length and thickness of the tooled edge, and edge modification type (unifacial microchipping, bifacial pressure flaking, etc.). Simple flake tools exhibit limited edge modification and/or retouch that may be intentional or the result of casual use. In contrast to formed flake tools, the basic outline of the original flake remains essentially unaltered; these are equivalent to "used" or "utilized" flakes. Simple flake tools were subjected to the same analysis as the formed flake tools.

Attributes collected for cores and core tools include the pattern of flake removals (nonpatterned, unidirectional, etc.), original artifact form (flake, cobble, etc.), and primary and secondary platform types (cortical, interior). For core tools, the number of worked edges (if applicable), the shape and length of worked edges, and the type of edge modification were also recorded. Core tools also show flake removals, with subsequent damage or use evident (e.g., grinding or battering of a flaked edge). As well as examining the same attributes as for cores, we examined type of modification (e.g., end battering, edge grinding, edge flaking), its extent, and angle of the working edge.

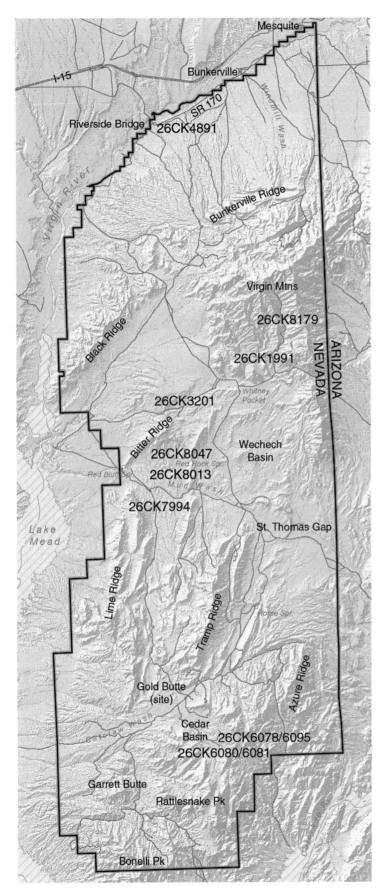

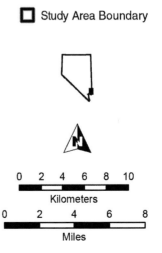

Study Area Boundary

0 2 4 6 8 10
Kilometers

0 2 4 6 8
Miles

FIGURE 6.1. Spatial distribution of excavated sites at Gold Butte.

A sample of the debitage from each single-component area was subjected to technological analysis. The vast majority of this material is composed of cryptocrystalline silicates (CCS), followed by much lower frequencies of obsidian and a variety of local toolstones (e.g., quartzite, basalt). Diagnostic flakes were initially grouped into two primary types, percussion and pressure. Percussion flake types were then sorted into primary decortication, secondary decortication, simple interior, complex interior, linear, early biface thinning, middle-stage biface thinning, late-stage biface thinning, angular shatter, and indeterminate percussion. Several nondiagnostic flake types were also recognized: edge preparation/pressure and indeterminate fragments.

Ground and Battered Stone

Ground and battered stone artifacts include millingstones, handstones, and battered cobbles. Basic metrical information for all ground stone artifacts was collected, as well as information on completeness, evidence of burning, material type, and presence and type of cortex. In the case of millingstones and handstones, additional attribute analysis was directed at overall planar shape, cross-sectional shape, number of surfaces, plan-view surface wear, and other types of wear (pecking, striations). The battered cobble analysis focused on characterization of both face and edge wear.

Flotation Analysis

Sediment samples were collected from the 14 single-component areas. A manual flotation technique for water separation was employed using 0.4-mm mesh (40 mesh per inch). The buoyant light fractions were dried and size-sorted using the following mesh sizes: 2 mm (10 mesh per inch); 1 mm (16 mesh per inch); 0.7 mm (24 mesh per inch); and 0.5 mm (35 mesh per inch). Light-fraction sorting was conducted by Eric Wohlgemuth with a binocular microscope at magnifications ranging from 7× to 30× power. Constituents were tallied and summed for all size grades by sample. Both charred seeds and uncharred modern contaminants were segregated from light fractions. Segregated constituents were sorted in translucent hard plastic centrifuge tubes with acid-free paper tags denoting site trinomial, sample number, size grade, and code for constituent type. All items of a single type or taxon are stored in plastic bags with acid-free paper labels.

Faunal Remains

Identification of faunal remains was made by analyst Tim Carpenter, based on comparisons with specimens held at the University of California, Davis. All specimens were initially sorted into identifiable and unidentifiable categories, first by element and then by taxon. Specimens were then identified to the genus or species level where possible. When that was not possible due to the condition of the bone, elements were identified to the family, order, or class level. Those that could not be assigned to class are listed as indeterminate bone (vertebrate). The unidentifiable mammal elements were further sorted into animal size categories, including medium-sized to large (i.e., artiodactyl), small to medium-sized (i.e., rabbit), and small (i.e., rodent).

26CK1991 (The Agave Ovens) Site Report

Site 26CK1991 is a large agave-processing and habitation site consisting of three large agave roasting pits, a smaller pit that is either a small roasting pit or a hearth, and two medium-sized depressions that may be either older, eroded roasting pits or possibly house pits (Figures 6.2 and 6.3). The site also contains a quite modest though diverse artifact assemblage consisting of flaked stone tools and debitage, milling equipment, and potsherds. Most of these were found on the surface and include six projectile points (four Elko, one dart-sized, one Cottonwood), two bifaces, one flake tool, six millingstones, one handstone, and 106 potsherds. The sherds are dominated by Patayan (n = 72) and Puebloan (n = 30) specimens; brown ware sherds are completely absent. In addition to the prehistoric artifacts, there is a scatter of historic materials. Some of the historic artifacts are old enough to raise the possibility that an ethnographic/postcontact period occupation occurred. Two of the large roasting pits (Pits 3 and 4) overlap each other, and the site was selected for excavation to explore the stratigraphic and temporal relationships between these pits.

Field Methods

Excavations focused entirely on Pits 3 and 4, and amounted to about four cubic meters of deposit. No attempt was made to explore other areas or features at the site, and no surface collection was made (all surface collections occurred during the survey phase of the project). Before excavation, a plan-view map of the two pits was drawn (Figure 6.4), as were surface profiles in cardinal directions (Figures 6.5 and 6.6). Pit 3, the larger of the two, is about 18 m in diameter. Pit 4 is about 10 m in diameter and overlies Pit 3. Pit 4 displays a very obvious ring of discarded burned limestone (burned rock midden) around the perimeter of a depression. Pit 3 has a less-pronounced configuration; its interior is in-filled with soil, and there is a less discrete scatter

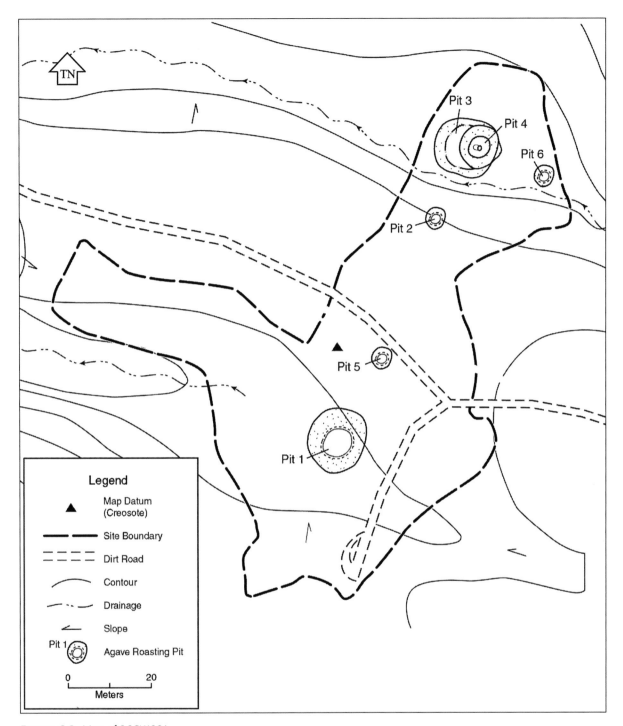

FIGURE 6.2. Map of 26CK1991.

of limestone cobbles around the perimeter. Both pits are filled with charcoal-rich, blackened soil mixed with burnt limestone.

A single 1-×-4-m excavation unit was laid out with the long axis running east-west, straddling the apparent boundary between the two pits (Figure 6.4). It was excavated stratigraphically, and elevation control was maintained by line level and string fixed to an arbitrary point next to the unit. As each stratigraphic boundary was identified, a profile was drawn of both the northern and southern sides of the unit. All excavated soil was screened through ⅛-inch mesh, and all large pieces of charcoal were collected and labeled according to stratum designation.

FIGURE 6.3. Overview of agave oven excavation at 26CK1991.

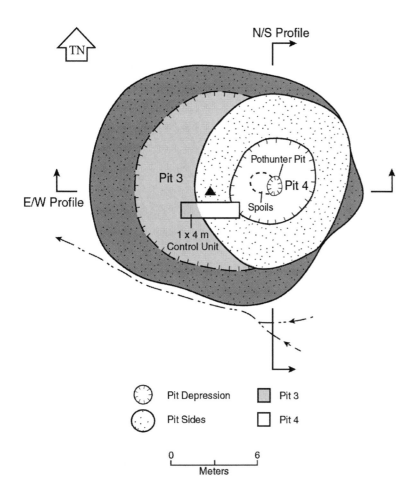

FIGURE 6.4. Plan view of Pits 3 and 4 at 26CK1991.

Site Structure and Chronology

The following section outlines the structural characteristics of the excavated roasting pits. A description of the chronological indicators from their deposits, consisting primarily of radiocarbon assays, is then provided.

Stratigraphic Profiles

After a thin layer of surface soils and vegetation was cleaned off, a clear differentiation of the pit fills was observable. The soil in Pit 4 was darker than that in Pit 3 and was superimposed above and cut into Pit 3 (Figure 6.7). Stratum I in Pit 4 was a mixture of discard and fill composed of loose sandy loam with charcoal and small gravel. Stratum II in Pit 4 was apparently discard material from the pit. It was black with a high content of small limestone cobbles and charcoal that formed a perimeter berm. At the bottom of this stratum there was a transition to a layer of gray ash, charcoal, and black pit fill. When this transition was first noted, it was thought to be another stratum of Pit 4, but because it crossed the boundary between the two pits and blended into the deposits of Pit 3, it was designated Stratum III in both pits (Figure 6.7).

Stratum III in Pit 3 was a dark brown fill of fine sandy loam intermixed with charcoal and a high amount of small burnt limestone cobbles and gravel. As the excavation continued, a concentration of stone was noted in the eastern side of Stratum III in Pit 3, and it became apparent that this concentration was different than the pit fill (Stratum VI, Figure 6.7). It consisted of dark

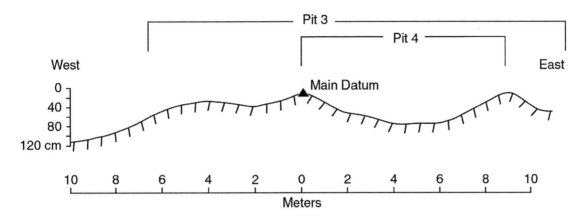

FIGURE 6.5. North-south surface profile of Pits 3 and 4 at 26CK1991.

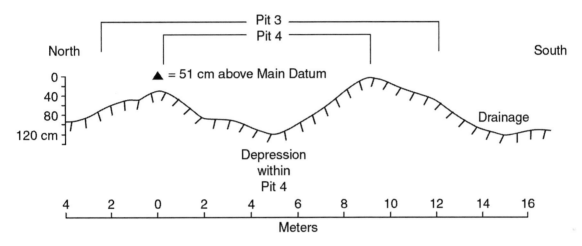

FIGURE 6.6. West-east surface profile of Pits 3 and 4 at 26CK1991.

brown to black fill around a dense concentration of large limestone cobbles (~30 cm in size). Some of the rock was burnt to white, almost transformed to lime, which would indicate a very high temperature burn (ca. 1,000–1,200°C). This seems rather high for a roasting pit but may indicate that the rock was in direct contact with the fuel. Given that the stone lies immediately below the Pit 4 berm (Stratum II) and curves downward toward the middle of Pit 4, as opposed to forming an acute angle with the bottom of Pit 3, it appears that Stratum VI was the stone lining of Pit 4 cut into the fill of Pit 3.

Stratum IV in Pit 3 was a loose sandy loam with small cobbles, gravel, and charcoal. It proved to be deep, extending to 110 cm below the surface. It ended on light brown very fine sand that appeared to be the original sediment that the pit was dug into. Excavation extended a short distance into this Stratum V to confirm that this was the case. It is interesting to note that no rock lined the bottom of the Pit 3, perhaps indicating that the larger stone lining occurred only around the perimeters of these roasting pits.

After the unit was drawn and photographed, six sediment samples were collected. Five were from the profile, and one control sample was from naturally deposited material away from the pits.

Radiocarbon Dates

A great deal of charcoal was collected, providing us opportunities to date the deposits of both pits and determine their chronological relationships. In addition, enough large intact pieces of charcoal were preserved so that identification of the fuel was possible.

Six dates from five sediment samples removed from discrete stratigraphic units were analyzed (Table 6.2; Figure 6.7). The results indicate multiple different firings of the ovens. The earliest date (AD 810) comes from Sample 4 in Pit 3, outside and below Pit 4. Three of the four dates from Pit 4 in addition to the other date from Pit 3 fall between AD 1580 and 1800, indicating repeated Late Prehistoric use. The less-than-perfect vertical sequence of the dates is attributed to the reuse, involving "cleaning" out the ovens for the next firing. The earlier

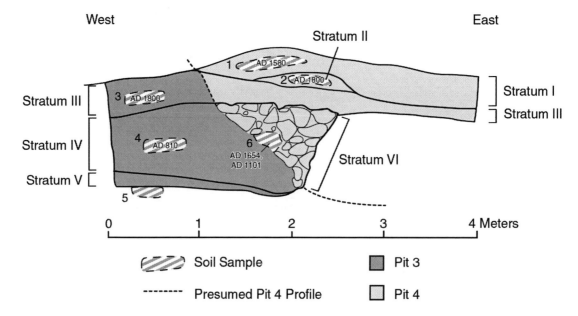

West   East

FIGURE 6.7. North wall profile of 1-x-4-m unit in Pits 3 and 4 at 26CK1991.

Stratum I -   Pit 4 discard and fill - 10YR 3/1 very dark gray loose fine sandy loam, with charcoal bits and small gravels.

Stratum II -   Pit 4 ash and charcoal - 10YR 4/1 dark gray, very loose ash with rock and charcoal (probable berm).

Stratum III -   Pit 3 fill and 4 - 10YR 4/1 to 3/1 dark gray soft fine sandy loam.

Stratum IV -   Pit 3 - 10YR 3/1 very dark gray loose fine sandy loam, with small cobbles and gravel charcoal.

Stratum V -   Sterile substrate - 7.5YR 6/4 light brown soft very fine silty sand with small to medium sized gravels.

Stratum VI -   Small boulders and rock - Pit 4 lining.

date from Sample 1, compared with Samples 2 and 3, even at the 2-sigma range (Table 5.1; Figure 6.7), is an indication of reverse stratigraphy, with spent fuel from an earlier firing being redeposited at the top of the profile.

Temporally Diagnostic Artifacts

The only temporally diagnostic artifacts recovered from excavation were sherds. Of the 18 recovered, 8 are Moapa, 8 are Tusayan, and the remaining 2 are unidentified. Both identified ceramic types date between AD 650 and 1200 and are consistent with the earliest radiocarbon date of AD 810 from Stratum IV in Pit 3. They were recovered from both pits with no apparent stratigraphic correlation, however, and probably represent a general presence of this artifact type in the churned sediments as a result of pit reuse.

TABLE 6.2. Radiocarbon Dates from 26CK1991.

Unit	Depth	Calibrated Intercept[a]	Conventional Age	Material
Pit 4	Stratum I	cal AD 1580 (cal BP 370)	330 ± 50 BP	Charcoal
Pit 4	Stratum II	cal AD 1800 (cal BP 150)	160 ± 40 BP	Charcoal
Pit 3	Stratum III	cal AD 1800 (cal BP 150)	160 ± 40 BP	Charcoal
Pit 3	Stratum IV	cal AD 810 (cal BP 1140)	1200 ± 60 BP	Charcoal
Pit 4	Stratum VI	cal AD 1101 (cal BP 849)	920 ± 30 BP	Charcoal
Pit 4	Stratum VI	cal AD 1654 (cal BP 296)	250 ± 30 BP	Charcoal

[a] See Table 5.1.

TABLE 6.3. Charred Plant Remains from 26CK1991.

Plant Remains	Pueblo I, Pit 3		Late Prehistoric, Pit 4		Total
	Stratum III	Stratum IV	Stratum I	Stratum II	
Sample Volume (Liters)	2.3	2.5	1.6	2.6	
Charred Nutshell					
Pinyon (*Pinus edulis/monophylla*)	—	1	—	—	1
Charred Seeds					
Goosefoot (*Chenopodium* sp.)	1	—	—	—	1
Filaree (*Erodium circutarium*)	—	—	—	1	1
Flowering Stems					
Agave (*Agave utahensis*)	27	21	34	85	167
Total	28	22	34	86	170

Component Definition

Two periods of occupation are represented by the excavation findings at 26CK1991. The early AD 810 radiocarbon date and the ceramics correspond to the beginnings of the Pueblo I period (AD 800–950). This component includes all materials from Pit 3. A later occupation is indicated by the four dates between AD 1580 and 1800. Although some earlier dating sherds occur in this context, Pit 4 is assigned to the Late Prehistoric component (post–AD 1250).

Artifact Inventory

Very few artifacts were recovered from the excavations. In addition to the potsherds outlined above, the assemblage is limited to one biface and 12 pieces of debitage from the Late Prehistoric component, and one flake tool, a core, and 48 pieces of debitage from the Puebloan component.

Floral and Faunal Remains

Charred plant remains from both components were dominated by flowering stems of agave (Table 6.3). A vitreous material was also found adhering to some of the agave fragments (Figure 6.8) and appears to be the charred remains of boiled-down juices from the plant. Other plant remains were one pine nut fragment and a single goosefoot seed from the Puebloan component, and a filaree seed from the Late Prehistoric sediments. The latter plant, a European import, was an invasive disturbance-following taxon used by Native peoples for food throughout California and the Great Basin (Wohlgemuth 2004). Its presence is not surprising in Pit 4, given the AD 1800 radiocarbon dates associated with this feature.

Faunal remains recovered during excavation were limited to 56 pieces of desert tortoise (*Gopherus agassizii*) carapace and bone. None showed signs of burning,

and they are likely the remains of a single individual that died in its burrow.

Summary

Archaeological data generated from the excavation of the agave oven complex at 26CK1991 reveal two intervals of use, one dating to the early end of the Pueblo I period (ca. AD 810) and the others corresponding to the Late Prehistoric period (ca. AD 1580 and AD 1800). The overlapping presence of these features is indicative of the long-term use of this site for agave roasting, which is consistent with other locations along the lower slopes of the Virgin Mountains at Gold Butte. Although the findings at 26CK1991 represent a very small sample, the several-hundred-year gap in the use of the oven complex (i.e., between AD 810 [or perhaps ca. AD 1100] and AD 1580) matches the chronological data collected from elsewhere at Gold Butte. Of the nearly 20 radiocarbon dates obtained from agave ovens at Gold Butte (Table 5.1), only this one anomalous result from mixed deposits in Pit 4 falls into the Pueblo II/III interval (AD 950–1250), when agricultural production and human populations reached their peak along the Virgin and Muddy Rivers. As is discussed in more detail in Chapter 8, it appears that intensive farming activities, particularly during the spring when planting and protection of small seedlings was critical, may have created scheduling problems for the collection and roasting of agave, as spring is also the most productive season for this resource (Bean and Siva Saubel 1972). Given that the good stands of agave at Gold Butte were located about 25 km east of the agricultural plots along the Virgin River, and because agave roasting took two or three days to accomplish, it is possible that the Puebloan farmers found it more beneficial to stay closer to home and tend to their crops.

Agave Interior
Actual Size

0   5

cm

Agave Interior
Magnified 200%

0   2.5

cm

Agave Exterior
Actual Size

0   5

cm

Agave Exterior
Magnified 200%

0   2.5

cm

FIGURE 6.8. Charred agave from 26CK1991.

26CK3201 (COLLAPSED ROCK SHELTER) SITE REPORT

Site 26CK3201 is a high-density scatter of flaked stone tools and debitage, battered cobbles, pottery fragments, and milling gear associated with a dark gray midden deposit. The artifacts and midden extend along a narrow terrace only one meter above a small wash that lies immediately to the south (Figures 6.9 and 6.10). The terrace is bounded on the north by an ancient upper terrace of cemented alluvium that has a vertical face about three meters high. The face of the upper terrace has been undercut by stream action, forming a series of small rock shelters that also have a limited amount of deposit in them. One of the shelters was relatively large at one point but collapsed onto the lower terrace midden, potentially capping the prehistoric deposit.

FIGURE 6.9. Overview of 26CK3201.

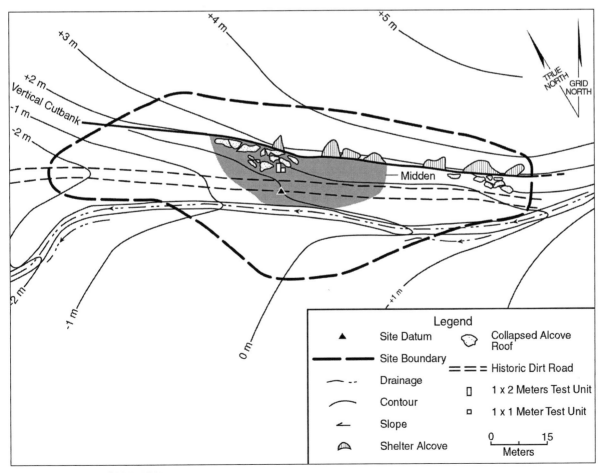

FIGURE 6.10. Map of 26CK3201.

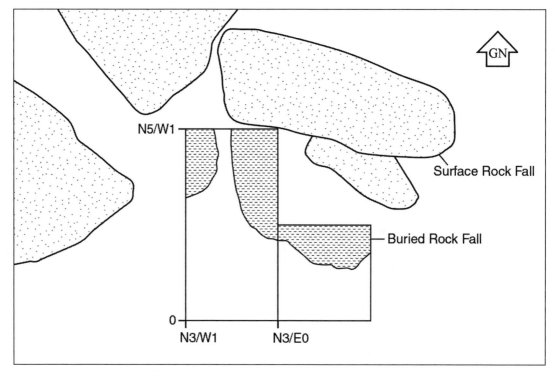

FIGURE 6.11. Plan view of surface and buried rock fall at 26CK3201.

Field Methods

Fieldwork began with the establishment of an east-west baseline, paralleling the orientation of the lower terrace and wash. This line is considered east for the purpose of the site grid but actually measures 120 degrees. Once the baseline was established, the field crew pin flagged all formed tools (including pottery); all material was mapped to a 10-cm degree of accuracy and then collected. The surface distribution showed that the flaked stone material was scattered across the lower terrace but the pottery was concentrated in an area just north of the datum. The flaked stone scatter was thought to be either Late Archaic or Basketmaker II in age due to the presence of a few Elko point fragments, while the pottery concentrated in the midden was obviously later in time.

As a result of these relationships, we placed a 1-×-2-m unit in the pottery area with the goal of finding a stratified deposit (a ceramic occupation on top and a preceramic occupation below). The unit (N3/W1) was oriented north-south, with the northern end adjacent to the collapsed rock shelter and the southern end moving down toward the wash (Figure 6.11). It was excavated to a depth of 140 cm, where bedrock was encountered. A second unit, 1-×-1-m N3/E0, was then connected to the exposure. It also encountered bedrock at about 140 cm below surface. The two units resulted in the excavation of 4.2 m³ (Table 6.4).

TABLE 6.4. Excavation Summary for 26CK3201.

Unit	Size (m)	Depth (cm)	Volume (m³)
N3/W1	1×2	140	2.8
N3/E0	1×1	140	1.4
Total			4.2

Site Structure and Chronology

A very complex stratigraphic sequence was encountered during the excavations (Figures 6.12 and 6.13). It begins with an A-horizon midden that includes a shallow layer of angular to subangular limestone gravel (A1) contained in a reddish yellow (7.5YR 6/6) silty midden matrix. Much of the gravel has washed down from the collapsed alcove adjacent to the north. The frequency of gravel decreases significantly in the A2 zone, where the silty-sandy midden becomes more brown in color (7.5YR 5/2). The midden reaches its darkest color in the A3 zone (dark brown; 7.5YR 3/2), where it comes in contact with a large slab of rock fall (2R) that lies on a surface about 80 cm below ground. The rock fall is the same cemented alluvium that has collapsed on the surface of the site and covers a large portion of the northern half of the exposure.

A new buried midden (3Ab) underlies the rock fall and extends south in the exposure. This is the surface that the rock fall collapsed onto; it was subsequently

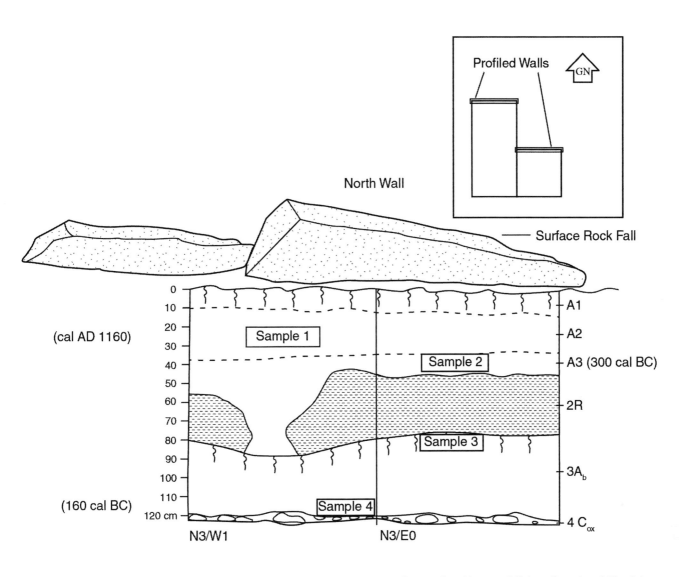

A1   Angular and subangular limestone gravel contained in a reddish yellow (7.5 YR 6/6) silty midden; much of the gravel has washed down from collapsed alcove to the north.

A2 - A3   Brown to dark brown (7.5 YR 5/2, 3/2) loosely compacted midden containing small gravels. The midden matrix is composed of powdery silts and sand. The midden is darker just above the contact with the rock fall (2R) in Unit N3/E0.

2R   Buried rock fall composed of cemented gravelly alluvium.

3A$_b$ Loosely compacted powdery silty-sand, pinkish gray (7.5 YR 6/2) midden containing small gravels.

4 C$_{ox}$ Combination of cemented alluvium, rounded stream gravels, and reddish yellow (7.5 YR 7/6) aeolian/alluvial fine grain silts and sand.

   Flotation Samples

FIGURE 6.12. North wall profile at 26CK3201.

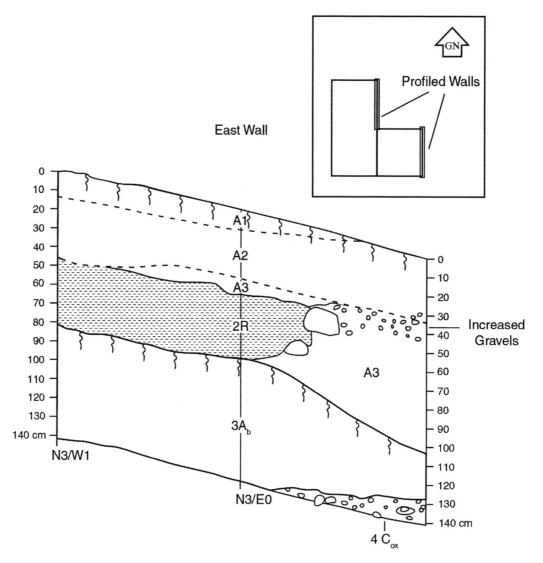

FIGURE 6.13. East wall profile at 26CK3201.

covered up by the accumulating A1, A2, and A3 sediments. Its texture is similar to that of the A2/A3 sediments, but it is pinkish gray in color (7.5YR 6/2). It eventually bottoms out on the sterile C-horizon sediments, which include chunks of the ancient, cemented alluvium mixed in with clean alluvial sands and gravel that form the lower terrace.

Four flotation samples were collected from this profile. One came from the upper A2 midden, one from the dark A3 deposits immediately above the rock fall, one from just below the rock fall, and the other from the base of the deposit (Figure 6.12).

Radiocarbon Dates

Three radiocarbon dates were obtained from the deposit (Table 6.5). The upper A2 midden produced a date of cal AD 1160, which corresponds to a Pueblo II occupa-

tion. A date of 300 cal BC was obtained from the slightly deeper A3 deposits, which probably represent a Basketmaker II use of the site. The final date from the deep contact between the lower 3Ab midden and the sterile 4C deposits produced what seems to be an anomalous (and too recent) date of 160 cal BC. As outlined in more detail below, the site seems to show a relatively high degree of stratigraphic integrity with regard to the vertical distribution of pottery, projectile points, and obsidian hydration readings, all of which indicate that the lower 3Ab midden should date to around 2500 cal BC.

Temporally Diagnostic Artifacts

Four data sets, aside from radiocarbon dates, indicate the age of the stratified deposits at this site: pottery, projectile points, a shell bead, and obsidian hydration rim values.

TABLE 6.5. Radiocarbon Dates from 26CK3201.

Unit	Depth (cm)	Calibrated Median Probability	Conventional Age	Material
N3/W1	20–30	cal AD 1160 (cal BP 790)	900 ± 40 BP	Charcoal
N3/E0	30–40	300 cal BC (cal BP 2260)	2200 ± 40 BP	Charcoal
N3/W1	126–146	160 cal BC (cal BP 2110)	2110 ± 40 BP	Charcoal

TABLE 6.6. Pottery from 26CK3201.

| | All Units | | | | |
	0–30 cm	30–80 cm	80–140 cm	Total	Surface Items
Brown Ware	13[a]	—	—	13	3
Paddle/Anvil	4	1	—	5	3
Logandale	1	—	—	1	—
Shivwits	17	2	—	19	—
Moapa	18	—	—	18	2
Tusayan	105[b]	3	—	108	12
Total	158	6	—	164	20
Unidentifiable Fragments	28	—	—	28	—

[a] Six are corrugated.
[b] Three are corrugated.

TABLE 6.7. Projectile Points from 26CK3201.

| | All Units | | | |
	0–30 cm	30–80 cm	80–140 cm	Total
Desert Side-Notched	2	—	—	2
Rose Spring	1	—	—	1
Arrow-Sized	2	—	—	2
Elko	—	2	—	2
Humboldt	—	—	1	1
Small Stemmed	—	1	—	1
Leaf-Shaped	—	1	—	1
Side-Notched	—	1	—	1
Dart-Sized	1	—	1	2
Total	6	5	2	13

Pottery

More than 160 diagnostic sherds were recovered from the excavations, and 96.3 percent came from the upper 30 cm of the deposit (Table 6.6). The vast majority (89.0 percent) are Puebloan types, which is consistent with the cal AD 1160 radiocarbon date obtained from this portion of the deposit. There are also a handful of Paiute brown ware and Patayan paddle and anvil sherds in the upper midden, indicating that site use was limited later in time as well. Notable among these are several pieces of brown ware on the surface and a few on the top 10 cm with either corrugation or heavy basketry impression (Figure 5.6b and c).

Projectile Points

Thirteen temporally diagnostic projectile points were recovered from the excavations (Table 6.7). All the arrow points are found in the upper 30 cm of the deposit, which is consistent with the radiocarbon dates and pottery. The single Rosegate point is coeval with the predominant Puebloan occupation, while the Desert series points are probably linked to the handful of Paiute brown ware sherds recovered from this location. All but one of the dart points are found below 30 cm, with the majority found in the A3 midden between 30 and 80 cm. This group includes two Elko forms and single examples of small stemmed, leaf-shaped, and side-notched implements. (None of the side-notched correspond to a classic point type for the region.) These findings match up well with the 300 cal BC radiocarbon date from this horizon and probably correspond to a Basketmaker II occupation.

The lower 3Ab midden (80–140 cm) has a single Humboldt series point and one undifferentiated dart fragment (Table 6.7). The project-wide projectile point study (see Chapter 5) shows that Humboldt series points are older (Early Archaic) than Elko points (Late Archaic/Basketmaker II) based on obsidian hydration data, and the depth of this specimen is consistent with such an age estimate. This finding also undermines the

validity of the 160 cal BC date obtained from the base of the 3Ab midden at 126–146 cm below surface.

Shell Bead

One *Olivella* tiny saucer (G1) bead was recovered from N3/W1 at 20–30 cm. Although tiny saucer beads are commonly found in post–AD 1500 contexts, which is consistent with the current finding, they also occur in many other time periods throughout southern California (Bennyhoff and Hughes 1987).

Obsidian Hydration Data

Obsidian hydration data also demonstrate a high degree of stratigraphic integrity at the site and indicate that three components are probably present (Table 6.8). The upper 30 cm has a tight cluster of relatively narrow rims from the three primary obsidian sources, as well as

TABLE 6.8. Source-Specific Obsidian Hydration Data from 26CK3201.

Source	Readings (Microns)	Mean	s.d.
Modena/Panaca Summit			
0–30 cm	2.2, 4.0, 4.0, 4.0, (7.3)	3.6	0.9
80–140 cm	9.0, 9.3, 9.3, 9.4, 10.1, 10.1, 10.1, 10.2, 10.4, 10.4, 10.4	9.9	0.5
Delamar Mountains			
0–30 cm	5.0	5.0	—
80–140 cm	11.9, 11.9, 12.0, 12.0, 12.0, 12.0, 12.0, 12.0, 12.0, 12.0, 12.3, 12.7	12.1	0.2
Kane Springs			
0–30 cm	4.0, 4.4, 4.5, 4.5, 5.1, 5.1, (10.1)	4.6	0.4
80–140 cm	(4.5), 9.0, 9.0, 9.1, 10.0, 10.5, 10.7, 10.8, 10.9	10.0	0.8
Partridge Creek			
0–30 cm	2.0, 2.1, 2.2	2.1	0.1
Unsourced			
30–50 cm	(4.6), 6.5, 6.7, 6.7, 7.0, 7.2, 7.3, 7.4, 7.4, 7.7, (13.4), (13.6)	7.1	0.4

Note: One reading of 4.5 microns from Wild Horse Canyon not included; values in parentheses are considered outliers and excluded from mean calculations; s.d. = standard deviation.

TABLE 6.9. Obsidian Hydration Summary from 26CK3201.

Depth (cm)	Number	Mean	Standard Deviation	Coefficient of Variation
0–30	11	4.3	0.8	0.19
30–50	9	7.1	0.4	0.06
80–140	31	10.8	1.2	0.11

Note: Includes all obsidian except Partridge Creek.

TABLE 6.10. Single-Component Areas at 26CK3201.

Unit	Transitional Early/ Late Archaic	Basketmaker II	Pueblo II
N3/W1	80–140 cm	30–80 cm	0–30 cm
N3/E0	80–140 cm	30–80 cm	0–30 cm

Note: All surface material is placed in an undated, residual category.

some Partridge Creek glass. When the Modena/Panaca Summit, Delamar Mountains, and Kane Springs source groups are combined into a single sample (Table 6.9), and two outliers are removed from the analysis, they produce a mean of 4.3 microns, which corresponds quite well with the cal AD 1160 radiocarbon date obtained from this context.

The next group of readings come from the A3 midden at depths ranging from 30 to 50 cm below surface (Tables 6.8 and 6.9) and correspond to the A3 radiocarbon date of 300 cal BC. After the removal of three outliers from this unsourced sample, it produces a mean of 7.1 microns, which also matches the associated radiocarbon date.

As we move down the profile into the 3Ab deposits, hydration readings from 80 to 140 cm show a clear contrast with the two samples from above (Tables 6.8 and 6.9). Modena/Panaca Summit and Kane Springs produced means of 9.9 and 10.0 microns, while Delamar Mountains yielded slightly thicker readings tightly clustered around a mean of 12.1 microns. When these sources are combined into a single group, they produce a mean of 10.8 microns, which does not correspond well with the lower radiocarbon date of 160 cal BC. Instead, we estimate that 10.8 microns probably corresponds to about 2500 cal BC (see Chapter 5).

Component Definition
Based on these findings, three components are defined at the site (Table 6.10). A Pueblo II component lies between 0 and 30 cm in both excavation units. A Basketmaker II occupation is represented at 30 to 80 cm below surface, while a Transitional Early/Late Archaic component is present between 80 and 140 cm. Finally, all surface materials from the site are placed in an undated, residual category.

Artifact Inventory
All three components at the site produced comparable amounts of flaked, ground, and battered stone tools, while the Puebloan assemblage also included an abundance of pottery (Table 6.11). Other artifacts such as bone tools, palettes, and non-utilitarian objects are absent, with the exception of a single shell bead recovered from the Puebloan component.

Puebloan Findings
The Puebloan component produced relatively high frequencies of sherds and flaked stone tools, the latter including bifaces, projectile points, flake tools, a core tool, and multiple cores (Table 6.11). Ground and bat-

TABLE 6.11. Assemblage by Temporal Component at 26CK3201.

	Transitional Early/Late Archaic	Basketmaker II	Pueblo II	Residual Undated	Total
Flaked Stone					
Projectile Point	2	5	7	3	17
Drill	1	—	—	—	1
Biface	37	30	22	11	100
Formed Flake Tool	—	3	1	1	5
Flake Tool	7	4	4	—	15
Core Tool	—	3	1	1	5
Core	5	9	5	2	21
Debitage	3,448	3,608	3,487	4	10,547
Battered & Ground Stone					
Battered Cobble	2	1	2	6	11
Handstone	2	—	—	2	4
Millingstone	3	—	2	1	6
Other					
Pottery	—	6	186	20	212
Shell Bead	—	—	1	—	1
Total	3,507	3,669	3,718	51	10,945

tered stone tools are much rarer, limited to two battered cobbles and two millingstone fragments.

Pottery

Most of the Puebloan sherds from the site are Tusayan (74.5 percent), followed by lesser frequencies of Moapa (12.8 percent), Shivwits (12.1 percent), and Logandale (0.7 percent; Table 6.6). Tusayan pottery is made throughout Virgin Anasazi territory, while Moapa and Shivwits originate from the Uinkaret Plateau, showing interactions with people from the east. Only three specimens are corrugated (all Tusayan), which may indicate greater use of the site during the earlier end of the Puebloan sequence (i.e., Pueblo I and II), as corrugated pottery tends to postdate AD 1050.

Flaked Stone Tools and Debitage

Analysis of the Puebloan flaked stone assemblage indicates that a full range of reduction activities took place at the site. Initial reduction is reflected by the presence of five cores (Table 6.12). This small collection is composed of split cobbles and large flake blanks that have been informally reduced by a combination of unidirectional/unifacial, bidirectional, multidirectional, and bipolar flake removals. Early-stage (Stage 1 and 2) and middle-stage (Stage 3) bifaces are both present, but in relatively low numbers, while near-finished (Stage 4)

and finished (Stage 5) tools are quite common, combining for 68.5 percent of the biface assemblage (Table 6.13).

Almost all the obsidian debitage is pressure flakes (86.3 percent), indicating that it arrived on site as finished or near-finished tools that were subsequently refined during the occupation (Table 6.14). Pressure flakes (63.9 percent) and late-stage thinning debris (5.9 percent) are also common in the chert assemblage, but a wider range of reduction activities is reflected by these data. Raw core reduction is evidenced by cortical debris (11.7 percent), while the intermediate stages are represented by interior (4.4 percent) and early biface thinning flakes (14.9 percent). Only a few quartzite flakes were found, and they indicate the reduction of locally available cobbles (i.e., cortical, thinning, and pressure flakes are all present).

The small sample of formed and simple flake tools, generally selected from the earliest reduction debris (largely cortical and interior flakes), showed various combinations of edge flaking, microchipping, and stepping/crushing. The single core tool has bifacial flake removals and battering on opposing edges of the tool.

Ground and Battered Stone

Both millingstones are small fragments (one margin and one interior piece) with what appears to be unifacial wear. One has a slightly concave surface with minimal

TABLE 6.12. Core Attributes by Period from 26CK3201.

Attribute	Transitional Early/ Late Archaic	Basketmaker II	Pueblo II	Total
Blank				
Globular Cobble	—	1	—	1
Split Cobble	2	—	2	4
Flake	1	2	3	6
Chunk	1	4	—	5
Indeterminate	1	2	—	3
Morphology				
Unidirectional/Unifacial	1	1	1	3
Bifacial	1	2	—	3
Multidirectional	2	2	2	6
Bidirectional	—	1	1	2
Bipolar	—	1	1	2
Indeterminate	1	2	—	3
Total Cores	5	9	5	19

TABLE 6.13. Biface Stages by Period from 26CK3201.

	Transitional Early/Late Archaic	Basketmaker II	Pueblo II	Total
Stage 1	2	1	2	5
Stage 2	3	4	2	9
Stage 3	16	9	2	27
Stage 4	3	5	4	12
Stage 5	8	9	9	26
Total	32	28	19	79
Indeterminate	5	2	3	10

polish and some pecking; the other has irregular polish on a flat surface. Of the two battered cobbles, one has pecking on one margin and was probably a hammerstone used for flaked stone reduction; the other shows more heavy-duty wear (pecking, grinding, flake removals) and was probably used for a variety of purposes.

Basketmaker II Findings

The Basketmaker II assemblage is composed almost entirely of flaked stone tools (n = 54), with ground and battered tools limited to a single battered cobble. The remainder of the collection is limited to a few sherds trickling down the profile from the overlying Puebloan occupation (Table 6.11).

Most of the flaked stone tools are bifaces (55.6 percent), followed by cores (16.7 percent), formed and simple flake tools (13.0 percent), projectile points (9.3 percent), and core tools (5.6 percent). The cores are made from a wide range of blanks (globular cobbles, flakes, chunks, indeterminate pieces) and show an informal variety of unidirectional/unifacial, bifacial, bidirectional, multidirectional, and bipolar flake removals.

A full range of reduction activities are reflected by the biface assemblage (Table 6.13): early Stage 1 and 2 (17.9 percent), Stage 3 (32.1 percent), Stage 4 (17.9 percent), and Stage 5 (32.1 percent) forms are all present. The chert debitage assemblage does not quite match this profile (Table 6.14), as pressure flakes dominate the assemblage (75.3 percent), which indicates a greater emphasis on tool finishing. Chert pressure flakes are followed by progressively lower frequencies of biface thinning flakes (early—9.7 percent; late—5.0 percent) and early-stage reduction debris (cortical—7.8 percent; interior—2.1 percent). Obsidian shows an even greater emphasis on tool finishing, with pressure flakes making up 87.0 percent of the assemblage. The small sample of quartzite shows no meaningful patterns.

Most of the formed and simple flake tools were made from early biface thinning flakes (57.7 percent), while the remainder includes single items made from interior, late biface thinning, and indeterminate flakes. All the simple flake tools show only microchipping, but the formed flake tools (two of which have serrated edges) exhibit much heavier wear in the form of edge flaking, stepping/crushing, and polish/grinding. Two of the three core tools are small fragments with indeterminate morphologies, while the other is a chunk with multidirectional flake removals; all have extensive amounts

TABLE 6.14. Technological Analysis of Debitage by Period from 26CK3201.

	Transition Early/Late Archaic						Basketmaker II						Pueblo II					
	Chert		Obsidian		Quartzite		Chert		Obsidian		Quartzite		Chert		Obsidian		Quartzite	
	#	%	#	%	#	%	#	%	#	%	#	%	#	%	#	%	#	%
Core Reduction																		
Percussion Decortication	84	10.2	—	—	7	58.3	40	7.8	1	4.3	0	0.0	71	11.7	—	—	1	25.0
Percussion Interior	19	2.3	—	—	—	—	11	2.1	—	—	1	50.0	27	4.4	2	14.3	—	—
Biface Reduction																		
Early Biface Thinning	132	16.0	3	3.2	1	8.3	50	9.7	2	8.7	0	0.0	91	14.9	—	—	1	25.0
Late Biface Thinning	64	7.7	10	10.5	—	—	26	5.0	—	—	0	0.0	36	5.9	—	—	—	—
Pressure	527	63.8	82	86.3	4	33.3	388	75.3	20	87.0	1	50.0	384	63.1	12	85.7	2	50.0
Diagnostic Total	826	100.0	95	100.0	12	100.0	515	100.0	23	100.0	2	100.0	609	100.0	14	100.0	4	100.0
Platform Prep./Pressure	233	—	32	—	—	—	161	—	9	—	0	—	99	—	3	—	—	—
Indeterminate Percussion	144	—	7	—	7	—	66	—	1	—	0	—	115	—	3	—	—	—
Indeterminate Fragment	374	—	10	—	8	—	175	—	6	—	2	—	221	—	5	—	1	—
Shatter	10	—	—	—	—	—	10	—	—	—	0	—	17	—	—	—	—	—
Sample Total	1587	—	144	—	27	—	927	—	39	—	4	—	1,061	—	25	—	5	—

Note: % = analytical percentage; all obsidian and quartzite debitage was analyzed. Chert debitage was sampled as follows: Pueblo II: N3/E3, 0–30 cm; Basketmaker II: N3/W1, 50–70 cm; Early/Late Archaic: N3/W1, 90–120 cm.

of edge battering. The one battered cobble has a small amount of pecking along its margins.

Transitional Early/Late Archaic Findings

A more diversified mix of tools was recovered from the Transitional Early/Late Archaic deposits at the site (Table 6.11). Although flaked stone tools are still dominant (n = 52), ground and battered stone tools were found in a slightly higher frequency (n = 7) than was the case in the Basketmaker II component.

Flaked Stone Tools and Debitage

Bifaces (71.2 percent) dominate the flaked stone assemblage, followed by a lesser number of cores (9.6 percent), flake tools (13.5 percent), projectile points (3.8 percent), and a single drill (1.9 percent). The small sample of cores is made from two split cobbles, a flake, a chunk, and an indeterminate fragment; their morphology is also quite variable, including specimens with unidirectional/unifacial, bifacial, multidirectional, and indeterminate flake removals (Table 6.12). The bifaces reveal a full range of reduction activities represented by early Stage 1 and 2 specimens (18.8 percent), Stage 3 bifaces (50.0 percent), and the more refined Stage 4 and 5 forms (34.4 percent; Table 6.13).

The chert debitage profile is somewhat consistent with these trends, as it includes small but significant frequencies of core reduction debris (cortical—10.2 percent; interior—2.3 percent) and biface thinning (early—16.0 percent; late—7.7 percent), but again a dominant presence of pressure flakes (63.8 percent; Table 6.14). Obsidian debitage shows an even greater dominance of pressure flakes (86.3 percent), followed by progressively lower frequencies of late (10.5 percent) and early (3.2 percent) biface thinning flakes. The small sample of quartzite seems to reflect the full reduction of locally available cobbles.

The flake tools are made from interior, early biface thinning, and indeterminate flake fragments. All seven show microchipping, and two also have edge flaking and stepping/crushing. The single drill is a long slender distal fragment that shows sided flaring toward its broken proximal end.

Ground and Battered Stone Tools

Both handstones are end fragments with unifacial wear. One has flat smooth polish, and the other has polish and pecking on a slight convex surface. The three milling-stones are all fragments (medial, margin, and end). One is bifacial with flat smooth polish and pecking on both faces; it has also been shaped by edge flaking and grinding. The other two also have flat smooth polish with

pecking on their single faces. Both battered cobbles have low levels of pecking and grinding along their margins.

Floral and Faunal Remains

Although four flotation samples totaling 21.3 liters were processed from the site, only six identifiable pieces of charred plants were found (Table 6.15): one pinyon nutshell, three goosefoot seeds, one phacelia seed, and a single agave fragment. This low yield of charred plant remains is consistent with the lack of features in the deposit and the low frequency of milling gear (4.7 percent) relative to flaked stone tools (95.3 percent) recovered during the excavation.

A better sample of faunal remains was recovered. Analysis of these remains focuses on bighorn sheep, undifferentiated artiodactyls, jackrabbits, cottontails, undifferentiated lagomorphs, and tortoise, as well as small fragments that can only be categorized as medium-to-large mammal (roughly sheep-sized) and small-to-medium mammal (roughly rabbit-sized; Table 6.16). We rely much less on unidentifiable fragments, intrusive rodents, and other minimally represented taxa due to their lower interpretive value. It is also important to note that multiple artiodactyl tooth enamel fragments within a single catalog entry are only given a frequency value of "1" because these fragile elements usually exfoliate during excavation and transport to the lab. The uncounted enamel fragments are listed in parentheses in Table 6.16.

Several interesting trends are exhibited by these data. First, the relative frequency of tortoise increases over time in the identifiable sample, beginning at 45.5 percent in the Transitional Early/Late Archaic component, rising to 79.2 percent in the Basketmaker II component, and reaching a high of 89.0 percent in the Puebloan component (Table 6.16). The relative percentage of bighorn sheep/artiodactyls versus rabbits/lagomorphs also produces a strong trend, with the former representing only 38.5 percent of the Transitional Early/Late Archaic assemblage, 50.0 percent of the Basketmaker II collection, and 88.9 percent of the Puebloan sample.

The relative frequency of medium-to-large mammal versus small-to-medium mammal follows a consistent pattern, with medium-to-large mammal making up 18.1 percent of the Transitional Early/Late Archaic component, 51.4 percent of the Basketmaker II sample, and 91.7 percent of the Puebloan collection. These general trends indicate an early preference toward small mammals and artiodactyls, followed by a growing focus on tortoise through time, augmented by much lower frequencies of artiodactyls.

TABLE 6.15. Charred Plant Remains from 26CK3201.

| | Transitional Early/Late Archaic | | Basketmaker II | Puebloan II | |
	N3/E0 71–86 cm	N3/W1 126–146 cm	N3/E0 30–40 cm	N3/W1 20–30 cm	Total
Charred Nutshell					
Pinyon (*Pinus edulis/monophylla*)	—	1	—	—	1
Charred Seeds					
Goosefoot (*Chenopodium* sp.)	1	1	—	1	3
Phacelia (*Phacelia* sp.)	—	1	—	—	1
Unidentified Seeds	—	1	—	—	1
Flowering Stems					
Agave (*Agave utahensis*)	—	—	—	1	1
Total	1	4	—	2	7
Sample Volume (Liters)	7.0	5.3	2.5	6.5	21.3

TABLE 6.16. Faunal Remains from 26CK3201.

	Transitional Early/Late Archaic	Basketmaker II	Pueblo II	Total
Bighorn Sheep	—	1	—	1
Artiodactyl	5 (3)	3 (2)	8 (14)	16 (19)
Jackrabbit	1	—	—	1
Cottontail	1	—	1	2
Lagomorphs	11	3	—	14
Tortoise	15	38	73	126
Medium-to-Large (Sheep-Sized)	28	18	22	68
Small-to-Medium (Rabbit-Sized)	127	17	2	146
Intrusive Rodents	5	6	—	11
Birds	2	—	—	2
Unidentifiable	49	23	25	97
Total	244	109	131	484

Note: Numbers in parentheses represent small tooth enamel fragments not included in the analysis.

Summary

Three periods of occupation are represented by the excavation findings at 26CK3201. The earliest, the Transitional Early/Late Archaic occupation, corresponds to a buried soil containing obsidian hydration readings tightly clustered around a mean of 10.8 microns and a Humboldt series projectile point. A radiocarbon date of 160 cal BC was also obtained from this stratigraphic unit but seems to have intruded from the upper Basketmaker II component. The assemblage is dominated by flaked stone tools and contains only a handful of ground and battered stone implements and only a few charred seeds. Faunal remains, although not numerous, reflect hunting activities focused on a mixture of small mammals, tortoise, and large mammals.

The Basketmaker II component corresponds to a radiocarbon date of 300 cal BC, a series of Elko and other dart-sized projectile points, and obsidian hydration data clustering around a mean of 7.1 microns. It maintains a rather focused, flaked stone production/hunting orientation: more than 50 flaked stone tools were recovered, but milling gear and plant remains were completely absent. Tortoise increases in importance, while large and small mammals are found in equal proportions.

Pottery dominates the Puebloan component, which also includes an obsidian hydration mean of

FIGURE 6.14. Overview of 26CK4891. Photo courtesy of Roy Miller.

4.3 microns, arrow-sized projectile points, and a radio-carbon date of cal AD 1160. Despite the high frequency of pottery, domestic features are absent and only trace amounts of milling gear and plant remains were recovered. Instead, flaked stone tools remain dominant, and tortoise becomes a primary focus of hunting, followed by low numbers of large game and a near absence of small mammal.

26CK4891 (RIVERSIDE PITHOUSE VILLAGE) SITE REPORT

Site 26CK4891 is an aerially extensive pithouse village located on the lip of the terrace on the south bank of the Virgin River (Figure 6.14). The site was first cursorily recorded in 1979 by R. F. Perkins; it was better documented in 1983 as part of Daniel Larson's (1987) dissertation research, which involved survey and limited testing of pithouses along the Virgin River. At that time it was characterized as a Basketmaker III village with seven pithouse depressions, seven cists, two separate storage unit alignments, and a combination pithouse/cist, distributed within an 80-x-75-m area.

The site remains in very good condition, especially given its proximity to a two-lane highway, with little obvious modern disturbance (few ATV tire tracks) and some debris within the 10- to 15-m-wide strip next to the road.

The 1983 record characterizes the site as a low-density scatter, from which nearly 100 sherds were collected. Today the surface assemblage is surprisingly meager, especially in light of the number, size, and type of features present. Then as now, several pieces of milling gear are present, in addition to a small quantity of (mostly plain gray ware) pottery, but even less debitage. The ground surface is a strongly developed desert pavement, and for that reason, the features evident in the 1980s are apparent today. Close-interval inspection of the site revealed four depressions, some with contiguous rock concentrations (Features 1, 3, 7/8/9 Complex, and 13) and six distinct rock concentrations/collapsed cists or storage units (Features 2/18, 5, 6, 11/12/14, 15, and 20). Due to differences in considered opinions, some features listed in 1983 were discarded when they could not be located again or were combined with an

TABLE 6.17. Comparison of Current Structures/Features and Those Distinguished in 1983 at 26CK4891.

Structure/ Feature	1983 Record (Larson 1987)	Current	Comment
1	Pithouse	Pithouse	Tested unit 5 (2 × 1 m).
2	Pithouse	Cleared area (not depression)	Blurs with Feature 18.
3	Pithouse	Pithouse	Tested units 3 (2 × 1) and 4 (1 × 1).
4	Cist	Not distinguished	Blurs with Structure 7/8/9 complex.
5	Cist	Cist	—
6	Cist	Cist	—
7	Pithouse	Not distinguished	Blurs with Structure 7/8/9 complex. Ephemeral/ambiguous.
8	Aligned storage units	Possible pithouse	Blurs with Structure 7/8/9 complex.
9	Pithouse and cist	Not distinguished	Blurs with Structure 7/8/9 complex. Ephemeral/ambiguous.
10	Pithouse	Not evident	No depression, no clearing.
11	Pithouse	Not evident	No depression, no clearing. May blur with Structures 12 and 13.
12	Cist	Cist	—
13	Pithouse	Pithouse	Tested units 1 (2 × 1) and 2 (1 × 1 m).
14	Cist	Not evident	May blur with Structures 12 and 13.
15	Cist	Not evident	No alignment, depression.
16	Metate	Could not locate	—
17	Cist	Indeterminate	Not plotted in 1983.
18	Aligned storage units	Cleared area (not depression)	Blurs with Structure 2.
19	Ceramic Cluster	Evident/intact	—

adjacent feature when they could not be individually distinguished (Table 6.17).

Field Methods

The field effort began with a walkover of the entire site area to identify artifact concentrations and features and correlate them with the 1983 site sketch map. A series of mapping datums was next established to facilitate topographic mapping and provide provenience control for feature scale-sketch maps and photographs. Of the four depressions large enough to be considered potential pithouses, three were selected for test excavation: Features 1, 3, and 13. No systematic surface collection was made. Only large hand tools and milling gear within 8 to 10 m of the features received in-field analysis.

For each of the three selected depressions, excavation began with a 2-x-1-m unit oriented to the north, placed in the middle of the depression or offset from the middle to intersect an edge of the basin. At Features 3 and 13 an additional 1-x-1-m unit was added to the end of the 2-x-1-m unit, resulting in a 3-x-1-m trench, in one instance to better expose the contact line between sterile/exterior and interior fill (Feature 13) and in both instances to provide a more complete cross section. The

TABLE 6.18. Excavation Summary for 26CK4891.

Structure	Unit	Size (m)	Depth (cm)	Volume (m³)
1	5	2 × 1	54	1.18
3	3	2 × 1	37	0.73
3	4	1 × 1	40	0.40
13	1	2 × 1	30	0.6
13	2	1 × 1	30	0.3
Total				3.21

three exposures removed a total of 3.06 m³ of deposit (Table 6.18).

Site Structure and Chronology

As shown in Figure 6.15, the features cluster in three separate areas 30 to 45 m apart. Features 1, 2/18, 3, 5, and 6 are within a 30-m area at the northwest edge of the site. Features 1, 5, and 6 are situated at the lip of the terrace and have begun to erode off the edge. The Feature 7/8/9 Complex (with the 1983 Features 4 and 10 no longer distinguishable) is at the north edge of the site, also near the terrace edge. Features 11/12/14, 13, and 15 are clustered at the southern edge of the site, well back from the terrace edges in the middle of the vast, open landform.

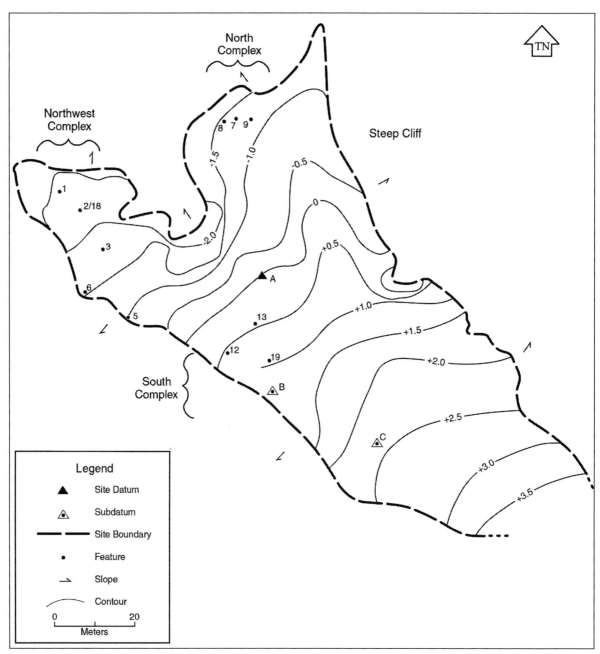

FIGURE 6.15. Map of 26CK4891.

Northwest Complex (Features 1, 2/18, 3, 5, and 6)

The Northwest Complex occurs within an area 305 m in diameter that is delimited on two sides by the steep, eroded terrace edge (Figure 6.15). The features include a large pithouse depression (Feature 1), an area 4 m to the south where the rocks appear to have been arranged (Feature 2/18), a shallow saucer-shaped depression (Feature 3) an additional 5 m to the southeast, a small slab-lined cist (Feature 6) 15 m farther to the south, and one more rock concentration (Feature 5) another 10 m to the southeast.

Feature 1

Feature 1 is the largest and topographically the most obvious pithouse structure at the site. On the surface, it is a 1.0–3.0-m-wide berm of cobbles surrounding a silty/pea-gravel surface 4 × 3 m in diameter that forms the floor of the depression (Figure 6.16). The berm rises 0.5 m above the basin along the southern part of the perimeter and 0.3 m above it along the northern perimeter. A 2-×-1-m excavation unit was placed inside the depression at the south edge, extending to the north. Overall, the unit was excavated to 54 cm below

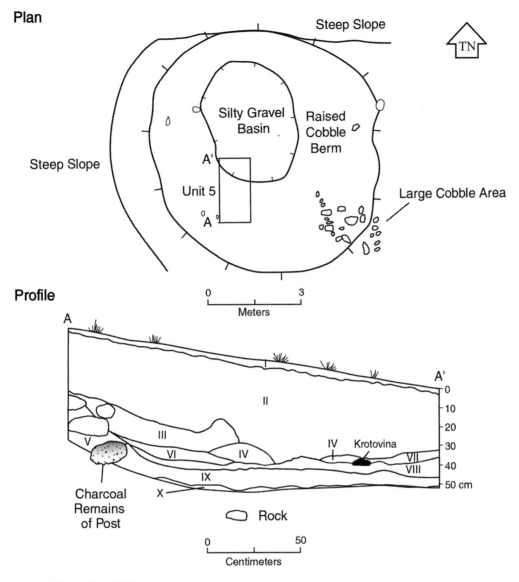

Plan

Steep Slope

Steep Slope

Silty Gravel Basin

Raised Cobble Berm

TN

A'

Unit 5

A

Large Cobble Area

0   3
Meters

Profile

A

II

III

V

VI

IV

IV   Krotovina

VII

VIII

IX

X

A'

0
10
20
30
40
50 cm

Charcoal Remains of Post

Rock

0   50
Centimeters

I   Topsoil, pebble crust.

II   Yellow-tan unconsolidated silt and subangular rounded (2-5 cm) pebbles.

III   Orangish clay-silt lens dipping north, with dispersed charcoal chunks and caliche-coated pea-gravel (wall fall/slump).

IV   Bright orange sand and clay-rich sediment with blocky structure; minimal charcoal (original structure roof coating likely).

V   In situ calcrete of fused gravel and cobbles with thick carbonate, off-white skin (original construction dug into this stratum).

VI   Mottled-orange silt with charcoal dappling (roof/wall slump).

VII   Yellow-tan silt with thin (0.4 cm) horizontal bed of clay from ponding (post-burn/ abandonment aeolian/alluvium).

VIII   Dark ashy lens, charcoal-rich with intermitted pockets of light wood ash (original roof burn).

IX   Orange-tan clay-rich stratum with subangular 2-3-cm (caliche-coated) gravel (prepared floor).

X   Water-laid, caliche-coated sand and gravel, horizontally bedded.

FIGURE 6.16. Plan and profile of Structure 1, 26CK4891.

surface, removing 1.08 m³ of deposit, terminating at the contact with a light-tan, caliche-coated, well-sorted coarse sand (a Pleistocene deposit underlying the desert pavement).

As revealed in the profile (Figure 6.16), the south wall of the pithouse was exposed at 35 cm below surface, extending 15 cm northward into the unit. A cluster of three rocks surrounding a large chunk of burned wood abutting the wall is interpreted as the vestige of a stone footing once supporting a vertical post. Ten strata are exposed in this 54-cm-deep unit, representing about 45 cm of overburden/fill (Strata I and II) and wall-fall/slump (Strata III, IV, VI), and a 2–5-cm-thick, charcoal-rich stratum of burned roof-fall (Stratum VIII) sitting on a 5–10-cm-thick, clean, prepared orange clay floor (Stratum IX). The floor, in turn, was placed on top of sterile, coarse-grained ancient sand (Stratum X).

While the stratigraphy is remarkably intact, the cultural assemblage is extremely meager, limited to only three sherds and one piece of debitage. Those items, however, were found in the 48–54-cm level within the floor zone of the structure. A sample of charcoal from the post provided a radiocarbon age assessment of cal AD 690, indicating it is a Basketmaker III period structure. The pottery is consistent with that ascription: two pieces were limestone-tempered Logandale sherds (Figure 5.5a), and the other was sand-tempered Tusayan plain gray.

A sediment sample from the prepared floor (Stratum IX) was submitted for pollen analysis. It was heavily dominated by low-spine Asteraceae pollen, to the point that it overwhelmed all other identified types. When the Asteraceae pollen is removed from consideration, the pollen profile reflects a weedy local vegetation community dominated by bursage. Quantities of both low- and high-spine Asteraceae reflect sunflower family plants as moderately abundant locally. Small quantities of pollen from other local plants include *Artemisia*, Boerhaavia type, Brassicaceae, *Cylindropuntia*, *Opuntia*, cheno-am, and *Ephedra nevadensis* type. The resulting impression is of a weedy sagebrush community with spiderling, members of the mustard family, cholla, prickly pear cactus, cheno-ams, Mormon tea, wild buckwheat, spurge, grasses, globe mallow, and evening primrose and rose family members. A few grains of maize pollen (*Zea mays*) constitute the only evidence of a cultivated crop. Creosote (*Larrea*) pollen is notably absent, indicating that the plant community shifted to its current form after site abandonment.

Flotation samples from Stratum VIII (4.3 liters) and Stratum IX (7.9 liters) were quite unproductive, other than yielding various quantities of highly fragmented charcoal. They contained just one seed identified to the sunflower family and four unidentifiable fragments.

The litter-free quality of the flotation samples is consistent with the litter-free overburden and a floor zone that is essentially devoid of artifacts. Overall, the impression is of a well-made structure at a site that was occupied for a surprisingly short period of time, so brief that no refuse accumulated in or around it, while the living surface was so clean as to appear virtually uninhabited.

Feature 3

On the surface, this is a shallow, silt-filled, saucer-shaped depression 3 m in diameter with a low, 1.0–1.5-m-wide berm wrapped around three sides (Figure 6.17). Fist-sized cobbles concentrated in the southeastern portion of the berm were loosely arrayed to form a 2-×-1-m rectangle, suggesting an associated storage unit. Excavations began with a 2-×-1-m unit placed to intersect part of this rock alignment and extend north into the depression. A subsequent 1-×-1-m unit extended the trench to the north to provide a more complete cross section (Figure 6.17). The resulting 3-×-1-m exposure was excavated to 37 cm, terminating on hard, white caliche/calcrete. A total of 1.08 m³ of deposit was removed.

The feature is a shallow, little-used pithouse. The cross section revealed four strata: Stratum I is a 5-cm-thick lens of topsoil; Stratum II is a 30-cm-thick, unconsolidated zone of silt/alluvium/aeolian; Stratum III represents the remnants of the occupational surface/living floor, indicated by intermittent thin (2–5 cm thick) patches of light-gray, charcoal-flecked, clay-rich sediment. This sits abruptly on an indurated calcrete sterile substratum (IV). In the southern 0.5 m of the trench, Stratum III is not represented, while Stratum IV is shallow, encountered at only 20 cm below surface, and then slopes quickly down to the north, interpreted as an indistinct wall/floor juncture. The structure was originally built by digging into this sterile substrate.

Although some of the rocks on the surface could be loosely construed as a rectangle, there was no subsurface indication of a storage unit or any intentional man-made feature. Rather, it seems likely that the loose "alignment" of rocks on the surface came from the original backdirt tossed at the perimeter, creating the slight berm.

Like Structure 1, regardless of the effort that went into building this structure, little in the way of an assemblage was recovered, limited to a biface, two core tools, 10 pieces of debitage, and 60 sherds, primarily within 15 cm of the ground surface. Only the heaviest items, the two core tools, were recovered at the contact between Stratum II/III, suggesting they were left on the

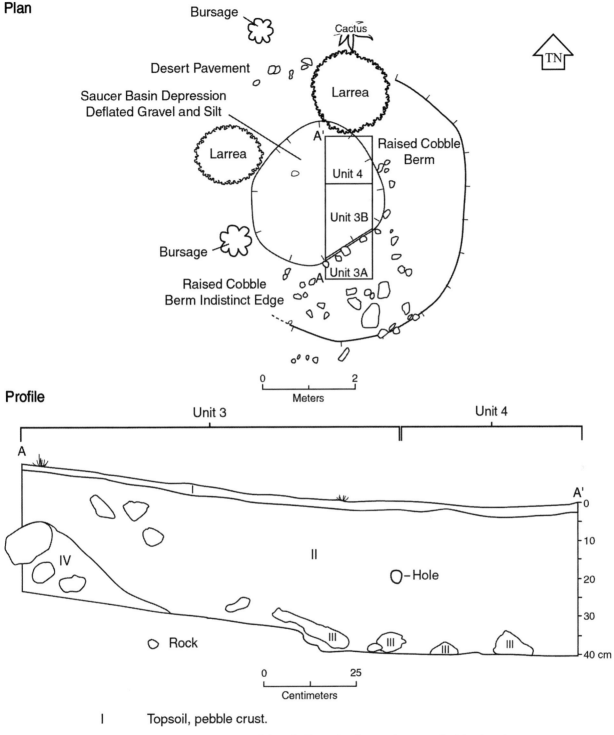

Plan

Bursage

Cactus

Desert Pavement

Larrea

TN

Saucer Basin Depression
Deflated Gravel and Silt

A'

Larrea

Raised Cobble
Berm

Unit 4

Unit 3B

Bursage

A

Unit 3A

Raised Cobble
Berm Indistinct Edge

0   2

Meters

Profile

Unit 3   Unit 4

A

A'

I

0

II

10

O – Hole

20

IV

30

III

O Rock   III

III   III   40 cm

0   25

Centimeters

I   Topsoil, pebble crust.

II   Yellow-tan unconsolidated silt and subangular rounded (2-5 cm)
        pebbles.

III   Light gray patches (charcoal flecked) remnant of cultural
        deposit, badly compromised by krotovina.

IV   In situ calcrete of fused gravel and cobbles with thick carbonate,
        off-white skin (original construction dug into this stratum).

FIGURE 6.17. Plan and profile of Structure 3, 26CK4891.

living surface. No floor features or other remnants of a structure were exposed.

A flotation sample from Stratum III (8.5 liters) contained little other than highly fragmented charcoal. A single cheno-am seed and two unidentifiable fragments were all that was recovered.

Feature 2/18

Feature 2/18 appears to be the remnants of a collapsed cist, indicated by a concentration of flagstone confined to a 2.75-×-1.2-m area. There remains only one upright slab, suggesting that the cist dimensions may once have been on the order of 1.7 × 1.1 m. The feature is surrounded by intact desert pavement.

Feature 5

Feature 5 is a concentration of fist-sized and larger rocks forming a small circular area 2.0 m in diameter. There was no obvious upright slab among them, nor was there any appreciable vertical relief that distinguished the rock concentration from the surrounding developed pavement. Its function is uncertain. It is inferred to be the remnants of a storage feature.

Feature 6

Feature 6 is made up of the intact remnants of a roughly circular, stone-lined cist with an interior dimension of 1.75 m. Several upright slabs extend 10–15 cm above the present ground surface and delimit the perimeter. The steep eroded terrace edge comes within 20 cm of its west edge; desert pavement extends outward in all other directions from it.

North Complex (Feature 7/8/9 Complex)

The 1983 site record describes and depicts three pithouses (Features 7, 9, and 10), a cist (Feature 4), and a storage unit alignment (Feature 8) in this vicinity. That struck us as an aggressive interpretation of the very modest cleared patches evident in the desert pavement at the north end of the site. We saw nothing that remotely equated with Features 4 and 10. In fact, there was but a single area about 7 × 5 m that contained two circular to oval areas, each 3–4 m across, where the rock has been removed from the pavement, leaving a patch of thin silt and small gravel. The rocks apparently had been tossed in a 2-m-wide zone between the cleared patches. This seems to accord fairly well with the originally defined Features 7 (west cleared area), 8 (rocky zone), and 9 (east cleared area). Several sherds from what appears to be a single vessel were scattered in and among Feature 8 rocks (Figure 5.6a).

Southern Complex (Features 13 and 11/12/14/15)

The 1983 record depicts four contiguous features within an area 12 m in diameter near the southern edge of the site, identifying them as three cists and a pithouse. Today there is a single slight depression that we recognized as Feature 13 and a discrete concentration of rocks over a 3.0-×-2.5-m area about 7 m to the southeast.

Feature 13 is a shallow, slightly dished basin 3.5–4.0 m in diameter surrounded by an indistinct cobbly apron that rises no more than 15 cm above it to grade into the surrounding desert pavement. Excavation began with a 2-×-1-m unit placed in the center of the depression. At a depth of approximately 20 cm a few silty-clay patches (Stratum II) were encountered in the unconsolidated fill (Stratum I), with hardpan sterile caliche (Stratum III) becoming exposed in the eastern portion of the unit, while the lightly charcoal-flecked unconsolidated fill (Stratum I with patches of Stratum II) continued to cover the western portion of the unit. A 1-×-1-m unit was opened extending to the north to more fully expose the contact line between sterile (exterior/eastern) deposits and the fill. Overall, the 3-×-1-m exposure was excavated to 30 cm, and 0.9 m³ of deposit was removed.

Although the sediment profile is unremarkable, Structure 13 produced the most robust assemblage of the three pithouses tested (Table 6.19). Nearly 250 sherds, two Rosegate projectile points, 41 pieces of debitage, 12 pieces of ground and battered tools, and one piece of modified bone were recovered from excavation or found adjacent on the surface. Nearly three-quarters of the sherds were on the surface or within the upper 15 cm of feature fill, while two large millingstone fragments on the surface extended 15 cm below the surface. From the 15- to 25-cm level, which best corresponds to an indistinct floor zone, an additional 50 sherds and two pieces of milling equipment were found. The five sherds recovered at a greater depth are attributed to bioturbation.

Only a few faint patches of charcoal-flecked sediment were noted. Consequently, our age assessment for Structure 13 is reliant on the time-sensitive artifacts—the Rosegate projectile points and Logandale and Tusayan ware sherds, which are consistent with Basketmaker III use.

Radiocarbon Dates

Only Structure 1 yielded enough charcoal to allow us to obtain a radiocarbon date. As indicated above, the charcoal was collected from a post mold at the southern edge of the structure. It provided a radiocarbon age

TABLE 6.19. Assemblage by Feature at 26CK4891.

	Structure 1		Feature 2/18	Structure 3		Feature 6	Feature 8	Structure 13			
	Surface	Subsurface	Surface	Surface	Subsurface	Surface	Surface	Surface	Subsurface	Surface	Total
Flaked Stone											
Projectile Point	—	—	—	—	—	—	—	—	2	—	2
Biface	—	—	—	—	1	—	—	—	—	—	1
Core Tool	—	—	—	—	2	—	—	—	1	—	2
Core	—	—	—	—	—	—	—	—	1	—	1
Debitage	—	1	—	—	10	—	—	—	41	—	52
Battered & Ground Stone											
Battered Cobble	—	—	—	—	—	—	—	—	1	—	1
Handstone	—	—	1	4	—	—	—	—	1	—	6
Millingstone	—	—	—	—	—	—	—	4	3	—	7
Hopper Mortar	—	—	—	—	—	—	—	1	—	—	1
Misc. Ground Stone	—	—	1	—	—	1	—	—	—	—	2
Other											
Pottery	—	3	—	—	60	—	34	—	236	—	333
Modified Bone	—	—	—	—	—	—	—	—	1	—	1
Quartz Crystal	—	—	—	—	—	—	—	—	1	—	1
Total	—	4	2	4	73	1	34	5	287	—	410
Sherds Collected in 1983	21	—	—	27	—	—	19	—	—	14	81

TABLE 6.20. Pottery from 26CK4891.

	Structure 1 Surface & Subsurface	Structure 3 Surface & Subsurface	Structure 13 Surface & Subsurface	Feature 8 Surface	Total
Paddle/Anvil	—	1	—	2	3
Logandale	2	10	61	3	76
Moapa	—	—	2	4	6
Tusayan	1	42	146	25	214
Total	3	53	209	34	299
Unidentifiable Fragments		7	28	—	35

assessment of cal AD 690, indicating use during the Basketmaker III period.

Temporally Diagnostic Artifacts

The temporally diagnostic artifacts recovered from the surface and excavations were two projectile points (Figure 5.3) and nearly 450 pieces of pottery. As reviewed below, all are consistent with Basketmaker III site use and corroborate the radiocarbon date.

Pottery

Nearly 300 diagnostic sherds were recently recovered from 26CK4891 (Table 6.20). Although the ratios between types differ from one structure to the next, Tusayan plain ware is prevalent in most contexts and at least a few Logandale sherds were recovered from each. At the site overall, most of the pottery is Tusayan plain ware (71.6 percent), followed by Logandale (25.4 percent). Only six olivine-tempered and three paddle and anvil manufactured sherds were recognized in the assemblage.

Regional archaeological literature indicates that Logandale pottery is best represented at the early end of the pottery sequence, in Basketmaker III/Pueblo I interval sites. In this regard, two out of the three sherds found in Structure 1 are Logandale, which is consistent with the Basketmaker III radiocarbon date obtained from this context. The near complete lack of olivine-tempered pottery at the site is also broadly consistent with the regional trend previously noted that such trade wares are most common in Pueblo II contexts.

Projectile Points and Obsidian Hydration Data

Both projectile points from the site were recovered from Structure 13 feature fill, and both are Rosegate points. Their occurrence is wholly consistent with the Basketmaker III age assignment for the site. One of them is the only piece of obsidian recovered from the site. It is made of Delamar Mountains obsidian and provided a hydration rim measurement of 4.7 microns. This is the final piece of chronological evidence consistent with a Basketmaker III occupation (Figure 5.10).

Component Definition

All indications are that site 26CK4891 was very briefly occupied only during the Basketmaker III interval. This is supported by the radiocarbon date from Structure 1, the projectile points recovered from Structure 13, and the sherds found throughout various contexts at the site. There is no clear indication of an earlier or a later site use. Furthermore, the meager amount of material culture at the surface or within the excavated structures suggests an extremely abbreviated occupation. Thus the site is interpreted as a single-component Basketmaker III occupation, and the material recovered from various contexts is reviewed as a single assemblage.

Artifact Inventory

The collective assemblage from 26CK4891 is dominated by sherds (see above), followed distantly by 16 pieces of milling equipment, three battered cobbles/core tools, three flaked stone tools, and 52 pieces of debitage (Table 6.19). Two other items—a small margin fragment of a piece of modified bone that appears to be part of a pin/awl, and a small angular fragment of a milky quartz crystal—are the only out-of-ordinary items found; they complete the assemblage.

Flaked Stone Tools and Debitage

What few flaked stone tools were recovered offer mute evidence of concern with hunting: two of the six are Rosegate projectile points, and a third is a nondiagnostic fragment of what is probably another point. The three remaining flaked stone tools consist of a unifacial core made on a CCS flake and two core tools. The latter are whole cobbles (9.0–11.0 cm across) that have at least one battered area along their flaked edges. As such, they might better be aligned with the ground and battered stone assemblage than with the flaked stone assemblage. The debitage reinforces this notion: most of it results from nonbifacial, cobble-core reduction activities; little results from biface manufacture and/or maintenance.

Of the small quantity of debitage recovered during excavation, most was from Structure 13, where near-equal quantities of CCS (n = 20) and quartzite (n = 18) flakes were found. Of these, the diagnostic CCS flake types reflect minimal biface reduction (seven percussion and two pressure flakes removed from bifaces) and even less nonbifacial core reduction (one decortication flake and four percussion interior flakes). The diagnostic quartzite flakes are exclusively from nonbifacial early-stage cobble/core reduction (five decortication flakes, two pieces of shatter, and seven percussion interior flakes). Three pieces of granite complete the flaked stone assemblage from Structure 13 (two percussion interior, one nondiagnostic fragment).

The ten flakes from Structure 3 mimic those from Structure 13: six are CCS (the four diagnostic pieces are two biface thinning flakes, one piece of shatter, and one percussion interior flake), and four are quartzite (the diagnostic pieces are limited to one decortication and one percussion interior flake). The only flake found in Structure 1 is an angular chunk of quartzite shatter.

Ground and Battered Stone

If we include the two cobble-core tools described above, the ground and battered implements from the site include ten millingstones (including two indeterminate fragments and one whole implement evocative of a flat hopper mortar), six handstones, and three battered implements. The millingstones that are whole or nearly so range from 24 to 34 cm long and about 23 cm wide. Collectively, they represent 14 worn faces, of which all are flat except one that is deeply concave/basined. No open-ended, three-quarter trough millingstones were present. Rather, the millingstones tend to be simple, rudimentary implements, with worn surfaces most frequently considered to have an incipient or indeterminate wear pattern. Of the handstones, three are bifacially worked and those complete or nearly whole are of a size routinely considered "one-hand" manos. They are between 10 and 17 cm across, 8 cm from front to back, and between 2 and 4 cm thick. To the two battered core tools, we can add one additional battered cobble that was noted but not recorded.

Floral and Faunal Remains

Given the depauperate artifact assemblage associated with the pithouses at the site, it is not a surprise that few subsistence remains were recovered, limited to nine scraps of dietary faunal remains and eight carbonized seeds of which only two are identifiable (one goosefoot and one sunflower family seed; see above). The faunal remains are limited to one piece of tortoise carapace, five fragments that can only be categorized as medium-to-large mammal (roughly sheep-sized), and three fragments that are small-to-medium-sized mammal (roughly rabbit-sized). Five of these are burned, providing clear indication that they are prehistoric food remains and not a result of modern roadside carnage.

Pollen analysis provides the only definitive evidence that maize was present on site. We can only wonder if the prehistoric residents ever experienced a successful crop or if the few pollen grains recovered reflect a failed attempt to cultivate the adjacent floodplain.

Summary

A single extraordinarily brief occupation of site 26CK4891 appears to have occurred exclusively in the Basketmaker III period. The site contains three spatially discrete clusters of features, each with at least one pithouse depression. Their spacing likely reflects what was considered appropriate social distance between three households. Of the three pithouse structures test excavated, Structure 1 is considerably more substantial and dug more deeply into the caliche natural sediment than either Structure 3 or 13. Yet in contrast to the number of structures and supporting features, the artifact assemblage is remarkably modest; two of the three houses provided meager evidence of having been lived in, while the third (Structure 13) was the most poorly defined yet had the most refuse incorporated in its fill. In light of how free of artifacts the floor zones were in all structures, how free of artifacts the fill zones were in two of the structures, and how little material is scattered across the surface of the site, it is difficult to imagine that the site was occupied year-round for even one year. The work that went into making these habitable structures (digging into hardpan) seems to have been largely a waste of effort, as it is difficult to imagine that the group resided here more than one or two seasons.

26CK6078/6095 (Cedar Basin Midden) Site Report

Site 26CK6078/6095 is a low-density artifact scatter located on a highly dissected northeast-trending ridge in Cedar Basin. Large weathered exposures of granite bedrock form the ridge, and numerous alcoves and nooks exist within the formation (Figure 6.18). Local vegetation is composed of juniper-pinyon woodland with an understory that includes dense thickets of Gambel oak, chamisa, and manzanita. A fast-moving forest fire passed through the area in 1999, reducing many of the juniper and pinyon trees to charred skeletons and

FIGURE 6.18. Overview of 26CK6078/6095.

allowing the understory plants to colonize the original woodland setting.

A dark gray midden area lies along the southeastern margin of the site and was designated Locus 1 during the survey phase of the project (Figure 6.19). Pottery and debitage, in addition to several pieces of milling gear, are concentrated in Locus 1. Two small, single-course rock rings (Features 1 and 2) also overlie the midden. The survey probe placed in Locus 1 found rich deposits extending to at least 50 cm. The midden contained pottery and a flaked stone assemblage, and indicated that flotation samples would probably render carbonized material.

A concentration of milling gear (milling station 1) was identified in one of the alcoves at the northwestern edge of the site, and a small arrastra is located less than 100 m away across a drainage to the southeast at 26CK6079. Ian's Rock Shelter (26CK6080/6081) is visible across the same drainage to the south less than 200 m away.

Field Methods

The field effort began with the establishment of a grid overlying Locus 1, where 100 percent surface collection was accomplished using 5-×-5-m cells. Detailed maps

were also made of Features 1 and 2. Surface collections outside Locus 1 were divided into a northeast lobe and a western lobe. The low-density dispersion of material was such that all portable artifacts in the northeast lobe were point provenienced and collected, while portable items other than debitage were point provenienced and collected from the western lobe. All larger pieces of milling gear were analyzed and left in place on the site.

A single 2-×-1-m unit was placed at S5/E1 in the center of the Locus 1 midden (Figure 6.19) approximately 6 m downslope and southeast of Feature 2. Subsurface yields were productive to a depth of 70 cm, yielding many sherds at the top of the profile and high frequencies of flaked stone tools and debitage throughout the deposit. The unit was closed at 80 cm, resulting in the excavation of 1.6 m³ of deposit.

Site Structure and Chronology

We begin by reviewing the structural characteristics of the site, providing descriptions of the milling station in the western lobe, Features 1 and 2 in Locus 1, and the stratigraphic relationships exposed during the excavation of the Locus 1 midden. We then review the chronological indicators found at the site, including radiocarbon dates, pottery, and projectile points.

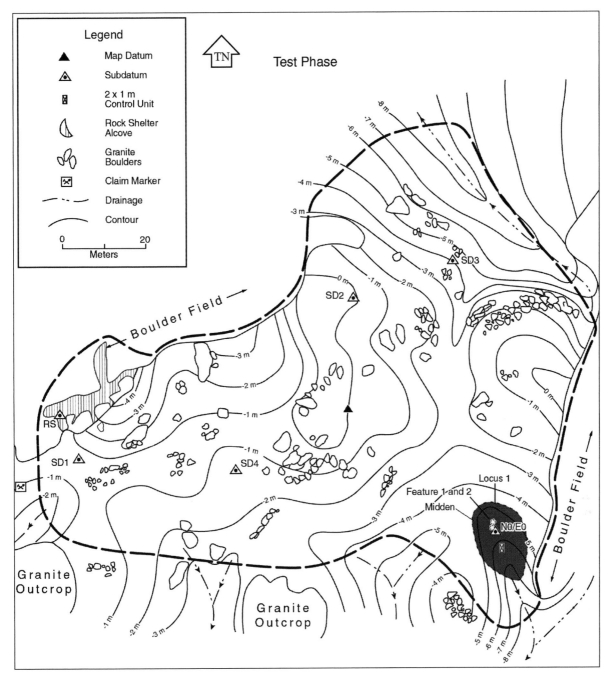

FIGURE 6.19. Map of 26CK6078/6095.

Features

Milling station 1 is situated at the northwest edge of the site. A narrow passage under overlapping bedrock boulders leads to an alcove approximately 20 × 5 m in size. Much of this area has little head room, but a smaller area (roughly 5 × 5 m) has a ceiling more than 1.5 m tall at the apex of the alcove. Two whole, large block millingstones, pieces of three handstones, and three sherds were found in this alcove. The floor of the alcove is tan-orange aeolian sand and silt, but is mostly coarse decomposing granite, with no potential for a subsurface deposit.

In the Locus 1 midden there are two features. Feature 1 is somewhat rectangular with its long axis parallel to the slope. Head-sized and larger granite cobbles form a single-course alignment, with exterior dimensions of 2.6 × 1.8 m and an interior dimension of 2.3 × 0.8 m. Feature 2 is about one meter farther downslope, southeast of Feature 1, and has less formal structure. It is a loose, circular concentration of fist- to head-sized granite

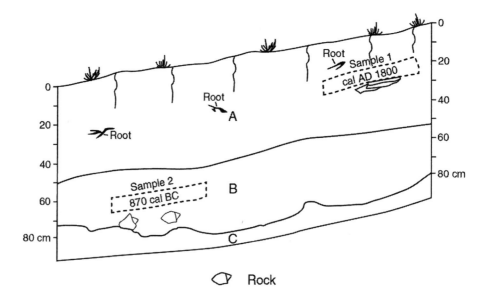

A   Loose very dark grayish brown (10YR 3/4) gravelly sandy silt.

B   Slightly compact dark yellowish brown (10YR 3/4) gravelly sandy silt.

C   Compact yellowish brown (10YR 5/4) decomposing granitic bedrock.

FIGURE 6.20. West wall profile of unit S5/E1 at 26CK6078/6095.

cobbles about 1.5 m in diameter, with an interior cleared area about 0.7 m across. The interiors of both features are slightly below the native ground surface and devoid of shrubs. These characteristics, in combination with the somewhat rectangular form of Feature 1 and the occurrence of about a half-dozen rusted cans in the general vicinity, suggest (but do not establish) that Features 1 and 2 are historic in age.

Stratigraphy

The vertical profile of the midden at Locus 1 represents a single stratigraphic unit (Figure 6.20). It begins with an upper A-horizon composed of a very dark grayish brown (10YR3/2) gravelly sandy silt with abundant decomposed granite gravel. At about 50 cm below surface it transitions to a more compacted B-horizon composed of yellowish brown (10YR3/4) silty sand (Stratum II). Between 70 and 80 cm below surface, a C-horizon of decomposing granite bedrock is encountered, resulting in a relatively distinct boundary and a considerably lighter yellow-brown (10YR5/4) matrix.

Radiocarbon Dates

Two radiocarbon dates were obtained from the Locus 1 midden, both from charcoal derived from flotation samples (Figure 6.20; Table 6.21). The first was collected from the upper A-horizon (20–30 cm) and produced a very late date of cal AD 1800. The other was collected from much deeper in the deposit (50–70 cm) and yielded a much older date of 870 cal BC. These findings reflect a relatively high degree of stratigraphic integrity and potentially two components: a lower Late Archaic deposit overlain by a Late Prehistoric upper deposit.

Temporally Diagnostic Artifacts

A variety of sherds and projectile points round out the chronological data sets.

Pottery

More than 240 sherds were recovered from the site (Table 6.22). Most were scattered across the surface (n = 173), but a large number were found in the subsurface deposits in Locus 1 (n = 70). The vast majority of the latter (91.4 percent) were found in the upper 30 cm of the deposit, which trends well with the vertical distribution of the radiocarbon dates. The pottery in the upper deposit, however, is dominated by Puebloan types (55 out of the 64 of the diagnostic fragments) that date between about AD 650 and 1200, substantially predating the cal AD 1800 radiocarbon date. The young date is a better fit to the interval when Paiute brown ware and certain types of paddle and anvil pottery were in use,

TABLE 6.21. Radiocarbon Dates from 26CK6078/6095.

Unit	Depth (cm)	Calibrated Intercept[a]	Conventional Age	Material
S5/E1	20–30	cal AD 1800/cal BP 150	170 ± 40 BP	Charcoal
S5/E1	50–70	cal BC 870/cal BP 2820	2730 ± 40 BP	Charcoal

[a] See Table 5.1.

but these late wares were present in significant numbers only on the surface, where they account for 60.1 percent.

Projectile Points

Twenty projectile points were recovered from the site: seven from the surface and 13 from the Locus 1 midden (Table 6.23). They are dominated by Elko (75.0 percent), followed by other dart forms (Gypsum, Humboldt, and dart-sized fragments; 15.0 percent). Only one arrow-sized fragment (5.0 percent) occurred, and it was on the surface. The near absence of arrow points at the site is surprising given the abundance of pottery on the surface.

Although the nine dart-sized points found between 30 and 70 cm in the Locus 1 midden are consistent with the lack of pottery and corroborates the Late Archaic radiocarbon date, four Elko points were found in the upper pottery-bearing deposit. As a result, it appears that the upper part of the midden at Locus 1 has Late Archaic material intermixed with Puebloan and Late Prehistoric material.

Component Definition

Based on the above findings, the data collected from 26CK6078/6095 are divided into three groups. All the subsurface material below 30 cm is assigned to a single Late Archaic component based on the 870 cal BC radiocarbon date, dominant presence of Elko points, and near absence of pottery. The upper 30 cm of the deposit, however, is considered chronologically mixed due to the co-association of the cal AD 1800 radiocarbon date (Late Prehistoric period), Puebloan pottery (potentially Basketmaker III and Puebloan I/II), and Elko projectile points (Late Archaic and Basketmaker II). Material from across the surface is also concluded to be mixed from the different use episodes over time.

Artifact Inventory

The Late Archaic artifact assemblage from 26CK6078/6095 is quite specialized (Table 6.24), composed of 25 flake stone tools and only one piece of milling gear (a single handstone). Bifaces (44.0 percent) and projectile points (36.0 percent) dominate the flaked stone assemblage, indicating that hunting activities were the primary focus of the Late Archaic occupation.

TABLE 6.22. Pottery from 26CK6078/6095.

	S5/E1			Surface	
	30–70 cm	0–30 cm	Subtotal	Items	Total
Brown Ware	0	0	0	18	18
Paddle/Anvil	0	9	9	74	83
Logandale	1	7	8	1	9
Shivwits	1	0	1	3	4
Moapa	1	14	15	10	25
Tusayan	3	28	31	47	78
Total	6	58	64	153	217
Unidentifiable Fragments	0	6	6	20	26

TABLE 6.23. Projectile Points from 26CK6078/6095.

	S5/E1				
	30–70 cm	0–30 cm	Subtotal	Surface	Total
Elko	7	4	11	4	15
Gypsum	1	—	1	—	1
Humboldt	—	—	—	1	1
Arrow-Sized	—	—	—	1	1
Dart-Sized	1	—	—	1	2
Total	9	4	13	7	20

While the upper mixed midden zone at Locus 1 also shows a dominance of flaked stone, the surface assemblage is fundamentally different, as it has a higher percentage of ground and battered stone implements (n = 42; 62.7 percent) than flaked stone tools (n = 25; 37.3 percent). The flaked stone assemblage remains rather specialized (mostly bifaces and projectile points), but the ground and battered stone collection includes a relatively even combination of millingstones (n = 17), handstones (n = 12), and battered cobbles (n = 12). Due to the chronologically mixed nature of the surface assemblage, it is impossible to determine the age of the ground and battered stone assemblage. But given that both brown ware and paddle and anvil pottery are abundant on the surface, in contrast to being absent from the upper deposit, it seems possible that much of the

TABLE 6.24. Assemblage by Temporal Component at 26CK6078/6095.

	Late Archaic	Mixed		Total
	Subsurface	Surface	Subsurface	
Flaked Stone				
Projectile Point	9	7	4	20
Drill	—	1	—	1
Biface	11	12	13	36
Formed Flake Tool	1	1	1	3
Flake Tool	3	1	2	6
Core	1	3	1	5
Debitage	411	186	784	1,381
Battered & Ground Stone				
Battered Cobble	—	12	1	13
Handstone	1	12	1	14
Millingstone	—	17	—	17
Pestle	—	1	—	1
Faunal Remains				
Bone	8	2	26	36
Other				
Ceramic	6	173	64	243
Historic/Modern	—	6	—	6
Total	451	434	897	1,782

ground/battered stone assemblage is essentially a Late Prehistoric phenomenon.

Flaked Stone Tools and Debitage

All bifaces recovered from the site are made from chert. The Late Archaic assemblage is dominated by Stage 3 and 4 specimens, indicating that some amount of late-stage thinning and tool finishing occurred on site (Table 6.25). The chronologically mixed assemblage is consistent with this pattern but shows a higher proportion of the finished, Stage 5 specimens.

The vast majority of debitage is also chert (Table 6.26). Late-stage biface thinning and pressure flakes combine for 67.0 percent of the Late Archaic diagnostic assemblage, which matches up well with the biface profile. Early-stage biface thinning debris (22.9 percent) accounts for most of the remainder of the assemblage. This profile is generally similar to that found in the temporally mixed assemblage, although pressure flakes are more common than late-stage thinning debris. The low frequency of cortical and interior flakes, combined with the paucity of cores (Table 6.26), indicates that most of the toolstone arrived on site as bifaces in various stages of reduction.

All the simple flake tools and formed flake tools are

TABLE 6.25. Biface Stages by Period from 26CK6078/6095.

	Late Archaic	Mixed Subsurface	Surface	Total
Stage 1	—	—	—	—
Stage 2	1	1	1	3
Stage 3	5	4	2	11
Stage 4	3	1	4	8
Stage 5	1	3	4	8
Total	10	9	11	30
Indeterminate	1	4	1	6

also made from chert. Most are made from cortical, interior, and early-stage biface thinning flakes, and two of the latter group have heavily worn tool edges.

Finally, a single drill was recovered from the surface. It is a small, extensively pressure-flaked biface that could be a reworked dart point. Its base has been squared off, and the tool bit shows polish and grinding.

Ground and Battered Stone

Fifteen of the 17 millingstones received formal analysis. Most are granite (n = 9), and the remainder are represented by a mixture of basalt, undifferentiated igneous

TABLE 6.26. Technological Analysis of Debitage by Period from 26CK6078/6095.

| | Late Archaic | | | | | | | | Mixed | | | | | |
| | Chert | | Obsidian | | Quartzite | | Quartz (milky) | | Chert | | Quartzite | | Quartz (milky) | |
	Count	%	Count	%	Count	%	Count	%	Count	%	Count	%	Count	%
Core Reduction														
Percussion Decortication	15	6.6	—	—	—	—	—	—	24	5.6	1	20.0	—	—
Percussion Interior	8	3.5	—	—	—	—	12	92.3	22	5.1	3	60.0	15	78.9
Biface Reduction														
Early Biface Thinning	52	22.9	—	—	1	100	—	—	91	21.3	1	20.0	1	5.3
Late Biface Thinning	89	39.2	—	—	—	—	1	7.7	127	29.7	—	—	1	5.3
Pressure	63	27.8	1	100	—	—	—	—	164	38.3	—	—	2	10.5
Diagnostic Total	227	100.0	1	100	1	100	13	100.0	428	100.0	5	100.0	19	100.0
Platform Prep./Pressure	2	—	—	—	—	—	1	—	4	—	—	—	3	—
Indeterminate Percussion	114	—	—	—	—	—	9	—	186	—	6	—	12	—
Indeterminate Fragment	35	—	—	—	1	—	—	—	100	—	—	—	3	—
Shatter	4	—	—	—	—	—	2	—	16	—	—	—	2	—
Sample Total	382	—	1	—	2	—	25	—	734	—	11	—	39	—

TABLE 6.27. Ground Stone from 26CK6078/6095.

	Polish	Polish & Pecking	Polish, Pecking, & Striations	Total
Millingstones				
Unifacial	7	1	1	9
Indeterminate	—	2	—	2
Bifacial				
Side 1	2	2	—	4
Side 2	2	2	—	4
Handstones				
Unifacial	2	1	1	4
Indeterminate	2	—	—	2
Bifacial				
Side 1	6	2	—	8
Side 2	6	2	—	8

material, schist, sandstone, and graywacke. Five are whole, and the others are either margin fragments or unidentifiable pieces. The majority have simple polish on a single worn surface, although a limited number of these also have pecking and striations (Table 6.27). Four millingstones have bifacial wear, two with simple polish on both faces, while the others exhibit polish and pecking on both worn surfaces.

The handstones show more material variability and a greater amount of wear, perhaps indicating that they stayed in the tool kit longer than the more cumbersome millingstones. All 14 handstones were analyzed: four were made from granite, four from quartzite, three from sandstone, two from dacite, and one from a metavolcanic stone. Eight of them have bifacial wear, with the majority showing simple polish and a few exhibiting pecking as well. The unifacial and indeterminate ones also have mostly simple polish, with a single example with secondary pecking and one with pecking and striations.

All but two of the 13 battered cobbles are white quartz; the others are sandstone and granite. All are rather small, fitting easily into the hand, and have extensive battering and grinding along multiple margins. These probably represent multiple functions, ranging from early-stage flaked stone reduction to processing vegetal products on millingstones, many of which show battering on their working surfaces.

Floral and Faunal Remains

Two flotation samples were collected from the Locus 1 midden, one from 20 to 30 cm (5.0 liters) and the other from 50 to 70 cm (6.5 liters). Although both relatively large samples produced limited amounts of charcoal, the charred plant assemblage is limited to a single pinyon nut fragment.

The faunal assemblage from the Locus 1 midden is also quite small, limited to 26 fragments from the upper mixed zone and eight pieces from the lower Late Archaic component. It is dominated by artiodactyls and medium-to-large mammal (sheep-sized) fragments (n = 19), followed by undifferentiated fragments (n = 6), and only one small-to-medium (rabbit-sized) fragment.

Summary

Site 26CK6078/6095 was intermittently occupied for a long period of time. It was first used during the Late Archaic period by people focused primarily on hunting. This is evident from the very narrow tool assemblage dominated by middle- to late-stage bifaces and Elko projectile points, and a few fragments of bone reflecting the butchering and consumption of large game. Later Puebloan and Late Prehistoric occupations are documented by temporally diagnostic pottery found in surface and near-surface contexts, intermixed with each other, as well as with flaked stone material from the earlier Late Archaic use. Due to this high degree of mixture, it is not possible to assign discrete artifact assemblages to these different periods of occupation. It is quite clear, however, that the surface assemblage has a much higher frequency of ground and battered stone tools than in the buried, Late Archaic component. The former assemblage probably reflects the use of the rich pinyon nut resource at Cedar Basin, as well as other small-seeded plants in the area.

26CK6080/6081 (IAN'S ROCK SHELTER) SITE REPORT

Site 26CK6080/6081 is a relatively large habitation site located in Cedar Basin. It lies in a rugged landscape of large granitic outcrops and boulders, covered with a relatively dense forest of pinyon, juniper, and scrub oak and an understory of yucca, Mormon tea, and various grasses. It includes two habitation loci, interspersed with a low-density scatter of flaked stone tools and debitage, milling gear, and sherds. Locus 1 contains a high density of these materials associated with a hearth. Locus 2 was the focus of our excavation because it consists of a large boulder rock shelter associated with a dark, rich midden deposit. Its surface contains pottery, milling equipment, flaked stone tools, and debitage. There is also a pile of limb wood with chopped ends (not sawed) placed near the drip line of the shelter (Figure 6.21). It is quite weathered and appears to be a cache of firewood, but we don't know its age or who placed it in this location. The survey probe produced sherds and debitage, as well as a robust assemblage of faunal remains.

Field Methods

Fieldwork began with the establishment of a grid at Locus 2 and a systematic collection of sherds and flaked stone tools. Each tool was mapped according to a 1-×-1-m grid, with the southwest corner providing the provenience for each cell. All surface milling gear was mapped, analyzed, and left in place. After this surface work was completed, a single 1-×-2-m unit was placed at S3/W5 (Figure 6.21). This location lies to the north of the core midden area but was chosen to avoid a disturbed area where pothunting may have occurred. The disturbed area has a shallow pit with a low berm on its south side.

Excavation in S3/W5 was quite productive, producing abundant pottery, four glass trade beads, Desert series projectile points, and other miniature arrow points. It bottomed out on shallow bedrock but reached 40 cm at either end of the unit. A concentration of fire-affected rock at the eastern end of the exposure prompted excavation of a 1-×-1-m unit at S3/W3, which exposed a substantial hearth/oven (Feature 1). An additional 1-×-1-m unit was excavated at the western end of the exposure (S3/W6), resulting in a 1-×-4-m trench.

After the work in the trench was completed, two additional units were excavated on either side of the exposure, one at S4/W6 (1 × 1 m) and the other at S2/W4 (0.5 × 1 m). Unit S4/W6 exposed a hearth (Feature 2) at 30–50 cm below surface, while S2/W4 was used to sample a small ash lens (Feature 3) observed in the north wall of the 1-×-4-m trench. The five units covered 5.5 m² and equaled about 3.1 m³ of excavation (Table 6.28).

Site Structure and Chronology

In this section we outline the structural characteristics of the site, including descriptions of the three features and the stratigraphic profile exposed during excavation. We then turn to the wide range of chronological indicators in the deposit, including radiocarbon dates, time-sensitive artifacts (e.g., projectile points, beads, pottery), and obsidian hydration data.

TABLE 6.28. Excavation Summary for 26CK6080/6081, Locus 2.

Unit	Size (m)	Depth (cm)	Volume (m³)
S3/W5	1 × 2	80	1.2[a]
S4/W6	1 × 1	60	0.5[a]
S3/W3	1 × 1	90	0.9
S2/W4	0.5 × 1.0	20	0.1
S3/W6	1 × 1	40	0.4
Total			3.1

[a] Reduction accounts for shallow bedrock in the exposure.

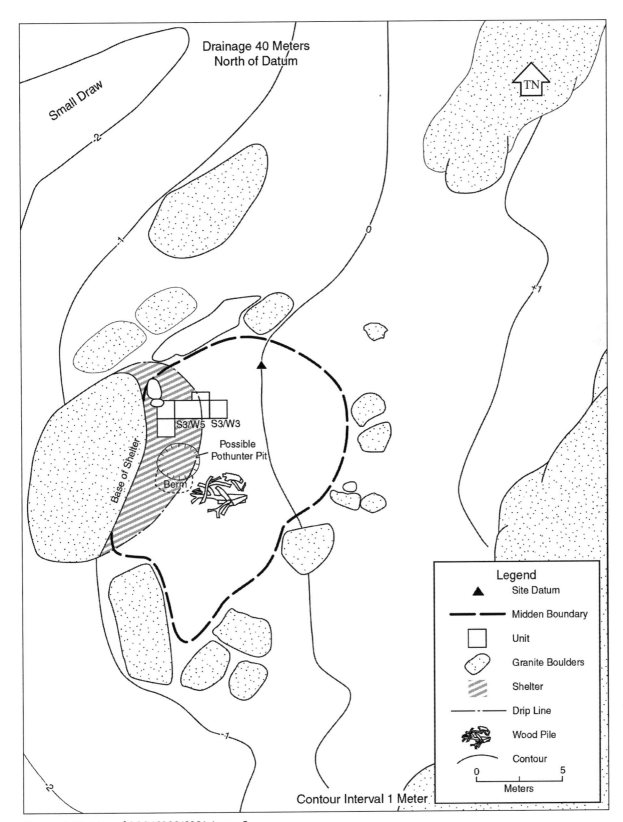

Drainage 40 Meters
North of Datum

Small Draw

TN

Base of Shelter

S3/W5 S3/W3

Possible
Pothunter Pit

Berm

Legend

▲ Site Datum

— · — Midden Boundary

☐ Unit

Granite Boulders

Shelter

Drip Line

Wood Pile

Contour

0   5

Meters

Contour Interval 1 Meter

FIGURE 6.21. Map of 26CK6080/6081, Locus 2.

Features

Feature 1 is a relatively large hearth/oven composed of more than 300 granite cobbles. The feature was discovered at about 30 cm below surface and formed a circle of rocks about one meter in diameter (Figure 6.22). After a good plan view was exposed of the feature, its northern half was excavated to reveal a profile. Due to its depth, excavations had to extend to 60 cm to expose a full profile. The profile, and subsequent excavation of its southern half, indicate that it was a rock-lined pit in the shape of a half sphere. Two flotation samples were collected from the Feature 1 fill, and the remainder of the matrix was screened separately from the nonfeature soils in the unit. The feature fill produced similar material to what was found in the nonfeature sediments, but a thick millingstone and large handstone were among the rocks used to build the feature.

Feature 2 is a smaller, less formal, rock-lined hearth (Figure 6.23). It is about 40 cm in diameter and only 10 cm deep, that is, it was found between 30 and 40 cm. It is unique, however, in having large sherds within it, perhaps indicating that a vessel broke during cooking. One of the sherds has a hole drilled through it, which could have supported a carrying rope or could have come from mending the bowl. Two flotation samples were collected from its matrix.

Feature 3 is a simple lens of gray (10YR 6/1) ash lacking rocks or associated artifacts (Figure 6.24). It is quite shallow (3–10 cm) and overlies solid bedrock. Given that the living surfaces associated with Features 1 and 2 are about 30 cm below the current surface, the bedrock underlying Feature 3 would have been exposed at that time. It follows, therefore, that Feature 3 could represent the most recent occupation at the site. One flotation sample was collected from this concentration.

Stratigraphy

Stratigraphic relationships within the 26CK6080/6081 deposit vary significantly across the exposure, depending on where bedrock was encountered (Figure 6.25). The profile begins with an upper A-horizon midden composed of a very dark grayish brown (10YR 3/2), loose sandy loam with abundant decomposed granitic gravel. This stratum is quite discrete where the bedrock is shallow, as it does not come into contact with any other soil or archaeological horizons. This occurs in much of S3/W5 and all of S2/W4, including Feature 3.

Where the deposit goes deeper, a buried 2Ab soil/midden horizon is encountered, particularly in S3/W3. It is composed of a very dark gray (10YR 3/1), loose sandy loam with abundant decomposed granitic gravel. It appears to be a buried soil due to its slightly darker color, and it forms the surface associated with Features

TABLE 6.29. Radiocarbon Dates from 26CK6081/6081, Locus 2.

Feature	Unit	Depth	Calibrated Intercept[a]	Conventional Age	Material
3	S3/W5	5–10	cal AD 1650 (cal BP 300)	250 ± 60 BP	Charcoal
1	S3/W3	35–45	cal AD 340 (cal BP 1610)	1710 ± 50 BP	Charcoal
—	S3/W5	66–80	40 cal BC (cal BP 1990)	2030 ± 40 BP	Charcoal

[a] See Table 5.1.

1 and 2. The profile bottoms out on a 2Cr horizon, which is a yellowish brown (10YR 5/4) accumulation of decomposed granitic gravel lacking midden soils. This stratum has been reworked by rodents, creating a blurred, undulating contact with the 2Ab horizon.

Radiocarbon Dates

Three radiocarbon dates were obtained from the site, one from Feature 3, one from Feature 1, and the other from the bottom of the buried 2Ab midden (Table 6.29). The upper Feature 3 assay produced a median probability date of cal AD 1650, which places it well into the Late Prehistoric period (post–AD 1250). Feature 1 returned a date of cal AD 340, which is consistent with the earlier buried soil/midden horizon and corresponds to the end of Basketmaker II. The sample collected from the bottom of the buried soil/midden also falls into the Basketmaker II period, producing a date of 40 cal BC.

Temporally Diagnostic Artifacts

A wide range of temporally diagnostic artifacts were recovered from the site. They include projectile points, sherds, glass beads, and shell ornaments.

Glass and Shell Artifacts

The glass bead collection includes five drawn specimens that are classified according to Kidd and Kidd (1970). As described in Chapter 5, drawn beads are manufactured by drawing or stretching molten glass into long canes that are then cut and shaped. Three of the beads are drawn, monochrome, and tumbled-oblate (DIIa), and are white, blue, and teal in color. The other two are drawn, polychrome, and tumbled-oblate (DIVa), and are red with a white interior. Manufactured in Venice, Italy, and used as trade goods by European colonists all over the world, all these bead types are common throughout California, the Great Basin, and the Southwest, and correspond to the earliest period of contact. All these specimens were found in the upper 20 cm of the deposit (Table 6.30), which roughly corresponds to a radiocarbon date of cal AD 1650.

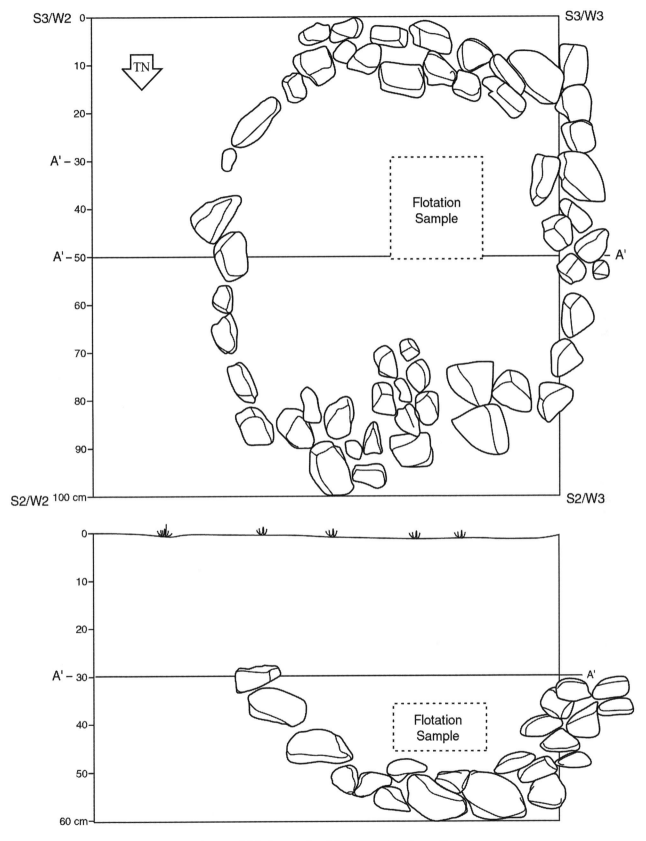

FIGURE 6.22. Feature 1 at 26CK6080/6081, Locus 2.

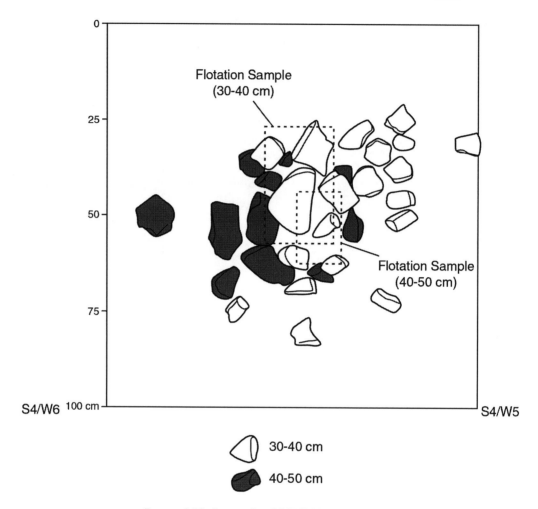

FIGURE 6.23. Feature 2 at 26CK6080/6081, Locus 2.

The three shell artifacts are also relatively high in the profile (Table 6.30). Two are quite fragmentary and cannot be easily identified. One might be a pendant fragment made from abalone or mussel, while the other is an indeterminate fragment of abalone shell. The final specimen is a complete abalone bead. It is relatively large (14 mm in diameter and 2.4 mm thick) and has a conical perforation measuring about 3.8 mm in diameter. It appears to be an abalone epidermis disk bead, which typically date to the Late Period in southern California (King 1990).

Pottery

A more complicated relationship is reflected by the sherds recovered from the site (Table 6.31). The upper midden zone contains the vast majority of sherds, and they are dominated by brown ware and paddle and anvil

TABLE 6.30. Glass Beads and Shell Artifacts from 26CK6080/6081, Locus 2.

Depth (cm)	Glass Beads	Shell Artifacts	Total
0–10	2	—	2
10–20	3	2	5
20–30	—	—	—
30–40	—	1	1
40–50	—	—	—
50–60	—	—	—
60–70	—	—	—
70–80	—	—	—
Total	5	3	8
Mean Depth (cm)	16.0	26.7	20.0

Note: All beads are from units S3/W5 and S4/W6.

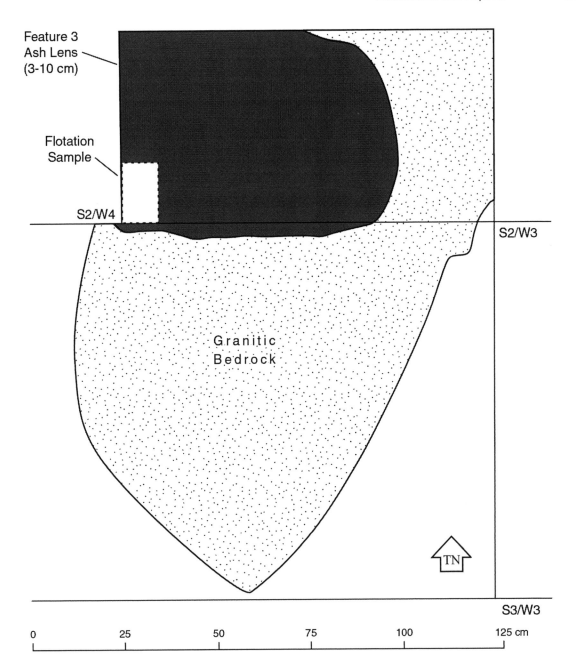

FIGURE 6.24. Feature 3 at 26CK6080/6081, Locus 2.

pieces (75.0 percent). This finding fits well with the site stratigraphy, radiocarbon dates, and beads, as brown ware postdates cal AD 1300 and the paddle and anvil wares postdate AD 1000.

The presence of Puebloan pottery, however, identifies a component not evident from the radiocarbon dates or beads. Although some of this pottery—including Moapa, Logandale, and Tusayan sherds, in addition to several worked sherds—was found in the upper midden (25.0 percent), a much higher percentage (51.5 percent) was found between 30 and 60 cm in the vicinity of

Feature 2 (in units S4/W6 and S3/W6). These include fragments of a Sosi black-on-white bowl in the middle of Feature 2; another Tusayan ware bowl sherd with a biconically drilled hole (of an indeterminate painted design); a worked sherd of Moapa plain gray (item 6080/6081-217); and a small, scalloped rim sherd (Figure 5.6e) of Tusayan plain gray. Not surprisingly, some of these Pueblo I and II sherds are mixed upward in the profile. Among them is another worked sherd, identified as Hildale black-on-gray (Tusayan ware; Figure 5.6d). The most general temporal range for the Feature 2

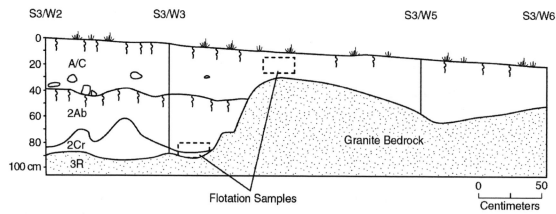

A/C   Upper A-horizon midden zone composed of a very dark grayish brown (10YR 3/2) loose sandy loam with abundant decomposed granitic gravels.

2Ab   Lower buried A-horizon midden zone composed of a very dark gray (10YR 3/1) loose sandy loam with abundant decomposed granitic gravels. It appears to be an earlier surface associated with Feature1.

2Cr   Yellowish brown (10YR 5/4) buried C-horizon composed of decomposed granite gravels lacking midden soils. This stratum has been reworked by rodents, creating the undulating contact with the 2Ab horizon.

3R   Granitic Bedrock.

FIGURE 6.25. South wall profile at 26CK6080/6081, Locus 2.

TABLE 6.31. Pottery from 26CK6080/6081, Locus 2.

	All Units[a] 0–30 cm	Feature 2[b] 30–60 cm	Lower Midden[c] 30–90 cm	Total	Surface Items
Brown Ware	108	7	3	118	14
Paddle/Anvil	411	25	5	441	30
Logandale	13	2	—	15	1
Shivwits	3	—	—	3	—
Moapa	33	9	1	43	11
Tusayan	124	23	6	153	10
Total	692	66	15	773	66
Unidentifiable Fragments	168	8	4	180	4

[a] Includes Feature 3.
[b] Includes units S4/W6 and S3/W6.
[c] Includes units S3/W5 and S3/W3 and Feature 1.

assemblage is AD 650 to 1200, which makes it older than the upper midden zone and younger than Feature 1 and the lower midden zone.

Finally, only a handful of sherds (1.6 percent of the total assemblage) were found in the lower midden/ Feature 1 zone, where the radiocarbon dates of cal AD 340 and 40 cal BC were obtained. These artifacts are intrusive, and their low number indicates a relatively high degree of depositional integrity.

Projectile Points
The vast majority (70 percent) of the projectile points from the upper midden zone fall into the Desert series

(Desert Side-notched and Cottonwood), which is consistent with all the previous findings (Table 6.32). A limited amount of stratigraphic mixing is also suggested, as the upper 30 cm includes a few Rosegate and Elko points and one Pinto. The Rosegate points presumably relate to the Puebloan occupation associated with Feature 2, while the Elko points would correspond to the radiocarbon dates obtained from the lower midden. The Pinto point does not link up with any component identified in the deposit.

Feature 2 and the stratigraphically inferior lower midden sustained some downward mixing, indicated by a few Desert series points (Table 6.32).

TABLE 6.32. Projectile Points from 26CK6080/6081, Locus 2.

	All Units[a] 0–30 cm	Feature 2[b] 30–60 cm	Lower Midden[c] 30–90 cm	Total	Surface Items
Desert Series	14	2	1	17	1
Rosegate	3	—	—	3	—
Elko	2	—	1	3	3
Pinto	1	—	—	1	—
Total	20	2	2	24	4
Arrow-Sized	4	—	—	4	1
Dart-Sized	4	—	—	4	—
Indeterminate	1	—	—	1	—

[a] Includes Feature 3.
[b] Includes S4/W6 and S3/W6.
[c] Includes units S3/W5 and S3/W3 and Feature 1.

Obsidian Hydration Data

Source-specific obsidian hydration data were obtained from two Desert series points, one Elko point, and debitage samples selected across the stratigraphic profile in units S3/W5 and S3/W3 (Table 6.33). Multiple obsidian sources are represented, the most common being Partridge Creek and Modena/Panaca Summit, followed by Unknown Variety 1, Black Tank, and Wild Horse Canyon. Most of the obsidian comes from the upper 30 cm of the deposit and displayed narrow bands regardless of source. The mean for each ranges from 1.8 to 2.4 microns, and when combined, they produce an overall mean of 2.1 microns. These are the lowest hydration values found in the study area and match up well with the 2.0 and 2.4 micron values for the two Desert series points at the site.

Hydration rim readings values obtained from the lower midden are problematic, probably due to a small sample size. Only three specimens (minus a 2.0 micron reading) make up the assemblage, and they range between 2.9 and 6.8 microns, producing a mean of 5.0 microns. Although wider than readings from the upper midden, they don't form a strong cluster that can be paired with the two radiocarbon dates from the lower midden. More than anything, it may suggest that obsidian was not routinely used at the site during the earliest occupation. An additional problem with the obsidian hydration sample is a 2.8-micron value obtained from an Elko point collected from the surface, which is much too thin for this point series.

Component Definition

Despite limited evidence of stratigraphic mixing, three relatively intact component areas are defined at the site (Table 6.34). The youngest is a Late Prehistoric period

TABLE 6.33. Source-Specific Obsidian Hydration Data from Units S3/W5 and S3/W3 at 26CK6080/6081, Locus 2.

Source	Readings (microns)	Mean	Standard Deviation
Partridge Creek			
0–30	2.0,[a] 2.0, 2.0, 2.1, 2.1, 2.2	2.1	0.1
40–70	(2.0), 2.9, 5.3	4.1	1.7
Modena/Panaca Summit			
0–30	1.0, 1.6, 2.4, 2.8, 2.9, (6.4)	2.1	0.8
50–60	6.8	6.8	—
Unknown Variety 1			
0–30	1.4, 1.4, 2.1, 2.2	1.8	0.4
Other			
0–30	2.4,[a] 2.5	1.4	0.1
All Sources			
0–30	n = 17	2.1	0.5
40–70	n = 3	5.0	2.0

Note: One Elko point from the surface yielded a value of 2.8 microns on Modena/Panaca obsidian. Values in parentheses are considered outliers and excluded from mean calculations.
[a] From a Desert series point.

occupation corresponding to the top 30 cm of the deposit in all excavation units, including Feature 3. This designation is supported by the cal AD 1650 radiocarbon date and the dominant presence of brown ware and paddle and anvil pottery, Desert series projectile points, glass and shell beads, and obsidian hydration readings of less than 2.6 microns.

A Puebloan occupation is present from 30 to 60 cm in units S4/W6 and S3/W6 and is largely associated with Feature 2. It is not as clean as the Late Prehistoric component, as it contains a 50-50 mixture of Puebloan

(Tusayan, Moapa, Logandale) and the later-dating brown ware and paddle and anvil pottery.

The earliest occupation is the lower Basketmaker II component found below 30 cm in units S3/W5 and S3/W3, which includes Feature 1. It is supported by the two radiocarbon dates of cal AD 340 and 40 cal BC, the near absence of pottery, a few relatively thick hydration readings, and a single Elko point. All surface material from the locus is placed into an undated, residual category.

Artifact Inventory

Most of the material recovered from the deposit is in the Late Prehistoric component (Table 6.35), and that rich assemblage appears to represent residential use. Although the artifacts recovered from the underlying Puebloan and Basketmaker II components are much lower in number, they too show multiple classes of tools, reflecting a relatively wide range of activities.

Late Prehistoric Findings

The Late Prehistoric component is dominated by sherds, with fewer flaked stone tools, ground and battered stone items, bone implements, glass and shell beads, and other non-utilitarian items such as ochre, ochre palettes, and a quartz crystal.

Pottery

We have already noted that most of the pottery is paddle and anvil or brown ware sherds. Given that the site is located well within ethnographic Southern Paiute territory, it is somewhat surprising to see paddle and anvil sherds (n = 411) at frequencies almost four times greater than brown ware sherds (n = 108). The former are usually associated with Yuman-speakers living south of the Colorado River, in this case the Hualapai, and most ethnographies do not mention them crossing the river and using these lands for subsistence purposes (e.g., Kelly and Fowler 1986; McGuire 1983). It should be noted, however, that none of the paddle and anvil pottery is painted, which could mean that much of it predates AD 1500, when the painted styles became popular. If that is the case, this Late Prehistoric component could reflect an ethnic replacement roughly dating to this period of time.

Flaked Stone Tools and Debitage

Bifaces (47.7 percent) dominate the Late Prehistoric flaked stone assemblage (Table 6.35), followed by lesser frequencies of flake tools (22.7 percent) and projectile points (22.0 percent), and relatively low numbers of cores (4.5 percent), form flaked tools (1.5 percent), and drills (1.5 percent). Most of the bifaces are late-stage

TABLE 6.34. Single-Component Areas at 26CK6080/6081, Locus 2.

	Basketmaker II[a]	Pueblo I/II[b]	Late Prehistoric[c]
S4/W6	—	30–60 cm	0–30 cm
S3/W6	—	30–40 cm	0–30 cm
S3/W5	30–80 cm	—	0–30 cm
S3/W3	30–90 cm	—	0–30 cm
S2/W4	—	—	0–20 cm

[a] Includes Feature 1. All surface material is placed in an undated, residual category.
[b] Includes Feature 2.
[c] Includes Feature 3.

forms (Stage 5 at 46.2 percent; Stage 4 at 21.2 percent), with Stage 3 specimens (28.8 percent) accounting for almost all the others (Table 6.36). This profile, combined with the relatively high frequency of projectile points, indicates that most bifaces arrived on site already thinned or in finished or near-finished condition.

Both drills in the late component are finely made, exhibiting a high degree of pressure flaking around their margins. One is the distal end of a long, slender bit with polish and rounding along its working end. The other is a complete tool with flared shoulders, a contracting stem, and a short bit, also worn along its distal end.

The reduction pattern reflected in the bifaces, projectile points, and drills is matched by the technological profile of the debitage (Table 6.37). Most of the diagnostic chert debitage is pressure flakes (61.5 percent), followed by lesser frequencies of late-stage (14.0 percent) and early-stage biface thinning flakes (12.1 percent), then cortical debris (9.1 percent) and interior flakes (3.2 percent). Obsidian shows a more pronounced version of this pattern, with a dominant presence of pressure flakes (79.1 percent), low frequencies of biface thinning flakes (11.7 percent) and interior flakes (9.3 percent), and no cortical debris at all.

The small sample of quartz and quartzite debitage reflects reduction of local cobbles (Table 6.37), as cortical flakes are common (13.3 percent and 50.0 percent), and interior and early-stage biface thinning debris combine for 33.3 percent and 25.0 percent of the respective assemblages. Some fine-grain material tool finishing is also evident, as a few pressure flakes are present.

Most of the flake tools and formed flake tools are made from early-stage flakes (Table 6.38), indicating that these relatively rare pieces of debitage were purposefully selected for tool use. These include cortical (14.3 percent), interior (38.1 percent), and early-stage biface thinning flakes (28.6 percent); late-stage biface thinning flakes (19.0 percent) were also used. Though informal, these tools show a great deal of use wear

TABLE 6.35. Assemblage by Temporal Component at 26CK6080/6081, Locus 2.

	Basketmaker II	Pueblo I/II	Late Prehistoric	Residual Undated	Total
Flaked Stone					
Projectile Point	2	2	29	4	37
Drill	—	—	2	—	2
Biface	9	11	63	8	91
Formed Flake Tool	—	—	2	1	3
Flake Tool	—	3	30	1	34
Core	—	2	6	—	8
Debitage	738	754	5,708	—	7,200
Ground & Battered Stone					
Battered Cobble	—	1	1	—	2
Handstone	1	1	1	—	3
Millingstone	2	—	2	1	5
Other					
Pottery	19	74	860	70	1,023
Glass Bead	—	1	5	—	6
Shell Bead	—	—	2	—	2
Modified Bone	1	1	8	—	10
Obsidian Needle	1	—	—	—	1
Ochre	1	—	2	—	3
Ochre Palette	—	—	2	—	2
Quartz Crystal	—	—	1	—	1
Misc. Stone	—	—	3	—	3
Total	774	850	6,727	85	8,436

TABLE 6.36. Biface Stages by Period from 26CK6080/6081, Locus 2.

	Basketmaker II	Pueblo I/II	Late Prehistoric	Total
Stage 1	—	1	—	1
Stage 2	—	—	2	2
Stage 3	3	1	15	19
Stage 4	2	6	11	19
Stage 5	4	2	24	30
Indeterminate	—	1	11	12
Total	9	11	63	83

(Table 6.38). A large number exhibit only microchipping (34.4 percent), but the majority (65.6 percent) have multiple forms of wear, including microchipping and more heavy-duty damage like edge flaking and stepping/crushing.

The small sample of cores shows little evidence of a formalized reduction system, probably due to the large number of thinned bifaces brought to the site. Although the Late Prehistoric core assemblage includes only six items, at least three blank forms are represented: tabular cobble, flake, and chunk (Table 6.39). Most of these are bifacially or multidirectionally flaked, but one unidirec-tional form is also present. The cores are quite small, clustering around a mean length of 5.3 cm.

Ground and Battered Stone
Only four tools in this class were recovered from the Late Prehistoric component—two millingstone fragments, one handstone, and one battered cobble. Both millingstones are small fragments (less than 6.0 cm long) and exhibit flat smooth polish on a single surface. The handstone is a margin fragment with unifacial polish on a flat, worn surface; it also has some pecking around its margin. The battered cobble is a small, thin,

TABLE 6.37. Technological Analysis of Debitage by Period from 26CK6080/6081, Locus 2.

	Basketmaker II								Pueblo I/II						Late Prehistoric							
	Chert		OBS		QTZT		Quartz		Chert		OBS		Quartz		Chert		OBS		QTZT		Quartz	
	#	%	#	%	#	%	#	%	#	%	#	%	#	%	#	%	#	%	#	%	#	%
Core Reduction																						
Percussion Decortication	27	8.8	—	—	1	100.0	1	14.3	21	5.5	—	—	1	11.1	45	9.1	—	—	2	50.0	2	13.3
Percussion Interior	8	2.6	—	—	—	—	2	28.6	9	2.3	—	—	1	11.1	16	3.2	4	9.3	—	—	3	20.0
Biface Reduction																						
Early Biface Thinning	51	16.6	—	—	—	—	1	14.3	57	14.8	—	—	2	22.2	60	12.1	3	7.0	1	25.0	2	13.3
Late Biface Thinning	53	17.2	1	12.5	—	—	—	—	45	11.7	2	28.6	—	—	69	14.0	2	4.7	—	—	1	6.7
Pressure	169	54.9	7	87.5	—	—	3	42.9	253	65.7	5	71.4	5	55.6	304	61.5	34	79.1	1	25.0	7	46.7
Diagnostic Total	308	100.0	8	100.0	1	100.0	7	100.0	385	100.0	7	100.0	9	100.0	494	100.0	43	100.0	4	100.0	15	100.0
Platform Prep./Pressure	69	—	—	—	—	—	4	—	82	—	—	—	—	—	58	—	6	—	—	—	1	—
Indeterminate Percussion	113	—	—	—	1	—	13	—	97	—	1	—	6	—	177	—	—	—	4	—	23	—
Indeterminate Fragment	190	—	1	—	—	—	17	—	143	—	1	—	19	—	164	—	7	—	—	—	32	—
Shatter	2	—	—	—	—	—	3	—	4	—	—	—	3	—	4	—	—	—	—	—	2	—
Sample Total	682	—	9	—	2	—	44	—	711	—	9	—	37	—	897	—	56	—	8	—	73	—

Note: OBS = obsidian; QTZT = quartzite; % = analytical percentage. All debitage was analyzed from the Basketmaker II and Pueblo I/II components. Analysis of the Late Prehistoric chert debitage was restricted to S3/W5, 0–30 cm; all other Late Prehistoric material types were fully analyzed.

TABLE 6.38. Simple and Formed Flake Tools by Period from 26CK6080/6081, Locus 2.

	Basketmaker II	Pueblo I/II	Late Prehistoric	Total
Flake Blank				
Cortical	—	—	3	3
Interior	—	—	8	8
Early Thinning	—	—	6	6
Late Thinning	—	—	4	4
Indeterminate	—	3	11	14
Total	—	3	32	35
Wear				
Rounding/Polishing; Edge Flaking	—	—	1	1
Stepping/Crushing; Microchipping	—	2	12	14
Stepping/Crushing; Edge Flaking	—	1	7	8
Microchipping	—	—	11	11
Microchipping; Edge Flaking	—	—	1	1
Total	—	3	32	35

TABLE 6.39. Core Attributes by Period from 26CK6080/6081, Locus 2.

	Basketmaker II	Pueblo I/II	Late Prehistoric	Total
Blank				
Tabular Cobble	—	—	1	1
Split Cobble	—	1	—	1
Flake	—	1	3	4
Chunk	—	—	1	1
Indeterminate	—	—	1	1
Total	—	2	6	8
Morphology				
Unidirectional/Unifacial	—	—	1	1
Bifacial	—	—	3	3
Multidirectional	—	1	2	3
Tested Cobble	—	1	—	1
Total	—	2	6	8

water-worn stone with light pecking at both ends, and could have been used as a hammerstone to reduce flaked stone material.

Modified Bone
All eight bone artifacts from the Late component—two tube beads, four probable awls, and two indeterminate pieces—are quite fragmentary. Both tube beads, probably made from rabbit long bones, show polish, striations, and evidence of burning. They also appear to have been cut or scored to facilitate breakage in a predictable location. Given that they are margin/end fragments and the scoring is still visible (and no end grinding is present), it seems likely that they broke during manufacture.

All four awls are small margin fragments showing polish and striations; three also have evidence of burn-ing. They are made from deer-sized long bones and represent only a small fraction of the original tool.

Other Artifacts
The other artifacts are two ochre palettes, two pieces of ochre, a single quartz crystal, and three modified stones. One of the palettes is a disk-shaped sherd (5.0 × 4.0 cm) with grinding along its entire margin. A small amount of orange ochre stains the concave surface of the piece. The second palette is made from a chert interior flake (3.4 × 2.5 cm). Its ventral surface is almost completely covered with bright red ochre. Both of the ochre chunks have maximum lengths of about 3.0 cm and are of the orange variety.

The quartz crystal is quite milky in color and is one elongate, five-sided piece (4.7 × 1.2 cm) fused with three other crystalline structures covered with cortex. It is not an impressive piece, but there is some evidence of battering on one of its ends. Two of the modified stones are flat pieces with edge flaking and grinding; they could have been used as palettes but show no pigment (perhaps they are blanks?). The other specimen is a small elongate tabular piece of stone (4.8 × 1.3 × 0.5 cm) that has been edge ground. It is difficult to know its function, but it may have been a gaming piece or some other non-utilitarian object.

Puebloan Findings

The assemblage from the Puebloan component is relatively small and is dominated by sherds, followed by flaked stone tools, and only a few examples of other artifact classes (Table 6.35). As discussed above, some Late Prehistoric artifacts appear to have trickled down into this component.

Pottery

The total sample of Puebloan sherds from excavation (i.e., irrespective of component) includes a dominant presence of Tusayan (69.1 percent), with Moapa (22.9 percent), Logandale (6.8 percent), and Shivwits (1.3 percent) also represented (Table 6.31). Tusayan pottery is made throughout Virgin Puebloan territory, while Logandale is thought to originate from the Virgin/Muddy River lowlands. Moapa and Shivwits, in contrast, show interactions with areas to the east on the Uinkaret Plateau. Only six of these are corrugated (all Tusayan), and such a low proportion may indicate use of the site at the early end of the Puebloan sequence (i.e., Pueblo I and II), as corrugated pottery tends to postdate AD 1050.

Flaked Stone Tools and Debitage

Bifaces dominate the flaked stone assemblage (61.7 percent), followed by much lower frequencies of flake tools (16.7 percent), projectile points (11.1 percent), and cores (11.1 percent). Most of the bifaces are in finished or near-finished condition (Stage 4 at 60.0 percent; Stage 5 at 20.0 percent), while single examples of Stage 1 and Stage 3 items are also present (Table 6.36). The three flake tools are small, indeterminate fragments that show a combination of stepping/crushing, microchipping, and edge flaking (Table 6.38). The two cores are made from a split cobble and flake, with the cobble showing minimal assaying and the flake showing multidirectional flake removals (Table 6.39).

Both the chert and obsidian debitage samples produced high frequencies of pressure flakes (65.7 percent and 71.4 percent), followed by late-stage biface thinning debris (11.7 percent and 28.6 percent). This indicates that most reduction activity was focused on tool finishing (Table 6.37). The small sample of quartz debitage is made up of diverse flake types that reflect the reduction of locally occurring cobbles into finished items.

Ground and Battered Stone

Of the two pieces in this artifact class, the one handstone from the Puebloan component is a margin fragment with smooth polish on a single flat surface. The other is a battered cobble showing extensive pecking, grinding, and flake removals along 50 percent of its margins. This tool was obviously used for a variety of heavy-duty pounding and grinding tasks.

Bone Tool

The one modified bone tool is a blunt, rounded end of a thin indeterminate tool (13.1 mm wide and 3.7 mm thick). It is highly ground and polished and could represent anything from a strigil to a gaming piece. Due to its fragmented condition (only 25.3 mm long), it is impossible to determine its original morphology or function.

Basketmaker II Findings

The Basketmaker II assemblage is quite small, limited to nine bifaces, two projectile points, one handstone, two millingstone fragments, a handful of intrusive sherds, one bone implement, an obsidian needle, and one small piece of ochre (Table 6.35).

Bifaces include a relatively high frequency of Stage 5 forms (44.4 percent), followed by Stage 3 (33.3 percent) and Stage 4 (22.2 percent) specimens (Table 6.36). Nearly all debitage is chert, and it reflects a wider range of stone-working activities than in the overlying components (Table 6.37). Although pressure flakes (54.9 percent) and late-stage thinning debris (17.2 percent) are still present in high frequencies, early-stage thinning (16.6 percent), interior flakes (2.6 percent), and cortical debris (8.8 percent) are more numerous than elsewhere. This indicates that people arrived at the site with a greater amount of unprocessed stone and conducted more comprehensive flaked stone reduction activities.

The single handstone is a complete bifacial specimen with smooth polish on both sides, shaped through pecking and grinding along its margins. Both millingstones are unifacial margin fragments with smooth polish, one on a slightly concave surface and the other on a flat working surface. The 19 sherds, which represent only 2.0 percent of the site total, show a similar mix of the types found in the upper component.

The piece of modified bone is a small indeterminate fragment with polish, striations, and evidence of

TABLE 6.40. Charred Plant Remains from 26CK6080/6081, Locus 2.

	Basketmaker II		Pueblo I/II		Late Prehistoric	
	S3/W3 (F1)	S3/W5	S4/W6 (F2)	S4/W6 (F2)	S3/W5	S2/W4 (F3)
	35–45 cm	66–80 cm	30–40 cm	40–55 cm	5–15 cm	5–10 cm
Charred Nutshell						
Pinyon (*Pinus edulis/monophylla*)	1	4	7	34	22	16
Charred Seed						
Goosefoot (*Chenopodium* sp.)	—	9	90	144	28	27
Tansy Mustard (*Descurainia* sp.)	—	—	4	—	—	—
Prickly Pear (*Opuntia* sp.)	1	—	—	—	—	—
Sunflower Family (Asteraceae)	—	—	—	4	—	—
Bean Family (Fabaceae)	—	—	—	—	—	—
Grass Family (Poaceae)	—	—	—	—	8	—
Unidentified Seeds/Fragments	—	—	3	11	2	19
Charred Berry Pits						
Manzanita (*Arctostaphylos* sp.)	—	—	3	—	—	—
Juniper (*Juniperus* sp.)	—	—	2	4	1	—
Charred Cone Scales						
Pinyon (*Pinus edulis/monophylla*)	—	—	13	6	2	—
Sample Volume (liters)	3.5	3.5	7.0	8.0	6.0	1.6

burning. The ochre piece is also quite small and bright red in color. Finally, the obsidian needle is a long sliver (24.6 × 3.7 × 3.4 mm), triangular in cross section. It is of Partridge Creek glass and appears to be a "tinkler" or natural sliver, given the silvery patina covering most of its surface. The patina is worn from the ends, and a hydration sample cut from one of them yielded a value of 2.9 microns, which suggests that it, like the sherds, is intrusive.

Floral and Faunal Remains

A relatively small but informative assemblage of subsistence remains was recovered from the site, including charred seeds, nuts, other plant parts, and vertebrate faunal remains.

Charred Plant Remains

Two flotation samples were obtained from each of the three components at the site (Table 6.40), amounting to 29.6 liters of sediment. Charred plant remains are quite sparse in the Basketmaker II component, limited to a handful of goosefoot and pinyon remains that may have trickled down from above. The Puebloan assemblage lacks evidence of domesticated taxa but shows a dominant presence of goosefoot (76.5 percent) and lower frequencies of pinyon (13.4 percent), other small seeds and fragments (7.2 percent), and berry pits (2.9 per-

cent), the last including juniper and manzanita. The combined Late Prehistoric period samples have a more even mix of goosefoot (44.4 percent), pinyon nutshell (30.6 percent), and undifferentiated grasses and other unknown seeds/fragments (24.2 percent), and only a single juniper pit (0.8 percent).

The presence of goosefoot and pinyon at the site may indicate that it was used during multiple seasons, as the former ripens during the late spring and summer and the latter in the fall. Alternatively, the goosefoot could have been harvested elsewhere and transported up to this pinyon zone to supplement the diet during the fall harvest. Chenopod, a known disturbance follower, was cultivated by ancestral Puebloan farmers in lowland settings (Adams and Fish 2006; Lyneis 1995). But if it were actually brought here from the adjacent lowlands (e.g., the Lost City fields), it seems likely that at least some sign of other domesticates (e.g., corn, beans, squash) would also be present.

Faunal Remains

The faunal remains indicate focus on bighorn sheep, undifferentiated artiodactyls, jackrabbits, cottontails, undifferentiated lagomorphs, and tortoise, as well as small fragments that can only be categorized as medium-to-large mammal (roughly sheep-sized) and small-to-medium mammal (roughly rabbit-sized; Table 6.41).

TABLE 6.41. Faunal Remains from 26CK6080/6081, Locus 2.

	Basketmaker II	Pueblo I/II	Late Prehistoric	Total
Bighorn Sheep	1	—	12	13
Artiodactyl	8	3 (2)	21 (44)	32 (46)
Cottontail	3	12	93	108
Lagomorphs	2	7	7	16
Tortoise	6	25	300	331
Medium-to-Large (Sheep-Sized)	77	115	1,167	1,359
Small-to-Medium (Rabbit-Sized)	22	29	249	300
Intrusive Rodents	—	—	55	55
Lizards	—	—	4	4
Birds	—	—	2	2
Carnivores	—	—	1	1
Unidentifiable	19	50	544	613
Total	138	241	2,455	2,834

Note: Numbers in parentheses represent small tooth enamel fragments not included in the analysis.

We rely much less on unidentifiable fragments, intrusive rodents, lizards, and other minimally represented taxa due to their lower interpretive value. It is also important to note that multiple artiodactyl tooth enamel fragments within a single catalog entry are given a frequency value of only 1 because these fragile elements usually exfoliate during excavation and transport to the lab. The uncounted enamel fragments are listed in parentheses in Table 6.41.

Several interesting trends are exhibited by these data. First, the relative frequency of tortoise increases over time, beginning at 30.0 percent in the Basketmaker II component, rising to 53.2 percent in the Puebloan component, and reaching a high of 69.3 percent in the Late Prehistoric deposits (Table 6.41). Bighorn sheep/artiodactyl follow a contrasting trend, reaching maximum relative frequencies in Basketmaker II times (45.0 percent) and dropping thereafter (Puebloan at 6.4 percent; Late Prehistoric at 7.6 percent). Rabbit frequencies begin at 25.0 percent in Basketmaker II, increase to 40.4 percent in the Puebloan deposit, and drop back down to 23.1 percent in the Late component.

The relative frequency of medium-to-large mammal versus small-to-medium mammal remains rather constant through time, with the former making up 77.8 percent of the Basketmaker II assemblage, 79.9 percent of the Puebloan, and 82.4 percent of the Late sample (Table 6.41). This contrasts with changes exhibited by the identifiable fraction of the assemblage, in which the relative abundance of large game declines over time. When the ratio of bighorn sheep/artiodactyl to medium-to-large mammal is calculated, however, it appears that the bone was processed much more extensively later in time (Basketmaker II—1:8.6; Puebloan—1:38.3; Late—1:35.4), creating the higher than expected counts of the medium-to-large mammal fragments.

Summary

Three periods of occupation are represented by the excavation findings at 26CK6080/6081. The earliest, the Basketmaker II occupation, corresponds to two radiocarbon dates of 40 cal BC and cal AD 340, a few relatively thick obsidian hydration readings (greater than 5.0 microns), and a single Elko series projectile point. This component includes a large rock-lined hearth/oven (Feature 1) associated with a small artifact assemblage composed of a limited number of biface and projectile point fragments, three pieces of milling gear, a bone tool, and a few other items.

Despite the presence of the hearth/oven feature, charred plant remains are nearly absent, limited to a few goosefoot seeds and pinyon nutshells. Faunal remains are slightly more abundant and reflect the hunting of multiple prey species, but with an emphasis on taking large game. These findings indicate that the site was used as a short-term, multiactivity occupation area during the Basketmaker II interval.

The Puebloan component also appears to represent a short-term, multiactivity occupation. It is largely associated with Feature 2 (a small rock-lined hearth) and has a high frequency of pottery, the most important being a Sosi black-on-white bowl fragment found in the middle of the hearth. As with the Basketmaker II component, however, some Late Prehistoric period artifacts (largely sherds) intrude into the deposit. The artifact assemblage includes a relatively diversified range of flaked stone tools (e.g., projectile points, bifaces, flake tools, cores), accompanied by one battered cobble, a handstone, and a single bone tool. Charred plant remains show no evidence of domesticated taxa. Instead, they are dominated by goosefoot seed and pinyon nutshell. Faunal remains reveal near-equal frequencies of tortoise and rabbit and much lower amounts of large game.

A more intensive occupation is reflected by the Late Prehistoric component, judging by the higher density and diversity of material recovered from this portion of the deposit. It corresponds to a cal AD 1650 radiocarbon date, glass and shell beads, a dominant presence of brown ware and paddle and anvil pottery, Desert series projectile points, and obsidian hydration readings of less than 2.6 microns. Flaked stone artifacts are abundant and include projectile points, drills, bifaces, flake tools, and cores, while ground and battered stone tools are also present but in reduced numbers. Bone tools are present, as are non-utilitarian items such as ochre, ochre-stained palettes, and a quartz crystal.

Charred plant remains from the Late Prehistoric component lack domesticated taxa and are dominated by goosefoot, pinyon, and much lower frequencies of a few other foods. Tortoise becomes a primary prey, followed by progressively smaller amounts of rabbits and large game. Both the plant and animal remains probably reflect an intensive use of the landscape, which is totally consistent with the diversified nature of the artifact assemblage.

A final issue involves the ethnicity of the Late Prehistoric period occupation. Most researchers would expect the occupation to be associated with the Southern Paiute, given that the site lies in their ethnographic territory. However, the high frequency of paddle and anvil pottery shows an unexpected connection to Patayan peoples living along the Colorado River (perhaps the Hualapai, who are today most proximal to the study area). These findings indicate that Cedar Basin, and its rich pinyon resources, was used by both the Hualapai and Southern Paiute late in time.

26CK7994 Site Report

Site 26CK7994 is a rock shelter located in a reddish yellowish sandstone formation that faces east toward an open valley. The drip line covers an area about 30 × 8 m and provides outstanding head room (more than 50 percent of the shelter is greater than 2 m high). Midden fills most of this area, and fire-affected limestone erodes out of the midden along the drip line. Tools and debitage are

TABLE 6.42. Excavation Summary for 26CK7994.

Unit	Size (m)	Depth (cm)	Volume (m³)
N7/W25	1 × 2.0	90	1.8
N14/W28.5	1 × 2.0	60	0.9 [a]
Feature 1	1 × 0.7	30	0.2
Total			2.9

[a] Shallow bedrock in the excavation exposure accounts for the low number of cubic meters.

also scattered along the drip line and on a lower terrace below the shelter (Figure 6.26).

Field Methods

We began the field effort by establishing a grid across the site and pin flagging all cultural material observed. Due to the relatively low density of material at the site, all tools and debitage were collected except for heavy milling gear, which was analyzed at the site and left in place. Tools were point provenienced, and debitage was collected according to a series of more generalized spatial units (i.e., midden versus lower terrace).

Excavation focused on three locations: one feature and two midden areas (Table 6.42). Feature 1 appeared to be a cist, due to the presence of a rectangular configuration of stones set on end. It was excavated in its entirety without a formal unit designation, and multiple flotation samples were collected from its fill. Two units were used to sample the midden, both 1 × 2 m in size. The first (N14/W28.5) was placed next to Feature 1 to provide a comparative context for interpreting the stratigraphic character of the cist. The other, unit N7/W25, was placed where the midden appeared to reach its maximum depth, as it seemed to be mounded up near a declivity in the shelter. Flotation samples were also collected from the intact, buried midden deposits in these units.

Site Structure and Chronology

The two excavation units exposed a similar profile, as shown in Figures 6.27 and 6.28. The N7/W25 profile is described as an example. It begins with a shallow (less than 10 cm) A-horizon of sterile, yellowish red (5YR 5/6) sand eroded from the roof of the shelter. These sterile sediments intermix with a buried midden to a depth ranging from 20 to 30 cm (2Ab1). The mixing is largely due to cattle tromping, as well as some rodent and tortoise activity.

An intact midden (2Ab2) is located below the mixed zone. It consists of a charcoal-rich, dark reddish gray (5YR 4/2), fine soft sand that contains a relatively dense accumulation of flaked stone tools, debitage, and a small

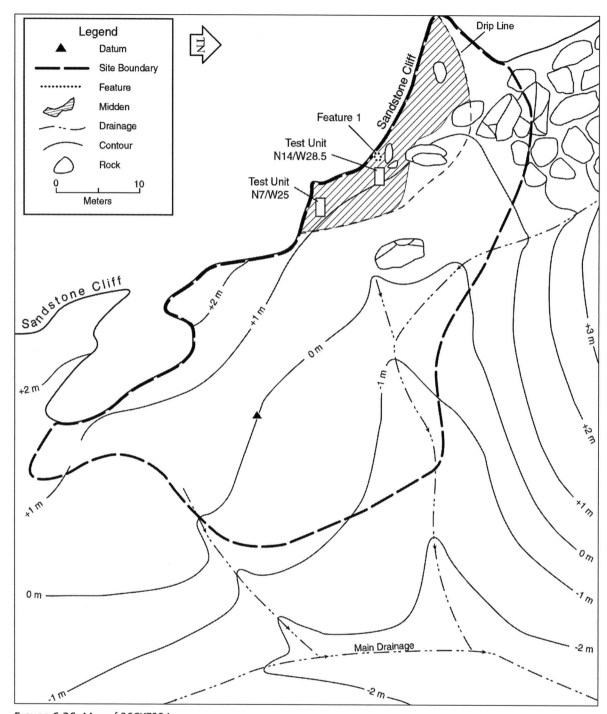

FIGURE 6.26. Map of 26CK7994.

amount of bone. The midden is rather homogeneous and truncates on bedrock at 90 cm in N7/W25 and at shallower depths in N14/W28.5.

Feature 1

Feature 1 is a stone-lined cist measuring 100 × 70 cm (Figures 6.29 and 6.30). It is located up against the back wall of the rock shelter at about N13.2/W32 (southwest corner). Because we excavated the entire feature con-

tents, no formal unit was established. The first phase of excavation began with the removal and screening of loose overburden containing modern plant material, cow droppings, and loose rocks, some of which may have been originally associated with the feature. The overburden included a battered cobble and some debitage; some knotted yucca fiber (prehistoric) and modern tortoise carapace were observed and collected from loose overburden northwest of the feature.

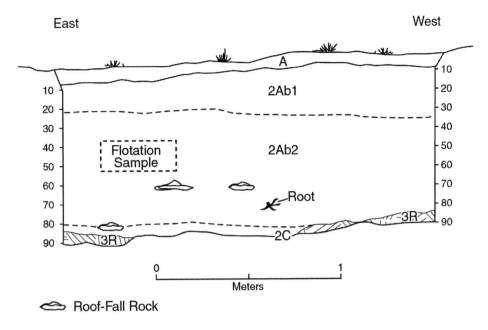

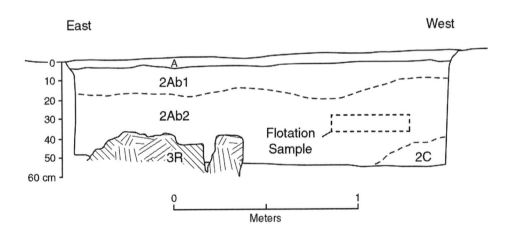

A   5YR 5/6 yellowish red, fine sand weathered from the roof.

2Ab1   Mixed surface sand/midden reworked by cattle tromping and rodent and reptile activity.

2Ab2   5YR 4/2 dark reddish gray midden deposit of fine soft sand.

2C   5YR 7/6 to 6/6 reddish yellow decomposed bedrock, slightly hard.

3R   5YR 7/6 reddish yellow bedrock.

FIGURE 6.27. South wall profile of N7/W25 at 26CK7994.

A   5YR 5/6 yellowish red, fine sand weathered from the roof.

2Ab1   Mixed surface sand/midden reworked by cattle tromping and rodent and reptile activity.

2Ab2   5YR 4/2 dark reddish gray midden deposit of fine soft sand.

2C   5YR 7/6 to 6/6 reddish yellow decomposed bedrock, slightly hard.

3R   5YR 7/6 reddish yellow bedrock.

FIGURE 6.28. South wall profile of N14/W28.5 at 26CK7994.

FIGURE 6.29. Feature 1, unit (*foreground*) and stone-lined cist (*background*), at 26CK7994.

TABLE 6.43. Radiocarbon Dates from 26CK7994.

Feature/Unit	Depth (cm)	Calibrated Intercept[a]	Conventional Age	Material
N14/W28.5	35–50	cal AD 580 (cal BP 1370)	1490 ± 40 BP	Charcoal
Feature 1	10–20	cal AD 130 (cal BP 1820)	1860 ± 50 BP	Yucca Fiber

[a] See Table 5.1.

Once the overburden was removed, a better view of the feature was exposed. It consisted of a rectangular configuration of slabs placed on end, filled with midden soils. Part of the fill was collected for flotation analysis, and the remainder was screened. This effort produced more modern tortoise shell, burnt bone, debitage, charcoal, and some matted yucca fiber. The floor of the feature was encountered at about 20 cm, where a few flat stones lined the bottom. The remaining fill at the bottom contained additional yucca fiber bundles.

During the exposure of the feature, more yucca fiber was found along the northwest margin. Judging from the condition and distribution of the tortoise shell, it appears that the animal dug into the cist, displaced some of the yucca fiber, and died in its burrow. It appears to have damaged the northwest corner of the feature, undercutting the two large rocks illustrated in Figure 6.30,

dragging overburden into the cist, and sending feature material out into the overburden.

Radiocarbon Dates

Two radiocarbon dates were obtained from the site (Table 6.43). The first was on a piece of yucca fiber from the bottom of Feature 1. It yielded a date of cal AD 130, which corresponds to a Basketmaker II (350 BC–AD 400) use of the site. The second date comes from 35 to 50 cm below surface in nearby unit N14/W28.5, and produced a younger date of AD 580, which falls into the Basketmaker III period (AD 400–800). Although it seems strange that the near-surface Feature 1 cist is older than the deposits in the adjacent excavation unit, it is important to note that the cist sits at the rear of the shelter where the basement rock meets the overhang, and little deposit has built up over time.

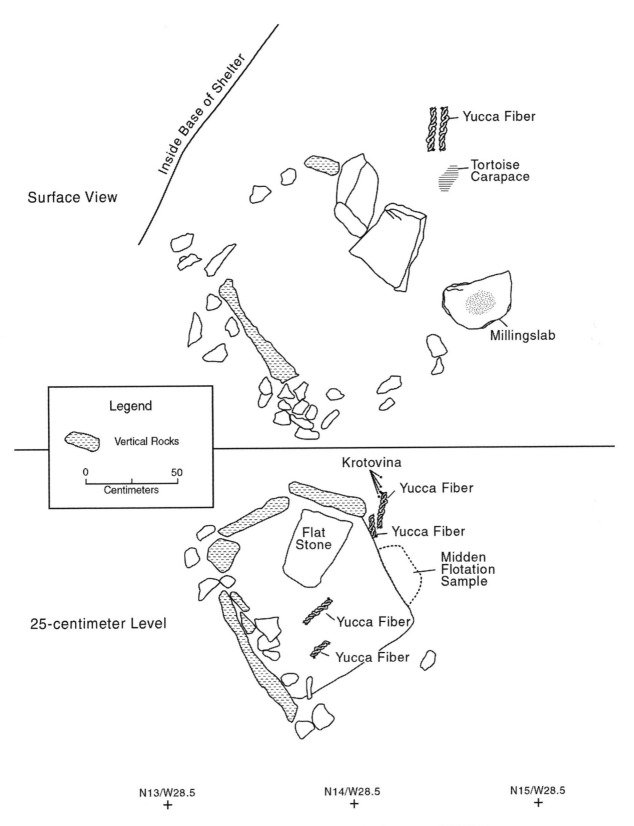

Surface View

Inside Base of Shelter

Yucca Fiber

Tortoise Carapace

Millingslab

Legend

Vertical Rocks

0   50
Centimeters

Krotovina

Yucca Fiber

Flat Stone

Yucca Fiber

Midden Flotation Sample

25-centimeter Level

Yucca Fiber

Yucca Fiber

N13/W28.5
+

N14/W28.5
+

N15/W28.5
+

FIGURE 6.30. Plan view of surface and 25-cm level, Feature 1, 26CK7994.

TABLE 6.44. Source-Specific Obsidian Hydration Data from 26CK7994.

Source	Readings (microns)	Mean	Standard Deviation
N14/W28.5			
Delamar Mountains			
20–30 cm	8.5, 9.9, 10.4	9.6	1.0
30–50 cm	8.0	8.0	—
Modena/Panaca Summit			
20–30 cm	2.4, 2.4, 2.8	2.5	0.2
30–50 cm	(1.7), 5.6, 6.1	5.8	0.4
Kane Springs			
20–30 cm	4.7	4.7	—
N7/W25			
Delamar Mountains			
50–70 cm	7.9, 8.0	8.0	0.1
Kane Springs			
50–70 cm	8.0, 8.0, 9.1	8.4	0.6
70–90 cm	8.1, 11.1	9.6	2.1
Shoshone Mountain			
70–90 cm	9.4	9.4	—
Black Tank			
50–70 cm	11.9	11.9	—

Note: Values in parenthesis are considered outliers and excluded from mean calculations.

TABLE 6.45. Single-Component Areas at 26CK7994.

Unit	Late Archaic	Basketmaker II	Mixed
Feature 1	—	0–30 cm	—
N7/W25	20–90 cm	—	0–20 cm
N14/W28.5	—	—	0–60 cm

Note: All surface materials placed in an undated residual category.

Temporally Diagnostic Artifacts

Pottery is absent from the site, and other temporally diagnostic artifacts are limited to four projectile points and one shell bead.

Projectile Points

One of the projectile points is a Humboldt specimen recovered from the surface of the site. The others, from excavation, are single Cottonwood and Elko points from 20 to 30 cm in N14/W28.5 and a dart-sized fragment from 20 to 30 cm in N7/W2.5. All three of the dart points are in accord with the cal AD 130 radiocarbon date, while the cal AD 580 date conceivably indicates site use when atlatl and dart technology was coming to an end. The Cottonwood series point does not correspond to either radiocarbon date and probably reflects an ephemeral visit to the site after AD 1250.

Shell Bead

The single shell bead recovered from the site is an *Olivella* saucer (G2). It was found on the surface and corresponds to the Middle period along the southern California coast (Bennyhoff and Hughes 1987). Although it is not from the excavations, it probably corresponds to the Basketmaker occupation of the site.

Obsidian Hydration Data

Obsidian hydration data reveal a degree of stratigraphic mixture in N14/W28.5 and a rather intact deposit in N7/W25 (Table 6.44). Unit N14/W28.5 has three hydration clusters at around 9.2, 5.5, and 2.3 microns. These values represent multiple time periods but cannot be separated from one another stratigraphically. The 9.2-micron cluster probably matches up with the Elko point, as obsidian Elko points produced a project-wide mean of 8.8 microns. Cottonwood/Desert Side-notched points yielded a project-wide mean of 2.2 microns, corresponding to the 2.3-micron cluster, while the 5.5-micron cluster comes close to the cal AD 580 radiocarbon date, according to the project-wide hydration rate. Despite these regular correspondences, there is no way of segregating the remaining material from the excavation unit into discrete units of time.

Delamar Mountains/Kane Springs hydration data from N7/W25 form a relatively tight cluster around a mean of 8.6 microns (s.d. = 1.2). The single hydration readings on Shoshone Mountain (9.4 microns) and Black Tank (11.9 microns) glass are slightly thicker, but we don't have a good understanding of the hydration rates associated with these sources. All these samples were collected from below 50 cm to avoid the disturbed portions of the deposit and probably represent a Late Archaic occupation dating to around 1000 cal BC.

Component Definition

Two single-component areas and two chronologically mixed locations are defined at the site (Table 6.45). A Late Archaic component is present between 20 and 90 cm in N7/W25, while the Feature 1 cist corresponds to a Basketmaker II occupation. All the material in N14/W28.5 is a mixture of multiple time periods (i.e., Late Archaic, Basketmaker, and Paiute periods), while the surface findings remain undated and are considered residual.

TABLE 6.46. Assemblage by Temporal Component at 26CK7994.

	Late Archaic	Basketmaker II	Mixed	Surface Residual	Total
Flaked Stone					
Projectile Point	1	—	2	1	4
Drill	—	—	—	1	1
Biface	4	1	13	2	20
Flake Tool	3	1	2	1	7
Core Tool	—	—	2	2	4
Core	1	—	3	6	10
Debitage	254	34	1,793	85	2,166
Battered & Ground Stone					
Battered Cobble	1	1	—	1	3
Handstone	—	—	1	—	1
Millingstone	—	—	—	2	2
Other					
Shell Bead	—	—	—	1	1
Floral Remains					
Bundle	—	1	—	—	1
Charcoal	3	2	3	—	8
Fiber	—	6	—	1	7
Wood	2	—	—	—	2
Total	269	46	1,819	103	2,237

Note: All surface finds were placed in the Surface Residual category.

Artifact Inventory

Unfortunately, most of the artifacts recovered from the site come from the chronological mixed deposits in unit N14/W28.5 and undated surface contexts; both locations produced flaked stone tools and debitage and little else (Table 6.46). The Late Archaic component also has an assemblage that is dominated by flaked stone tools, while the Basketmaker II assemblage from the cist includes an interesting assortment of perishable artifacts made from fibrous material.

Late Archaic Findings

The Late Archaic assemblage includes four bifaces, three flake tools, one projectile point, a core, and a single cobble tool (Table 6.46). The bifaces reflect the later end of the production sequence, as the assemblage includes two Stage 3 specimens, a Stage 4, and a Stage 5 form. The chert debitage, in contrast, includes a large number of core reduction flakes (cortical and interior, both at 15.2 percent), fewer biface thinning debris flakes (early at 12.8 percent, late at 1.6 percent), but a dominant presence of pressure flakes (55.2 percent). Obsidian debitage shows an even greater emphasis on tool finishing,

with pressure flakes at 76.9 percent, followed by lower frequencies of late-stage (15.4 percent) and early-stage (7.7 percent) biface thinning flakes (Table 6.47).

One flake tool each is made from a cortical, early-stage biface thinning flake and a late-stage biface thinning flake. Wear is as variable as form, with microchipping, edge flaking, and polishing/grinding represented. The single cobble tool has light pecking along one of its margins.

Two slightly charred sticks were also recovered from the Late Archaic deposits (Figure 6.31). They are made from a heavy, dense wood (not *Pluchea sericea* [arrow weed]) and have been minimally whittled. Their function is unknown.

Basketmaker II (Feature 1) Findings

The Feature 1 assemblage is limited to a biface fragment, a flake tool, a battered cobble, and a few pieces of debitage. Much more interesting is the perishable assemblage, which consists of a possible sandal, six bunches of yucca fiber in various stages of production, and a cache of juniper bark (or possibly sagebrush) fiber. The possible sandal appears to be a margin fragment of a

TABLE 6.47. Technological Analysis of Debitage from 26CK7994.

| | Late Archaic | | | | | | | | Basketmaker II | |
| | Chert | | Obsidian | | Quartzite | | Limestone | | Chert | |
	#	%	#	%	#	%	#	%	#	%
Core Reduction										
Percussion Decortication	19	15.2	—	—	—	—	1	100.0	1	11.1
Percussion Interior	19	15.2	—	—	—	—	—	—	2	22.2
Biface Reduction										
Early Biface Thinning	16	12.8	1	7.7	—	—	—	—	3	33.3
Late Biface Thinning	2	1.6	2	15.4	—	—	—	—	—	—
Pressure	69	55.2	10	76.9	1	100.0	—	—	3	33.3
Diagnostic Total	125	100.0	13	100.0	1	100.0	1	100.0	9	100.0
Platform Prep./Pressure	12	—	—	—	—	—	—	—	3	—
Indeterminate Percussion	41	—	—	—	—	—	1	—	3	—
Indeterminate Fragment	46	—	—	—	2	—	1	—	6	—
Shatter	10	—	—	—	—	—	—	—	—	—
Sample Total	234	—	13	—	3	—	3	—	21	—

Note: % = analytical percentage.

sole (Figure 6.32). Although the specimen is in poor condition, it appears to be constructed from a series of twisted bundles, forming a figure-eight stitch woven back and forth across a looped cord. It is probably similar in construction to specimens from the Shivwits area illustrated by Lowie (1924:207, Figure 5a); see also the illustration from the California desert provided by Bean (1978:580).

Two of the yucca fiber bundles are nearly identical (Figure 6.33). They appear to be cleaned, bunched together, and bent in half (a U-shaped configuration). Another item is a loose accumulation of cleaned yucca fibers, not yet spun into a strand, twine, or bundle (Figure 6.34). The juniper/sagebrush material is quite similar, as it is a loose assortment of cleaned fibers (Figure 6.35); neither sagebrush nor juniper exists in the vicinity of the site. Another specimen is partially cleaned yucca fiber that is knotted (Figure 6.36), and the last appears to be twisted yucca fiber, but the exact configuration is difficult to determine because it is mixed with an unknown type of excrement (Figure 6.37).

Floral and Faunal Remains

Charred plant remains were essentially absent in the Late Archaic and mixed portions of the deposit but were relatively abundant in the cist (Table 6.48). The quantity of carbonized material recovered from the flotation samples suggests that the cist previously also served as a hearth at some point during its use life. Its assemblage includes a comparatively high frequency of goosefoot (n = 26) and pinyon nutshell (n = 18) and lesser numbers of desert tomato (n = 4), as well as a handful of undifferentiated seeds belonging to the grass, mallow, and bean families. The presence of pinyon is particularly interesting, as the nearest groves are currently 16 km to the northeast in the Virgin Mountains or 22 km to the south in Cedar Basin. Pinyon nuts, which ripen in the fall, combined with the spring-summer ripening seeds of goosefoot, also indicate multiple seasons of occupation, or the storage and later use of one of these important food resources.

Faunal remains follow a different pattern from the plants, as they are essentially absent from the cist but present in low numbers elsewhere in the deposit (Table 6.49). The tortoise bone found in the cist is considered problematic because a modern tortoise burrowed into the edge of it and died, and we attempted to remove its remains from the excavation sample but may not have gotten it all. Rabbits dominate the Late Archaic component (81.8 percent), followed by artiodactyls (9.1 percent) and tortoise (9.1 percent). The relative frequency of medium-to-large mammal versus small-to-medium mammal follows a consistent pattern, with small-to-medium mammal making up 80.8 percent and medium-to-large only 19.2 percent.

The mixed deposits have a much higher relative abundance of tortoise and higher frequencies of large versus small game. The significance of these findings is difficult to assess, however, due to the uncertain age of the material.

Whittled

26CK7994 -101
Actual Size

0   5
cm

FIGURE 6.31. Charred and whittled sticks from the Late Archaic component at 26CK7994.

Summary

Multiple periods of occupation are evident at the site and include brief visits during the Late Archaic, Basketmaker II, Basketmaker III, and Late Prehistoric periods. Unfortunately, however, only the Late Archaic component in unit S7/W25 and the Basketmaker II cist (Feature 1) retain chronological integrity, as multiple components are hopelessly mixed in unit N14/W28.5. Flaked stone tools and debitage dominate the Late Archaic component and probably reflect hunting-oriented use of the site. This is supported by a small faunal assemblage of mostly small game but some artiodactyl,

26CK7994 -38 Side A

26CK7994 -38 Side B

0   5 cm

FIGURE 6.32. Probable yucca sandal fragment from Feature 1, cist, at 26CK7994.

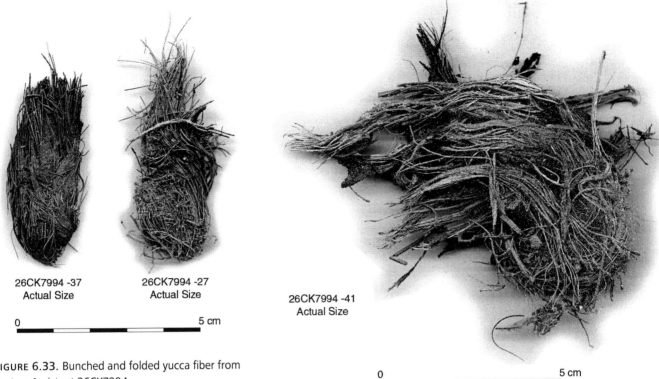

26CK7994 -37
Actual Size

26CK7994 -27
Actual Size

0   5 cm

FIGURE 6.33. Bunched and folded yucca fiber from
Feature 1, cist, at 26CK7994.

26CK7994 -41
Actual Size

0   5 cm

FIGURE 6.34. Loose accumulation of cleaned yucca fibers from
Feature 1, cist, at 26CK7994.

26CK7994 -49
Actual Size

0   5 cm

FIGURE 6.35. Loose accumulation of bark fibers (juniper or sagebrush) from Feature 1, cist, at 26CK7994.

26CK7994 -50
Actual Size

0 _____ 5 cm

FIGURE 6.37. Possible knotted yucca fiber from Feature 1, cist, at 26CK7994.

26CK8013 (DUNE FIELD)
SITE REPORT

Site 26CK8013 is a late-dating habitation area located in a dune field near Red Rock Springs. It consists of ground and flaked stone tools, debitage, pottery, and a fire-affected rock scatter approximately 150 × 40 m in extent. This material is concentrated in two areas, Locus 1 and 2, in the central site area (Figure 6.38). Locus 1 is mostly a scatter of tools, flakes, and fire-affected rocks, whereas Locus 2 is predominantly a pottery concentration dominated by corrugated brown ware. Also documented at the site is a hearth and an associated buried living surface (Feature 1 Area) situated in a nonlocus context in the east-central part of the site (Figure 6.38).

The site is situated along a narrow alluvial finger separating two drainages associated with Red Rock Springs. This finger is capped by a thin veneer of sand in the site vicinity. The site itself is located on a low-relief saddle fronting the north side of the southernmost drainage (Figure 6.38). A series of active dunes—sand hummocks 2–3 m high—are found near the center of this saddle along with Loci 1 and 2. Both drainages are active with areas of surface water and riparian vegetation (even in November, when fieldwork at this site was undertaken). The site is within the blackbrush vegetation community and has a sparse cover of creosote, yucca, ephedra, and grasses. Catclaw was noted along the drainage immediately fronting the site.

Field Methods

Fieldwork included boundary definition and surface collection, mapping, and the excavation of several exploratory control units and surface scrapes, as well as feature exposure and documentation. The initial field

26CK7994 -55
Actual Size

26CK7994 -50
Actual Size

0 _____ 5 cm

FIGURE 6.36. Knotted yucca fiber from Feature 1, cist, at 26CK7994.

and the near-absence of features, plant remains, and milling gear.

The Basketmaker II cist (Feature 1) contains a mixture of charred seeds, perishable artifacts, and little else. The plants are primarily pinyon nuts and goosefoot seeds. The perishable remains include a possible yucca sandal fragment, a mass of juniper or sagebrush fiber, and several small bundles or hanks of yucca fiber that seem to have been cleaned/processed. These last were likely either cached for future use or discarded as by-products from the manufacture of an item such as a sandal.

TABLE 6.48. Charred Plant Remains from 26CK7994.

	Late Archaic (N7/W25 36–53 cm)	Basketmaker II (Feature 1)	Mixed	Total
Charred Nutshell				
Pinyon (*Pinus edulis/monophylla*)	—	18	—	18
Charred Seeds				
Goosefoot (*Chenopodium* sp.)	—	26	1	27
Desert Tomato (*Lycium* sp.)	—	4	—	4
Mallow Family (Malvaceae)	—	2	—	2
Bean Family (Fabaceae)	—	1	—	1
Grass Family (Poaceae)	—	9	—	9
Unidentified Seeds	—	27	—	27
Total	—	87	1	88
Sample Volume (Liters)	3.3	16.7 [a]	4.5	23.7

[a] Combines three samples of 2.9, 7.5, and 6.3 liters.

TABLE 6.49. Faunal Remains from 26CK7994.

	Late Archaic	Basketmaker II (Feature 1)	Mixed	Total
Artiodactyl	1	—	13	14
Jackrabbit	5	—	—	5
Cottontail	2	—	7	9
Lagomorphs	2	—	7	9
Tortoise	1	11 [a]	93	105
Medium-to-Large (Sheep-Sized)	5	—	27	32
Small-to-Medium (Rabbit-Sized)	21	—	84	105
Intrusive Rodents	2	—	4	6
Lizards	4	1	4	9
Birds	—	—	1	1
Unidentifiable	6	2	41	49
Total	49	14	281	344

[a] Most are probably intrusive.

effort involved making a systematic inventory of the site, pin flagging all formal artifacts, noting artifact concentrations, and revising as necessary all locus and site boundaries. A datum and grid were established (E-W grid line at 82 degrees), and a contour map was developed. All tools and artifacts were plotted using the total station and subsequently collected. Larger items (e.g., ground stone) were analyzed in the field and left at the site.

Exploratory testing commenced at Locus 1 with the excavation of a single 1-×-2-m unit (S1/E23). It exposed about 20 to 25 cm of low-density, artifact-bearing de-posit before terminating abruptly on compacted, miner-alized sand. Because Locus 2 appeared to be primarily a surface pottery scatter, subsurface sampling was limited to the excavation of a single 2-×-2-m surface scrape to depth of 10 cm (N15.5/E8). The unit yielded an abun-dance of corrugated brown ware and also confirmed the surficial nature of deposits in this area.

The final excavation unit turned out to be the most fortuitous. Located adjacent to a small concentration of chipping debris in a nonlocus area east of Locus 1, the unit (N0/E50) yielded evidence of a hearth and an associated stained living surface (both referred

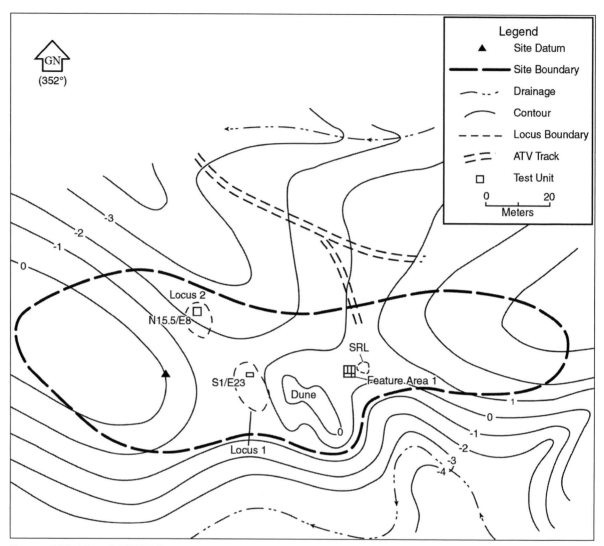

FIGURE 6.38. Map of 26CK8013.

to as the Feature 1 Area) just below the sandy surface (10–15 cm). A 3-×-3-m block exposure in the feature area was dug with adjoining 1-×-1-m and 1-×-2-m units (Table 6.50; Figure 6.38). The block exposure was excavated with respect to two stratigraphic units: the sand veneer just above the feature (fill) and the underlying hearth and adjoining stained living surface (floor and subfloor). The hearth was sectioned, illustrated, and photographed; flotation samples were obtained for radiocarbon and archaeobotanical analysis.

Site Structure and Chronology

As previously mentioned, there are three major activity zones at 26CK8013: Locus 1, Locus 2, and the Feature 1 Area. Surrounding these is a more diffuse surface artifact scatter. Excavations at the site revealed that all deposits are shallow, with most cultural material confined to the uppermost 20 cm of dune sand.

Locus 1

Locus 1 is an area about 15 by 10 m, with tools, flakes, and fire-affected rock scattered across it. It is located in the saddle of two prominent dune fields at the site (Figure 6.38). It, too, is a surface manifestation; most cultural materials are confined to the surface or the upper 25 cm of sand that blankets most of the site. The profile in the excavated unit (S1/E23) consists of an upper 20 to 25 cm of reddish sand overlying whitish, very compact mineralized sand, that is, caliche (Figure 6.39). This profile is probably consistent across much of the site, including the Feature 1 Area (see below). No temporal indicators were recovered from Locus 1.

Locus 2

Locus 2, in the northwest site area (Figure 6.38), is a discrete concentration of surface and near-surface corrugated brown ware (n = 86). With the exception

TABLE 6.50. Excavation Summary for 26CK8013.

Unit	Context	Size (m)	Depth (cm)	Volume (m³)
S1/E23	Locus 1	1×2	0–30	0.6
N15.5/E8	Locus 2	2×2	0–10	0.4
N0/E49	Feature 1 Area: Floor/Fill Zone	1×2	0–10	0.2
N0/E50	Feature 1 Area: Floor/Fill Zone	1×2	0–10	0.2
N0/E51	Feature 1 Area: Floor/Fill Zone	1×2	0–10	0.2
S1/E49	Feature 1 Area: Floor/Fill Zone	1×2	0–10	0.2
S1/E51	Feature 1 Area: Floor/Fill Zone	1×1	0–10	0.1
N0/E50	Feature 1 Area: Floor/Subfloor	1×2	10–15	0.1
N0/E51	Feature 1 Area: Floor/Subfloor	1×2	10–15	0.1
Total				2.1

Note: Feature 1 is a hearth and associated living surface.

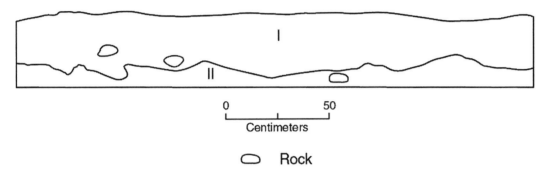

0   50
Centimeters

◯ Rock

I 5YR6/6 reddish yellow loose to slightly compact fine dune sand.

II 10YR8/1 white very compact, minor fine sand (caliche).

FIGURE 6.39. South wall profile of S1/E23 at 26CK8013, Locus 1.

of four flakes, no cultural material was recovered. The brown ware concentration most likely represents a pot drop dating to the Late Prehistoric period and may be chronologically related to the Feature 1 Area (see discussion below).

Feature 1 Area

Located east of Locus 1, this area has a thin layer of aeolian sand that has formed a protective cover over Feature 1. In plan, this area consists of a hearth (Feature 1a) and an associated living surface. The living surface includes a thin zone (less than 3 cm thick) of slightly compacted, darker, discolored soil that extends throughout the northern three-quarters of the block exposure. A discrete zone of darker charcoal staining (Feature 1b) was documented on the living surface in the northeast corner of the exposure. A distinct perimeter of the living surface is apparent in the southern part of the exposure (Figure 6.40), although the overall extent and shape of this surface was not determined.

The hearth (Feature 1a), approximately 80 cm in diameter, is an intact fire-affected rock cluster laced with pockets of charcoal. In section, it is dish-shaped and no more than 8 cm thick (Figure 6.41). Several more compacted, slab-like sections of floor deposit were observed immediately adjacent to the hearth. A radiocarbon sample obtained from Feature 1a returned a date of cal AD 1650, indicating a Late Prehistoric occupation (Table 6.51). Also recovered from this feature area were eight brown ware sherds consistent with this time frame. Noteworthy, however, is that all the sherds from the Feature 1 Area are plain with no surface decoration whereas all the Locus 2 sherds have a corrugated surface treatment.

Further confirmation of Late Prehistoric use is provided by two Desert Side-notched points with the feature and a third recovered nearby in a nonlocus context. The only obsidian recovered from the site is from the Feature 1 Area. Two unmodified obsidian flakes yielded hydration values of 12.0 (Modena/Panaca Summit) and

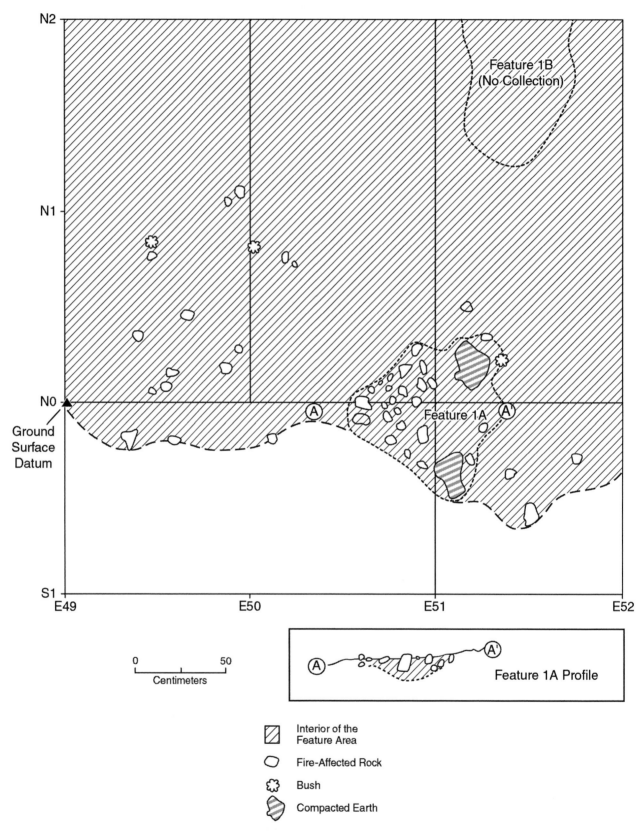

FIGURE 6.40. 26CK8013, Feature 1 Area.

Feature 1B
(No Collection)

N2

N1

N0

Ground
Surface
Datum

S1

E49   E50   E51   E52

Feature 1A

Ⓐ   Ⓐ'

0   50
Centimeters

Ⓐ   Ⓐ'   Feature 1A Profile

▨ Interior of the
   Feature Area

◯ Fire-Affected Rock

✿ Bush

▨ Compacted Earth

FIGURE 6.41. North wall profile of Feature 1A at 26CK8013.

TABLE 6.51. Chronological Data from 26CK8013.

	Description	Mean	Material/Source	Date
Feature 1				
S1/E49 and S1/E51	0–15 cm	—	Charcoal	cal AD 1650 (cal BP 300)
Obsidian Studies				
Feature 1: N0/E50	Flake	12.0	Modena/Panaca Summit	—
	Flake	1.6	Kane Springs	—
Projectile Points				
Surface Artifact 14	Desert Side-notched	—	—	—
Feature 1: N0/E51	Desert Side-notched	—	—	—
Feature 1: S1/E49	Desert Side-notched	—	—	—

1.6 (Kane Springs) microns. The latter is consistent with the Late Prehistoric period whereas the larger value likely reflects Late Prehistoric scavenging of an older flake from somewhere on the landscape.

Component Definition

Site 26CK8013 contains two components, each dating to the Late Prehistoric period: Locus 2, a pot drop; and the Feature 1 Area, a hearth and living surface. Furthermore, no brown ware sherds were found in nonlocus contexts on site. Although undated, Locus 1 lies roughly

between them and no more than 20 m from these dated components, and exhibits a flaked and ground stone assemblage broadly similar to theirs. The evidence at hand indicates that the entirety of 26CK8013 is a single Late Prehistoric manifestation (Table 6.51).

Artifact Inventory

The assemblage at 26CK8013 includes a handful of flaked and ground stone tools as well as more ubiquitous amounts of debitage, pottery, and bone. Also recovered was a single lead musket ball (Figure 6.42),

26CK8013

Lead Musket Ball
Actual Size

0 ——————————— 5
cm

FIGURE 6.42. Lead musket ball at 26CK8013.

TABLE 6.52. Assemblage at 26CK8013.

Type	Locus 1	Locus 2	Feature 1	Nonlocus	Total
Flaked Stone					
Projectile Point	—	—	2	1	3
Biface	—	—	1	2	3
Flake Tool	—	—	2	1	3
Debitage	19	4	316	1	340
Battered & Ground Stone					
Handstone	—	—	—	4	4
Millingstone	4	—	2	4	10
Other					
Pottery	—	86	8	6	100
Musket Ball	—	—	—	1	1
Total	23	90	331	20	464

the only indication of postcontact visitation. The assemblage is arrayed by activity area in Table 6.52.

Flaked Stone Tools and Debitage

Along with the Desert Side-notched points, the flaked stone assemblage contains three bifaces, three flake tools, and 340 unmodified flakes. The points are all proximal end fragments fashioned from chert. As previously mentioned, two were recovered in direct association with the Feature 1 Area. The only biface found in a datable context was from the Feature 1 Area; it is a pressure-finished, Stage 5 margin fragment made of chert. The other two bifaces are also Stage 5 fragments, one of chert, the other of a quartz-like material. Two fragmentary flake tools were also recovered from the Feature 1 Area, both fashioned from chert and exhibiting unifacial wear in the form of step fractures and microchipping.

A total of 340 pieces of debitage was recovered, almost all of it chert and from the Feature 1 Area (Table 6.52). A technological analysis of a sample revealed that it is dominated by pressure flakes (74.5 percent), followed by much lesser amounts of biface thinning (17.7 percent), percussion interior (4.7 percent), and decortication (3.1 percent) flakes. The emphasis on pressure thinning is consistent with the tool maintenance and rejuvenation that might be expected in a domestic living area.

Ground Stone

Ten millingstones and four handstones are documented at the site, attesting to the importance of plant resources. Two of the millingstones were recovered

from the Feature 1 Area. Both are small margin fragments that have been burned, suggesting they may have had secondary use as heat mass in the associated hearth. The remainder of the millingstones were found widely scattered across the surface of the site. Two are whole or near-complete, and the rest are fragmentary. As a class, they appear to be mostly expedient processing tools; most are unshaped and have a single, flat, worn surface.

Complementing the millingstones, four handstones were also recovered. All were found on the surface in nonlocus context. Sandstone, followed by quartz, was the preferred material for these specimens. Most are fragmentary, unshaped, and limited to unifacial use wear.

Historic Item

The only historically manufactured item at the site is a lead musket ball found on the surface (Figure 6.42). It is a .54-caliber projectile made from a two-part mold. It measures 0.61 × 0.53 inches (15.6 × 13.6 mm) and appears never to have been discharged from a weapon. This type and size of musket ball is consistent with Spanish-era weapons of the seventeenth century. According to Dougherty (2009), "smooth bore muskets that fired round lead bullets about 0.50 to 0.75 inches in diameter" were also common in the early nineteenth century. If the musket ball is the same age as the Late Prehistoric occupation, it may reflect Spanish intrusion into this area. Since no other definitive evidence of such has been found in this area, it is more likely an AD 1800s artifact that reflects interaction with early Euro-American explorers, hunters, or immigrants.

TABLE 6.53. Faunal Remains from the Feature 1 Area, 26CK8013.

	Total
Artiodactyl	16
Desert Tortoise	118
Rabbit/Cottontail	1
Small-to-Medium (Rabbit-Sized)	7
Medium-to-Large (Sheep-Sized)	9
Unidentifiable	2
Total	153

Faunal and Floral Remains

A total of 153 pieces of bone was recovered, all from the Feature 1 Area (Table 6.53). Most is desert tortoise (mostly carapace fragments). Interestingly, a number of artiodactyl and medium-to-large mammal fragments (also probably artiodactyl remains) were recovered from the same context. While working at this site, we observed a herd of bighorn sheep near the adjacent spring. Perhaps this area was good bighorn habitat throughout the Late Prehistoric period.

Although some of the feature matrix (7.5 liters) was subjected to flotation analysis, no seed remains were recovered. The substantial ground stone assemblage from the site indicates considerable plant processing, but little evidence remains of food that was prepared at Feature 1.

Summary

By all accounts, 26CK8013 is a habitation site dating to the Late Prehistoric period. All the 100 sherds are brown ware consistent with Southern Paiute use. A single radiocarbon date of cal AD 1650 from an intact hearth feature pinpoints the period of active use. If the musket ball dates to the Spanish era of initial exploration of the Southwest, it would be the first physical evidence of such.

The site has most of the elements of a typical Numa foraging camp—a hearth and associated small living surface, a couple of cooking pots, a discrete scatter of milling equipment, and a modest flaked stone assemblage. As previously noted, the site is located near several drainages with an active flow, which not only provided a dependable source of water but also supported a stable plant habitat and animals. The only direct dietary refuse at the site, however, is faunal remains. Two primary taxa were of importance, desert tortoise and artiodactyls, the latter most likely bighorn sheep. The prevalence of tortoise remains is consistent with other late-dating sites throughout the Mojave Desert. The predominance of bighorn sheep may reflect local hunting conditions and the nearby springs, a critical water source for these herds.

26CK8047 (DART SHAFT SHELTER) SITE REPORT

Site 26CK8047 consists of several rock shelters, three hunting blinds, and a sparse scatter of flaked stone tools and debitage, milling gear, and some pottery. Most of the shelters lack archaeological deposits, but Rock Shelter 5 contains midden, possible hearth features, and two noteworthy perishable items: a straight shaft of wood consistent in form and size with a dart shaft and a small corncob. Because of the presence of perishable material, Rock Shelter 5 was selected for excavation.

Field Methods

After all formal tools were pin flagged and collected at the site, excavations were initiated in Rock Shelter 5. A single 1-x-3-m unit (S1/W4) was laid out along the southern edge of the shelter (Figures 6.43 and 6.44), overlying the features observed on the surface. Feature 1 was a small concentration of charcoal at the east end of the unit, and Feature 2 was a concentration of fire-affected rock at the west end of the exposure.

Feature 1 was mapped and excavated separately. The next phase of work was the excavation of the 1-x-3-m unit (S1/W4). It was dug stratigraphically (rather than in 10-cm levels) and avoided Feature 2 until the unit reached sterile sediments around its margins. The first stratigraphic unit consisted of 2 to 3 cm of aeolian sand with some midden soils mixed in. It was brushed off and screened until a more compact midden was encountered on an undulating surface between 5 and 10 cm below the surface.

This upper midden zone was removed using the same methods applied to the aeolian sand zone. The upper midden did not cover the entire floor of the unit. Instead, it formed a half-circle extending to the north end of the unit (Figure 6.44). Once the midden was removed, a near-sterile matrix of loose dry sand was encountered (2Ab). This stratigraphic unit contained two additional features (Figure 6.45), a fire pit with charcoal and rock (Feature 3) and a pit filled with gray ashy silt (Feature 4). Both of these features were then excavated, and the unit excavations continued downward.

A lower midden zone was next found just below and east of Feature 4 (Figure 6.46), and this thin stratum was taken out in its entirety as a flotation sample. Sterile sediments were encountered below Features 3 and 4 and the lower midden zone. Finally, Feature 2 was

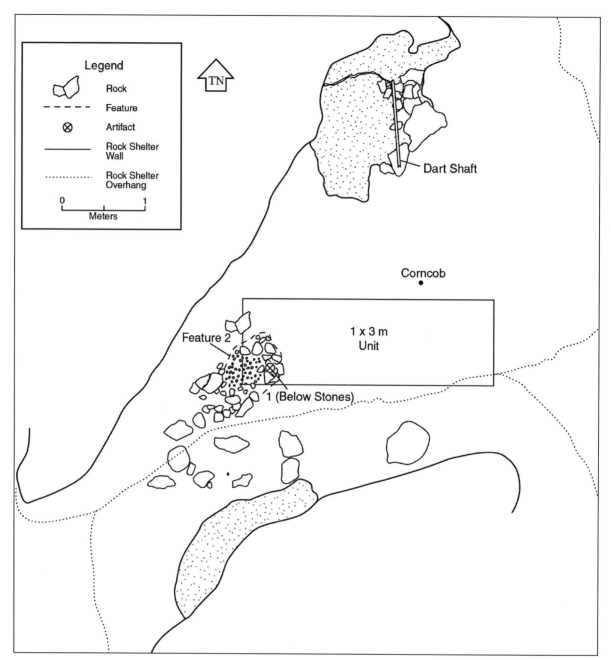

FIGURE 6.43. Map of 26CK8047, Rock Shelter 5.

sectioned and a flotation sample was collected from its fill.

A maximum depth of 25 cm was reached along the eastern two-thirds of the exposure, while excavations extended down to only 15 cm along the western third of the unit. Based on these relationships, we estimate that 0.65 m³ was excavated at the site.

Site Structure and Chronology

A great deal of stratigraphic complexity was found within Rock Shelter 5 even though the deposit was quite shallow. This is probably because the shelter saw only limited use on a couple of occasions. Otherwise, the activity of humans would have mixed up the loose sandy deposit and blurred the thin, ephemeral strata observed. The following discussion describes the structural aspects of the deposit, focusing on the features, soil profiles, and radiocarbon dates that correspond to these discrete occupational events.

Features

Feature 1 was a circular concentration of charcoal-rich soil measuring 65 × 60 cm. It lacked hearth stones but seemed to have more fire-affected rock than the adjacent

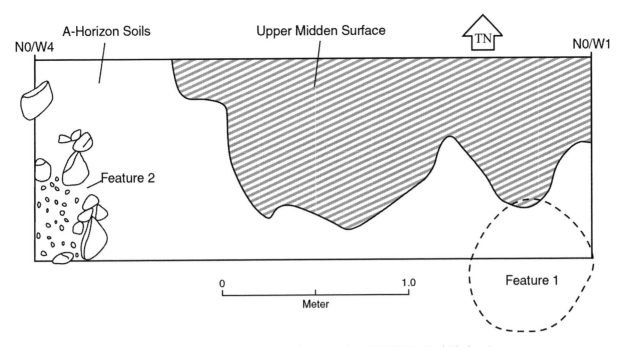

FIGURE 6.44. Plan view of near-surface deposit at 26CK8047, Rock Shelter 5.

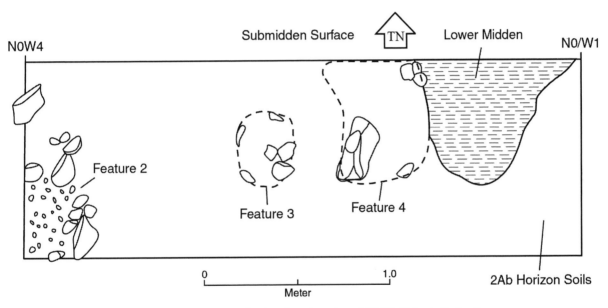

FIGURE 6.45. Plan view of subsurface deposit at 26CK8047, Rock Shelter 5.

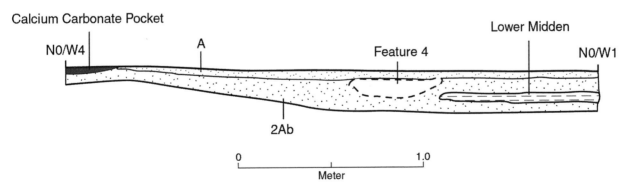

A   5YR 5/4 Loose dry reddish brown blow sand and upper midden deposits.

2Ab   7.5YR 7/6 Loose dry reddish yellow soil containing a lens of the gray (5YR 5/10) lower midden.

FIGURE 6.46. North wall profile at 26CK8047, Rock Shelter 5.

midden smears. Its depth ranged from 2 to 5 cm below surface, and it may represent a single-event feature. Due to its small size, the entire matrix was removed as a flotation sample.

Feature 2 was a circular configuration of rocks at the west end of the 1-×-3-m unit. We sectioned the feature by first removing all small rocks from the interior (which weighed 8 pounds) and then pulling the large perimeter rocks from its eastern half (28 pounds). Once the rocks were removed, the eastern half of the feature fill was excavated. It contained rock, calcium carbonate, and light-colored soil, and produced a biface, some debitage, and a few pieces of bone. No concentration of charcoal or other discrete strata were observed.

Feature 3 was located immediately below the upper midden and consisted of a small fire pit with dense charcoal and fire-affected rock. It measured 40 × 30 cm, but no artifacts were found with it. A large portion of this very dark gray matrix (5YR 3/1) was collected for flotation analysis.

Feature 4 was also located immediately below the upper midden, and it consisted of a small pit filled with a clean, fine-grained silt that was gray in color (5YR 6/1). Some fill was screened, but nothing was found. The remainder was collected for flotation analysis.

Stratigraphy

Figure 6.46 shows the north wall profile of the 1-×-3-m exposure. It begins with a thin A-horizon of aeolian sand and the upper midden, created by loose, dry sand eroding from the roof of the sandstone shelter and through aeolian transport. A buried 2Ab submidden deposit lies immediately below the upper midden and is lighter in color (7.5YR 7/6, reddish yellow). A portion of Feature 4 can be seen in the profile, with its concentration of gray (5YR 6/1), very fine-grained silt. The thin lower midden is visible at the eastern end of the unit and is gray (5YR 5/1), dry, loose sand. Finally, a light gray (5YR 7/1) pocket of calcium carbonate was exposed at the west end of the unit near the surface.

Radiocarbon Dates

Two radiocarbon dates were obtained from the site (Table 6.54). The first is from the corncob collected from the surface. It was found about one meter north of the excavation unit and produced a date of cal AD 220, which corresponds to the Basketmaker II period. The second assay was obtained from the lower midden and yielded a date of cal AD 1910. These findings indicate that the corncob is an isolated item deposited many years before the formation of the shallow archaeological deposit that we excavated. Given that the late radiocarbon date came from the deepest stratigraphic unit in the deposit,

TABLE 6.54. Radiocarbon Dates from 26CK8047, Rock Shelter 5.

Unit	Depth	Calibrated Intercept[a]	Conventional Age	Material
N0.2/W1.8	Surface	cal AD 220 (cal BP 1730)	1820 ± 40 BP	Corncob
S1/W4	Lower Midden	cal AD 1910 (cal BP 40)	90 ± 40 BP	Charcoal

[a] See Table 5.1.

it seems likely that it reflects very recent occupation, either Southern Paiute or even historic.

Temporally Diagnostic Artifacts

Diagnostic artifacts are limited to a single dart-sized projectile point, six sherds, and the wooden dart shaft fragment. The dart-sized projectile point was found on the surface 15 m east of the shelter, well away from the excavation unit, and does little more than indicate hunting sometime before AD 400. The pottery includes five Puebloan (four Tusayan and one Shivwits) sherds and one brown ware sherd. Four of mixed types were from the surface, and two Tusayan sherds were found in the unit. The former merely indicates multiple brief episodes of site use by the Southern Paiute (possibly in historic times) and by Puebloan groups. The worked wooden shaft is classified as dart-sized based on its 11-mm diameter. If we ascribe a terminal date of ca. AD 500 to the period when atlatl and dart weaponry was supplanted by bow-and-arrow technology, it conceivably is contemporaneous with the Basketmaker II corncob.

Component Definition

The shallow deposit exposed in unit S1/W4 produced two Puebloan sherds but a subsurface radiocarbon date reflecting a Southern Paiute/historic period use. The dart shaft and corncob from the surface and a subsurface radiocarbon date of cal AD 220 point to Basketmaker II use of the site. Combined, they show that the deposit is mixed and it is not possible to isolate single-component assemblages that correspond to the separate use episodes. As a result, the artifacts and faunal remains are presented here according to whether they were found in excavation or on the surface, while the plant remains obtained from flotation samples are associated with their precise feature or stratigraphic context.

Artifact Inventory

As outlined above, both the corncob and atlatl dart shaft were found on the surface within the shelter. The corncob is a distal end fragment (53 × 14 mm) and has

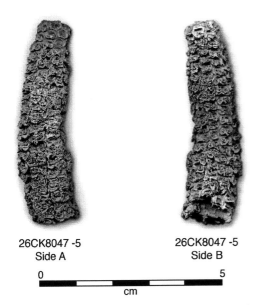

26CK8047 -5
Side A

26CK8047 -5
Side B

0   5
cm

FIGURE 6.47. Corncob fragment from 26CK8047, Rock Shelter 5.

eight rows (Figure 6.47). The dart shaft is 11.0 mm in diameter, significantly thicker than the threshold of 8 mm that is commonly used to separate arrows from dart shafts (e.g., Harrington 1933; Buck and DuBarton 1994; Gilreath 2009; Winslow et al. 2003b). It is 102.5 cm long, is longitudinally cracked, and appears cut or rudimentarily v-notched. Although it is somewhat shaped, it is not completely smooth and may represent a work in progress.

Most of the flaked stone tools—six bifaces, three flake tools, a drill, and a core—were found in subsurface contexts (Table 6.55). The surface tools were the dart point fragment and one biface. Overall, the bifaces are mostly Stage 5 fragments (n = 4), with a single Stage 3, Stage 4, and indeterminate fragment. The drill is almost complete, missing only a small portion of its distal end. The proximal end is flat and wide, allowing the user to apply plenty of torque to the task at hand.

Floral and Faunal Remains

Flotation samples were processed from Features 1, 2, and 3 and from the upper and lower midden deposits. The samples were extremely unproductive: five samples totaling 18.8 liters produced only one unidentifiable seed fragment.

All the faunal remains come from subsurface contexts (Table 6.56). They consist of a relatively even mix of tortoise (46.2 percent), lagomorphs (33.3 percent), and artiodactyls (20.5 percent). A different pattern is found among the more fragmentary mammal sample, however, in which small-to-medium mammal bone (88.6 percent) is much more abundant than medium-to-large (11.4 percent).

TABLE 6.55. Assemblage at 26CK8047, Rock Shelter 5.

Artifact	Excavation	Surface	Total
Flaked Stone			
Projectile Point	—	1	1
Drill	1	—	1
Biface	6	1	7
Flake Tool	3	—	3
Core	1	—	1
Debitage	167	—	167
Ground & Battered Stone			
Battered Cobble	—	1	1
Handstone	—	2	2
Miscellaneous Ground Stone	1	—	1
Pottery			
Brown Ware	—	1	1
Shivwits	—	1	1
Tusayan	2	2	4
Perishable Material			
Arrow Shaft	—	1	1
Corncob	—	1	1
Total	181	11	192

TABLE 6.56. Faunal Remains from 26CK8047, Rock Shelter 5.

	Number
Bighorn Sheep	—
Artiodactyl	8
Jackrabbit	5
Cottontail	5
Lagomorphs	3
Tortoise	18
Medium-to-Large (Sheep-Sized)	5
Small-to-Medium (Rabbit-Sized)	39
Intrusive Rodents	5
Lizards	11
Unidentifiable	5
Total	104

Summary

Rock Shelter 5 at 26CK8047 produced subsurface and surface materials spanning the Basketmaker II, Puebloan, and Late Prehistoric periods. Unfortunately, due to the shallow nature of the deposits, single-component assemblages could not be separated from one another. Despite the multiple periods of use, artifacts and subsistence remains are not abundant, indicating that visits to the site were extremely brief. These visits included multiple activities, reflected by the few but varied flaked stone tool types, ground and battered stone implements, and pottery.

Perhaps the most important discovery at the site is the corncob dating to cal AD 220. This is the only agricultural product found during the entire project, and it is noteworthy that it dates to the Basketmaker II interval, not to the Puebloan periods, when human populations and agricultural production reached their zenith. Although this is just a single finding, it is consistent with the project-wide land-use pattern database, which shows that Puebloan people did not visit the hinterland with nearly the same intensity as earlier or later groups.

26CK8179 (Sheep Shelter) Site Report

Site 26CK8179 was first recorded in November 2006, during the random-sample survey phase of this study. It is located in a steeply sloping, southwest-trending drainage that empties into a large, south-trending canyon draining a large part of the southern Virgin Range. Access to the site is via a dirt road passing along the bottom of this canyon, about 600 m southwest of the site. (The road is washed out several miles downstream, however, requiring a long walk to the site.) The site lies at an elevation of 5,680 feet (1,730 m). Local vegetation is a pinyon-juniper forest with a dense understory of various cacti, yucca, sage, and grasses. The site is situated against the base of a prominent, northeast-facing limestone outcrop or cliff that is about 20 m tall and has a concavity at its base that forms a large shelter with a comparatively level floor (Figure 6.48). The roof at the very back of the shelter is steep, leaving less than a meter of vertical clearance (head space) over a large area. Due to the orientation of the cliff, the shelter is in shade for all but a few hours each day, year round.

The surface of the site is dominated by an apparent agave oven, consisting of a large mound of fire-cracked and discolored limestone cobbles which is constructed within and adjacent to the shelter's overhang and which appears to overlie a deposit of habitation debris, including flaked stone tools and debitage, milling equipment, scraps of wood and fiber, and faunal remains. The latter includes fragments of large mammal bone and a sheep horn core. A roughly oval concentration of boulders in the upslope, eastern part of the overhang suggested the possibility of an intact feature, perhaps a rock-lined storage pit. Discolored soil (occupational midden, charcoal-rich soil from the agave oven, or a combination of the two) and fire-affected rock extend north and west about 20 m from the shelter area. The site seems very well preserved, although the presence of a shallow pit in the central shelter area (Figure 6.49) suggests the possibility of some informal collection at the site.

The site was chosen for test excavation for several reasons. First, the juxtaposition of the agave oven and midden/habitation debris suggested the possibility that the oven might cap or abut an intact, likely single-component habitation deposit. If such were the case, then the deposit's age could be established by radiocarbon dating the oven. Second, the placement and construction of the oven appeared to be unique since other agave ovens in the area are typically at lower elevations and in open-air settings. The setting of this oven seemed a good opportunity to explore methods of construction and use of these features. Finally, surface collection and a shovel probe during the survey phase suggested that the shelter had a rich and deep cultural deposit, including various faunal and floral remains.

Field Methods

We began our work at the site by establishing a grid, using the datum placed during the survey phase. The grid was oriented at 328 degrees relative to true north to allow excavation units to run perpendicular to the shelter's back wall. A 2-×-1-m unit was laid out at S4.5/W1.5, about a meter from the back wall, on the back side of the berm of the mounded agave oven (Figure 6.50). This and all units were excavated in surface-parallel 10-cm levels with spoils passed through ⅛-inch mesh. Fire-affected rock from each level was collected, weighed, and discarded.

Excavation of the uppermost levels of unit S4.5/W1.5 proved difficult because of the amount of burned limestone rock, making sidewall maintenance problematic. A range of material, mostly flaked stone tools, debitage, and faunal remains, was interspersed throughout the rocky matrix in the uppermost levels. Additionally, organic materials were abundant, including agave leaves, some appearing quite fresh, as well as loose masses of agave fiber and fragments of charred and uncharred wood. As excavation of the unit progressed, the quantity of burned rock gradually decreased, giving way to a loamy, dark brown midden (Figure 6.51). No clearly defined bottom to the agave oven was apparent. This unit continued down to 70 cm below surface, where excavation was finally halted due to continually decreasing quantities of cultural material. At no point did a bedrock floor become apparent, though several large roof-fall boulders were encountered, particularly in the northern end of the unit (Figure 6.52).

A second unit was opened adjacent to the south, abutting the back wall of the shelter. The uppermost

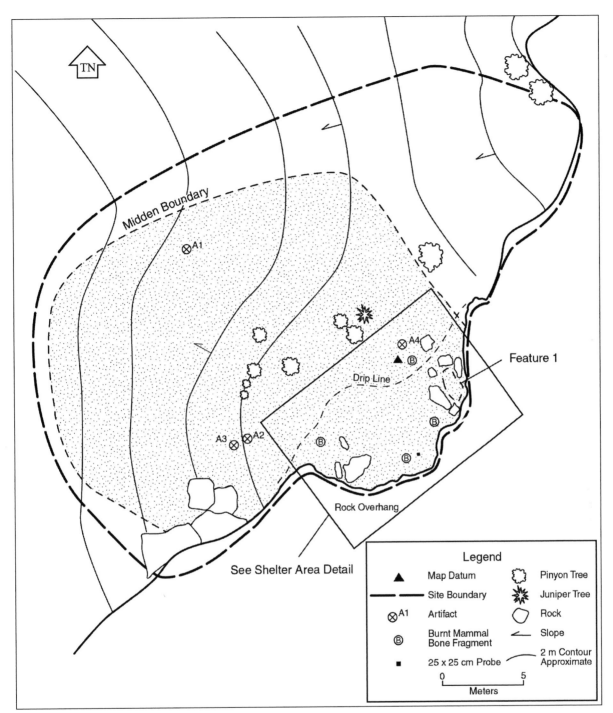

FIGURE 6.48. Map of 26CK8179.

levels were similar to those of the first unit, heavily dominated by fire-cracked limestone but with even more organic material. This gradually gave way to a more uniform, but still very rocky, midden. As excavation progressed, the rear wall of the shelter continued to recede south until it became a near-horizontal overhang. The south limit of the unit was established at S6.5/W1, and excavation proceeded normally but with some

difficulty due to the tight quarters. The uncompacted clay deposit in the south end of the unit suggested that cultural deposits continued farther south under the overhang. This indicated that the usable floor area of the shelter was considerably larger when it was initially occupied and that the shelter has since filled in, reducing its floor space. A large roof-fall boulder in the floor of unit S6.5/W1 was exposed at about 70 cm (Figure 6.52).

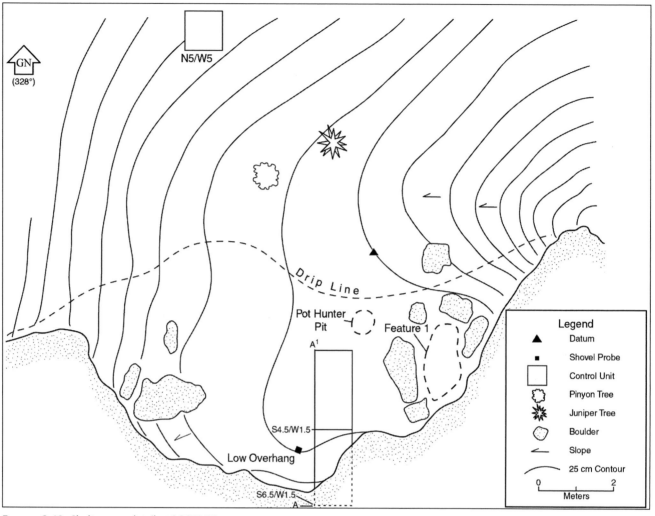

FIGURE 6.49. Shelter area detail at 26CK8179.

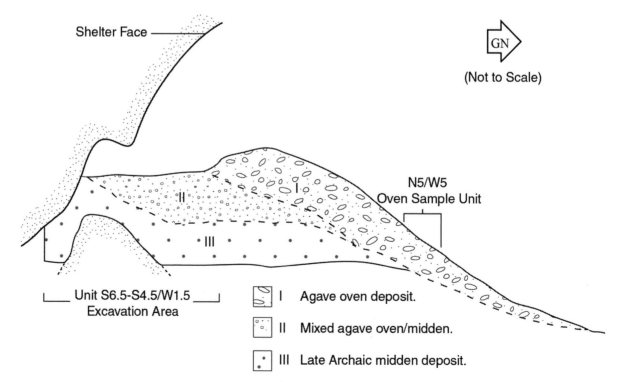

Unit S6.5-S4.5/W1.5
Excavation Area

I   Agave oven deposit.

II   Mixed agave oven/midden.

III   Late Archaic midden deposit.

FIGURE 6.50. Schematic profile of 26CK8179.

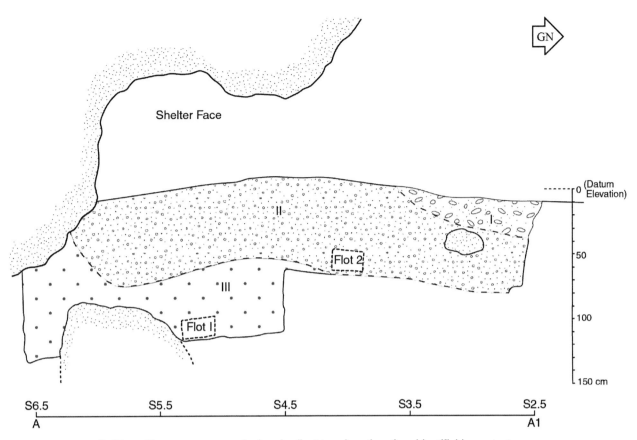

Shelter Face

GN

(Datum Elevation) 0

II

Flot 2

50

III

100

Flot I

150 cm

| S6.5 | S5.5 | S4.5 | S3.5 | S2.5 |

A   A1

Soil transitions are very gradual and reflect trends rather than identifiable contacts.

I   Angular, fire-cracked limestone cobbles with very little soil matrix.

II Loose, very dark gray (10YR 3/1) powdery loam with very abundant limestone fire-cracked rock cobbles (75% of overall volume) and abundant organic material that includes fresh agave spines and pine cone scales. Abundant charcoal. Rodent runs throughout. Occasional slabs of roof-fall rock.

III Loose, very dark gray (10YR 3/1) loam with a smaller quantity of limestone cobbles (25-50% of volume) and much less frequent organic material, though not entirely absent. Large slabs of roof-fall rock throughout.

FIGURE 6.51. West wall profile, units S4.5/W1.5 and S6.5/W1.5 at 26CK8179.

Excavation continued to 120 cm deep, until several other boulders covered most of the floor.

Aside from these two units, the rock feature in the eastern part of the shelter was dismantled. This was originally identified as a possible rock-lined storage pit, but as abundant fire-cracked rocks were removed, it became apparent that the feature was a natural declivity formed by roof-fall boulders. The concavity subsequently filled with fire-cracked rock and other debris, perhaps related to the use of the oven or to more recent pot hunting. Very little sediment was among the loose, unconsolidated rocks. A few artifacts were recovered, however, as described below.

To further explore the structure of the agave oven, we placed a 1-x-1-m unit in the apron of midden northwest of the shelter (N5/W5; Figures 6.49 and 6.50). We anticipated that this unit was at the downhill, outer edge of the oven and would expose a comparatively shallow lens of fire-affected rock. Instead, it exposed a deep and dense deposit of burned rock in a loose, heavily charcoal-stained soil matrix. The rocks in this outer apron were distinctly larger and more heavily fire-affected than those in the shelter. Excavation progressed to a depth of 80 cm, at which point the bottom of the fire-affected rock deposit had still not been reached; however, no artifacts of any kind had been recovered.

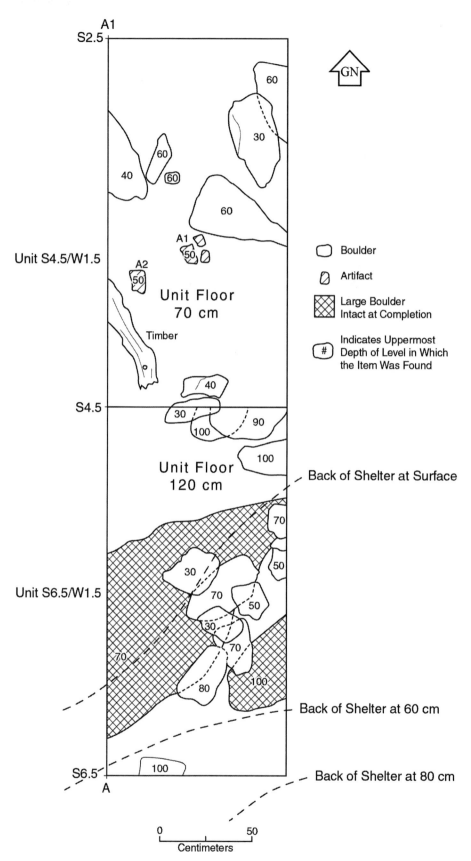

Figure 6.52. Plan view of units S4.5/W1.5 and S6.5/W1.5 at 26CK8179.

After excavation, plan and profiles were drawn, flotation samples were collected, and all units were backfilled. Accounting for the irregular size of the unit in the back of the shelter as well as the many large boulders in the shelter units, we estimate that approximately 4.05 m³ of deposit was processed at the site.

Site Structure and Chronology

Chronological data from the site consist of two radiocarbon assays, source-specific obsidian hydration measurements on 24 obsidian items, and 14 diagnostic artifacts, namely projectile points.

Radiocarbon Dates

The two radiocarbon assays were of wood charcoal recovered from flotation samples, one from S6.5/W1.5 at 100–115 cm (in the deepest part of the excavated shelter) and the other from N5/W5 at 40–70 cm (in the outer apron of the oven). The first returned a date of 1440 cal BC; the second was substantially older, at 2870 cal BC. The first one places use of the site in the Late Archaic period, and the second falls near the Early Archaic/Late Archaic boundary. It thus appears likely that the agave oven represents distinct but partially overlapping features rather than parts of the same single-use feature, as was assumed at the outset. This interpretation helps to explain the markedly different appearance of the small, burned rocks in a loamy matrix within the shelter versus the large and mostly rocky matrix in the outer apron, as well as the considerable depth in the outer apron. While the site may thus have seen repeated use, it appears that all or nearly all of the artifacts and ecofacts are associated with the younger date and come from the shelter deposit.

Obsidian Hydration Data

The source-specific obsidian hydration data are somewhat difficult to interpret, given the diverse sources represented (Table 6.57), the uncertainty of source-specific hydration rates, and the effect of the site's high altitude (cold setting) on effective hydration temperature. The 24 obsidian tools and flakes submitted for sourcing and hydration analysis include most of the obsidian found at the site: ten pieces from Kane Springs, six from the Delamar Mountains (including one of the two Elko Corner-notched points), six from the Modena/Panaca Summit, and two from Wild Horse Canyon, Utah. As Table 6.57 shows, the averages for the three most common sources are substantially smaller than for most other Late Archaic sites in the Gold Butte area (see Chapter 5), owing no doubt to the high-elevation (cool) temperature effects and perhaps the sheltered setting.

TABLE 6.57. Source-Specific Obsidian Hydration Data from 26CK8179.

Source	Readings (microns)[a]	Mean	Standard Deviation
Delamar Mountains	(3.0), 4.3, 5.0,[b] 6.0, 6.9, 7.1	5.9	1.2
Kane Springs	3.7, 4.0, 4.0/(5.4), 4.9, 4.9, 4.9/(5.9), 5.0, 5.0, 6.0, 6.1	4.8	0.8
Modena/Panaca Summit	2.5, 3.2, 4.0, 4.1 (6.0), (16.0)	3.4	0.8
Wild Horse Canyon, Utah	5.4/(8.5), 7.1/(8.5)	6.2	1.2

[a] Values in parentheses are considered outliers and excluded from mean calculations; values behind slashes are second bands.
[b] Denotes projectile point.

If we discount statistical outliers (removed via Chauvenet's criterion), the results for each source group are internally cohesive and support the interpretation of a single component associated with the more recent of the two radiocarbon dates.

Projectile Points

The 14 projectile points at the site consist of nine Elko Corner-notched, one Gypsum, one Humboldt, one large concave-base specimen, one indeterminate dart-sized fragment, and one leaf-shaped serrated item. All are consistent with a Late Archaic occupation and with the younger of the two radiocarbon dates. The points occur throughout the stratigraphic profile in the shelter, without any particular pattern to their distribution.

Discussion

All lines of evidence indicate that the site contains a single Late Archaic component, associated with the agave oven in the central shelter. This partially overlies an earlier agave oven which lacks associated artifacts and which dates to the recent end of the Early Archaic period. The relationship of the cultural assemblage to the oven in the shelter area is still somewhat enigmatic, however, as no clear base or outline to the oven was found and the assemblage appears thoroughly intermixed with the dense deposit of fire-affected rock. No strong trend in the vertical distribution of cultural materials is apparent, though densities are generally highest between 40 and 80 cm. It seems likely that construction of the oven in the shelter disturbed a preexisting midden, vertically mixing the assemblage. It is noteworthy that the only three pieces of milling gear recovered from the site were from the 50–60-cm and 60–70-cm levels in the shelter units. Assuming that these items are less

TABLE 6.58. Assemblage from 26CK8179.

	Total
Flaked Stone	
Projectile Point	14
Biface	17
Drill	1
Formed Flake Tool	1
Flake Tool	5
Core	9
Debitage	380
Ground Stone	
Handstone	2
Millingstone	1
Ornament	
Shell	1
Modified Bone	6
Total	437
Faunal & Floral Remains	
Bone	1,135[a]
Plant Material	132

[a] 61 small fragments recovered in heavy fraction of flotation samples are not included.

TABLE 6.59. Technological Analysis of Debitage from 26CK8179.

	Chert		Obsidian		Quartzite	
	#	%	#	%	#	%
Core Reduction						
Primary Decortication	3	1.3	—	—	—	—
Percussion Interior	20	8.8	1	4.8	—	—
Biface Reduction						
Early Biface Thinning	73	32.0	1	4.8	1	50.0
Late Biface Thinning	53	23.2	5	23.8	—	—
Pressure	79	34.7	14	66.6	1	50.0
Diagnostic Total	228	100.0	21	100.0	2	100.0
Platform Prep./Pressure	3	—	2	—	—	—
Indeterminate Percussion	86	—	3	—	—	—
Indeterminate Fragment	19	—	8	—	—	—
Shatter	8	—	—	—	—	—
Sample Total	344	—	34	—	2	—

Note: % = analytical percentage.

prone to vertical mixing, this suggests that the original occupation surface may have been at about this depth.

Artifact Inventory

Excavation yielded a modest collection of flaked and ground stone tools as well as a large and diverse assortment of faunal and floral remains (Table 6.58).

Flaked Stone Tools and Debitage

The flaked stone assemblage consists of the 14 projectile points, a drill, 17 bifaces, nine cores, a formed flake tool, five simple flake tools, and 381 pieces of debitage. The great majority of the assemblage is fashioned from chert, with only 39 obsidian specimens and one each of quartzite and a metavolcanic material. Many of the chert pieces are potlidded and thermally crazed, a result of uncontrolled burning.

As noted above, the 14 points are the only Late Archaic period forms. All are made of chert except for two Elko points made of obsidian. Most are proximal fragments, though the large leaf-shaped point, the Gypsum point, and three of the Elko are complete or nearly so.

Of the bifaces, 14 were made of chert and three of obsidian. They are mostly middle-stage (n = 6) and late-stage (n = 8) fragments. Several of the latter are distal tips of complete/finished projectile points that do not retain diagnostic elements.

The single drill is also made of chert. It is complete, with a long, narrow, bifacial bit and a nicely made, bifacially flaked, convex-shaped, unnotched base.

The single formed flake tool is chert. It, too, is complete, with invasive, steep-sided modification along one margin. Five flake tools were also recovered, most made on large flakes and displaying microchipping on one or two margins.

The nine cores recovered are all chert except for one large specimen of metavolcanic rock. Four of the chert specimens retain cortex.

All debitage recovered was subjected to technological analysis (Table 6.59). It consists of 344 pieces of chert, 34 of obsidian, and two of quartzite. The assemblage shows an emphasis on tool finishing (pressure flakes) and biface reduction rather than core reduction.

Ground and Battered Stone

Three pieces of ground stone were recovered, and a fourth was noted on the surface. The surface item is part of a bifacially worn handstone made of a purple, distinctive sandstone conglomerate. Of the subsurface items, a millingstone margin and a handstone were found in the 50–60-cm level of S4.5/W1.5 and an end fragment of a handstone was recovered from the 60–70-cm level of S6.5/W1. The millingstone is made from rhyolite. It is in three conjoining pieces that together make up a margin fragment; it shows bifacial wear—both flat worn surfaces have a smooth polish, and one of them is also pecked. The nearby handstone is made from metavolcanic rock. It is complete (13.6 × 8.5 × 5.2 cm) and has bifacial wear and evidence of shaping on the margins. Both worn surfaces are basically flat, with smooth polish on them and pecking on one. The final handstone fragment is an end piece made from sandstone, unshaped, and showing bifacial wear. Both surfaces are smooth-polished and slightly convex. One surface retains a reddish residue.

Modified Bone

Six pieces of modified bone were recovered. One of these (cat. no. 97) was recovered from the mass of jumbled small cobbles and loose fill in Feature 1. It is a large, complete awl fashioned from a split long bone of a medium-to-large mammal (likely artiodactyl), with heavy polish and striations on one end but without evidence of fire-hardening. The rest of the modified bone tools were recovered from the shelter units. Item 175 is a fragmentary tool that may be an unfinished awl. It is made from the distal end of a bobcat ulna and has light polish and some striations. The rest are small fragments made on unidentified long bone fragments. Item 107 is a sharp distal end of a possible needle, with minimal shaping and lacking evidence of polish, striations, or fire hardening. Items 26CK8179-57, -83, and -89 are medial or distal fragments of awls or pins, all showing high polish, striations, and fire-hardening.

Shell Artifact

Two slivers of a single *Dentalium* shell (Figure 6.53) were recovered from S6.5/W1.5 at a depth of 70–80 cm. It is 20.3 mm long and has split longitudinally so that only a half remains; also, the outer surface has exfoliated so that the item is now in two pieces. Although not a finished ornament, it is one of a very small number of marine shell artifacts found in the Gold Butte study, the others being fashioned from *Olivella* or *Haliotis* (see Chapter 5).

This shell originates from the Oregon/Washington coast and is rarely found in archaeological contexts in the Great Basin. Bennyhoff and Hughes (1987) note that it is sometimes found in mostly Late Prehistoric contexts in northern Nevada (e.g., Lovelock Cave, Humboldt lake bed, Churchill County). Janetski (2002) reports a few occurrences in Fremont contexts in northern Utah. It is not represented in the extensive array of shell ornaments reported by Haury (1965) at Snaketown, Arizona, nor is it reported in the available Virgin Branch archaeology literature. Given that its occurrence in southern Nevada is aberrant, and that its presence in a Late Archaic context has interesting implications about long-distance trade through various groups to the northwest, we had its identification confirmed by

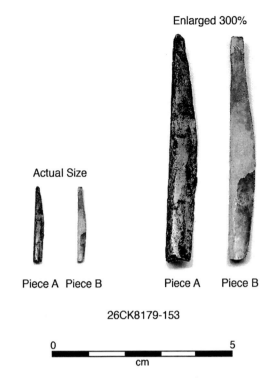

Enlarged 300%

Actual Size

Piece A   Piece B   Piece A   Piece B

26CK8179-153

0   5
cm

FIGURE 6.53. *Dentalium* shell ornament from 26CK8179.

Randall Milliken, a well-regarded expert in California and Great Basin trade beads (e.g., Hughes and Milliken 2007; Milliken and Bennyhoff 1993).

Floral and Faunal Remains

As mentioned above, subsistence remains, both faunal material and plant macrofossils, were well represented in the deposit, especially below the drip line in the protected shelter.

Plant Remains

A large amount of plant material was recovered from screens, much of it unburned and some of it rather fresh-looking. While this material was found throughout the profile, it was most abundant in the uppermost 30 cm of the deposit, interspersed among the loose cobbles dominating this part of the profile. Most of this material was made up of agave leaves and fibers, but some pinyon cone scales, pinyon needles, and partially burned fragments of wood were also recovered.

Two flotation samples were processed, one from the outer apron of the oven (N5/W5) and the other from the lowermost level in the back of the shelter (S6.5/W1). In all, 9.8 liters of sediment were processed. The sample from the outer apron of the oven produced only a single prickly pear (*Opuntia* sp.) seed. The shelter sample, by contrast, was productive, yielding 87 pinyon (*Pinus* sp.) nut hulls, 14 manzanita (*Arctostaphylos* sp.) berry pits, a

TABLE 6.60. Faunal Remains from 26CK8179.

	Burned	Unburned	Total
Mammals			
Bighorn Sheep	6	65	71
Artiodactyl	22	57	79
Medium-to-Large (Sheep-Sized)	125	274	399
Bobcat	—	7	7
Badger	—	5	5
Long-Tailed Weasel	—	2	2
Medium Carnivore	1	4	5
Medium Mammal	—	2	2
Jackrabbit	—	21	21
Cottontail	2	47	49
Hare/Rabbit	—	11	11
Small-to-Medium (Rabbit-Sized)	13	137	150
Shrew	—	1	1
Desert Woodrat	—	22	22
Botta's Pocket Gopher	—	4	4
New World Mice	—	13	13
Squirrel	5	145	150
Rodent	1	81	82
Small Mammal	—	2	2
Indeterminate-Sized	8	20	28
Birds			
Burrowing or Screech Owl	—	1	1
Perching Birds	—	1	1
Reptiles			
Desert Tortoise	2	1	3
Nonvenomous Snake	—	2	2
Rattlesnake	—	5	5
Snake	—	2	2
Lizard		2	2
Vertebrates			
Unidentified Vertebrate	—	16	16
Total	**185**	**950**	**1,135**[a]

[a] 61 small fragments from heavy fraction of flotation samples are not included.

hackberry (*Celtis laevigata*) pit, and nine unidentifiable seeds or seed fragments. Both samples yielded abundant wood charcoal.

Faunal Remains

A large assemblage of faunal remains was recovered, totaling 1,135 pieces of bone or teeth (Table 6.60). Nearly half of the identifiable remains (49 percent) are from medium-to-large mammals, almost certainly artiodactyls. A smaller number were identified specifically as desert bighorn sheep. Nearly 30 percent of the medium-to-large-mammal remains show evidence of burning; a few also show cutmarks. Small mammals, almost entirely rodents, are the next most common (24 percent of identifiable remains), though most of these remains are probably intrusive, given that they rarely are burned. Following these in abundance are lagomorphs (jackrabbits, cottontails) and small-to-medium mammals, the latter probably also lagomorphs, in total making up 21 percent of identified remains. Carnivores (bobcat, badger, weasel), birds, and reptiles make up the remainder of the identifiable assemblage.

Summary

Based on projectile point types and obsidian hydration data, site 26CK8179 appears to be a single-component, Late Archaic period occupation. The two radiocarbon dates indicate a longer period of use, extending into the recent end of the preceding Early Archaic period. However, we argue here that the great majority, if not the entirety, of the assemblage is associated with the more recent of the two dates, taken from the shelter area where the material was recovered. The earlier date from the downhill, outer apron area is not physically associated with an artifact assemblage and may represent a site use episode focused exclusively on agave.

Whatever the specifics of its depositional history, the site presents a uniquely detailed view of Late Archaic subsistence practices. It is the earliest dated example of agave processing in the region (see Chapter 5). The robust faunal assemblage also provides an important window into Late Archaic high-elevation hunting practices, which appear focused mainly on bighorn and less on small, rabbit-sized game.

EXCAVATION SUMMARY

The nine prehistoric archaeological sites test excavated as part of the Gold Butte project resulted in the discovery of 14 single-component areas. Identification of these areas was based on the presence of discrete strata and features dated with various combinations of radiocarbon assays, time-sensitive projectile points, temporally diagnostic pottery, and obsidian hydration readings. The earliest component was found at 26CK3201, where occupation occurred at about 2500 cal BC, or at the very beginning of the Late Archaic period (2500–350 BC). Three additional Late Archaic components were found at 26CK6078/6095, -7994, and -8179, roughly spanning the remainder of this temporal interval. Basketmaker II/III occupations (350 BC–AD 800) were found at four sites (26CK3201, -4891, -6080/6081, and -7994). Three sites (26CK1991, -3201, and -6080/6081) have components corresponding to the Puebloan interval (AD 800–1250), while the Late Prehistoric period (post–AD 1250) is also represented at three sites (26CK1991, -6080/6081, and -8013). With the exception of 26CK1991, where excavations focused on agave ovens generally lacking artifacts, all the other components represent at least some amount of residential activity.

Artifact Assemblages

The data presented in Table 6.61 are organized according to general artifact class (flaked stone, ground and battered stone, other domestic items, and ceramics) and include more specific artifact types within these generalized groups (e.g., projectile points, handstones, bone tools, pottery). Sherds are excluded from some of the initial analyses that follow because they do not occur in Late Archaic assemblages and, therefore, are not conducive to interperiod comparisons across the entire occupational sequence. With regard to chronological organization, each single-component area is placed under its more generalized time period. Rather than focus on the individual component areas, most of the discussions that follow rely on the combined counts of artifacts from each generalized time period (see subtotals in Table 6.61).

Flaked stone tools dominate the aceramic assemblages during all time periods (Table 6.61). They range from a high of 86.7 percent in the Late Archaic to a low of 82.4 percent in the Late Prehistoric. This dominance remains relatively constant across all the single-component areas except 26CK4891 (a Basketmaker III pithouse village), where the combined frequency of ground and battered stone and other domestic items (63.6 percent) is actually higher than that of flaked stone tools (36.4 percent). When the rest of the Basketmaker components are separated from 26CK4891, flaked stone tools represent 88.9 percent of their assemblages. These findings probably indicate a high degree of settlement differentiation at this time, with large residential sites being established near the Virgin River (but still in the Gold Butte study area) and short-term camps being used in the hinterland.

Bifaces are the most common flaked stone tool type from all time periods, making up 60.3 percent of the Basketmaker flaked stone assemblage and progressively lower percentages of the Puebloan (55.9 percent), Late Archaic (53.1 percent), and Late Prehistoric (47.8 percent) assemblages (Table 6.61; Figure 6.54). Projectile points (19.2 percent) are slightly more abundant than flake tools (15.4 percent) and cores (12.3 percent) in Late Archaic contexts. All three are found in near-equal frequencies in Basketmaker and Puebloan assemblages (ranging between 15.3 and 11.8 percent) but diverge in the Late Prehistoric period, when flake tools (25.0 percent) and projectile points (22.8 percent) increase and cores reach an all-time low (4.4 percent). As illustrated in Figure 6.54, the increase in projectile points and flake tools gives the Late Prehistoric period the most even mix of flaked stone tools in the entire occupational sequence.

Biface manufacturing patterns also change over time (Table 6.62; Figure 6.55). The frequency of early-stage bifaces (Stage 1 and 2) stays relatively constant in Late Archaic (15.5 percent), Basketmaker (13.5 percent), and Puebloan (17.2 percent) assemblages but drops to 3.1 percent in Late Prehistoric contexts. Stage 3 bifaces reach maximum frequencies in the Late Archaic (50.0 percent), decrease steadily through the Basketmaker (29.7 percent) and Puebloan (10.3 percent) components, and increase again late in time (23.1 percent). Late-stage bifaces (Stage 4 and 5) follow an opposite trend, producing their lowest frequencies in the Late Archaic (34.5 percent), steadily increasing when moving into the Basketmaker (56.8 percent) and Puebloan (72.4 percent) periods, and leveling off thereafter (Late Prehistoric at 68.5 percent). These general trends indicate that a fuller range of biface reduction took place during the earlier periods of occupation than was the case later in time, when tool finishing and maintenance were more common activities.

Debitage follows a similar but more muted pattern (Table 6.62; Figure 6.56). Early- and late-stage biface thinning flakes match up with the Stage 3 bifaces, reaching maximum frequencies in the Late Archaic (34.2 percent), decreasing in the Basketmaker periods (22.4 percent), but staying steady thereafter (Puebloan at 24.3 percent; Late Prehistoric at 23.9 percent). Pressure flakes, matching the Stage 4 and 5 biface frequencies, start low in the Late Archaic (52.5 percent), increase in Basketmaker (66.5 percent), and level out in Puebloan (62.8 percent) and Late Prehistoric (65.1 percent) contexts. Core-reduction flakes (decortication and percussion interior flakes) are minimally represented throughout the sequence.

Due to the low number of ground and battered stone tools recovered during the test excavations, few definitive patterns are apparent. Handstones, millingstones, and battered cobbles are present in every component area except at the agave ovens (26CK1991), largely because we selected midden deposits (and hence habitation zones) for excavation. One potentially important change over time is the relative frequency of millingstones versus handstones and battered cobbles. Millingstones begin with a low of 33.3 percent in the Late Archaic, increase in Basketmaker (50.0 percent), drop

TABLE 6.61. Artifact Summary of the Fourteen Single-Component Areas Test Excavated at Gold Butte.

Site (26CK)	Late Archaic					Basketmaker II and III					Pueblo I and II				Late Prehistoric				Total
	3201	6078/6095	7994	8179	Total	3201	4891	6080/6081	7994	Total	1991	3201	6080/6081	Total	1991	6080/6081	8013	Total	Total
Flaked Stone																			
Projectile Points	2	9	1	13	25	5	2	2	—	9	—	7	2	9	—	29	2	31	74
Bifaces	37	11	4	17	69	30	1	9	1	41	—	22	11	33	1	63	1	65	208
Flake Tools	7	4	3	6	20	7	—	—	1	8	1	5	3	9	—	32	2	34	71
Cores	5	1	1	9	16	9	1	—	—	10	1	5	2	8	—	6	—	6	40
Subtotal	51	25	9	45	130	51	4	11	2	68	2	39	18	59	1	130	5	136	393
Ground & Battered Stone																			
Battered Cobbles	2	—	1	—	3	1	1	—	1	3	—	2	1	3	—	1	—	1	10
Millingstones	3	—	—	1	4	—	3	2	—	5	—	2	—	2	—	2	2	4	15
Handstones	2	1	—	2	5	—	1	1	—	2	—	—	1	1	—	1	1	2	10
Subtotal	7	1	1	3	12	1	5	3	1	10	—	4	2	6	—	4	3	7	35
Other Domestic Items																			
Bone Tools	—	—	—	6	6	—	1	1	—	2	—	—	1	1	—	8	—	8	17
Drills	1	—	—	1	2	—	—	—	—	—	—	—	—	—	—	2	—	2	4
Non-utilitarian	—	—	—	—	—	—	1	2	—	3	—	1	1	2	—	12	—	12	17
Subtotal	1	—	—	7	8	—	2	3	—	5	—	1	2	3	—	22	—	22	38
Total	59	26	10	55	150	52	11	17	3	83	2	44	22	68	1	156	8	165	466
Ceramics																			
Pottery	—	6	—	—	6	6	299	20	—	325	10	186	74	270	8	871	88	967	1,568
Grand Total	59	32	10	55	156	58	310	37	3	408	12	230	96	338	9	1,027	96	1,132	2,034

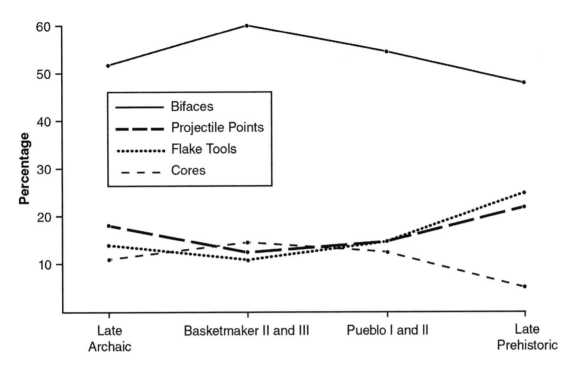

FIGURE 6.54. Relative frequency of flaked stone tool types across time.

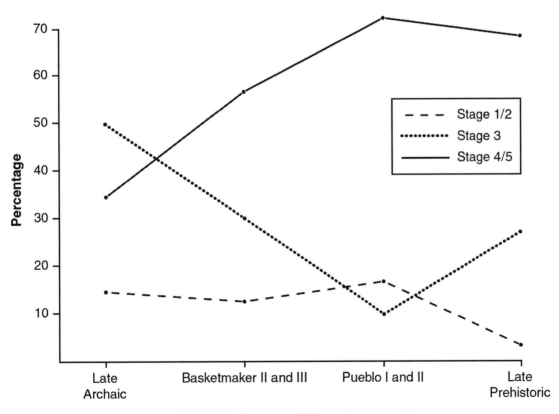

FIGURE 6.55. Relative frequency of biface stages across time.

TABLE 6.62. Biface Stage and Debitage Type by Period.

	Late Archaic	Basketmaker II and III	Pueblo I and II	Late Prehistoric	Total
BIFACE					
Stage 1	5	1	3	—	9
Stage 2	4	4	2	2	12
Stage 3	29	11	3	15	58
Stage 4	8	7	10	11	36
Stage 5	12	14	11	26	63
Indeterminate	6	3	4	11	24
Total	64	40	33	65	202
DEBITAGE					
Core Reduction					
Decortication	121	69	93	51	334
Interior	66	25	39	25	155
Biface Reduction					
Early Thinning	273	107	157	72	609
Late Thinning	208	82	93	93	476
Pressure	738	562	646	450	2,396
Diagnostic Total	1,406	845	1,028	691	3,970
OTHER					
Platform Prep./Pressure	250	233	181	66	730
Indeterminate Percussion	385	192	218	227	1,022
Indeterminate Fragment	473	372	365	227	1,437
Shatter	32	13	25	10	80
Total	2,546	1,655	1,817	1,221	7,239

Note: Data are from chert only.

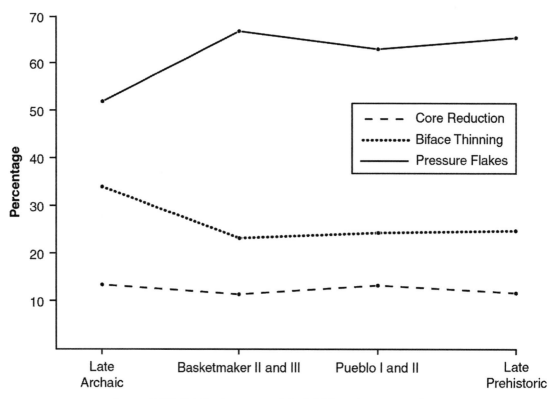

FIGURE 6.56. Relative frequency of chert debitage types across time.

again in Puebloan (33.3 percent), and reach a new high in Late Prehistoric contexts (57.0 percent). Given that these items are typically part of the site furniture (i.e., they are rarely transported), they might signal a higher degree of occupational stability late in time.

This general theme is supported to a limited degree by the category of "other domestic items," which are minor contributors the Late Archaic (5.3 percent), Basketmaker (6.0 percent), and Puebloan (4.4 percent) assemblages but increase in the Late Prehistoric period (13.3 percent; Table 6.61). This category includes bone awls and stone drills that were used to manufacture and maintain other things (e.g., clothing, basketry), as well as non-utilitarian items such as beads, paint palettes, ochre, and quartz crystals. While the drills and awls are found in low numbers in multiple locations, the non-utilitarian items are concentrated in Late Prehistoric contexts, particularly 26CK6080/6081.

Sherds were found in all late Basketmaker (BM-III), Puebloan, and Late Prehistoric contexts (Table 6.61). They contribute equally to the Basketmaker (79.6 percent) and Puebloan (79.9 percent) assemblages and increase in relative frequency in Late Prehistoric contexts (85.4 percent). Although their frequency roughly parallels that of the other artifact classes, they are more highly correlated with the combined totals of ground and battered stone and other domestic items ($r = 0.97$) than with flaked stone tools ($r = 0.84$), perhaps indicating a pull toward more residential contexts.

Floral and Faunal Remains

More than 124 liters of sediments were subjected to flotation analysis, yielding a rather small sample of charred seeds. Yields were lowest in Late Archaic (3.9 seeds/liter) and Basketmaker (2.3 seeds/liter) contexts but increased in the Puebloan (14.6 seeds/liter) and Late Prehistoric (12.6 seeds/liter) deposits. The data obtained from sites with positive results show that domesticated plants are completely absent, and pinyon nutshell, *Chenopodium* (goosefoot) seeds, and agave fragments are the most important constituents of the overall assemblages (Table 6.63).

When pinyon, goosefoot, and agave frequencies are combined by period and separated by habitat (pinyon upland versus desert lowlands), several interesting patterns emerge (Table 6.64). Beginning in the pinyon zone, pinyon nuts are dominant in the Late Archaic but surpassed by goosefoot later in time, while agave is never present. In the lowlands, small amounts of pinyon and goosefoot are present early on (i.e., in Late Archaic and Basketmaker components) but are essentially replaced by agave over time.

Combining the pinyon zone and lowland samples provides a better view of these relationships (Table 6.64; Figure 6.57). Pinyon remains are dominant in the Late Archaic, but the diet breadth expands to include goosefoot during the Basketmaker periods. Goosefoot reaches maximum importance in the Puebloan periods, and agave becomes a contributor for the first time. The final phase of intensification occurs during the Late Prehistoric period, when agave becomes dominant and goosefoot is more abundant than pinyon.

These patterns reflect a broadening of the diet breadth, beginning with pinyon and then moving to pinyon/goosefoot and, ultimately, to pinyon/goosefoot/agave. Pinyon ripens in the fall and is a highly ranked food, so it makes good sense that it was a dominant resource early on and used throughout the sequence. Goosefoot is the next plant added to the diet during Basketmaker and Puebloan times, and why it came before agave may also have a seasonality connection. Agave is best harvested in the spring before it sends up its stalk, while goosefoot seeds become available in late spring and early summer. It may be that the near-absence of agave in the Basketmaker and Puebloan excavated components, particularly the latter, relates to a scheduling problem, as spring was when the agricultural crops needed to be planted and extra attention given to the young seedlings, creating a disincentive to travel 25 km from the Virgin River to the agave zone at Gold Butte. By the Late Prehistoric period, when the scheduling constraints of agriculture production were removed, local Southern Paiute populations may have intensified the use of agave like never before.

Like the plant remains, archaeofaunal samples are rather small and fragmentary for most of the project sites (Table 6.65). The most precise levels of identification in our analysis are genus/species (e.g., bighorn sheep, jackrabbit, cottontail, desert tortoise) and order (e.g., artiodactyls, lagomorphs), while a more generalized level of identification includes fragmentary pieces that can only be categorized as medium-to-large mammal (mostly sheep-sized) and small-to-medium mammal (mostly rabbit-sized). Other taxa have been identified at some of the sites, but their numbers are quite low and are not presented here. Squirrel bone is present but at only one site (26CK8179). Due to the restricted distribution of this taxon, with regard to both time and space, its comparative value is limited, and therefore we excluded it from this analysis. As a result, the following discussion focuses on artiodactyls, lagomorphs, and tortoise.

Beginning with the pinyon uplands (Table 6.66), artiodactyl (i.e., bighorn sheep and artiodactyl) is quite

TABLE 6.63. Plant Macrofossil Remains from Key Gold Butte Sites.

| | Late Archaic | | | Basketmaker II and III | | Pueblo I and II | | | Late Prehistoric | | |
	3201[a]	7994[b]	8179[b]	6080/ 6081[b]	7994[a]	1991[a,c]	3201[a]	6080/ 6081[b]	1991[a]	6080/ 6081[b]	Total
Charred Nutshell											
Pinyon (*P. edulis/monophylla*)	1	—	87	5	18	1	—	41	—	38	191
Charred Seeds											
Goosefoot (*Chenopodium* spp.)	1	—	—	9	26	—	1	234	1	56	328
Tansy Mustard (*Descurainia* spp.)	—	—	—	—	—	—	—	4	—	—	4
Filaree (*Erodium cicutarium*)	—	—	—	—	—	—	—	—	1	—	1
Prickly Pear (*Opuntia* spp.)	—	—	—	1	—	—	—	—	—	—	1
Desert Tomato (*Lycium* spp.)	—	—	—	—	4	—	—	—	—	—	4
Phacelia (*Phacelia* spp.)	1	—	—	—	—	—	—	—	—	—	1
Sunflower Family (Asteraceae)	—	—	—	—	—	—	—	4	—	—	4
Bean Family (Fabaceae)	—	—	—	—	1	—	—	—	—	1	2
Mallow Family (Malvaceae)	—	—	—	—	2	—	—	—	—	—	2
Grass Family (Poaceae)	—	—	—	—	9	—	—	—	—	8	17
Unidentified Seed Fragments	1	—	9	—	27	—	—	14	—	21	72
Charred Berry Pits											
Manzanita (*Arctostaphylos* spp.)	—	—	14	—	—	—	—	3	—	—	17
Juniper (*Juniperus* spp.)	—	—	—	—	—	—	—	6	—	1	7
Charred Cone Scales											
Pinyon (*P. edulis/monophylla*)	—	—	—	—	—	—	—	19	—	2	21
Flowering Stems											
Agave (*Agave utahensis*)	—	—	—	—	—	21	1	—	146	—	168
Total	4	—	110	15	87	22	2	325	148	127	840

[a] Desert lowlands.
[b] Pinyon upland.
[c] Dates to early Pueblo I (AD 810).

TABLE 6.64. Plant Macrofossils by Period and Habitat.

	Late Archaic	Basketmaker II and III	Pueblo I and II	Late Prehistoric	Total
Pinyon Zone					
Pinyon	87	5	41	38	171
Chenopodium	—	9	234	56	299
Agave	—	—	—	—	—
Subtotal	87	14	275	94	470
Lowland Zone					
Pinyon	1	18	1	—	20
Chenopodium	1	26	1	1	29
Agave	—	—	22	146	168
Subtotal	2	44	24	147	217
All Zones					
Pinyon	88	23	42	38	191
Chenopodium	1	35	235	57	328
Agave	—	—	22	146	168
Total	89	58	299	241	687

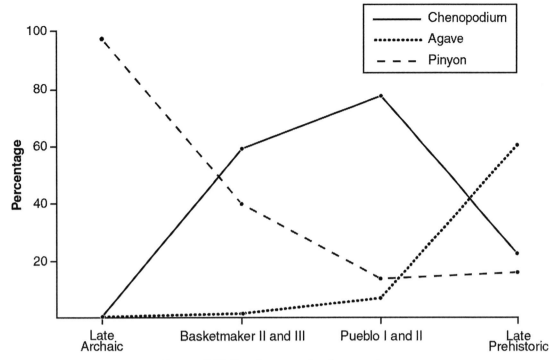

FIGURE 6.57. Key plant macrofossils across time.

TABLE 6.65. Archaeofaunal Remains from Key Gold Butte Sites.

	Late Archaic				Basketmaker II and III			Pueblo I and II			Late Prehistoric			
	3201[a]	7994[a]	8179[b,c]	Total	3201[a]	6080/ 6081[b]	Total	3201[a]	6080/ 6081[b]	Total	6080/ 6081[b]	8013[a]	Total	Total
Bighorn Sheep	—	—	76(4)	76	1	1	2	—	—	—	12	—	12	90
Artiodactyl	5(3)	1	61(9)	67	3(2)	8	11	8(14)	3(2)	11	21(44)	3(12)	24	113
Jackrabbitt	1	5	21	27	—	—	—	—	2	2	—	—	—	29
Cottontail	1	2	49	52	—	3	3	1	12	13	93	1	94	162
Lagomorphs	11	2	11	24	3	2	5	—	7	7	7	—	7	43
Tortoise	15	1	3	19	38	6	44	73	25	98	300	118	418	579
Medium-to-Large	28	5	398	431	18	77	95	22	115	137	1,167	9	1,176	1,839
Small-to-Medium	127	21	150	298	17	22	39	2	29	31	249	5	254	622
Total	188	37	769	994	80	119	199	106	193	299	1,849	136	1,985	3,477

Note: Numbers in parentheses represent small tooth enamel fragments not included in the analysis; sites 26CK1991, -4891, -6078/6095, and -8047 not included due to mixed components or insufficient sample sizes.
[a] Desert lowlands.
[b] Pinyon uplands.
[c] Squirrels present but not included (see site report for details).

abundant relative to lagomorphs and tortoise in the Late Archaic (62.0 percent) and slightly less so in Basketmaker times (45.0 percent), but drops precipitously during the Puebloan (6.1 percent) and Late Prehistoric (7.6 percent) periods (Figure 6.58). Artiodactyls are never abundant in the arid lowlands, but they reach a peak in Late Archaic components (13.6 percent), drop slightly in Basketmaker (8.9 percent) and Puebloan

(9.8 percent) contexts, and drop again in the Late Prehistoric (2.4 percent).

The relationship between tortoise and lagomorphs also shows major changes over time (Table 6.66; Figure 6.59). The relative abundance of tortoise versus lagomorphs is quite low in the pinyon zone during the Late Archaic (3.6 percent) but increases in the Basketmaker (54.5 percent) and Puebloan (54.3 percent) periods

TABLE 6.66. Identified Faunal Remains by Period and Habitat.

	Late Archaic	Basketmaker II and III	Pueblo I and II	Late Prehistoric	Total
Pinyon Zone					
Artiodactyl	137	9	3	33	182
Lagomorph	81	5	21	100	207
Tortoise	3	6	25	300	334
Subtotal	221	20	49	433	723
Desert Zone					
Artiodactyl	6	4	8	3	21
Lagomorph	22	3	1	1	27
Tortoise	16	38	73	118	245
Subtotal	44	45	82	122	293
All Zones					
Artiodactyl	143	13	11	36	203
Lagomorph	103	8	22	101	234
Tortoise	19	44	98	418	579
Total	265	65	131	555	1,016

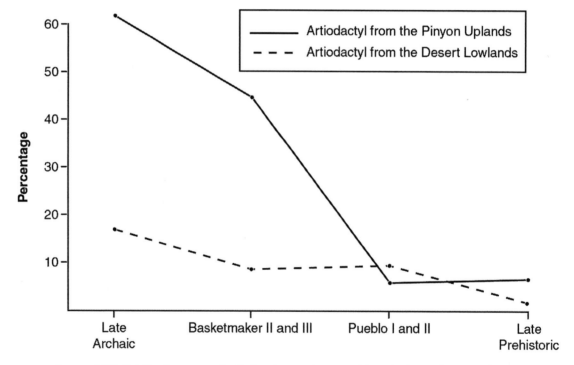

FIGURE 6.58. Relative frequency of artiodactyl versus lagomorph/tortoise by environmental zone.

and again during the Late Prehistoric (75.0 percent). A parallel trend is produced by the arid lowlands sample, with tortoise beginning at a low of 42.1 percent in the Late Archaic, showing a major increase in Basketmaker times (92.7 percent), and increasing and staying high thereafter (Puebloan at 98.6 percent; Late Prehistoric at 99.7 percent).

The decline in the use of artiodactyls over time is accompanied by a strong shift in the degree of bone fragmentation, perhaps indicating differences in the intensity of butchering and use (Table 6.67; Figure 6.60). Dividing the frequency of medium-to-large mammal bone fragments by the number of identifiable artiodactyl bone gives a rough estimate of the amount of bone fragmentation. During the Late Archaic the ratio of artiodactyls to medium-to-large mammal bone is only 1:3.0. The ratio increases significantly in the Basketmaker (1:7.3) and Puebloan (1:12.5) periods and jumps

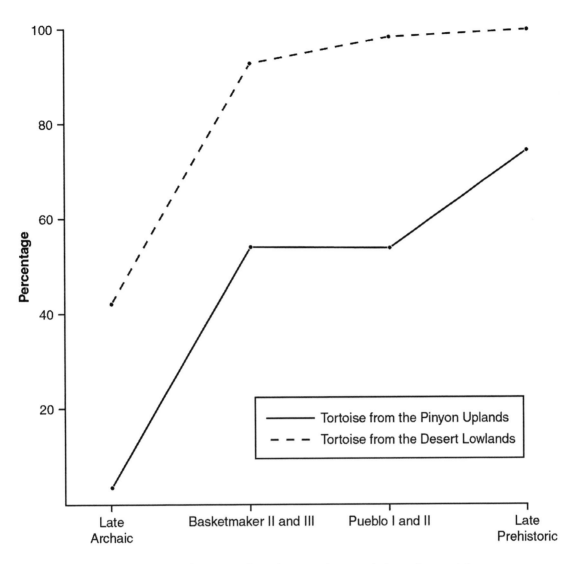

FIGURE 6.59. Relative frequency of tortoise versus lagomorphs by environmental zone.

TABLE 6.67. Relationship between Identifiable and Fragmentary Faunal Remains.

	Late Archaic	Basketmaker II and III	Pueblo I and II	Late Prehistoric
Artiodactyl	143	13	11	36
Medium-to-Large	431	95	137	1,176
Artiodactyl:Medium-to-Large	1:3.0	1:7.3	1:12.5	1:32.7
Lagomorph	103	8	22	101
Small-to-Medium	298	39	31	254
Lagomorph:Small-to-Medium	1:2.8	1:4.9	1:1.4	1:2.5
Average Weight of Medium-to-Large (g)	1.06	0.43	0.27	0.27

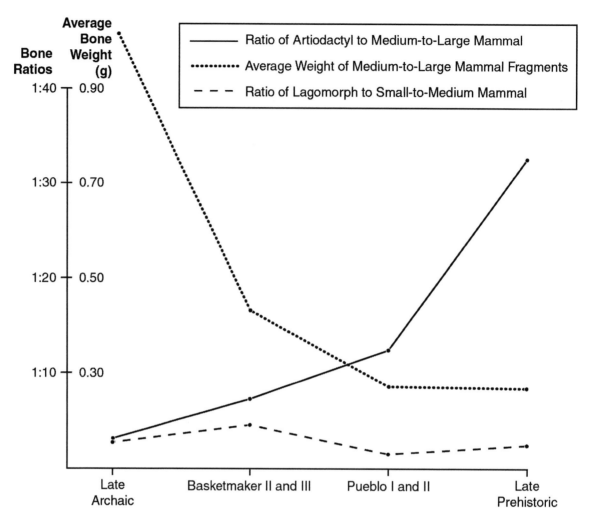

FIGURE 6.60. Relationship between identifiable and fragmentary faunal remains.

again in the Late Prehistoric to 1:32.7. This relationship is confirmed by calculating the average weight of the medium-to-large mammal fragments (Table 6.67; Figure 6.60). It begins in the Late Archaic at 1.06 g per bone, decreases to 0.43 g in the Basketmaker components, and continues to decline into the Puebloan (0.27 g) and Late Prehistoric (0.27 g) periods. This decrease in the size of medium-to-large mammal bone over time (most likely bighorn sheep) was probably due to more intensive use of important by-products such as marrow and fat.

Discussion

When the floral and faunal remains are combined, it appears that the Late Archaic peoples tended toward high-grade resources from the Gold Butte hinterland, focusing on hunting bighorn sheep and harvesting pinyon nuts probably during the fall and winter months. The relatively low frequencies of tortoise (burrowed in winter, more available at other times), agave processing (optimal in spring), and goosefoot seeds (late

spring-summer) indicate that Gold Butte was used less often and less intensively than was the case later in time.

The diet breadth and seasonal use of Gold Butte expanded during Basketmaker times, as goosefoot, lagomorphs, and tortoise were added to the diet, extending the fall-winter occupations into the warm seasons of the year. Although there is limited evidence for the addition of agave during the Puebloan periods, the intensive use of agave does not occur until the Late Prehistoric period, when it surpasses all other plant remains in the excavated samples. This intensive use can also be seen in the proliferation of roasting ovens radiocarbon dated to the Late Prehistoric period throughout the Gold Butte area (see Chapter 5). The expanding use of Gold Butte over time is also reflected in the artifact assemblage data outlined above, particularly during the Late Prehistoric period, when subtle trends in the mix of flaked stone tools and milling gear, and increasing frequencies of bone tools, drills, sherds, and non-utilitarian items, point to a higher degree of residential stability.

7 Rock Art

Our study of the rock art at Gold Butte relies primarily on inter- and intraregional stylistic comparisons. As mentioned earlier, there are four broad categories with temporal significance: Desert Archaic, representational, Protohistoric, and Early Historic (Figure 7.1). In this chapter we start with a review of the different styles found in the surrounding regions, their defining characteristics and rough age parameters. Then we describe the methods we used at Gold Butte to inventory and characterize the rock art present there. We provide atemporal summary data and indicate the number of sites, panels, and kinds and quantities of motifs encountered. Finally, we review the stylistic affiliation of the different concentrations, revealing some engaging temporal trends and suggesting the dynamic prehistory of the area.

BACKGROUND

In developing a context for understanding the rock art at Gold Butte, we rely as a starting point on the work primarily of Schaafsma (1971, 1980) to appreciate the Southwestern and Puebloan rock art tradition; Christensen and Dickey (2001) and Hedges (2003) to appreciate the rock art tradition associated with groups located along the Lower Colorado River and out into the Colorado Desert; and Heizer and Baumhoff (1962) and Heizer and Clewlow (1973) for guidance on the characteristics best associated with Great Basin rock art tradition.

Desert Archaic Rock Art

The basal rock art form throughout the Great Basin and Colorado Desert is pecked abstract designs of curvilinear and rectilinear forms. Hedges (1982) defined

this as the Western Archaic, and it has since had broad application in the southern Great Basin and southern California. Heizer and Baumhoff's (1962) Abstract Curvilinear and Abstract Rectilinear, though less rigorously defined, roughly equate. There is some indication that curvilinear shapes are dominant early on (before 2000 BC) and were eventually supplanted by rectilinear shapes (Gilreath and Hildebrandt 2008), though abstract designs see persistent use throughout all of prehistory.

Representational Rock Art

In the Southwest, by 2000 BC, representational art becomes widespread, with shapes of sheep (quadrupeds) and anthropomorphs recognizable. The earlier tradition of manufacturing designs by pecking continues, but elaborate, representational, polychrome pictographs make a seemingly abrupt appearance at about this same time. Both techniques, however, depict a similar suite of design elements. And from 2000 BC to AD 1250, variations in how sheep and human forms were pecked and painted largely serve to differentiate separate styles in the region. For representational work, general time-transgressive trends are for figures to shift from complex to plain, from large to small, and from exquisite to mundane in execution.

East/southeast of Gold Butte, along the sandstone canyon walls in the Colorado River drainage, three well-documented pre-Basketmaker rock art styles have been defined (Figure 7.2). Along the North Rim of the Grand Canyon are elaborate, large, polychrome anthropomorphs of the Grand Canyon Esplanade style; up from the confluence of the Little Colorado River and into the San Juan drainage are Glen Canyon Linear

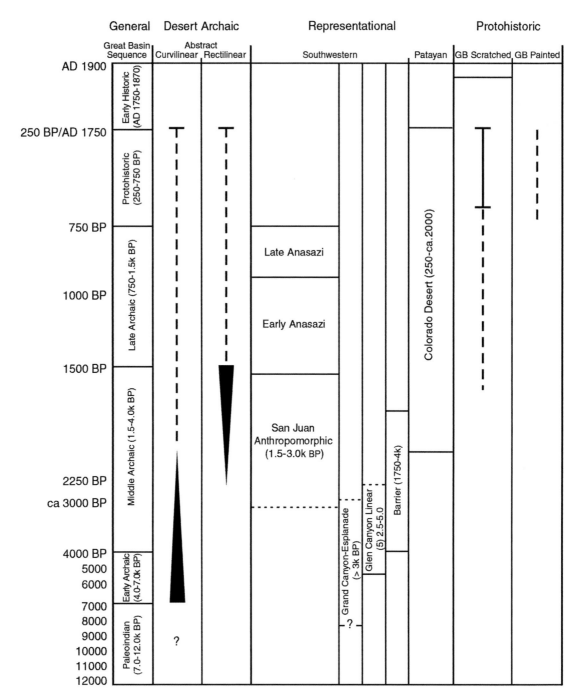

FIGURE 7.1. Rock art style chronology.

(Style 5) petroglyphs; and yet farther upstream, the artwork shifts back to polychrome pictographs of large anthropomorphs of the Barrier Canyon style. Though not especially well documented, terminal dates for these three hunter-gatherer representational rock art styles appear to be on the order of 1000 BC, 500 BC, and AD 250, respectively. Absolute dates are uncommon: Tipps (1995:68) reports dates of 3850 to 1640 radiocarbon years BP associated with Barrier Canyon panels,

which Cole (2004:40) reasonably converts to 2000 BC and AD 400. Shared characteristics of these three styles are their portrayal of "humanlike forms…heroic and supernatural in appearance," their use of elongated forms, and their "fine-line and highly detailed work" (Cole 2004:41).

Grand Canyon Esplanade and Barrier Canyon representational rock art are polychrome and less often monochromatic pictographs. Hallmarks of the former

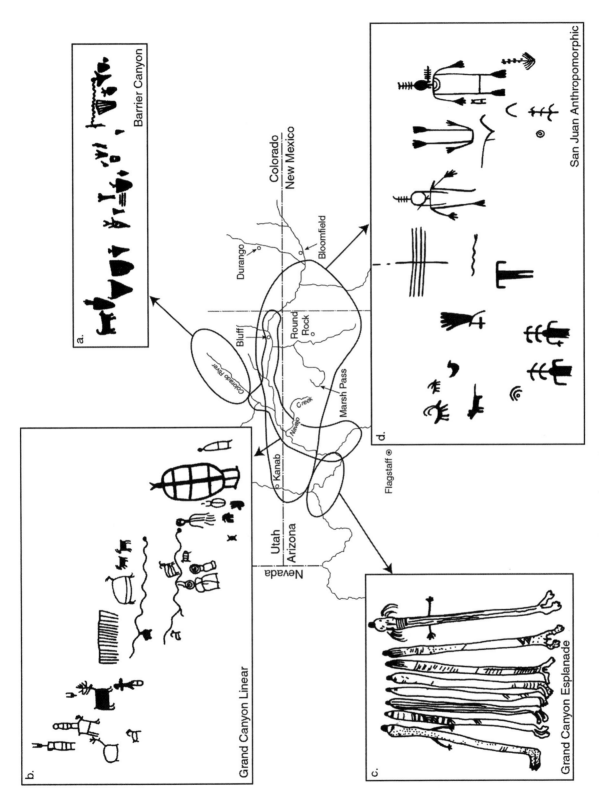

FIGURE 7.2. Southwestern Archaic and Basketmaker II rock art styles.

include a wide range of pigment colors and large (often life-sized) "outlined humanlike subjects with detailed interior body and facial embellishments frequently composed of stripes, dots, bands, and blocks" (Cole 2004:47). Both styles have compositions that include a row of static, large, front-facing anthropomorphs "attended" by miniature birds, quadrupeds, and stick-men figures (Cole 2004; Schaafsma 1980:61) that hover, flank, or perch on their shoulders. Other shared traits are their much-reduced heads (often a simple tab on Esplanade elements) and arms and legs that are missing or inconsequential. In contrast to Barrier Canyon style, Esplanade anthropomorphs may have feet, shown in profile or splayed to the sides, and an obvious phallus, in addition to a high incidence of superpositioning and a high percentage (56 percent) of nonrepresentational, geometric-abstract designs, often associated with the human-like figures (Allen 1998; Christensen and Dickey 2004; Dickey and Christensen 2009). Barrier Canyon rock art is dominated by large (often life-sized) ethereal human forms with elongate, tapering torsos, often with hunched shoulders, and a variety of head shapes and headdress types, but lacking appendages. One other contrast is that about half the Esplanade-style anthropomorphs are polychrome, compared with only 20 percent of the Barrier Canyon ones (Dickey and Christensen 2009:108).

Grand Canyon Linear rock art is essentially made as petroglyphs (not pictographs). Hallmarks are the rectilinear outlined bodies of humans and sheep with parallel and vertical interior body designs (Castleton 1987; Cole 2004:43; Turner 1963, 1971). Sheep tend to be large with rectangular bodies; anthropomorphs are generally 0.2 to 1.0 m tall, with vertically elongated trapezoidal to rectangular bodies, often with a phallus, but without arms, and characteristically with two-horn or ear headdresses.

Turning to the west, Heizer and Baumhoff (1962) defined Great Basin Representational as a petroglyph style. There is general agreement that their initial dating of AD 1 to 1500 is too young (1962:234), and a span on the order of 2000 BC to AD 1000 seems to be more in line now with the rest of the archaeological record. Grant et al. (1968) studied the age of the representational petroglyphs concentrated in the Coso Range in the western Mojave Desert and concluded that much of it fell roughly between 1000 BC and AD 1000. They also noted that the proportion of representational elements (relative to abstract ones) increased over time, the manner of execution improved, and designs became more highly stylized. By the end of the florescence of representational rock art in the Coso Range

TABLE 7.1. Proportion of Representational Rock Art Tallied by Heizer and Baumhoff (1962).

	Count	Percent	Total Elements
Inyo County, CA (Coso)	161	41	393
Clark County, NV	439	45	980
Rest of Great Basin	78	4	1,919
Total	678	21%	3,292

ca. AD 1000, numerous well-executed, highly stylized, and highly detailed sheep were being made, and archers (in contrast to human figures holding what are often interpreted as atlatl paddles and/or bundles of dart foreshafts) were being depicted with some frequency, as were large, patterned-bodied anthropomorphs. Subsequent work in the Coso Range supports the abstract-to-representational-to-scratched rock art chronology (Gilreath 1999, 2003; Gilreath and Hildebrandt 2008; Hildebrandt and Ruby 1999) and confirms the 1000 BC to AD 1000 span for the florescence of the highly localized Coso representational style.

As a result of the term Heizer and Baumhoff chose, there is a common misconception that Great Basin Representational rock art is a pan–Great Basin phenomenon. But even by their accounting, a more accurate characterization is that there are a few spots in the Great Basin where appreciable amounts of it occur (Table 7.1): in Inyo County, California, caused by the occurrence of Coso-style rock art, which is about 41 percent representational; and in Clark County, Nevada, where 45 percent of the designs are representational. Their compiled data for the rest of Nevada show merely that 4 percent of the elements are representational, and these are thinly spread throughout the state, with no one county having more than 3 percent. Heizer and Baumhoff specifically note that sheep are especially concentrated in Clark County and to a lesser degree in Lincoln County. (The few Lincoln County sites they review highlight the occurrence of sheep and pictographs; Pahranagat-style anthropomorphs were essentially unknown to them.) The temporal significance of representational art appears to differ on a somewhat local level. In the Coso Range it appears to be primarily an AD 1 to 1000 phenomenon that ramped up just before the time when the bow and arrow replaced atlatl and dart hunting technology (Gilreath and Hildebrandt 2008). The frequency with which atlatls (bifurcated circles) supplanted by archers are depicted provides general support for this interpretation.

Several lines of evidence suggest that Late Archaic/pre-Basketmaker hunter-gatherers along the Colorado

River and into the eastern Mojave Desert practiced a similar underlying religion or belief system, with a limited set of symbols represented by anthropomorphs of heroic proportion, bighorn sheep, and the atlatl. In western Colorado River canyons these life-size anthropomorphs are attended by small quadrupeds. In the eastern Great Basin, at Pahranagat for example, what could be taken for superheroes are often depicted wielding atlatls (Holmes and Carter 2009), and the atlatl design is found at Archaic rock art sites throughout the eastern Great Basin and Mojave Desert (e.g., Atlatl Rock [CK1] in Valley of Fire [Heizer and Baumhoff 1962]). While Late Archaic hunter-gatherers' proclivity for polychrome designs is manifest in the pictographs on the Colorado Plateau, it is manifest in the hunting gear of eastern Mojave Desert people. This is suggested by the ceremonial caches of dart shafts with elegant, fine lines and dots of green, red, maroon, and white paint adorning cane and wooden implements in caves such as Firebrand (Blair 2006) and Gypsum (Gilreath 2009). In select places like the Coso Range, the rock art underscores the symbolic importance of the bighorn sheep. Elsewhere split-twig figurines indicate their widespread symbolic importance to Late Archaic people. These items have been found secreted away in Cowboy Cave (Jennings 1980) in the northern Great Basin, in Stanton's Cave in the Grand Canyon (Euler 1978), and in Etna and Newberry caves (Fowler 1973; Davis and Smith 1981) in the southern Great Basin/Mojave Desert. In northern Utah along Green River these figures have been radiocarbon dated between 2150 and 1500 BC (Coulam and Schroedl 2004:52); in the Mojave Desert they are radiocarbon dated between about 2000 and 1000 BC (Davis and Smith 1981); in the Grand Canyon they are somewhat younger. Emslie et al. (2005:169; see also Tuohy 1986:229–231) report dates on the order of 1200 BC to AD 500. In some instances, they are "attended" by highly decorated hunting gear.

Basketmaker/Puebloan Rock Art

The term Basketmaker/Puebloan rock art, as used here, is inclusive of what has been considered Basketmaker II, as well as what has been differentiated as Early and Late Anasazi rock art. While various design and compositional variations have been articulated for different locations and for different subunits of time, there is a broad Basketmaker/Ancestral Puebloan rock art stylistic tradition throughout northern Arizona and Utah which continuously depicted representational designs, with particular emphasis on anthropomorphs, zoomorphs, and tracks/prints. Castleton and Madsen (1981) provide distributional maps of various motifs that indicate

a stylistic and geographic separation between Fremont to the north and the Puebloan art work found in southern Utah.

At the early end, San Juan Anthropomorph style (Figure 7.2) is associated with Basketmaker II sites and temporally overlaps with the end of the Late Archaic hunter-gatherer rock art styles; it dates between ca. 1000 BC and AD 500. The signature element of this style is the "large, broad-shouldered...figures depicted in rows, in pairs, or scattered across a cliff surface" (Schaafsma 1980:109), with adornment such as headgear, necklaces, earrings, and/or sashes. The body is typically an elongated trapezoid that tapers to the bottom, with simple arms that drop from the shoulders, and legs that extend down from the outer edge of the torso. They generally are from 0.6 to 1.5 m tall. A geometric, rectilinear object often projects from one side of the head. Vertical stacks of a repeated shape, such as mushroom caps or plant-like shapes, are also common. Like their Archaic antecedents, the anthropomorphs are in a full frontal and static position (Cole 1990).

Schaafsma (1971, 1980) defines three geographical variations of Virgin Anasazi rock art: Eastern and Western, commonly drawn as petroglyphs, and Cave Valley representational pictographs (Figure 7.3). Furthermore, she differentiates Early and Late styles. Cave Valley pictographs (which she associates with the Early Anasazi) are dominated by blunt, stubby anthropomorphs in a variety of colors, sometimes accompanied by birds, a flute player, and the usual complement of curvilinear abstract elements such as dots, spirals, concentric circles, and wavy lines. The Cave Valley type site and panels of this style are most prevalent in the vicinity of Zion National Park. In comparing Virgin with Kayenta representational, Schaafsma (1980:153) notes that the former has "less variation in subject matter" and that "stylistically shapes become rounded, moving away from the crisp forms of central Kayenta petroglyph elements. Stick-figure lizards and flute players are less common, as are pottery and textile motifs. Mountain sheep continue to be represented in large numbers, and deer with elaborate antlers are depicted.... Hooked ladder motifs increase, and unformalized abstract designs, perhaps borrowed from the Great Basin Abstract Style, appear to be contemporaneous."

Schaafsma perceives a stylistic shift ca. AD 500 and differentiates the Early Anasazi rock art style from earlier Basketmaker II compositions. Anthropomorphs are much reduced in size, importance, and elaboration and are characterized by two tendencies: some are simple, imbalanced "X"-shaped figures, with a solid, elongated triangle for a torso and with legs turned out to the side;

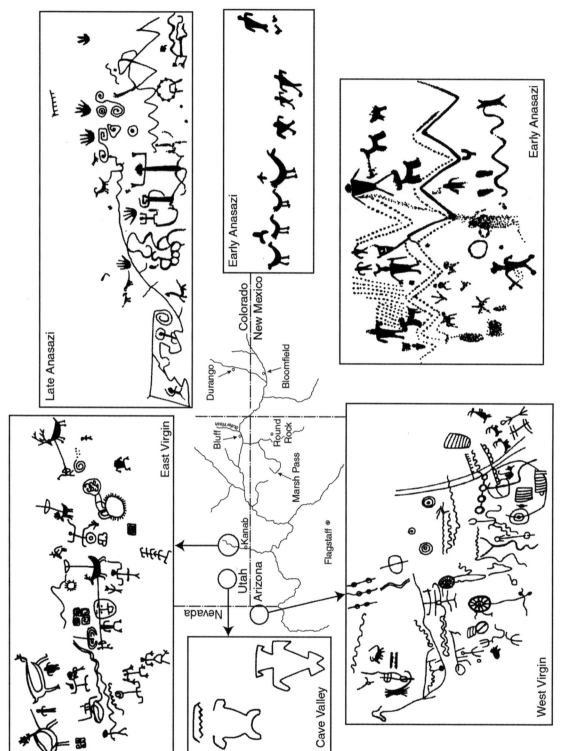

FIGURE 7.3. Virgin Anasazi rock art styles.

others are stick figures often "engaged in a variety of seemingly ordinary activities—walking, running, sitting in groups, and so on" (Schaafsma 1980:122). The flute player makes an occasional appearance (without the hump and phallus indicative of Late Anasazi panels). Bird-like figures are common, standing or flying singly or in groups and sometimes serving as a headdress on the simple anthropomorphs. Sheep are much less frequently depicted than in earlier sites, and they tend to be rendered simply. Early Anasazi panels are as often petroglyphs as monochrome or two-toned pictographs.

Schaafsma perceives yet another stylistic shift ca. AD 850 and differentiates Late Anasazi designs from earlier ones. The Late Anasazi style equates with Turner's Grand Canyon Style 4 petroglyphs, which have diagnostic designs that include "birds, flute players, hunting scenes, anthropomorphs with enlarged appendages and genitals, bird-bodied, open-mouthed, cloven sheep, concentric circles, and watchspring scrolls" (Turner 1963:7). The human shape is yet again reduced in size and further simplified to a rectilinear stick figure, now with arms that extend out at a right angle and turn skyward at the elbows. Lizards make a strong contribution, though the distinction between "men" and "lizards" is often arbitrary. Late Anasazi petroglyphs were commonly placed on cliff faces, while the more modest pictographs tend to be associated with rock shelters. This style occurs over a vast region and is interpreted as indicative of the expansion of Pueblo II populations. The terminal date for this style correlates with the Puebloan retraction throughout the greater Southwest and is placed generally around AD 1250 for the Gold Butte area.

Patayan Rock Art

For western Arizona and the Colorado Desert, the Patayan tradition temporally overlaps at the early end with the Puebloan occupations throughout the Southwest and extends closer to the present. The Patayan adaptation begins around AD 1 and has a terminal date of about AD 1750 for the Colorado Desert. The rock art associated with the Patayan tradition includes Grapevine and Colorado Desert styles found along the Lower Colorado River and throughout the Colorado Desert. Hedges (1973) draws attention to the persistent presence of digitate anthropomorphs in rock art sites across the southern desert, and notes that this motif is uncommon in Great Basin sites to the north. In his more recent analyses Hedges (2002, 2003) associates digitate anthropomorphs with ancestral Yuman cultures in the Colorado Desert, but whether this motif reflects a deep-time distinction between southern and more northern desert cultures, or whether it is an added element to the

pan-Western Archaic tradition, remains, in his opinion, an open question (2002:34).

Signature characteristics of the Grapevine style are its rectilinear, symmetrical, and geometric forms; the prevalent motifs are rectangles and subrectangles with interior elements, denticulated images, concentric plus signs, and capital "H" and "I" designs, as well as "mask-like" motifs (Christensen and Dickey 2001). Both of these styles—Grapevine and Colorado Desert—are well represented throughout the southern California desert and are associated with Patayan/Yuman archaeological sites attributed to the ancestral Mohave.

Protohistoric Rock Art

At the recent end of the prehistoric sequence, Great Basin Scratched and Great Basin Painted styles are recognized (Heizer and Baumhoff 1962:207–208), both generally placed between AD 1350 and 1800. Great Basin Scratched, also referred to as Numic Scratching, is firmly dated in the western Mojave Desert to the last 600 years (Gilreath 2003). Characteristics of this style are fine, incised lines quickly and lightly scratched into desert varnish, in a range of designs that favor cross-hatching, closely set roughly parallel lines, and rayed circles or sunbursts. Great Basin Painted designs are generally monochrome daubs, short thick lines, dots, circles, or simple starbursts painted in red, white, or yellow. Individual elements tend to be small, seldom more than 10–20 cm across, with one or a few elements forming a panel.

Early Historic Rock Art

Human-like figures wearing a cowboy hat or Euro-American clothing, riding a horse, holding a rifle or pistol, and so forth were made in postcontact time, within the last 150 years or so. When made using traditional pecked, scratched, or painting techniques, the artwork is usually attributed to Native Americans.

Distinct from Native American Historical rock art are Euro-American pictographs and petroglyphs. These are commonly initials, names, dates, a rancher's brand, and the like. They may be applied with an oily, colored material like axle grease or carved with a knife into a rock. They are readily distinguished from prehistoric and precontact Native American rock art based on their content or message and their manner of execution.

METHODS

An initial inventory of rock art sites in the study area was built from a conventional records search to identify known sites; from an Internet search during which we compiled posted images of panels in or near the study

TABLE 7.2. Summary Quantities of Rock Art Sites, Panels, and Elements.

	Random Survey	Nonrandom Survey	Not Reexamined	Total
No. of Sites (trinomials)	9	29[a]	4[b]	42
No. of Concentrations	11	56	4	71
No. of Panels	38	298	43	379
No. of Petroglyph Elements	449+	2,429	300+	3,178+
No. of Pictograph Elements	2	56	53	111

Note: + indicates that inventory counts of elements are incomplete.
[a] 26CK5608/Site 1 and 5608/Site 3 are counted separately here.
[b] Sites 26CK1968/1969, -3420, -6580, and -8097.

area; and from informal interviews with several individuals active in southern Nevada rock art interest groups. This resulted in (1) a concordance between trinomials and local site or place names; (2) basic information about Gold Butte rock art which was not included in the formal records (e.g., an appreciation for the number of co-occurring panels, their condition, design compositions, and the distinctive panels); and (3) a determination of which clusters of panels had not been previously documented (or were only poorly documented) so that they could be located and slated for formal recordation. At the end of this prefield exercise, 51 concentrations were identified, many of which could be generally associated with 34 different trinomials but at least a dozen concentrations that had never been recorded in any fashion.

In the subsequent field study phase, six sites with rock art were newly discovered during random survey, and 31 concentrations were encountered in the course of nonrandom survey, including the dozen previously mentioned. In total, 71 loci/sites with rock art have been identified in the study area (Tables 7.2 and 7.3). All but four were field-examined; 37 were recorded for the first time, and supplemental observations were made and an updated record completed for 30. They contain a total of 379 panels, which display more than 3,000 pecked elements and more than 100 painted elements.

For each panel, a tally of the quantity of different design elements was made based on review of panel photos or sketches, and/or in-field observations. At this stage, information for all the known panels was reviewed, and general impressions were drawn concerning the range of variability in the designs and condition of the body of work, as well as the varying quality and kind of information provided in field notes and on site records.

As indicated from the background review, a number of different styles were expected. In the interest of gauging how much of whose rock art is present in Gold

Butte, each of the 71 rock art concentrations was classified according to the style or styles of rock art present, with the classification categories limited to Early Historic, Protohistoric/Southern Paiute, Patayan, Basketmaker/Puebloan, and Desert Archaic.

Early Historic rock art was easily distinguished and consists of English initials and dates carved, incised, or painted with a black greasy substance (axle grease?). (Obvious recent and modern markings were noted as graffiti and vandalism and receive no further consideration here.)

Attributes used to define Protohistoric/Southern Paiute rock art at the late end of the sequence from Desert Archaic rock art at the early end were fairly direct. At the late end, any/all prehistoric pictographs or pigment is presumed to be Paiute rock art. At the early end, if the rock art was only abstract—whether curvilinear or rectilinear—it was classified as Desert Archaic. Distinguishing Basketmaker/Puebloan from Patayan rock art was more problematic since both styles make considerable use of both representational and abstract designs.

At the next analytical step, after review of information available for the panels and loci, several keystone rock art publications were again consulted, and a suite of signature icons distinctive to Basketmaker/Puebloan and Patayan rock art which occur with some frequency at Gold Butte were identified. Those suites of icons then served as the comparative or reference collection, and a second review of the panel slides and sketches was made to determine the style(s) prevalent at each concentration. For each concentration, specific panels and/or elements were noted on which the stylistic classification was based. No doubt, as our understanding of the distinguishing characteristics of different styles and the relationship between them improve, some of these assignments may be proven to be in error. At this juncture, though, the concern is less with being infallible than with being transparent and explicit about the factors that determine stylistic classification so that they may

TABLE 7.3. Baseline Information on Gold Butte Rock Art Sites.

Site (26CK), Locus	Action	Other Names or Numbers Applied	Temporary Field Number	Panel Data Source	Location
1968/1969	Not recorded	Raven Rock, CK1643 (location cf. CK8153 in part)	(cf. 088-35/088-36)	Original site record	ND
1978	Update	Sheep Procession	084-31-2	New	R
1984	Update	CK1645	089-41-1	New	NR
3093	Update		094-46-2	New	NR
3096	Update	Includes CK1985	090-41	New	NR
3206, L3	Update	Piedmont 75/76/83/84m	076-28/077-28-1, etc.	New	R
3420	Not recorded	CK143 = panel 20 only, Mud Wash	n.a.	NRAF, Gilreath et al. 2006	ND
5179, LE1	Update	CK5179, L1 & 2, Solemn Prayer	069-26	NRAF, FW sup	NR
5179, LE2	Update	CK5179, L1 & 2, Solemn Prayer	069-26	NRAF	NR
5179, LK/K1	Update	CK5179, L3, Looters Rock	068-26	NRAF, FW sup	NR
5608/Site 1	Not recorded	NRAF's CK5608/Site 1 on field map, Red Racer	Not found		ND
5608/Site 3	Update	NRAF's CK5608/Site 3, CK3205	078-30-4	NRAF, FW sup	NR
6543	Update	Lollipop	075-30	NRAF, FW sup	NR
6544	Update	Uno	075-30	NRAF, FW sup	NR
6580	Not recorded	Hobgoblin	n.a.	NRAF, Gilreath et al. 2006	ND
6641	Update	Waffle	069-26	NRAF, FW sup	NR
6642	Update	Chase Ridge	068-26	NRAF, FW sup	NR
6643	Update	Ascending Sheep	068-26	NRAF, FW sup	NR
6666, L1	Update	Jump Rope A	073-29	NRAF, Gilreath et al. 2006	R
6666, L2	Update	Jump Rope A	073-29	NRAF, Gilreath et al. 2006	R
6666, L3	Update	Jump Rope B	072-29	NRAF, FW sup	R
6672, L1	Update	Babe's Bluff	068-27	NRAF, FW sup	NR
6672, L2	Update	" "	" "	NRAF, FW sup	NR
6672, L3	Update	" "	" "	NRAF, FW sup	NR
6672, L4	Update	" "	" "	NRAF, FW sup	NR
6672, L5	Update	" "	" "	NRAF, FW sup	NR
6672, L6	Update	" "	" "	NRAF, FW sup	NR
7029, L1	Update		068-26	NRAF, Gilreath et al. 2006	NR
7029, L2	Update	" "	" "	NRAF, FW sup	NR
7029, L3	Update	" "	" "	NRAF, FW sup	NR
7029, L4	Update	" "	" "	NRAF, FW sup	NR
7029, L5	Update	" "	" "	NRAF, FW sup	NR
7029, L6	Update	" "	" "	NRAF, FW sup	NR
7029, L7	Update	" "	" "	NRAF, FW sup	NR
7996	New	—	069-26-3	New	NR
7997	New	—	069-27-1	New	R
8019	New	—	074-29-1	New	NR
8062	New	—	076-30-5	New	NR
8064	New	—	076-30-7	New	NR
8065	New	—	076-30-8	New	NR
8070	New	—	077-27-3	New	NR
8071	New	NRAF's CK5608/Site 6 on field map	077-27-4	New	NR

TABLE 7.3. (cont'd.) Baseline Information on Gold Butte Rock Art Sites.

Site (26CK), Locus	Action	Other Names or Numbers Applied	Temporary Field Number	Panel Data Source	Location
8084	New	NRAF's CK5608/Site 8 on field map	078-30/077-30-1	New	NR
8086	New	—	078-30-2	New	NR
8087	New	NRAF's CK5608/Site 4 on field map	78-30-3	New	NR
8093	New	—	080-30-2	New	NR
8096	New	—	081-29-1	New	R
8097	New	—	081-29-2	New	R
8098	New	—	081-29-3	New	R
8100	New	—	081-30-2	New	R
8123	New	—	084-30/083-30-1/H	New	NR
8129	New	CK1979	084-31-4	New	R
8136	New	—	085-32-1	New	NR
8140, L3	New	—	086-31/086-32/ 085-31-1	New	NR
8140, L4	New	CK1974	" "	New	NR
8140, L5	New	CK1975	" "	New	NR
8140, L6	New	CK1973	" "	New	NR
8140, L7	New	—	" "	New	NR
8140, L8	New	—	" "	New	NR
8140, L9	New	—	" "	New	NR
8140, L10	New	—	" "	New	NR
8140, L11	New	—	" "	New	NR
8140, L12	New	—	" "	New	NR
8140, L13	New	—	" "	New	NR
8140, NL Area 2	New	—	" "	New	NR
8140, NL Area 3	New	—	" "	New	NR
8140, NL Area 4	New	—	" "	New	NR
8140, NL Area 5	New	—	" "	New	NR
8156	New	—	089-40-1	New	NR
8165	New	—	094-42-2	New	NR
8166	New	—	094-42-3	New	NR

Note: R = random sample survey unit; NR = nonrandom sample survey unit; ND = outside survey units; NRAF = site and panels recorded/ sketched by precursor of Nevada Rock Art Foundation; FW Sup = augmented by Far Western fieldwork.

be applied elsewhere, that is, so that the classification is replicable.

In developing the short list of icons considered Basketmaker/Puebloan, we relied on Schaafsma (1971, 1980). She depicts anthropomorphs in many variants (Figure 7.4). Iconic forms include bodies that are large and rectangular, hourglass-shaped, or triangular; figures that are action-oriented (running, jumping, falling, flute playing, dancing); heads that are bucket- or malycephalic-shaped; stick figures in a strong, squatting position and stick figures with arms angled upward. Basketmaker/Puebloan-style sheep are far less variable than the anthropomorphs. They are mostly chunky, with oblong bodies that may grade into well-proportioned, rectangular bodies and pseudo-boat-shaped bodies.

Along with these common designs, other representational designs classified as Basketmaker/Puebloan include birds and sundry tracks or prints (bird tracks, handprints, bear paws, etc.).

In developing the short list of icons considered to be Patayan, we relied on Christensen and Dickey (2001) and Hedges (2003). Both of these studies are of sites that have minimal Basketmaker/Puebloan influence. Compared with Basketmaker/Puebloan forms, there are few Patayan anthropomorph variants (Figure 7.4): they have digitate and elephantine hands and feet; arms and legs that take the shape of back-to-back Cs; and simple, stick figures with arms straight out or angled down, often with small, round, simple heads (an opened circle or solid-pecked ball). Patayan sheep

Basketmaker/Puebloan

— Representational —

Anthropomorphs

Sheep

Patayan

— Representational —

Anthropomorphs

Sheep

— Abstract —

H and I

Crenellated Rectilinear Enclosed

Diamond Chain

Vertical Ball Series

FIGURE 7.4. Iconic Basketmaker/Puebloan and Patayan elements.

characteristically have an elongate, skinny, rectilinear form. Aside from the anthropomorphs and sheep, Patayan rock art commonly depicts what are often tallied as plants or stalk designs, as well as open, angular bug-like designs. There are also a few iconic Patayan abstract designs (Figure 7.4): I and H designs, which can become elaborate, crenellated vertical elements or sometimes rectangular rug-like shield designs; other vertical designs, especially three balls connected with a line; diamond or triangular sequences that are fringe- or net-like; and fairly large-format, open, angular designs.

When the rock art style was classified for a concentration, if the abstract designs appeared to be the same vintage as the representational designs, based on weathering and panel composition, then they were presumed to be either Basketmaker/Puebloan or Patayan. If the abstract designs appeared to be a different vintage than the representational designs, the concentration received an Archaic assignment.

Each rock art locus was classified according to the styles that could readily be distinguished. When a locus contained several panels and a number of elements that were indicative of a particular style, that style was considered to be "well represented"; if a few iconic elements indicated that a different style was present but they were numerically or graphically overwhelmed by the prevalent style, the subordinate one was charted as a "minority." In instances where panels were too indistinct to be classified with much confidence, or designs were ambiguous or atypical, the rock art locus was classified as indeterminate. Eight loci remain classified as Indeterminate style.

Atemporal Findings

Of the 377 prehistoric sites identified in the lands inventoried, rock art is known to be present at 38, as well as at four additional sites previously recorded by others. In total, 379 panels have been documented in some fashion at these 42 sites (Table 7.4). But rather than being scattered throughout the area, all the rock art is confined to the few small islands of Aztec sandstone that makes up only about 4 percent of the study area. As is evident in Figure 7.5, the Red Rock formations are conspicuous from a great distance. In a similar vein, the rock art was, in general, made to be conspicuous within the Red Rock formations. If we project from the 38 percent of the Red Rock formation that was intensively inventoried, there is an estimated total of 900 panels. Since this area has been much visited by rock art aficionados and outdoor recreationalists, it is highly likely that all large, elaborate panels, like those shown in Figure 7.6, have been discovered. Thus the panels not yet recorded probably are small and simple.

As summarized in Figure 7.7, the rock art typically occurs in clusters of six or fewer panels. It is also the case that the panels tend to be relatively small, typically less than 2 m across, and simply constructed (Figure 7.8): 76.6 percent (n = 281) have no more than ten elements, and only 3.3 percent (n = 12) have more than 35 elements. The one concentration with an aberrantly high number of panels (n = 58) is 26CK5179/Locus K, which is unusual in a number of ways and is discussed later. Atypically large—anywhere from 10 to nearly 60 m long—and elementally rich panels such as those shown in Figure 7.6 occur at only seven locations.

The rock art at Gold Butte is overwhelmingly petroglyphs. Only ten Scratched designs are recorded, and they are confined to one panel each at four locations. Slightly more than 100 painted elements are present at only 14 locations (31 panels), but nearly half of them are at a single location (26CK3420/Mud Wash) and are Early Historic writing. Of the remainder, 348 panels were made exclusively by pecking, and pecked and painted designs co-occur on only nine panels.

Excluding scratched and modern designs, there are 357 documented panels, which contain at least 3,090 pecked elements (Table 7.5). Just over half (53.7 percent) of elements on them are abstract, just over one-fourth (26.3 percent) are representational, and one-fifth (20.0 percent) are indeterminate pecked areas of little interpretive value and dismissed from further consideration. As summarized in Figure 7.9, nearly half (44.6 percent) of the panels have abstract-only designs, and abstract designs are more abundant than representational designs on another 27.2 percent of the panels. Representational designs have at least a minimal presence on just over half of the panels (55.4 percent) and are the only diagnostic elements present on 13.6 percent of them.

The prevalent abstract motifs are circular designs, with a number of variations well represented (31.4 percent). Other abstract designs that find fairly common expression at Gold Butte are rakes, dot patterns, and grids. Less distinctive lines and curvilinear or rectilinear marks are also commonplace. The three most prevalent representational designs are sheep (45.8 percent), anthropomorphs (23.2 percent), and various kinds of tracks (12.0 percent), including bird tracks and hand- or paw prints.

Temporal Trends

Even though Gold Butte experienced patterned use for at least the last 5,000 years and the rock art was placed within a small part of the area throughout all that time, surprisingly few concentrations have appreciable amounts of stylistically different rock art in co-

TABLE 7.4. Summary Attributes of Panels by Concentration.

Site (26CK)	Locus	No. of Panels	Modern	Historic Grease	Protohistoric Pictographs	Protohistoric Scratched	Abstract	Petroglyphs Representational	IPA	Element Total	Petroglyphs Motifs	Elements per Panel Mean	Elements per Panel S.D.
1968/1969	n.d.	6	15	0	0	0	17	2	0	34	8	3.2	n.d.
1978	n.a.	3	0	0	0	0	24	77	80	181	13	60.3	96.7
1984	n.a.	1	0	0	22	0	0	0	0	22	0	0.0	—
3093	n.a.	3	0	0	0	0	10	6	2	18	8	6.0	3.6
3096	n.a.	2	0	0	0	0	7	5	3	15	9	7.5	0.7
3206	3	2	0	0	0	0	47	1	0	48	4	24.0	4.2
3420	n.d.	21	9	44	0	0	37	23	15	128	16	3.6	9.5
5179	E1	6	0	0	0	0	34	3	6	43	15	7.2	8.7
5179	E2	1	0	0	0	0	3	0	0	3	3	3.0	—
5179	K/K1	13	0	0	0	0	63	36	6	105	24	8.1	11.4
5608/Site 1	n.a.	1	0	0	9	0	0	0	0	9	0	0.0	—
5608/Site 3	n.a.	8	0	0	0	0	75	144	5	224	24	28.0	40.3
6543	n.a.	5	0	0	0	0	70	3	1	74	9	14.8	17.2
6544	n.a.	1	0	0	0	0	8	0	4	12	4	12.0	—
6580	n.a.	15	0	0	0	0	78	43	61	182	25	12.1	9
6641	n.a.	1	0	0	0	0	20	5	7	32	12	32.0	—
6642	n.a.	3	0	0	0	0	18	2	11	31	10	10.3	8.7
6643	n.a.	1	0	0	0	0	0	2	1	3	3	3.0	—
6666	1	1	0	0	0	0	28	9	31	68	20	68.0	—
6666	2	10	0	0	0	0	48	8	35	91	21	9.1	17.4
6666	3	5	0	0	0	0	10	2	1	13	9	2.6	1.3
6672	1	1	0	0	0	0	0	5	0	5	4	5.0	—
6672	2	2	0	0	0	0	20	13	3	36	14	18.0	17
6672	3	9	0	0	0	0	10	11	6	27	8	3.0	3.3
6672	4	3	0	0	0	0	39	19	1	59	17	19.7	13.3
6672	5	5	0	0	0	0	16	4	1	21	10	4.2	3.8
6672	6	1	0	0	0	0	0	1	0	1	1	1.0	—
7029	1	58	29	0	0	6	170	18	92	315	32	4.9	5.2
7029	2	11	0	0	4	1	77	15	68	165	18	14.6	11.1
7029	3	12	0	0	9	0	31	1	14	55	11	3.8	3.8
7029	4	27	0	0	4	1	94	16	76	191	23	6.9	7.9
7029	5	1	0	0	0	0	0	9	0	9	1	9.0	—
7029	6	3	0	0	0	0	31	12	2	45	8	15.0	0
7029	7	18	0	0	0	0	106	6	14	126	17	7.0	7.3
7996	n.a.	6	0	0	0	0	24	5	0	29	13	4.8	5.1
7997	n.a.	1	2	0	0	0	2	2	0	6	3	4.0	—

TABLE 7.4. (cont'd.) Summary Attributes of Panels by Concentration.

| Site (26CK) | Locus | No. of Panels | Historic | | Protohistoric | | Petroglyphs | | | Element | Petroglyphs | | |
| | | | Modern | Grease | Pictographs | Scratched | Abstract | Representational | IPA | Total | Elements per Panel | | |
											Motifs	Mean	S.D.
8019	n.a.	2	0	0	0	0	10	1	0	11	5	5.5	0.7
8062	n.a.	2	0	0	0	0	6	1	0	7	5	3.5	2.1
8064	n.a.	5	0	0	0	0	30	1	0	31	12	6.2	6.8
8065	n.a.	1	0	0	0	0	12	2	2	16	12	16.0	—
8070	n.a.	1	0	0	0	0	1	0	0	1	1	1.0	—
8071	n.a.	2	0	0	0	0	2	0	0	2	2	1.0	0
8084	n.a.	1	0	0	0	0	6	0	0	6	3	6.0	—
8086	n.a.	3	0	0	0	0	18	2	0	20	8	6.7	6.7
8087	n.a.	1	0	0	0	0	3	0	0	3	2	3.0	—
8093	n.a.	1	0	0	0	0	1	0	1	2	2	2.0	—
8096	n.a.	6	0	0	0	0	9	2	0	11	6	1.8	1.6
8097	n.a.	1	1	0	0	0	0	0	0	1	0	0.0	—
8098	n.a.	5	0	0	0	0	14	7	0	21	8	4.2	4.1
8100	n.a.	3	0	2	2	0	0	2	0	6	2	0.7	0.6
8123	n.a.	2	0	0	0	0	0	2	0	2	2	1.0	0
8129	n.a.	1	0	0	0	0	1	3	3	7	3	7.0	—
8136	n.a.	2	0	0	0	0	1	14	3	18	4	5.5	0
8140	3	14	9	0	1	0	72	47	31	160	22	10.7	12.3
8140	4	1	0	0	6	0	0	0	0	6	0	0.0	—
8140	5	7	3	0	4	2	20	9	1	39	13	4.6	5.1
8140	6	5	1	0	1	0	5	6	0	13	7	2.2	3.3
8140	7	10	0	0	3	0	57	39	0	99	15	9.6	9
8140	8	3	0	0	0	0	8	3	3	14	8	4.7	3.2
8140	9	4	0	0	0	0	11	27	0	38	11	9.5	11.8
8140	10	6	0	0	0	0	46	38	0	84	20	14.0	19.8
8140	11	9	1	0	0	0	57	50	26	134	21	14.8	38.2
8140	12	1	0	0	0	0	1	0	0	1	1	1.0	—
8140	13	1	0	0	1	0	0	0	0	1	0	0.0	—
8140	nla2	2	0	0	0	0	10	3	0	13	8	6.5	3.5
8140	nla3	1	0	0	0	0	4	5	0	9	3	9.0	—
8140	nla4	3	0	0	0	0	10	15	2	27	9	9.0	13.9
8140	nla5	1	0	0	3	0	11	2	0	16	7	13.0	—
8156	n.a.	1	5	0	0	0	2	2	0	9	4	4.0	—
8165	n.a.	1	0	0	0	0	4	2	0	6	6	6.0	—
8166	n.a.	3	3	0	0	0	11	19	0	33	10	10.0	9.8
Total		379	78	44	69	10	1660	812	618	3294		8.9	11.5

Note: n.a. = not applicable; n.d. = data not available; nla = nonlocus area; IPA = indeterminate pecked area; S.D. = standard deviation.

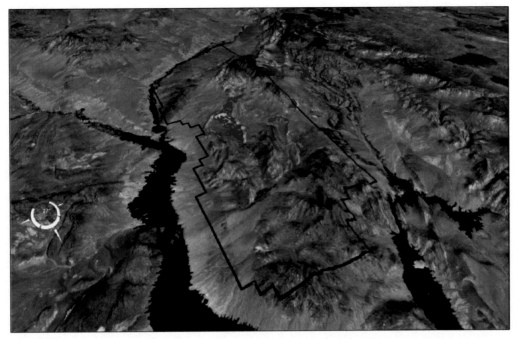

a

b

FIGURE 7.5. Aztec sandstone formation from the air (a) and from the ground (b).

a. Site 26CK8140, Locus 10, Panel 4: Mixture of Patayan (solid cones, simple stickman, digitate anthropomorph, elongate narrow sheep) and Basketmaker/Puebloan designs (squatting anthropomorph, oblong-bodied sheep).

b. Site 26CK5608, Site 3, Panel 2: Predominantly Patayan (H/I, crenellate elements) and fewer Basketmaker/ Puebloan designs (flute player on his back; well-made sheep, and large anthropomorph with head ornament/ ear bobs).

FIGURE 7.6. Large-scale petroglyph panels at Gold Butte with mixture of Basketmaker/Puebloan and Patayan rock art.

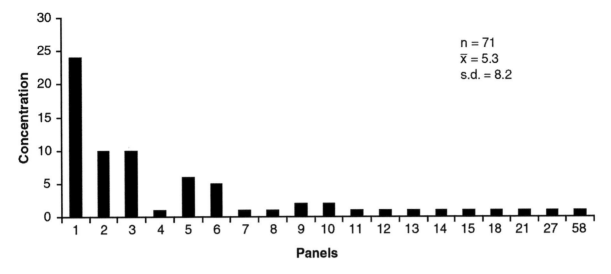

FIGURE 7.7. Panel quantities per concentration.

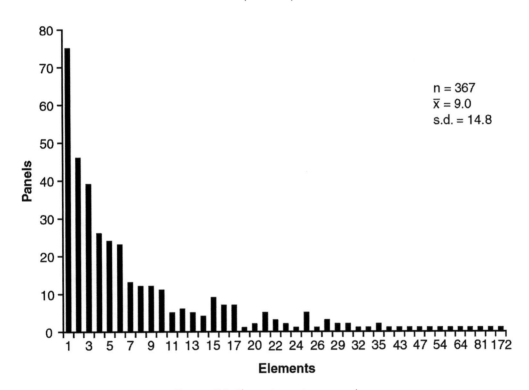

FIGURE 7.8. Element counts per panel.

association, figured at less than 20 percent (Table 7.6). Over two-thirds (70.0 percent) of the concentrations are classified as having a single style well represented, with a similar number of locations having Archaic only, Basketmaker/Puebloan only, or Patayan only. This spatial patterning in itself suggests the importance that different groups placed on maintaining their separate identities, with those who made the rock art intentionally choosing to practice their tradition at different spots in a comparatively uniform red rock landscape.

Desert Archaic

Sixteen locations are classified as having only Archaic abstract designs well represented, while six have co-associations of Archaic and later style designs (Table 7.6). A minor amount of Archaic designs were noted at seven other concentrations. The single-style locations contain nearly 100 panels with nearly 500 abstract elements, and an average of 7.8 elements per panel (Table 7.7). Examples of some single-period panels and individual elements are provided in Figure 7.10;

TABLE 7.5. Rock Art Elements by Concentration.

Site (26CK)	Locus	No. of Panels	Representational													Abstract								
			Sheep	Sheep Head	Anthropomorph	Tracks/Prints	Medicine Bag	Snake	Deer	Quadruped	Lizard/Turtle	Bird	Insect	Plant	Subtotal	Circles	Atlatls	Lollipop	Connected Circles	Circle String	Circle Cluster	Reticulated Circles	Dots	Rake/Comb
1968/1969	n.d.	6	1	—	1	—	—	—	—	—	—	—	—	—	2	5	—	—	—	—	—	—	1	—
1978	n.a.	3	65	—	6	—	—	4	—	—	—	—	—	2	77	—	—	2	3	1	—	—	—	—
1984	n.a.	1	—	—	—	—	—	—	—	—	—	—	—	—	0	—	—	—	—	—	—	—	—	—
3093	n.a.	3	—	—	2	—	—	2	1	1	—	—	—	—	6	2	—	—	—	—	—	—	—	—
3096	n.a.	2	2	—	1	—	—	—	—	—	—	—	2	—	5	1	—	1	—	—	—	—	—	—
3206	3	2	—	—	—	1	—	—	—	—	—	—	—	—	1	—	—	—	—	—	—	—	—	—
3420	n.d.	21	6	—	13	—	—	2	—	—	—	—	—	2	23	3	—	—	—	—	—	—	9	—
5179	E1	6	—	—	1	—	—	—	—	—	—	—	—	2	3	8	—	—	—	1	2	—	—	1
5179	E2	1	—	—	—	—	—	—	—	—	—	—	—	—	0	—	—	—	1	—	—	—	—	—
5179	K/K1	13	19	—	6	4	—	3	—	1	—	—	—	3	36	17	—	—	1	—	—	—	4	2
5608/Site 1	n.a.	1	—	—	—	—	—	—	—	—	—	—	—	—	0	—	—	—	—	—	—	—	—	—
5608/Site 3	n.a.	8	71	—	31	12	—	5	1	4	3	12	2	3	144	4	2	2	4	—	—	—	—	—
6543	n.a.	5	—	—	2	—	—	—	—	—	—	—	—	1	3	35	—	—	—	—	—	—	1	—
6544	n.a.	1	—	—	—	—	—	—	—	—	—	—	—	—	0	5	—	—	—	—	—	—	—	—
6580	n.a.	15	10	9	4	10	—	—	—	1	2	1	5	1	43	32	1	—	—	1	1	2	4	4
6641	n.a.	1	—	—	3	1	—	—	—	—	—	—	—	1	5	2	—	—	—	1	—	—	1	2
6642	n.a.	3	—	—	1	—	—	1	—	—	—	—	—	—	2	5	1	—	—	—	—	—	—	3
6643	n.a.	1	1	—	1	—	—	—	—	—	—	—	—	—	2	—	—	—	—	—	—	—	—	—
6666	1	1	—	—	3	1	1	—	—	—	1	2	1	—	9	10	2	—	—	1	—	—	1	3
6666	2	10	2	1	1	1	—	—	—	1	—	1	—	1	8	10	—	—	2	—	—	1	1	5
6666	3	5	—	—	2	—	—	—	—	—	—	—	—	—	2	3	—	—	1	1	—	—	—	—
6672	1	1	2	—	—	1	—	1	—	1	—	—	—	—	5	—	—	—	—	—	—	—	—	—
6672	2	2	4	—	7	1	—	—	1	—	—	—	—	—	13	3	—	—	2	—	—	—	3	—
6672	3	9	1	—	9	1	—	—	—	—	—	—	—	—	11	1	—	—	2	—	—	—	—	—
6672	4	3	—	—	4	6	—	5	1	1	—	—	—	2	19	3	—	—	1	—	2	—	—	19
6672	5	5	1	1	—	1	—	1	—	—	—	—	—	—	4	—	—	—	—	—	—	1	—	—
6672	6	1	—	—	1	—	—	—	—	—	—	—	—	—	1	—	—	—	—	—	—	—	—	—
7029	1	58	—	3	8	2	—	—	1	—	—	—	—	4	18	62	7	0	1	12	1	4	7	2
7029	2	11	5	4	2	2	—	—	1	1	—	—	—	—	15	34	—	—	—	3	—	—	16	—
7029	3	12	—	—	—	1	—	—	—	—	—	—	—	—	1	16	1	—	—	—	—	—	—	1
7029	4	27	1	3	5	3	—	—	—	—	—	2	2	—	16	11	—	—	—	—	3	3	3	3
7029	5	1	—	—	—	—	—	—	—	—	—	—	—	9	9	—	—	—	—	—	—	—	—	—
7029	6	3	9	—	2	—	—	1	—	—	—	—	—	—	12	7	—	—	—	—	—	—	13	—
7029	7	18	1	3	—	1	—	—	—	—	—	—	1	—	6	10	—	—	—	5	—	1	47	4
7996	n.a.	6	1	—	1	1	—	1	—	—	—	—	1	—	5	1	—	—	—	1	1	—	—	—
7997	n.a.	1	2	—	—	—	—	—	—	—	—	—	—	—	2	—	—	—	—	—	—	—	—	1
8019	n.a.	2	—	—	—	—	—	—	—	—	—	—	—	1	1	3	—	—	—	—	—	—	—	1
8062	n.a.	2	—	—	—	1	—	—	—	—	—	—	—	—	1	2	—	—	—	—	—	—	—	1
8064	n.a.	5	—	—	—	—	—	—	—	—	—	—	—	1	1	1	—	3	6	3	—	—	—	1
8065	n.a.	1	1	—	—	—	—	1	—	—	—	—	—	—	2	1	—	—	2	3	—	—	—	—

Abstract																			Other Prehistoric Petroglyph Elements					
Grid	Staff	Shield	Checkerboard	Ladder	Fringe	Pit/Groove/Cupule	Nested Curves	Spiral	Star	Cross	Cone	Triangle	Tally	Lines	Curvilinear	Rectilinear	Unique	Subtotal	Indet. Pecked Area	Scratched	Subtotal	Pictograph Grease Elements	Modern/Graffiti	Total
—	—	—	—	1	—	—	—	—	—	—	—	—	—	1	8	1	—	17	0	0	19	0	15	34+
3	—	—	—	—	—	—	3	—	—	1	—	—	—	—	1	10	—	24	80	0	181	0	0	181
—	—	—	—	—	—	—	—	—	—	—	—	—	—	—	—	—	—	0	0	0	0	22	0	22
—	—	—	2	—	—	—	3	—	—	—	—	—	—	3	—	—	—	10	2	0	18	0	0	18
—	—	—	—	—	—	—	—	—	—	—	—	—	—	2	2	1	—	7	3	0	15	0	0	15
—	—	—	—	—	—	—	—	—	—	—	—	—	40	—	1	—	6	47	0	0	48	0	0	48
—	1	—	—	—	1	—	1	1	1	6	—	—	—	3	6	5	—	37	15	0	75	44	9	128
1	—	2	—	1	—	—	—	1	1	—	—	—	—	4	10	2	—	34	6	0	43	0	0	43
—	—	—	—	1	—	—	1	—	—	—	—	—	—	—	—	—	—	3	0	0	3	0	0	3
8	2	5	—	3	—	2	1	1	—	3	—	3	—	3	1	1	6	63	6	0	105	0	0	105
—	—	—	—	—	—	—	—	—	—	—	—	—	—	—	—	—	—	0	0	0	0	9	0	9
1	—	—	—	1	—	—	2	13	1	8	19	—	—	6	7	5	—	75	5	0	224	0	0	224+
—	—	—	—	—	—	—	—	1	—	—	—	—	—	7	14	12	—	70	1	0	74	0	0	74
—	—	—	—	—	—	—	—	—	—	—	—	—	—	2	1	—	—	8	4	0	12	0	0	12
2	1	—	—	—	—	2	1	1	2	3	—	—	—	11	10	—	—	78	61	0	182	0	0	182
4	—	—	—	—	—	—	2	—	—	—	—	—	—	7	1	—	—	20	7	0	32	0	0	32
—	—	3	—	—	—	—	1	—	—	—	—	—	—	—	3	2	—	18	11	0	31	0	0	31
—	—	—	—	—	—	—	—	—	—	—	—	—	—	—	—	—	—	0	1	0	3	0	0	3
2	1	—	—	—	—	—	1	—	—	1	—	—	—	1	2	2	1	28	31	0	68	0	0	68
—	3	—	—	1	—	2	—	—	—	4	—	—	—	7	7	4	1	48	35	0	91	0	0	91
—	—	2	—	—	—	—	—	—	—	—	—	—	—	1	1	1	—	10	1	0	13	0	0	13
—	—	—	—	—	—	—	—	—	—	—	—	—	—	—	—	—	—	0	0	0	5	0	0	5
—	—	—	—	—	—	—	1	2	2	—	—	—	—	1	3	3	—	20	3	0	36	0	0	36
—	—	—	—	—	—	—	—	—	—	—	—	—	—	—	5	—	2	10	6	0	27	0	0	27
2	—	1	—	—	—	—	—	1	—	—	—	—	—	3	4	3	—	39	1	0	59	0	0	59
—	—	—	—	—	—	—	2	—	—	1	—	—	—	1	11	—	—	16	1	0	21	0	0	21
—	—	—	—	—	—	—	—	—	—	—	—	—	—	—	—	—	—	0	0	0	1	0	0	1
2	2	2	1	4	1	1	4	1	1	4	1	0	1	12	31	3	3	170	92	6	286	0	29	315
1	—	1	—	1	—	—	—	1	—	—	—	—	—	2	15	3	—	77	68	1	161	4	0	165
—	1	—	—	—	—	—	1	1	—	—	—	—	—	2	2	6	—	31	14	0	46	9	0	55
24	—	1	5	1	—	—	—	1	—	1	—	1	—	20	7	10	—	94	76	1	187	4	0	191
—	—	—	—	—	—	—	—	—	—	—	—	—	—	—	—	—	—	0	0	0	9	0	0	9
—	—	—	—	—	—	—	—	—	—	—	—	—	—	9	2	—	—	31	2	0	45	0	0	45
1	—	4	—	—	—	—	—	—	—	—	—	1	—	15	12	5	1	106	14	0	126	0	0	126+
3	1	—	—	—	—	8	—	—	—	—	—	—	—	8	1	—	—	24	0	0	29	0	0	29
—	—	—	—	—	—	—	—	—	—	—	—	—	—	—	—	1	—	2	0	0	4	0	2	6
—	—	—	—	—	—	—	—	—	—	—	—	—	—	3	3	—	—	10	0	0	11	0	0	11
—	—	—	—	—	—	—	—	—	—	—	—	—	—	2	—	1	—	6	0	0	7	0	0	7
—	—	—	—	2	—	—	—	2	—	—	—	—	4	2	4	2	—	30	0	0	31	0	0	31
1	—	1	—	1	—	—	—	1	—	—	—	—	—	—	1	1	—	12	2	0	16	0	0	16

TABLE 7.5. (cont'd.) Rock Art Elements by Concentration.

Site (26CK)	Locus	No. of Panels	Representational													Abstract								
			Sheep	Sheep Head	Anthropomorph	Tracks/Prints	Medicine Bag	Snake	Deer	Quadruped	Lizard/Turtle	Bird	Insect	Plant	Subtotal	Circles	Atlatl	Lollipop	Connected Circles	Circle String	Circle Cluster	Reticulated Circles	Dots	Rake/Comb
8070	n.a.	1	—	—	—	—	—	—	—	—	—	—	—	—	0	—	—	—	—	—	—	—	—	—
8071	n.a.	2	—	—	—	—	—	—	—	—	—	—	—	—	0	—	—	—	—	—	—	1	—	—
8084	n.a.	1	—	—	—	—	—	—	—	—	—	—	—	—	0	4	—	—	—	—	—	—	—	—
8086	n.a.	3	—	—	1	1	—	—	—	—	—	—	—	—	2	3	—	—	—	—	—	1	—	—
8087	n.a.	1	—	—	—	—	—	—	—	—	—	—	—	—	0	—	—	—	—	—	—	—	—	1
8093	n.a.	1	—	—	—	—	—	—	—	—	—	—	—	—	0	1	—	—	—	—	—	—	—	—
8096	n.a.	6	—	—	—	2	—	—	—	—	—	—	—	—	2	—	—	—	—	3	—	—	—	2
8097	n.a.	2	—	—	—	—	—	—	—	—	—	—	—	—	0	—	—	—	—	—	—	—	—	—
8098	n.a.	5	5	—	—	2	—	—	—	—	—	—	—	—	7	2	—	—	—	—	—	—	—	—
8100	n.a.	3	—	—	1	1	—	—	—	—	—	—	—	—	2	—	—	—	—	—	—	—	—	—
8123	n.a.	2	1	—	—	—	—	1	—	—	—	—	—	—	2	—	—	—	—	—	—	—	—	—
8129	n.a.	1	3	—	—	—	—	—	—	—	—	—	—	—	3	—	—	—	—	—	—	—	—	—
8136	n.a.	2	9	—	5	—	—	—	—	—	—	—	—	—	14	1	—	—	—	—	—	—	—	—
8140	3	14	15	—	16	11	—	—	1	1	—	—	—	3	47	9	1	—	4	—	3	—	—	—
8140	4	1	—	—	—	—	—	—	—	—	—	—	—	—	0	—	—	—	—	—	—	—	—	—
8140	5	7	5	—	1	1	—	—	1	—	—	—	—	1	9	—	1	—	1	—	—	—	3	—
8140	6	5	3	—	1	—	—	2	—	—	—	—	—	—	6	2	—	—	—	—	1	—	—	—
8140	7	10	30	—	4	1	—	2	—	2	—	—	—	—	39	25	—	1	—	—	2	—	—	4
8140	8	3	3	—	—	—	—	—	—	—	—	—	—	—	3	2	—	—	—	—	—	—	1	—
8140	9	4	21	—	3	2	—	—	—	1	—	—	—	—	27	2	—	—	—	—	—	—	1	1
8140	10	6	19	—	6	4	5	—	—	1	1	—	—	2	38	16	—	—	—	2	1	—	1	1
8140	11	9[a]	15	—	23	1	—	6	—	—	1	2	—	2	50	14	—	—	—	—	—	—	—	3
8140	12	1	—	—	—	—	—	—	—	—	—	—	—	—	0	—	—	—	—	—	—	—	—	—
8140	13	1	—	—	—	—	—	—	—	—	—	—	—	—	0	—	—	—	—	—	—	—	—	—
8140	nla2	2	—	—	—	2	—	—	—	1	—	—	—	—	3	4	—	—	—	1	1	—	—	—
8140	nla3	1	1	—	—	4	—	—	—	—	—	—	—	—	5	4	—	—	—	—	—	—	—	—
8140	nla4	3	3	—	—	12	—	—	—	—	—	—	—	—	15	3	—	—	—	—	—	—	—	—
8140	nla5	1	1	—	1	—	—	—	—	—	—	—	—	—	2	4	—	—	—	—	—	1	—	1
8156	n.a.	1	—	—	—	—	—	1	—	1	—	—	—	—	2	—	—	—	—	—	—	—	—	—
8165	n.a.	1	1	—	1	—	—	—	—	—	—	—	—	—	2	1	—	—	—	—	—	—	—	—
8166	n.a.	3	8	—	8	2	—	1	—	—	—	—	—	—	19	—	—	—	—	—	—	—	—	5
Total	71	371	348	24	188	97	6	40	5	17	12	20	14	41	812	394	16	9	29	41	18	15	117	71

Note: + indicates incomplete counts; n.a. = not applicable; n.d. = data not available; nla = nonlocus area.
[a] 11 panels assigned differently between first and second recordation episode.

						Abstract													Other Prehistoric Petroglyph Elements					
Grid	Staff	Shield	Checkerboard	Ladder	Fringe	Pit/Groove/Cupule	Nested Curves	Spiral	Star	Cross	Cone	Triangle	Tally	Lines	Curvilinear	Rectilinear	Unique	Subtotal	Indet. Pecked Area	Scratched	Subtotal	Pictograph Grease Elements	Modern/Graffiti	Total
—	—	—	—	—	—	—	—	—	—	—	—	—	—	—	—	1	—	1	0	0	1	0	0	1
—	—	—	—	—	—	—	—	—	—	—	—	—	—	—	—	1	—	2	0	0	2	0	0	2
—	—	—	—	—	—	—	—	1	—	—	—	—	—	1	—	—	—	6	0	0	6	0	0	6
—	—	—	—	—	—	1	—	2	—	—	—	—	—	7	4	—	—	18	0	0	20	0	0	20
—	—	—	—	—	—	—	—	—	—	—	—	—	—	—	2	—	—	3	0	0	3	0	0	3
—	—	—	—	—	—	—	—	—	—	—	—	—	—	—	—	—	—	1	1	0	2	0	0	2
1	—	—	—	—	—	—	—	—	—	1	—	—	—	—	—	2	—	9	0	0	11	0	0	11
—	—	—	—	—	—	—	—	—	—	—	—	—	—	—	—	—	—	0	0	0	0	0	1	1
—	1	—	—	—	—	—	—	1	—	—	—	—	1	6	3	—	—	14	0	0	21	0	0	21
—	—	—	—	—	—	—	—	—	—	—	—	—	—	—	—	—	—	0	0	0	2	2	0	4
—	—	—	—	—	—	—	—	—	—	—	—	—	—	—	—	—	—	0	0	0	2	0	0	2
—	—	—	—	—	—	—	—	—	—	—	—	—	—	1	—	—	—	1	3	0	7	0	0	7
—	—	—	—	—	—	—	—	—	—	—	—	—	—	—	—	—	—	1	3	0	18	0	0	18
1	2	—	—	—	7	2	1	—	1	1	—	—	2	20	11	7	—	72	31	0	150	1	9	160
—	—	—	—	—	—	—	—	—	—	—	—	—	—	—	—	—	—	0	0	0	0	6	0	6
—	—	—	—	—	—	—	—	—	—	—	—	—	—	11	1	3	—	20	1	2	32	4	3	39
—	—	1	—	—	—	—	—	—	—	—	—	—	—	—	—	1	—	5	0	0	11	1	1	13
—	—	—	—	—	—	—	—	1	—	1	—	—	2	4	10	7	—	57	0	0	96	3	0	99+
1	1	—	—	—	—	—	—	—	—	—	—	—	—	1	2	—	—	8	3	0	14	0	0	14
—	—	—	—	1	1	—	—	—	—	1	—	—	—	—	4	—	—	11	0	0	38	0	0	38
—	2	1	—	1	—	—	—	1	—	2	—	—	3	9	6	—	—	46	0	0	84	0	0	84+
1	3	2	—	—	—	—	2	8	1	1	5	—	—	5	2	10	—	57	26	0	133	0	1	134
—	—	—	—	—	—	—	—	—	—	—	—	—	—	—	—	1	—	1	0	0	1	0	0	1
—	—	—	—	—	—	—	—	—	—	—	—	—	—	—	—	—	—	0	0	0	0	1	0	1
—	—	—	—	—	—	—	—	—	—	—	—	—	1	—	2	1	—	10	0	0	13	0	0	13
—	—	—	—	—	—	—	—	—	—	—	—	—	—	—	—	—	—	4	0	0	9	0	0	9+
—	—	—	—	1	—	2	—	1	1	—	—	—	—	—	2	—	—	10	2	0	27	0	0	27
—	—	—	—	—	—	—	—	—	—	—	1	—	4	—	—	—	—	11	0	0	13	3	0	16
—	—	—	—	—	—	1	—	—	—	—	—	—	—	—	—	—	1	2	0	0	4	0	5	9
—	1	—	—	—	—	—	—	—	—	—	—	—	—	1	—	1	—	4	0	0	6	0	0	6
—	1	—	—	1	—	—	—	—	—	1	—	—	—	1	2	—	—	11	0	0	30	0	3	33
59	23	26	6	22	11	19	18	49	13	42	26	6	50	204	230	125	21	1,660	618	10	3,100	113	78	3,288

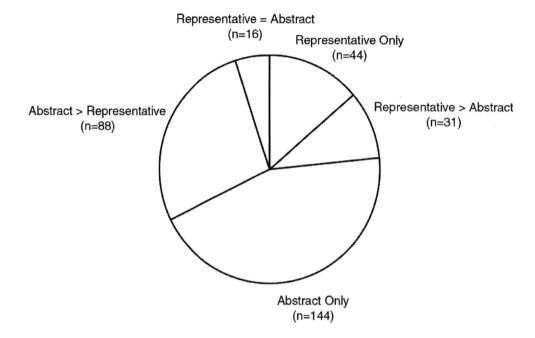

FIGURE 7.9. Proportion of design classes on panels.

examples of Archaic designs overlain with subsequent styles are shown in Figure 7.11. As they suggest, these early panels and their abstract designs may be quite difficult to make out, sometimes as a consequence of superpositioning and sometimes because of extreme weathering.

Basketmaker/Puebloan

Fourteen locations are classified as having only Basketmaker/Puebloan designs well represented, while they co-occur with appreciable amounts of earlier and/ or later styles in 11 locations. Trace amounts were noted in eight additional places. The single-style locations contain nearly 50 panels, with more representational than abstract elements portrayed, at 270 and 227, respectively (Table 7.7). In addition to a fundamental shift in the nature of the elements drawn, these panels are considerably more complex than earlier ones, with an average of 11.0 elements per panel. Examples of the various ways in which anthropomorphs were depicted are provided in Figure 7.12. Some are chunky Cave Valley–like figures (7.12a); others have broad-shouldered, tapered, triangular torsos (7.12c); yet others have hourglass bodies (7.12b). Both action-oriented figures, which Schaafsma associates with Basketmaker II/early Pueblo II times (Figure 7.12d–f), and highly stylized, stick figures with right-angle appendages (Figure 7.12g), which she associates with later Puebloan periods, are also noted. Hump-backed and flute-playing figures are uncommon but readily distinguished (Figure 7.12f; see also bottom

of Figure 7.6). Well-made sheep, with bodies that range from oblong to nearly boat-shaped, but always with horns in profile, are common. Some designs show single birds, flocks in flight formation, and bird-like tracks (Figure 7.12l). Other animals are also recognizable, including tortoise-like elements and bear paw prints.

Patayan

Although the number of locations with Patayan-only designs well represented is similar to that with Basketmaker/Puebloan-only designs, the former contain nearly twice the number of panels but nearly the same number of elements as the latter (Table 7.7). In short, the Patayan created considerably more panels of considerably less complex design than their immediate predecessors (Figure 7.13). In addition, the composition shifts dramatically: the ratio of representational to abstract designs reverses from 1.0:0.8 in the Basketmaker/Puebloan body of art to 1.0:2.0 in the Patayan. Typical representational Patayan elements are shown in Figure 7.13, including simple anthropomorphs with exaggerated digitated hands and/or feet and appendages at an acute angle to the body, as well as processions of skinny quadrupeds. Abstract elements especially well represented are vertical ball-and-string sequences and open-lattice plant and bug-like designs. Based on these co-associations, visually dominating H/I and cone-shaped elements (Figure 7.6) and thick, solid-bodied anthropomorphs (Figure 7.13b) are judged to be Patayan.

TABLE 7.6. Stylistic Classification of Rock Art Concentrations.

Site (26CK), Locus	Archaic	Basketmaker-Puebloan	Patayan	Paiute	Historic	Indeterminate	Site (26CK), Locus	Archaic	Basketmaker-Puebloan	Patayan	Paiute	Historic	Indeterminate
1968/1969	—	—	√	—	—	—	8065	—	√	√	—	—	—
1978	√	√	√	—	—	—	8070	—	—	—	—	—	√
1984, L1	—	—	—	√	—	—	8071	—	—	—	—	—	√
3093	—	√	—	—	—	—	8084	—	—	—	—	—	√
3096	—	√	—	—	—	—	8086	—	√	—	—	—	—
3206, L3	√	Mn	—	—	—	—	8087	√	—	—	—	—	—
3420	—	Mn	√	—	√	—	8093	—	—	—	—	—	√
5179, LE1	—	Mn	√	—	—	—	8096	—	—	√	—	—	—
5179, LE2	—	—	—	—	—	√	8097	—	—	—	—	—	(van-dalism)
5179, LK/K1	—	Mn	√	—	—	—	8098	—	—	√	—	—	—
5608-1	—	—	—	√	—	—	8100	—	—	√	Mn	—	—
5608-3	—	√	Mn	—	—	—	8123	—	√	—	—	—	—
6543	—	—	√	—	—	—	8129	—	√	—	—	—	—
6544	√	—	—	—	—	—	8136	—	√	√	—	—	—
6580	√	√	√	—	—	—	8140, L3	√	√	√	Mn	—	—
6641	—	√	√	—	—	—	8140, L4	—	—	—	√	—	—
6642	√	—	Mn	—	—	—	8140, L5	—	√	√	Mn	—	—
6643	—	√	—	—	—	—	8140, L6	—	√	—	Mn	—	—
6666, L1	√	Mn	—	—	—	—	8140, L7	Mn	√	Mn	Mn	—	—
6666, L2	√	—	Mn	—	—	—	8140, L8	√	Mn	—	—	—	—
6666, L3	√	—	—	—	—	—	8140, L9	Mn	√	Mn	—	—	—
6672, L1	—	√	—	—	—	—	8140, L10	Mn	Mn	√	—	—	—
6672, L2	—	√	√	—	—	—	8140, L11	—	√	√	—	—	—
6672, L3	Mn	Mn	√	—	—	—	8140, L12	√	—	—	—	—	—
6672, L4	√	—	Mn	—	—	—	8140, L13	—	—	—	√	—	—
6672, L5	√	—	—	—	—	—	8140, NLA 2	Mn	—	√	—	—	—
6672, L6	—	—	√	—	—	—	8140, NLA 3	—	—	—	—	—	√
7029, L1	√	—	√	—	—	—	8140, NLA 4	Mn	√	—	—	—	—
7029, L2	√	—	√	Mn	—	—	8140, NLA 5	√	√	—	Mn	—	—
7029, L3	√	—	—	Mn	—	—	8156	—	—	—	—	—	√
7029, L4	√	—	—	Mn	—	—	8165	—	—	√	—	—	—
7029, L5	—	—	√	—	—	—	8166	—	—	√	—	—	—
7029, L6	—	√	—	—	—	—							
7029, L7	√	—	—	—	—	—	**Totals**						
7996	Mn	√	√	—	—	—	Only Well-Represented	16	14	15	4	1	8
7997	—	√	—	—	—	—	Co-associated Well-Represented	6	11	12	—	—	—
8019	√	—	—	—	—	—	Minor Presence	7	8	6	9	—	—
8062	—	—	—	—	—	√							
8064	√	—	—	—	—	—							

Note: Mn = minor presence.

TABLE 7.7. Summary of Prehistoric Rock Art Concentrations by Well-Represented Styles.

Style	Concen-trations	Panels	Abstract	Representational	Indeterminate Pecked	Scratched	Painted	Total	Modern
Paiute Only	4	4	—	—	—	—	38	38	—
Patayan Only[a]	15	88	325	161	34	—	2	522	18
BM-Puebloan Only	14	47	227	270	18	—	4	519	3
Archaic Only	16	99	497	73	191	1	13	775	—
Indeterminate	8	10	25	8	1	—	—	34	5
Mixture of Styles									
Patayan/BM-Puebloan	7	28	154	98	42	2	4	300	4
Patayan/Archaic	2	69	247	33	160	7	4	451	29
BM-Puebloan/Archaic	1	1	11	2	—	—	3	16	—
Patayan/BM-Puebloan/Archaic	3	32	174	167	172	—	1	514	9
Total	70	378	1,660	812	618	10	69	3,169	68

Note: BM = Basketmaker.
[a] Excludes grease and carved writing at 26CK3420/Mud Wash.

Protohistoric/Paiute Pictographs

Thirteen locations contain between one and six panels that have a handful of painted designs. None is elaborate, and nearly all are monochrome and red (Figure 7.14). The most extensive concentration is in a small alcove at 26CK1984, where 22 red and black elements were distinguished. As described above, pictographs are presumed to be late based on a review of regional literature. Two features confirm that they are the most recent style of prehistoric rock art in Gold Butte: in a few instances red pigment has been painted on top of earlier pecked abstract and representational designs (Figure 7.14d and e); and in one instance a red anthropomorph is on a raw, unweathered surface that recently spalled off (Figure 7.14a). The latter instance is also associated with a pecked design of what appears to be a horse and rider.

Scratched designs are quite rare, limited to only ten and confined to one panel each at four locations. They are neither elaborate nor extensive. In light of how uncommon pictographs and scratched designs are, it is significant that pictographs co-occur at three of the four locations where scratched designs were recorded. While the data are not definitive, they support the interpretation that like simple pictographs, scratching is a late prehistoric style.

Early Historic Rock Art

Twelve panels concentrated in Mud Wash (26CK3420) consist of historic writing, mostly initials and dates, painted in what is thought to be axle grease, alongside a few initials and similarly recent designs carved into the sandstone. A brief record of the site made in October 1979 noted "the initials D.H. 1844 and another name and date [of] 1927." Sketches of the panels made in 2005 show nothing quite as definitive as dates or initials, only short, linear markings that conceivably are remnants of lettering. The discrepancy between the 1979 and 2005 information may relate in part to panel degradation in the 25+ years between the records and/or to analysts' perceptions. In any event, this is the only historic pictograph site that has been identified at Gold Butte.

The purported marking of "D.H. 1844" is of particular interest, since Fremont's party traveled up the Old Spanish Trail that year, moving from southwest to northeast, generally following the Virgin River corridor. At this point, it must remain purely speculative that the markings here are directly related to that event. Based on the material with which they were made and the manner of execution, most of the writing likely dates to the Mormon period (post–AD 1857), when Mud Wash was well traveled, connecting Littlefield, Arizona, toward the east, to the St. George crossing on the Virgin River toward the west.

CONCLUSIONS

Examination of the rock art underscores several major aspects of prehistoric land-use patterns for Gold Butte. First, it suggests a land-use history considerably more complicated than that constructed by Larson and Michaelsen (1990). As we discuss in Chapter 8, their population reconstruction creates the impression that

a

b

c

d

FIGURE 7.10. Desert Archaic abstract petroglyphs at Gold Butte. (a) Site 26CK6642, Panel 3, (b) Site 26CK7029, Locus 2, Panel 11, (c) Site 26CK 7029, Locus 3, Panel 2, (d) Site 26CK7029, Locus 7, Panel 14.

around AD 500 there was a Southwestern expansion into what was essentially an empty landscape, that these Southwestern people experienced a rapid but short-lived florescence and then rapidly retracted, leaving behind unoccupied terrain. In contrast, the rock art reflects the fact that Gold Butte experienced successive waves of use, with Archaic occupants supplanted by Southwestern-influenced groups, who were in turn supplanted by Patayan and then Southern Paiute groups. And as it turns out, the rock art's complexity is in good agreement with any number of other local archaeological data sets.

The analytical method of using rock art studies from the surrounding areas, where presumably little stylistic mixing exists, to identify the keystone elements for dif-

ferent styles has been productive, allowing us to recognize distinct styles at Gold Butte that have temporal as well as cultural significance. If it weren't for the rock art analysis, evidence of a Patayan occupation in Gold Butte would be founded exclusively on pottery, and the two data sets combined clearly support a local occupation rather than ephemeral travel-through events or a trade relation with Puebloans.

In addition, the discovery that Basketmaker/ Puebloan and Patayan rock art co-occur here prompted a reassessment of Schaafsma's characterization of the West Virgin style. In short, this analysis does not sustain the notion of a West Virgin style (e.g., Figure 7.3) but instead reveals that it is a mixture of two distinct styles. The West Virgin variant appears simply to be East Virgin

e

f

g

FIGURE 7.10. Desert Archaic abstract petroglyphs at Gold Butte.
(e) Site 26CK8140, Locus 9, Panel 4, (f) Site 26CK8087, Panel 1,
(g) Site 26CK6672, Locus 4, Panel 3.

a

b

FIGURE 7.11. Petroglyph panels at Gold Butte with a mixture of abstract Desert Archaic and subsequent representational Basketmaker/Puebloan and Patayan rock art. (a) Site 26CK8140, Locus 3, Panel 2, (b) Site 26CK8140, Locus 7, Panel 9.

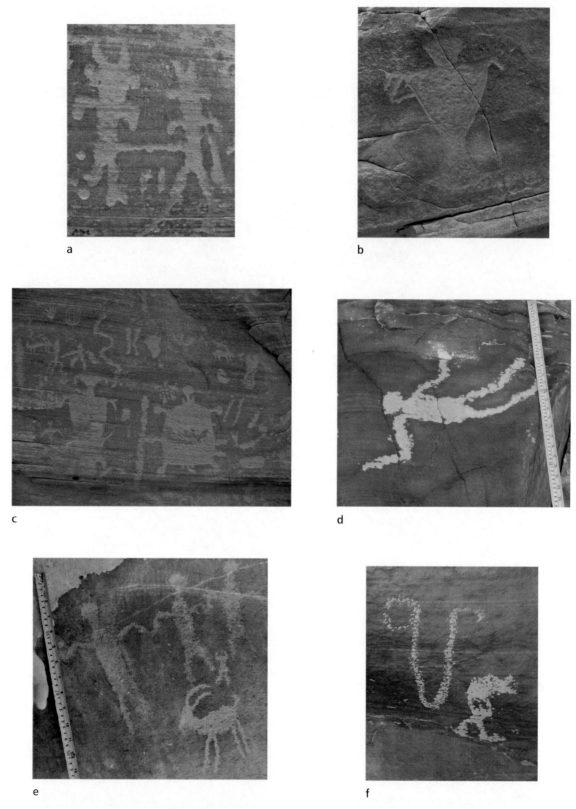

FIGURE 7.12. Basketmaker/Puebloan representational petroglyphs at Gold Butte. (a) Site 26CK5608, Site 3, Panel 1, (b) Site 26CK5608, Site 3, Panel 1, (c) Site 26CK5608, Site 3, Panel 1, (d) Site 26CK8140, Locus 6, Panel 3, (e) Site 26CK8140, Locus 11, Panel 6, (f) Site 26CK8140, Locus 11, Panel 1.

Figure 7.12. Basketmaker/Puebloan representational petroglyphs at Gold Butte. (g) Site 26CK8140, Locus 11, Panel 5, (h) Site 26CK8140, Locus 7, Panel 4, (i) Site 26CK5608, Site 3, Panel 1, (j) Site 26CK5608, Site 3, Panel 1, (k) Site 26CK5608, Site 3, Panel 1, (l) Site 26CK8140, Locus 11, Panel 1.

FIGURE 7.13. Patayan representational and abstract petroglyphs at Gold Butte. (a) Site 26CK7029, Locus 1, Panel 5, (b) Site 26CK5179, Locus 1, Panel 3, (c) Site 26CK7029, Locus 1, Panel 55, (d) Site 26CK1978, Panel 1.

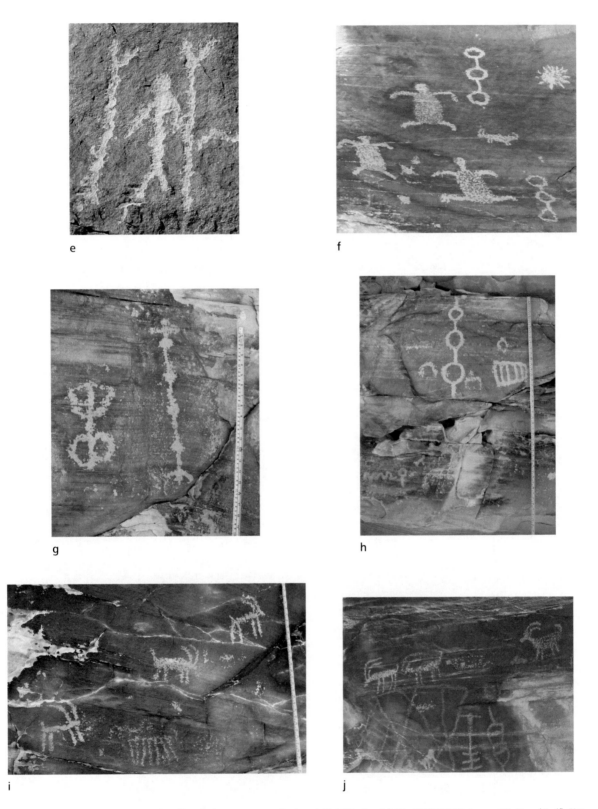

FIGURE 7.13. Patayan representational and abstract petroglyphs at Gold Butte. (e) Site 26CK8140, Locus 10, Panel 1, (f) Site 26CK8140, Locus 11, Panel 3, (g) Site 26CK8140, Locus 10, Panel 2, (h) Site 26CK8140, Locus 11, Panel 2, (i) Site 26CK8140, Locus 7, Panel 5, (j) Site 26CK1978, Panel 1.

FIGURE 7.14. Paiute pictographs at Gold Butte. (a) Site 26CK8140, Locus 13, Panel 1, (b) Site 26CK8140, Locus 4, (c) Site 26CK8140, Locus 5, Panel 7, (d) Site 26CK8140, Locus 7, Panel 1, (e) Site 26CK8140, NLA 5, Panel 1.

with an overlayer of mainstream Patayan elements. With the dismissal of a West versus East Virgin rock art style, cultural unity rather than intragroup differentiation seems to better describe the ancestral Puebloan groups throughout southern Utah and the Arizona Strip. That southern Utah, the Arizona Strip, and Gold Butte are an integrated unit, and stand in contrast to Fremont-style rock art found in the northern two-thirds of Utah, is given further support by Castleton and Madsen (1981).

In the early stage of this project, the possibility that we would find evidence of Fremont influences from the north and northeast was raised. As summarized by Schaafsma (1980:166), "The hallmark of Fremont rock art everywhere is the broad-shouldered human figure in ceremonial regalia. Typically it has a tapering torso and horned or other elaborate headgear. Adornment varies from region to region, but common embellishments are heavy necklaces represented with dots or as solid yokes, very large ornamental earrings or 'hairbobs,' and sashes. Facial features, especially eyes, may be depicted. Feet usually point out to either side, and fingers are splayed. Many figures hold small shields." The rock art at Gold Butte presents us with no compelling evidence of Fremont influences. Among the human-like figures, shield bearers are unknown, horned/elaborate headgear is atypical, and items of adornment such as necklaces and earbobs are atypical, as are detailed faces. Beyond the rock art, the conventional archaeological data sets from Gold Butte similarly provide little evidence of a Fremont influence: there is just a single Fremont sherd and not a single Nawthis Side-notched or Parowan-style arrowhead.

Finally, most (but not all) of the rock art in Gold Butte was made in conspicuous places. A number of functions have been ascribed to publicly displayed rock art. Foremost among these are that it functioned to promote group cohesion, that it pronounced jurisdictional claim on land, and that it delimited territorial boundaries, informing outsiders that they were potentially transgressing. Two adjacent loci in the vicinity of 26CK7994 (Figure 6.1; 26CK7029, Loci 1 and 2) are noteworthy exceptions to this pattern. Though still set in the Red Rock zone, they are found in a small offset island of sandstone on the south side of Mud Wash, apart from the main area (Figure 7.5a). Collectively, these two loci contain 69 panels, a much higher-density concentration than anywhere else. And rather than being conspicuous, the panels are tucked away within the recesses of dark, narrow passages and dead-end natural tunnels in the formation. Stylistically, these locations have a mixture of both Patayan and Archaic designs, heavily dominated by abstract with very few representational elements. The context of the panel placement suggests that they were made in private as individual acts. Beyond that inference, the large amount of Patayan and lack of Puebloan-style rock art here reinforces the notion of a boundary of sorts between Puebloan and Patayan territory or spheres of influence. As a comparison of Figure 6.1 and Figure 8.6 indicates, Mud Wash corresponds to the least-effort travel corridor from the Shivwits Plateau; Patayan (paddle and anvil) pottery is heavily distributed in sites south of Mud Wash.

8 Synthesis

In this chapter we track prehistoric land-use intensity at Gold Butte across the Holocene using a variety of indices. Insofar as the rise of Formative lifeways along the nearby Virgin and Muddy river corridors is critical to our understanding of the study area, we pay particular attention to the ceramic signatures of land-use intensity during the Basketmaker and Puebloan occupation. Also relying principally on ceramic assemblages, we identify a Late Prehistoric Patayan occupation, as well as the ascendance of the Southern Paiute during ethnographic times. With this basic cultural-historical and land-use intensity framework established, we then attempt to integrate survey and excavation data into a broader review of lifeways associated with each of the major time periods: Paleo-Archaic and Early Archaic; Late Archaic and Basketmaker II; Basketmaker III and Pueblo I–III; and Late Prehistoric. We conclude with a discussion of the role of hinterland and marginal resource tracts in adjacent farming and nonfarming settlements.

A PROFILE OF HOLOCENE LAND-USE INTENSITY AT GOLD BUTTE

Several data sets potentially track shifting land-use patterns during the Holocene, including obsidian hydration, time-sensitive projectile points, ceramics, and radiocarbon assays. While it might be statistically more revealing to present only those data emanating from the sample survey, sample sizes associated with projectile points and radiocarbon assays are relatively small. For this reason, we have combined both survey and test evaluation results for these two classes of chronological data. Conversely, obsidian hydration data from well-controlled survey contexts are more robust, and

thus we have chosen to highlight survey-level data as potentially more representative of shifting land-use practices. Notwithstanding these sampling issues, we wish to emphasize the directionality of these three proxy data sets, which, as we demonstrate below, all seem in general agreement.

It is worth reiterating at this point that much of the Gold Butte study area sits within the view shed of the Virgin River and the well-documented Basketmaker and Puebloan settlements that flank the river corridor. At least in this context, Gold Butte must be viewed as a hinterland, but a hinterland situated next to a major population center. If Larson and Michaelsen's (1990) demographic reconstructions are correct, populations along this corridor jumped thirty-fold within a 750-year period, from about AD 500 to 1250, before collapsing. To what degree are these wholesale changes reflected in the Gold Butte study area? Or did the florescence of Formative village life in some way mitigate the need to intensively use hinterland resources? These questions are paramount as we review the data outlined in previous chapters.

In Chapter 5 we reviewed the hydration characteristics of the three main source groups represented: Kane Springs, Delamar Mountains, and Modena/Panaca Summit. Their hydration rim development rates appear to be similarly influenced by effective hydration temperature (EHT), and the case is made that all three sources hydrate at about the same rate. These project data are arrayed in Figure 8.1 and reveal a series of subtle peaks and valleys along the time periods they are inferred to represent.

As might be expected, given the documentation

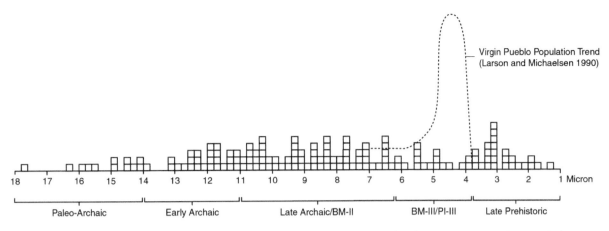

FIGURE 8.1. Project-wide hydration array for dominant obsidian source groups (Modena/Panaca Summit, Kane Springs, and Delamar Mountains).

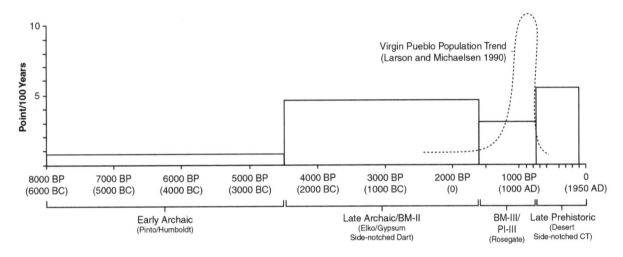

FIGURE 8.2. Frequency of time-sensitive projectile points in the study area (standardized per 100 years of occupation).

of Stemmed series projectile points in the study area, there is a Paleo-Archaic signature in the hydration database evinced by a small number of readings greater than 14.0 microns. The profile then exhibits a reasonably robust and stable Early and Late Archaic presence, reflected in those readings between 14.0 and 6.2 microns. Perhaps the most significant aspect of this profile is the dip in readings that correspond to the Puebloan period (6.2 to 3.8 microns), which is then followed by a spike in values associated with the Late Prehistoric period (3.8 to 1.0 microns). The Puebloan dip occurs at roughly the same time as the thirty-fold jump in populations along the Virgin River corridor (Larson and Michaelsen 1990). Furthermore, the obsidian profile spikes after the collapse of local Puebloan populations at about AD 1250.

This overall pattern is corroborated by the time-sensitive projectile point data obtained from the sample survey (Figure 8.2). Here the representation of various point forms has been standardized with regard to the

frequency of points per 100 years of occupation for each time period. Again, the relationship between those point forms representing the Late Archaic, Puebloan, and Late Prehistoric periods is the most relevant. What we find is that point frequencies remain relatively robust through the Late Archaic period, dip somewhat during the Puebloan periods, and then rebound to their highest level during the Late Prehistoric period.

The project radiocarbon profile again confirms the overall pattern (Figure 8.3) but also provides more fine-grained resolution to some of these broader changes. Thus, for example, the dip in radiocarbon dates appears to be narrowly confined to AD 950 to 1250, the Pueblo II and III periods. By contrast, Basketmaker III and Pueblo I use of the study area appears to be steadily increasing. Another key observation is that there is no uptick in the profile for at least 200 years after the Puebloan collapse at about AD 1250. But after this hiatus, the radiocarbon profile increases dramatically. This

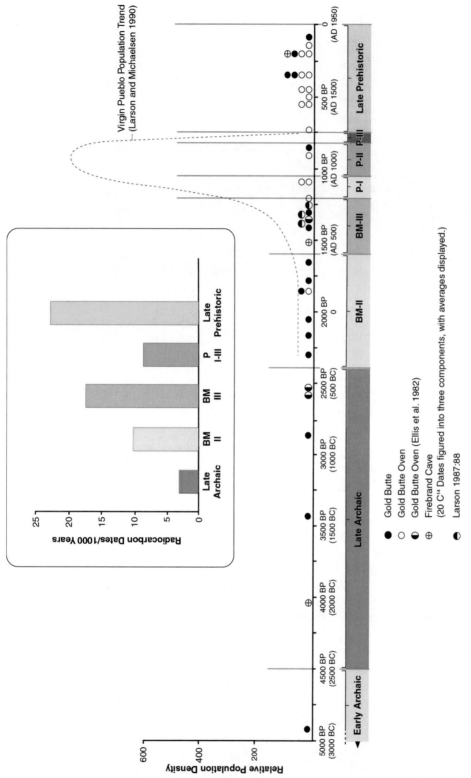

Note: Includes radiocarbon data from Firebrand Cave (Blair 2006), three dates obtained from agave ovens by Ellis et al. 1982, and three dates from Larson 1987:88. The twenty dates from Firebrand Cave represent three different temporal components. Only the average date for each component is plotted.

FIGURE 8.3. Project-wide radiocarbon date profile (calibrated) plotted against estimated relative population of Virgin Branch Puebloans (from Larson and Michaelsen 1990).

discontinuity has implications for both the subsequent Patayan and Southern Paiute occupations of the study area during the Late Prehistoric period (see discussion below).

LAND-USE INTENSITY: BASKETMAKER III AND PUEBLOAN PERIODS

There are several pottery data sets that allow further refinement of land-use intensity during the Basketmaker III/Puebloan periods. Larson and Michaelsen (1990) make use of the seriation potential of two key time-transgressive trends: the relative frequencies of olivine-tempered pottery and corrugated pottery. Under the current classification, the olivine-tempered sample includes all (noncorrugated) Moapa and Shivwits wares; corrugation occurs on some Moapa, Shivwits, and Tusayan sherds.

The fact that corrugation was most popular at the latter end of the Puebloan sequence (i.e., Late Pueblo II and Pueblo III) has been recognized locally (Allison 2000; Hayden 1930:72; Larson and Michaelsen 1990; Lyneis 1986, 2008), as well as in other core areas of the Southwest (e.g., Plog and Hantman 1986). Larson and Michaelsen (1990:233) make the case that olivine tempering is relatively more common at the early end of the Puebloan period (Basketmaker III, Pueblo I), somewhat less so during Pueblo II times, and mostly absent from Late Pueblo II/III contexts. Both Lyneis (1986) and Allison (2000:133) acknowledge Larson and Michaelsen's seriation but argue that olivine-tempered ceramics (Moapa and Shivwits wares) continued to be popular through middle Pueblo II times before mostly disappearing by Pueblo III. For example, at Main Ridge, Lyneis (1986:35) places the Moapa series at about 20–30 percent of the site assemblage. Allison's and Lyneis's studies, however, mostly lack well-dated Basketmaker III and Pueblo I contexts from which to assess the early use of olivine-tempered ceramics. Notwithstanding these differences, corrugated surface treatment and olivine tempering appear to have been most popular at slightly different times. Insofar as they often co-occur in the same contexts, they are amenable to seriation analysis.

Larson and Michaelsen go on to organize their project-wide ceramic sample from the Lower Virgin River Basin along this basic seriation principle, assigning various room blocks, components, and sites to specific time periods (Larson and Michaelsen 1990:Table 2). A summary of Larson and Michaelsen's seriation frequencies for olivine-tempered versus corrugated surface treatment, as well as the thresholds they assign to the various periods, is illustrated in Figure 8.4. These pro-

TABLE 8.1. Seriation of Sites Based on Frequency of Olivine-Tempered and Corrugated Pottery.

Site (26CK)	Olivine Tempered		Corrugated	
	n	%	n	%
Basketmaker III (AD 400–800)				
4891	6	2.0	—	—
6084	1	10.0	—	—
3208	2	13.3	—	—
8047	1	20.0	—	—
7992	7	46.7	—	—
8168	4	50.0	—	—
6082	13	54.2	—	—
8170	47	59.5	—	—
6672	49	59.8	—	—
1991	18	60.0	—	—
8035	19	90.5	—	—
8032	29	78.4	—	—
065-046-2	27	90.0	—	—
7921	33	97.1	—	—
7893	1	100.0	—	—
8001	58	100.0	—	—
Pueblo I (AD 800–950)				
6078/6095	29	23.8	2	1.6
3201	39	24.4	3	1.9
6080/6081	57	23.8	6	2.5
7574	7	30.4	1	4.3
Pueblo II and III (AD 950–1250)				
7966	106	43.3	28	11.4
6088	7	43.8	2	12.5
7892	17	77.3	4	18.2
1988	5	35.7	3	21.4
7983	1	33.3	1	33.3

Note: Percentage frequencies derived from the total of all Puebloan sherds collected. Temporal-seriation breaks based on Larson and Michaelsen 1990:Table 2.

vide a useful framework for evaluating the Gold Butte Puebloan ceramics.

With respect to the project-wide pottery sample from Gold Butte, only 50 of the 1,924 Puebloan series sherds identified exhibited corrugated surface treatment, that is, 2.6 percent. Conversely, 30 percent of this same sample exhibits olivine temper. Based on the seriation summary in Figure 8.4, the profile for the Puebloan period occupation of the study area is therefore decidedly early, trending toward Basketmaker III and Pueblo I.

The result is much the same when we look at the seriation results for specific project sites (Table 8.1). Of the 25 components containing pottery with either olivine temper or corrugated surface treatment, fully

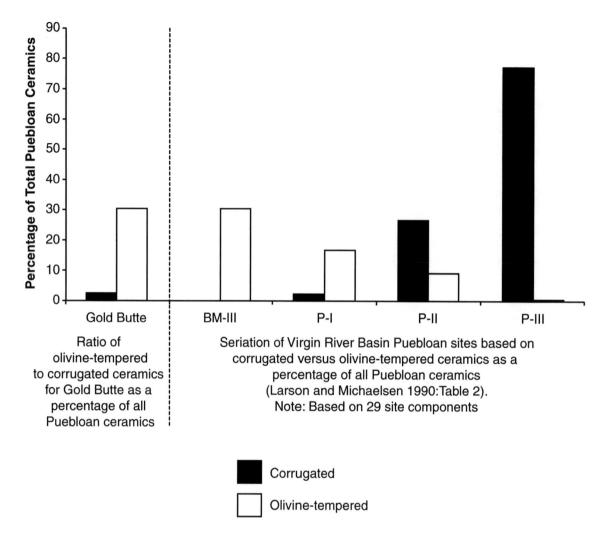

FIGURE 8.4. Gold Butte and Virgin River Basin Puebloan ceramics.

16 seriate to the Basketmaker III period (i.e., they are represented by olivine-tempered sherds but no corrugated specimens). An additional four sites seriate to the Pueblo I period, and the remaining five to Pueblo II or possibly Pueblo III times. Thus fully 64 percent of the project sites containing one or both of these two classes of pottery date to Basketmaker III, and almost 80 percent to either Basketmaker III or Pueblo I times. In a now familiar pattern at Gold Butte, these ceramic data indicate that the intensity of land use in the hinterland appears to be dropping as populations are rising along the adjacent river corridors.

This pattern is also confirmed by the feature inventory along the small portion of the study area that fronts the Virgin River. In total, 51 house pits were documented in this zone (Table 4.7). Most, if not all, of these features date to Basketmaker III times, although only a few have been radiocarbon dated. Conversely, no features or architectural manifestations of Pueblo I, II, or early

Pueblo III were identified in the study area, although sizable farming settlements (population aggregates) dating to this time span are located elsewhere in this river basin.

Several conclusions can be drawn from the ceramic and other data sets. First, there is no reason to believe that the rise of ancestral Puebloan village life along the river corridor, with its attendant population increases, resulted in increased use of the adjacent hinterland. In fact, the opposite seems to have occurred: the demands of intensive agricultural production may have limited options associated with the foraging of wild resources in hinterland habitats. Put another way, there simply may have been less of a need for these farming populations to exploit the outlying resource tracts.

The Puebloan level of commitment to intensive agriculture appears to have far outstripped the commitment of earlier-dating Basketmaker II and III populations. As measured in radiocarbon dates, we see a steady Basketmaker II and III rise in the use of the Gold Butte hinterland in relation to the Late Archaic level (Figure 8.3). The pattern suggests a more sustained commitment to the hunting and gathering of wild resources, at least in relation to the subsequent Puebloan period. While there is good regional evidence for the cultivation of maize in Basketmaker times, these data indicate that this activity may been relatively less systematic and/or intensive—the plant-and-harvest technique as described by Barlow (2005; see also discussion below).

COMPONENT STRUCTURE AND LIFEWAYS: A PERIOD REVIEW

Now that we have outlined several parameters of changes in land-use intensity through time, it remains to integrate survey and excavation data into a broader review of the lifeway associated with each major time period represented in the archaeological record at Gold Butte. An initial component summary of excavation data has already been presented (see the excavation summary in Chapter 6); the implications of these data for subsistence-settlement patterns and prehistoric lifeways, as well as some theoretical issues raised in Chapter 3, are further explored here.

We have previously reviewed atemporal patterns associated with the frequency, type, and distribution of cultural resources documented during the survey program (see Chapter 4). Here we place these findings in a more explicit chronological context. This analysis of survey data, however, is hampered by the high level of settlement concentration in a few specific areas (Cedar Basin and the Red Rock zones) and the inordinate degree of overprinting of assemblages of different ages. We have addressed this issue in several ways, specifically by relying on an "artifact" as opposed to a "site" analysis (e.g., see land-use intensity discussion above) and by standardizing various artifact/feature ratios by time period to reveal overall trend lines. We also rely on the identified single-component areas defined at the tested sites to gain insight into feature and assemblage structure associated with the specific time periods. Finally, it should be mentioned that our excavation sample was directed mostly at "habitation" sites, predominantly rock shelters and open-air middens. Thus our excavation results tend to be biased toward one particular site type. With all this in mind, let us turn to a synthetic discussion of each major time period.

Paleo-Archaic and Early Archaic (Pre–2500 BC)

Perhaps the most elusive parts of the archaeological record at Gold Butte are the assemblages and components predating 4,000 years ago, that is, the Paleo-Archaic

and Early Archaic periods. The study area is bereft of pluvial basins that elsewhere in the Great Basin and Mojave Desert often attracted prehistoric populations during this time. Datable evidence of this period is limited to a moderate number of projectile points (n = 37; Table 5.3), including Great Basin Stemmed and Silver Lake variants, as well as Pinto and Humboldt forms (Early Archaic). In addition, upward of 25 percent of the obsidian hydration rim values from the dominant source groups (Kane Springs, Delamar Mountains, and Modena/Panaca Summit) are greater than 11.0 microns, which we use as the divide between the Early and Late Archaic periods (Figure 5.9).

Clearly, then, there is an early presence at Gold Butte. But where was the focus of this occupation? Figure 8.5 graphs the frequency of time-sensitive projectile points for each major period recovered during the survey in each of the three primary environmental strata. These values are standardized against the percentage of survey coverage in each of these zones. Thus, for example, the general desert (lowland stratum) constituted 55 percent of the project inventory area, but only 20 percent of the Paleo-Archaic/Early Archaic points were recovered from this area, resulting in a 35 percent spread below the expectation. When these data are arrayed for each time period, Figure 8.5 reveals that, more than any subsequent time period, Paleo-Archaic/Early Archaic points are concentrated in the Red Rock stratum.

Of course, Figure 8.5 also reveals that the Red Rock stratum was the preferred area for all time periods (although the smallest deviation from the expectation was recorded for the Late Archaic period; see discussion below). Atemporal analyses of the broader survey results confirm this pattern (see Chapter 4). As we discuss, the Red Rock stratum is where all Late Archaic, Puebloan, and Late Prehistoric rock art occurs, indicating its centrality for ritual and ceremonial activities. Its geographic extent also takes in most of the primary trade corridors modeled for the Puebloan period (see discussion below). The fact that the Red Rock stratum was the focus of prehistoric activity in the Early Archaic period *well before* any of these subsequent and more substantial cultural developments suggests a more fundamental attraction, namely, water.

The Red Rock stratum is characterized by a series of massive, Jurassic-age, Aztec sandstone outcrops. In several locations, active springs and short riparian corridors are found in this formation. The sandstone also has an impermeable quality that tends to impound surface water in small declivities and basins (i.e., tenajas) after short-term and seasonal rains. These water resources

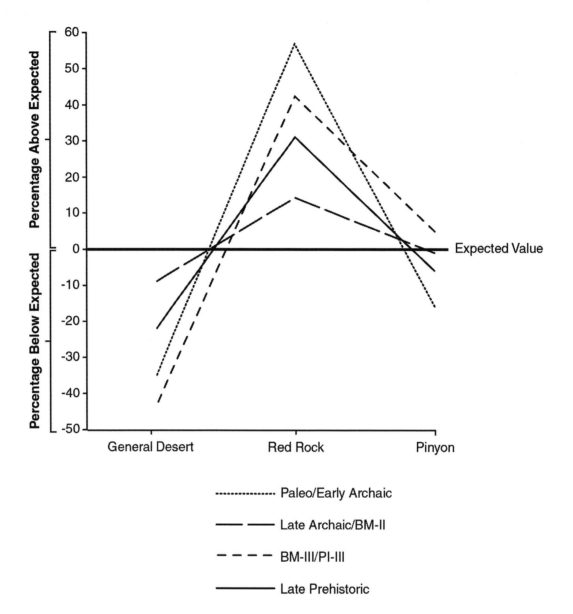

FIGURE 8.5. Frequency of time-sensitive projectile points by environmental stratum.

also attract a variety of game and, at the more productive springs, sustain a limited amount of riparian vegetation. But away from the major river corridors that flank the study area, it is difficult to overstate the stark aridity of Gold Butte and the overall importance of these oases.

Beyond survey-level results, it remains a challenge to adequately characterize the lifeway of these early inhabitants of Gold Butte; no components dating to the Paleo-Archaic/Early Archaic were excavated. One clue, however, is in the relatively high levels of milling equipment from single-component sites dating to this time discovered during survey (Table 8.2), standardized as a ratio of flaked stone tools to milling tools in Figure 8.6. The relative amount of milling gear is higher than in the

subsequent Late Archaic but lower than in the much later-dating Basketmaker III/Puebloan or Late Prehistoric components.

As we further detail below, the presence of milling equipment is particularly sensitive to site function, work and gender organization, and residential patterns. We interpret the more even balance of hunting weaponry and milling tools at Paleo-Archaic/Early Archaic sites— at least in comparison to subsequent Late Archaic manifestations—as more typical of a settlement framework characterized by small, demographically inclusive foraging groups consisting of men, women, and children. As documented throughout the Mojave Desert and Great Basin for this time frame, these groups were probably

TABLE 8.2. Key Artifact Assemblages and Features from Single-Component Survey Sites.

	Paleo-Archaic/Early Archaic Pre–2500 BC		Late Archaic/BM II 2500 BC–AD 400		BM III/PI–III AD 400–1250		Late Prehistoric Post–AD 1250		
	#	Average	#	Average	#	Average	#	Average	Total
Flaked Stone									
Projectile Points	16	1.6	21	1.5	6	0.2	0	0.0	43
Bifaces	24	2.4	23	1.6	28	0.7	7	0.5	82
Other Tools	12	1.2	11	0.8	11	0.3	5	0.4	39
Subtotal	52	5.2	55	3.9	45	1.1	12	0.9	164
Ground Stone									
Millingstones	18	1.8	8	0.6	23	0.6	35	2.7	84
Handstones	3	0.3	3	0.2	14	0.4	9	0.7	29
Subtotal	21	2.1	11	0.8	37	1.0	44	3.4	113
Features									
Hunting Blinds	0	0.0	6	0.4	0	0.0	0	0.0	6
Agave Ovens	10	1.0	8	0.6	8	0.2	14	1.1	40
Total	83	8.3	80	5.7	90	2.3	70	5.4	323

Note: Single component refers to sites with temporal indicators (e.g., projectile points, pottery sherds) from only a single time period.

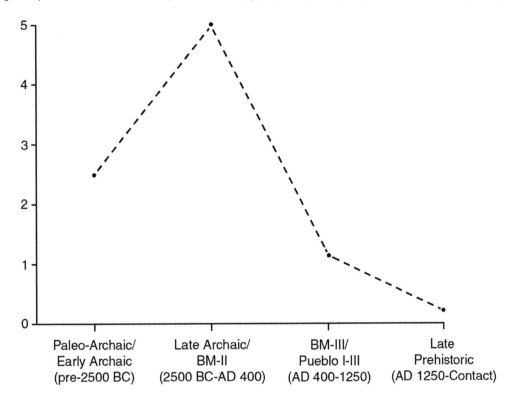

FIGURE 8.6. Ratio of flaked stone tools to milling tools at single-component survey sites.

more residentially mobile and ranged over a wider territory than during subsequent time periods (Bird et al. 2009; Basgall 1996, 2000; Delacorte 1999). A crucial stop in this settlement round appears to have been the springs and tenajas among the Aztec sandstone at the Red Rock stratum.

Late Archaic and Basketmaker II
(2500 BC–AD 400)

Along any number of dimensions, use of Gold Butte seems to have expanded during the Late Archaic and Basketmaker II periods. We find higher relative frequencies of projectile points in relation to the previous

Paleo-Archaic and Early Archaic periods (Figure 8.2). A number of caves, rock shelters, and open-air sites seem to have been first occupied during this period (as such, we have relatively robust excavation samples), and it is probably during this time that rock art production dramatically increases.

As reviewed in Chapter 3 (see also Gilreath et al. 2006), these changes, rather than simply reflecting a continuation of Early Archaic land-use patterns albeit with higher population densities, may represent a more fundamental shift in settlement structure. In this scenario, the hinterland of Gold Butte was less the locus of residential activity and more the domain of logistical forays primarily associated with large-game hunting, at least in comparison to the periods before and after. And continuing with this scenario, residential bases were strategically situated near productive resource tracts (e.g., the Virgin River) from which long-range hunting forays emanated. To the extent that this settlement system emphasizes large-game hunting—presumably directed mostly at bighorn sheep—it is also thought to incorporate a social and symbolic context (Blair 2006; Byrd et al. 2005; Gilreath 2009; Heizer and Baumhoff 1962; Hildebrandt and McGuire 2002; McGuire et al. 2007; McGuire and Hildebrandt 2005).

With respect to survey results, we find some initial corroboration of this pattern. As previously reviewed in Figure 8.6 (see also Table 8.2), the ratio of flaked stone tools to milling implements reaches its highest level at this time and is nearly five times higher than in subsequent periods. In addition, it is during this period that the only hunting blinds are documented (Table 8.2). In essence, assemblages dating to this time are dominated by hunting weaponry—projectile points and bifaces—generally associated with taking large game. To the extent that large game (especially bighorn sheep) was pursued by males on long-distance hunting forays, this argues for a more logistically oriented land-use pattern in the Gold Butte hinterland. Residential activity was probably more concentrated in productive resource tracts near the major river corridors, although there is scant evidence of such sites dating to this time in or near the study area. The comparative lack of milling equipment in site assemblages in the hinterland suggests a reduction in residential activity consistent with this emphasis on logistical hunting.

Given this characterization of Late Archaic/Basketmaker II land use—intensified residential occupation along the river corridors and increasing long-distance logistical forays—it is perhaps not surprising that Elko and Gypsum series projectile points dating to this time are more evenly dispersed across a variety of environmental zones (Figure 8.5). Certain habitats and landforms may have been more routinely targeted, but this emphasis on long-range logistical mobility probably meant that these hunters stopped in and/or passed through a comparatively wide portion of the Gold Butte landscape.

Given the trend toward the taking of large game inferred from survey-level information, it follows that we should find corroboration in data sets derived from the excavation of several Late Archaic components. Artiodactyl remains, mostly bighorn sheep, reach their highest relative frequencies during the Late Archaic period, whereas tortoise remains are only minimally represented (Figure 8.7a; see also the excavation summary in Chapter 6). More broadly, and in combination with the archaeobotanical evidence, Late Archaic peoples appear to have used high-grade resources from the Gold Butte hinterland, additionally focusing on pinyon nuts (Figure 8.7b). Bighorn sheep and pinyon nuts present a strong fall/winter signal of seasonal occupation. Negative evidence, as indicated by the near-absence of tortoise remains (burrow hibernation in winter but available in warmer months), agave processing (optimal in spring), and goosefoot seeds (late spring-summer ripening), suggests reduced settlement activity in spring, summer, and perhaps early fall.

There is one additional element to this Late Archaic hunting focus that pervades the archaeological record of Gold Butte, and that is its symbolic dimension, reflected in the abundance of rock art dating to this time in the Red Rock zone, as well as by site 26CK5434. In Chapter 7 we identify five major temporal and cultural rock art styles at Gold Butte: the two most relevant to this discussion are Desert Archaic and Basketmaker/Puebloan. The temporal parameters for each of these styles/periods are not easily reconciled with the chronological sequence used in this presentation; for example, the Basketmaker/Puebloan tradition (which includes Basketmaker II) commences at about 300 BC, thus overlapping the Late Archaic–Basketmaker II period by some 700 years. This overlap is potentially of even longer duration if Late Archaic–Basketmaker II components are recognized by the presence of either Elko or Gypsum dart points, which may have persisted until AD 600–700.

Notwithstanding these temporal issues, it seems clear that there was a transition from abstract to more representational designs in this region, commencing at about 300 BC and continuing through the Basketmaker III/Puebloan period. But as we have previously noted, Gold Butte probably sustained more intense occupation at the earlier end of the Basketmaker-

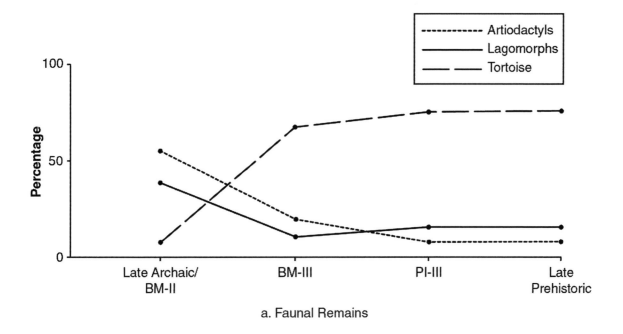

a. Faunal Remains

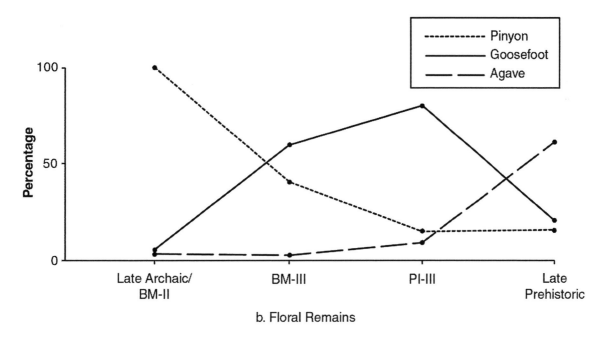

b. Floral Remains

FIGURE 8.7. Faunal (a) and floral (b) remains from excavated sites at Gold Butte.

Puebloan period (specifically Basketmaker II and III, Pueblo I), and thus it is likely that most of the representational elements and panels date between 350 BC and AD 950.

In the symbolic dimension of the hunt at Gold Butte, bighorn sheep, which are depicted with oblong to nearly boat-shaped bodies but always with horns in pro-file, are a key stylistic element of the representational inventory. A total of 372 such elements were documented in the study area from 38 different sites—all in the Red Rock zone. Depictions of sheep constitute the dominate form, making up about 46 percent of all representational elements (Table 7.5). Although of uncertain Great Basin and/or Southwestern origin, this emphasis on bighorn sheep, as well as depictions of various hunting scenes and weaponry, has been tied to the Late Holocene rise of logistical large-game hunting observed throughout the West (Gilreath and Hildebrandt 2008; Hildebrandt and McGuire 2002; McGuire and Hildebrandt 2005; see also Broughton et al. 2008; Broughton and Bayham 2003; and Byers and Broughton 2004 for further discussion of Late Holocene faunal trends). In sum, the technological, subsistence, and symbolic dimensions of Late Archaic–Basketmaker II hunting seem very much on display at Gold Butte.

One final aspect of this Late Archaic–Basketmaker II hunting focus now recognized in the study area is represented at site 26CK5434. This site, with its obscured entrance, crawlways, and back chambers, as well as its caches of decorated hunting weaponry and firebrands or torches, strongly resembles other specialized "hunting magic" sites that date to the same period. Recognized as such by the recovery of split-twig figurines depicting bighorn sheep, caches of hunting weaponry, and other artifacts of ritual use, this list includes nearby Gypsum Cave (Gilreath 2009; Harrington 1933), as well as Newberry Cave (Davis and Smith 1981), Stanton's Cave in the Grand Canyon (Euler 1978), and Etna Cave (Fowler 1973). The calibrated radiocarbon dates from 26CK5434 (Table 5.2) cluster between 2000 and 1500 BC, indicating that this complex of hunting-related cultural expression was well under way toward the beginning of the Late Archaic period.

Basketmaker III (AD 400–800) and Pueblo I–III (AD 800–1250)

As previously outlined, the Basketmaker III and Pueblo I–III intervals experienced an explosion in human population, largely due to the development of agricultural-based economies in the Virgin-Muddy river lowland (Larson and Michaelsen 1990). This increase is evident in the Gold Butte hinterland during the Basketmaker III period (AD 400–800), particularly from the radiocarbon dates generated from the series of pithouse villages overlooking the Virgin River along the northern margins of our study area (see also Larson 1987). By Puebloan times (AD 800–1250), however, the intensity of land use surprisingly declined at Gold Butte, in counterpoint to when lowland populations peaked.

We now take a closer look at the archaeological record of Gold Butte to explore why this demographic reorganization took place. One of the first and most obvious factors contributing to these differences in land use is the lack of a strong monsoonal weather pattern in the study area, which prevented the development of dry-land farming (see Chapter 2). Unlike much of the greater Southwest, where field houses and cultivated plots were common in the hinterlands, agricultural sites are completely absent at Gold Butte during Puebloan times, when farming activities were entirely focused on the riverine lowland.

This lowland focus most certainly influenced the range of wild plant and animal resources that were used in the hinterland, but there is little agreement among archaeologists regarding the interplay between wild and domestic foods during this important period of prehistory. Larson and Michaelsen (1990:243), for example, propose that Basketmaker II subsistence was largely dependent on wild resources, while Lyneis (1995) argues for a primary role for agricultural foods in both Basketmaker and Puebloan communities. Despite the priority Lyneis gives to domesticates, she recognizes that wild plants such as pine nuts, acorn, agave, mesquite, and small seeds were also used, although she does not speculate as to their overall economic utility (Lyneis 2000: 222–223). She also notes that maize was probably the lone cultigen in Basketmaker contexts and that beans and squash were not added to the diet until Puebloan times (i.e., after AD 800).

"Plant and Harvest" versus "Typical Agriculture"

When attempting to understand when and why people shift from foraging adaptations to those dependent on farming, researchers have found it useful to rank the caloric return rates of both wild and domestic foods. These types of analyses show that lower-ranked foods are often added to the diet when the availability of higher-ranked foods is diminished (Kennett and Winterhalder 2005). Barlow (2005) has addressed this issue among the Fremont by comparing the caloric return rates of wild plant foods with cultivated maize; Figure 8.8 shows rates for the Virgin Branch Puebloans. Return rates for wild plants show that mesquite (2,080 Kcal/Hr) and pine nuts (1,200–1,700 Kcal/Hr) offer the highest returns, while agave (730 Kcal/Hr) and small seeds such as goosefoot (500 Kcal/Hr) are much less productive. Two approaches to cultivation are proposed by Barlow. "Plant and harvest" refers to situations in which minimal tending of the fields occurs, and this approach offers relatively high return rates (1,300–1,700 Kcal/Hr). "Typical agriculture" entails a much higher investment, including more weeding/cultivation and greater use of irrigation, and produces much lower return rates (100–1,100 Kcal/ Hr). It should be noted, however, that the extra labor costs for both types of agriculture (especially the intensive form) result in greater production per unit of land (see the x-axis of Figure 8.8). These basic relationships

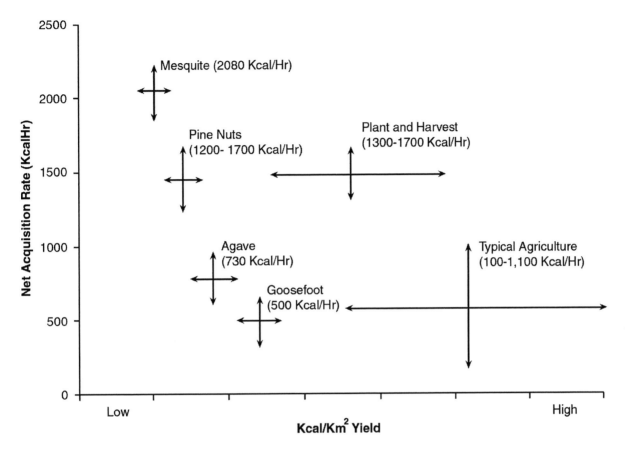

FIGURE 8.8. Caloric return rates for key wild and domestic plants relevant to the Virgin Branch Puebloans.

indicate that low-density hunter-gatherers could choose to optimize efficiency while higher-density agricultural groups along the Virgin River would eventually need to optimize yield.

This diet-breadth model shows that mesquite and pine nuts have higher return rates than maize, except for the most productive forms of the low-investment plant-and-harvest strategy. Agave and goosefoot, in contrast, have lower return rates than all production levels of the plant-and-harvest approach, and are also surpassed by typical agriculture when production levels are relatively high. Given that Gold Butte contains stands of pinyon, agave, and a variety of small-seeded plants, we can use changes in the use of these and other wild foods to indirectly measure the success of farming along the Virgin lowlands, particularly by monitoring the use of low-ranking foods like agave and small seeds. If the reduced use of the Gold Butte hinterland during Puebloan times was linked to a highly productive agricultural system, then visits to the area should reflect the use of highly ranked foods like pinyon nuts and large game. If, on the other hand, these visits reflect intensive foraging for lower-ranked foods, particularly those with lower

return rates than the agricultural products, this could signal that the agricultural system was supplemented from time to time with noncultivated foods.

The data outlined below indicate that the latter was probably the case. Our first hint regarding the importance of hinterland foraging is the ratio of flaked stone tools to milling tools obtained from single-component sites discovered during the survey (Table 8.2 and Figure 8.6). Whereas the Late Archaic–Basketmaker II interval has a predominance of rather specialized hunting-related assemblages, the combined Basketmaker III and Puebloan components have a much higher percentage of milling gear. Although the percentage of milling gear is not as high as in the Late Prehistoric period, it surely indicates the importance of plant processing in hinterland areas.

Plant macrofossil data also reflect the importance of wild plant foods. With the exception of a single corncob found at 26CK8047, our excavations failed to produce evidence of domesticated plants at Gold Butte. It is important to note, however, that the radiocarbon date of cal AD 130 on that corncob corresponds quite closely with radiocarbon samples obtained from several other

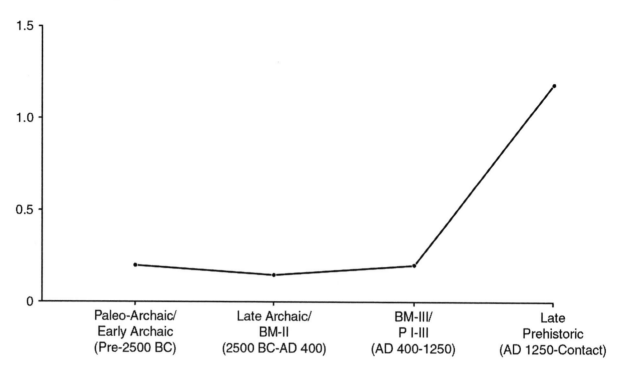

FIGURE 8.9. Ratio of agave ovens to flaked stone tools at single-component survey sites.

corn and gourd fragments found in other places away from the Virgin lowlands. Black Dog Cave, for example, produced three dates (cal AD 330 on corn; cal AD 40 on corn; cal AD 170 on a gourd; Winslow et al. 2003b), while a single date of AD 228 was obtained from a corncob recovered at 26CK5434 (Blair 2006). All these dates correspond to the Basketmaker II period and indicate that people regularly augmented their diets with domesticates while foraging for wild foods. This mix of domesticated and wild foods, combined with the relatively highly visible Basketmaker sites at Gold Butte (see radiocarbon dates in Figure 8.3), probably indicates that Barlow's (2005) plant-and-harvest strategy was in play at this time, as the lower investments directed toward cultivation resulted in higher mobility and a greater emphasis on foraging in outlying areas. The lack of radiocarbon dates on domesticates in outlying areas during Puebloan times, even though agricultural production was at its peak, probably reflects the emergence of the typical agriculture strategy, as greater labor investments in the lowlands resulted in reduced use of the hinterland.

The most important wild plants obtained from the project flotation samples were pinyon nutshell, goosefoot seeds, and agave fragments. As outlined above (Figure 8.7b), pinyon remains are dominant in the Late Archaic, but the diet breadth expanded to include goosefoot during Basketmaker III. Goosefoot reaches maximum importance in the Puebloan period, and

agave becomes a minor contributor for the first time. The final phase of intensification occurs during the Late Prehistoric period, when agave becomes dominant and goosefoot remains more abundant than pinyon. The importance of pinyon and the lack of agave during Basketmaker III times fits the expectation of our diet-breadth model, as pinyon return rates are higher than most forms of plant-and-harvest agriculture, and agave returns are lower. The abundant presence of the small-seeded goosefoot was not expected, however, as its return rates are slightly lower than those of agave. Goosefoot frequencies continue to increase into Puebloan times, which is less surprising given the lower return rates for typical agriculture, but agave still lags behind.

The low frequency of agave macrofossils is matched by the temporal distribution of agave ovens found during the survey. Of the 19 radiocarbon dates obtained from these features (Figure 8.3), only one falls within the Pueblo II/III interval (AD 950–1250). Moreover, the relative abundance of agave ovens located at single-component sites discovered during the survey, as measured against the frequency of flaked stone tools, remains quite low through the sequence until the Late Prehistoric period, when they spike in frequency (Table 8.2; Figure 8.9).

Why agave processing lags behind the intensive use of goosefoot is probably related to the optimal season of harvest for these two plants. Agave is best harvested in the spring before it sends up its stalk (see Chapter 2), while goosefoot reaches peak production in summer. The low frequency of agave processing in Puebloan times may well relate to a scheduling conflict, as spring planting and the care of young seedlings would have interfered with traveling 25 km to the agave zone at Gold Butte. By the Late Prehistoric period, when agricultural production had ceased, local Southern Paiute populations greatly intensified the use of agave.

Summer foraging at Gold Butte during Puebloan times is also supported by the faunal remains obtained from the project sites (Figure 8.7a). Unlike the Late Archaic period, when artiodactyls and lagomorphs are abundantly present and tortoise is rarely found (probably reflecting fall and winter visits), tortoise makes up almost 75 percent of the Puebloan assemblages. Tortoises are best taken during the warm seasons of the year when they are out of their winter burrows, and their high numbers in Puebloan components are fully consistent with people moving across large tracts of lands harvesting goosefoot. Taken together, the high frequency of milling gear, small seeds, and tortoise and the smaller amounts of other foods like pinyon and rabbits probably reflect periodic forays to the Gold Butte hinterland to supplement the agricultural diet during years when crop yields were reduced.

Floral and faunal remains from a recent excavation at the Main Ridge site allow us to compare Gold Butte profiles with a Pueblo II occupation along the Virgin-Muddy river lowlands (Table 8.3), adding support for the importance of periodic foraging. These data were collected from excavations in Room 20 (Harry 2008); the plant remains were reported by Cummings (2008) and the faunal remains by Watson (2008). Gold Butte and Main Ridge both have quantities of cheno-ams, but this is where the similarities begin and end. Pinyon and agave, although found in low numbers, are present at Gold Butte but completely absent at Main Ridge, while both maize (abundant) and beans (rare) are present at Main Ridge but absent at Gold Butte. The lack of transport of these key resources between Gold Butte and Main Ridge seems rather strange, but it probably indicates that Puebloan peoples were largely foraging in the hinterland during crop failures and not making special, logistically organized trips back and forth during periods of plenty; otherwise, high-ranked resources like pinyon would have been transported to places like Main Ridge (Rhode 1990).

The faunal remains also produce little evidence for resource transport (Figure 8.7a). Logistical forays to the Virgin Mountains for sheep and deer would produce relatively high frequencies of these highly ranked animals

TABLE 8.3. Faunal and Floral Remains from Puebloan Components at Gold Butte and Main Ridge.

	Gold Butte	Main Ridge	Total
Faunal Remains			
Artiodactyl	11	48	59
Lagomorph	22	83	105
Tortoise	98	46	144
Total	131	177	308
Artiodactyl:Lagomorph	1:2.0	1:1.7	1:1.8
Plant Remains			
Agave	22	—	22
Pinyon	42	—	42
Cheno-am	235[a]	163[b]	398
Tansy Mustard	4	19	23
Corn	—	242	242
Beans	—	11	11
Total	303	435	738

[a] Includes *Chenopodium* (goosefoot).
[b] Includes goosefoot, *Amaranthus* (pigweed, amaranth), and *Atriplex* (saltbush, shadscale).

both at the hunting camps and back at the residential base (Dean 2001, 2007; Pickrell 2005; Szuter and Bayham 1989; Diehl and Waters 2005), but this is not the case for Puebloan assemblages at either location. Although the ratio of artiodactyls to lagomorphs is slightly better at Main Ridge (1:1.7) than at Gold Butte (1:2.0), the differences are quite minor. In fact, the only significant difference between the two places is the greater abundance of tortoise at Gold Butte. This difference may also reflect the seasonality of habitation. If Gold Butte was used mostly in the summer, when tortoise reached maximum availability, and Main Ridge was occupied year round, including the winter dormant stage of the tortoise, cool-season hunting of lagomorphs and artiodactyls may have increased their overall contribution to the diet.

These findings indicate that Late Archaic peoples visited Gold Butte on a limited basis, focusing on the highest-ranked resources (artiodactyls, pinyon) mostly during fall and winter. The earliest evidence of domesticates in the local area occurs during Basketmaker II times, and it appears that the local population practiced a plant-and-harvest approach to agricultural production through the Basketmaker III period (or until about AD 800). This allowed them to systematically exploit a broad mix of both domesticated and wild foods, and is reflected by a broadening of the diet (adding goosefoot and tortoise) and extending the season of use at Gold Butte into the summer. By Puebloan times, the high-investment traditional agriculture strategy restricted the use of Gold Butte, as more labor investment (weeding/cultivation, irrigation) was required to successfully grow an expanded crop (beans and squash, in addition to maize) and to support an expanding population.

Although much diminished, use of Gold Butte did not altogether cease during the Puebloan period. But rather than reflect a systematic subsistence-settlement strategy based on a mix of domesticated and wild foods, we suspect this occupation was more of an emergency response to low crop yields or even catastrophic failures, which apparently occurred with some regularity among Southwestern agriculturalists (Mabry 2005). The one exception to this overall land-use characterization was the continuing use of the Aztec sandstone formations at Gold Butte for the production of rock art, much of it classified as Basketmaker/Puebloan (see Chapter 7). Although many of these panels may have been produced more toward the early end of this time frame, as discussed above, it seems clear that these highly visible Red Rock formations continued to attract prehistoric artisans throughout the Puebloan period.

Puebloan Interregional Exchange and Other Social Relationships

Although local Puebloan peoples generated a livelihood based on farming in the lowlands and foraging in outlying areas such as Gold Butte, direct subsistence was not the sole focus of their economic system. Archaeological data from Lost City show that they intensively mined salt, and the scale of these operations suggests that this commodity was traded widely (Shutler 1961). They may also have grown cotton, which would have set them apart from many of their upland neighbors on the Shivwits and Uinkaret Plateaus, as cotton is more successfully grown with irrigation than with the dry-land farming system used by most of these upland peoples (Lyneis 1992). Another valued commodity, turquoise, is thought to have been obtained through direct access to mines near Boulder City, Searchlight, and even Halloran Springs in the Mojave Desert. Some of this material is found in Lost City burials (Lyneis 1992), but much of it was probably traded to the east as well. All these items are quite rare in the archaeological record, due to either preservation issues (salt, cotton) or their extreme value/rarity (turquoise), so we have little quantitative data to evaluate how interregional exchange influenced local lifeways in the past. Exotic pottery types, exotic obsidians, and marine shell beads, in contrast, survive well in the archaeological record and provide a glimpse of this elusive part of the prehistoric past.

Pottery is the most useful of these items, as nonlocal wares from the east were commonly traded into the Virgin area and could represent the reciprocal side of the exchange relationships outlined above (i.e., exchanged for salt, cotton, or turquoise). The dominant ceramic trade wares for this period are Moapa Gray/White and Shivwits Gray. The former is recognized by its distinctive crushed olivine-rich xenolith temper. This mineral is found associated with lava flows in the Mount Trumbull area on the Uinkaret Plateau (Allison 2000; Lyneis 1988; Menzies et al. 1987), and most researchers think that Moapa pottery was manufactured in this general area (but see Jensen [2002] and Sakai [2000] for other possibilities). Shivwits Gray was fashioned from dark-fired, iron-rich clay tempered with crushed Moapa sherds, and Lyneis (1988, 1992) believes that it was produced on the Shivwits Plateau. A small but persistent amount of San Juan Red and Tsegi Orange wares, produced east of the Uinkaret Plateau, also find their way into Virgin Puebloan sites. The sand-tempered Tusayan Gray Virgin series and limestone-tempered Logandale Gray, in contrast, were produced in the local area (Allison 2000; Lyneis 1992).

Allison (2000) and Jensen (2002) have thoroughly studied the temporal and geographic distribution of these pottery types in the region but focus more on subsistence issues than on the exchange of nonfood commodities. Allison suggests that the Virgin Branch Puebloans engaged in rather small-scale exchange systems, with most households obtaining the eastern wares through their own trade networks (2000:134). He views this as a mutualistic system of exchange, designed to minimize the risk of periodic downturns in subsistence productivity. Jensen (2002:44) agrees, arguing that farming in the uplands to the east was high risk compared with farming along the lowland floodplains to the west, where water from the reliable spring-fed Muddy River was available. In her constructed model of exchange, the eastern upland populations provide pots in exchange for corn from the western lowland populations. Thus the upland people engaged in trade in order to buffer the risk of starvation, while the lowland groups traded to maintain social ties and/or to obtain valued items. These explanations don't entirely square with the emerging character of late Puebloan subsistence-settlement practices at Gold Butte described above, however, and the presumption that these populations were periodically and routinely the victims of crop failures. It is hard to imagine how trade in a small number of exotic pottery vessels could have much alleviated these occasional catastrophes.

Regardless of which resources were heading to the east, the question remains as to how these exchange items made their way to consumer populations located

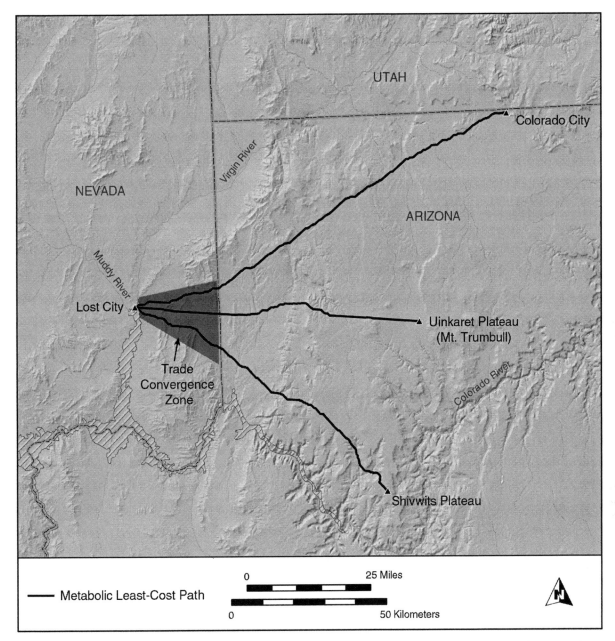

FIGURE 8.10. Least-effort travel corridors from pottery production locations at Mt. Trumbull, the Shivwits Plateau, and major Puebloan settlements near Colorado City.

along the Virgin and Muddy River Basins to the west, and what role the study area played in the movement of these goods. To determine the most efficient trade corridors from the pottery production centers on the Uinkaret and Shivwits plateaus to the Lost City settlements along the lower Virgin River Basin, we used a GIS-based least-cost algorithm to plot the metabolically most efficient routes (Pandolf et al. 1977). Although it is not a pottery production center per se, we also include a Virgin Branch population center to the northeast near Colorado City (Fowler and Madsen 1986) in recogni-

tion of the likely contacts this area also had with settlements in the lower Virgin River Basin. To operationalize this analysis, we selected specific UTM grid coordinates at Lost City, Colorado City, and the two pottery production zones.

The results of this metabolic least-cost analysis (Figure 8.10) are perhaps not too surprising, as they form more or less straight lines from each population/ production center. The northern route (Colorado City to Lost City), however, is perhaps most noteworthy in that it does not follow the Virgin River, which was one

TABLE 8.4. Ratio of Local to Traded Puebloan Sherds in the Least-Cost Trade Convergence Zone.

	Local Wares	Trade Wares
Inside Corridor	925 (70.2%)	393 (29.8%)
Outside Corridor	758 (79.7%)	205 (21.3%)

of several major alignments of the Old Spanish Trail in historic times.

With respect to Gold Butte, the energetic model points to a geographic convergence of these routes in a broad triangle in the center of our study area, with the apex pointing to Lost City (Figure 8.10). If the exotic wares from the east were directly transported to the Lost City pueblos along these routes, then we expect Moapa Gray/White, Shivwits Gray, and other trade wares to be more concentrated within this trade convergence zone than the locally made wares (i.e., Tusayan and Logandale Gray).

To test this hypothesis, we examined the ratio of trade to locally produced wares, both inside and outside the hypothesized trade corridor (Table 8.4). The results show a higher ratio of trade wares in the corridor than in the adjacent outlying area. Although the contrast between these two areas is not dramatic, it is statistically significant ($p = 0.05$). From this, we conclude that a large portion of the ceramic wares imported from production centers on the Uinkaret and Shivwits Plateaus to Puebloan settlements located along the lower reaches of the Virgin River Basin and Moapa Valley passed through the center of Gold Butte.

One additional data set is relevant to the issue of interregional relationships among the Virgin Branch Pueblo: rock art. Schaafsma (1971, 1980) identifies two geographic variations of Virgin Branch rock art—Eastern and Western—implying separate cultural traditions. As reviewed in Chapter 7, the Western Virgin variant now appears to be the same as the Eastern Virgin style, the only difference being that the former often has an overlay of Patayan elements. With the dismissal of this east versus west distinction, cultural unity rather than intragroup differentiation seems to better characterize the ancestral Puebloan groups throughout southern Nevada, southern Utah, and the Arizona Strip (see also Castleton and Madsen 1981).

Late Prehistoric (Post–AD 1250 to Contact)

Puebloan culture collapsed abruptly along the Virgin River at about AD 1250 (Larson and Michaelsen 1990). Identifying the reasons for the Puebloan collapse has been the subject of debate throughout the Southwest for many decades. This is certainly the case for the Virgin Branch, where various scenarios have been proposed, including abandonment due to devastating droughts, withdrawal due to violent conflict with the Southern Paiute, and assimilation with the Southern Paiute and a return to a foraging way of life. Larson and Michaelsen (1990) are the primary proponents for a drought-induced abandonment, but discrepancies between the timing of the final drought event (AD 1120–1150) and the AD 1200–1250 collapse led Lyneis (1995) to suggest that other factors must have been involved, including complex interactions with Numic-speaking peoples from the west (i.e., the Southern Paiute). The nature of Southern Paiute–Puebloan interactions has also been the subject of debate, as it is unclear whether the Southern Paiute moved into an abandoned area, actively displaced the farming population (Ambler and Sutton 1989; Hayden 1930), or assimilated the Puebloans into their hunter-gatherer culture (Huffman 1993; Janetski 1993; Lyneis 1994, 1995).

The results of our study suggest that this traditional formulation—ancestral Puebloan groups in some sense giving way to the Southern Paiute—is probably not correct or at best is incomplete. What is new here is the documentation of a substantial ancestral Yuman—that is, Patayan—occupation, recognized by a large and spatially extensive assemblage of paddle and anvil pottery and by a large and stylistic cohesive rock art inventory. Judging from the estimated age of paddle and anvil pottery recovered from Gold Butte, the Patayan were actively using this area between AD 1000 and 1500. It is also important to emphasize that brown ware pottery, a signature of Southern Paiute occupation, is thought to postdate AD 1300.

Enter, then, the Patayan into the Late Prehistoric conversation at Gold Butte. They may well have overlapped the Puebloan occupation on the adjacent river lowlands by as much as 200 to 250 years. It is also likely that it was the Patayan, not Puebloan groups, who were encountered by the Southern Paiute when they first encroached on Gold Butte. Evidence of these disparate occupations, and the nature of their interaction, is reviewed below.

The Patayan

Aside from their rock art and distinct paddle and anvil pottery, little is known regarding the lifeways of the Patayan, although they are thought to be ancestral Yuman-speakers related to the ethnographic Hualapai and Mohave, the former bounding the study area on the south (Figure 2.3). They were also referred to more generically as the Hakataya (Schroeder 1979), and their core settlements appear to have been oriented along the lower Colorado River, although they practiced a dispersed land-use strategy relying on a variety of seasonally available wild plant and animal resources. It also seems clear that the Hualapai and their ancestors engaged in some level of agricultural production—Kroeber (1935) felt that this activity was probably intermittent by ethnographic times, while Dobyns and Euler (1976) argue that it was much more important during precontact (i.e., Patayan) times. This mixed use of both domesticates and wild foods is reminiscent of the more informal plant-and-harvest strategy described above for Basketmaker and perhaps Pueblo I populations. As we are outside the summer monsoonal boundary for effective dry-land farming, it also means that the local Patayan agricultural system necessitated some seasonal settlement focus on the floodplain of the lower Colorado River.

Our analysis of Patayan lifeways at Gold Butte, however, is hindered by the lack of resolution afforded by our excavation data. Owing to temporal overlap resulting from the mixing of subsurface materials, no "pure" Patayan spatio-temporal component was identified as such, although the Patayan surely constitute an important aspect of what is classified as Late Prehistoric.

As mentioned above, two archaeological data sets provide exceptions to these constraints: the substantial inventory of rock art panels and the large and extensive assemblage of paddle and anvil pottery, both ascribed to Patayan occupation. With regard to rock art, Patayan petroglyphs were documented at a frequency rivaling their Basketmaker/Puebloan counterparts at Gold Butte, although panel design is generally less complex and trends toward comparatively abstract representations (Table 7.7). As with all rock art at Gold Butte, Patayan panels are concentrated in the Red Rock zone and are often co-associated with Archaic and/or Basketmaker/Puebloan panels. If nothing else, these rock art panels provide a striking example of Patayan cultural expression at Gold Butte. The second exception is found in the frequency, distribution, and co-associations reflected in paddle and anvil pottery. This more robust data set potentially provides a window into Patayan relationships with the Puebloans and the Southern Paiute. The evidence is reviewed below.

Patayan Interactions with the Puebloans and Southern Paiute

As we have seen, the evidence for Patayan occupation at Gold Butte is overwhelming: paddle and anvil sherds actually outnumber brown ware (Southern Paiute) sherds. Table 8.5 reveals several noteworthy aspects of the cultural geography associated with these two

TABLE 8.5. Frequency of Patayan (Paddle/Anvil) and Southern Paiute (Brown Ware) Pottery in the Northern and Southern Portions of the Study Area.

	North	South	Total
Sites			
Brown Ware	7	—	7
Paddle/Anvil	4	11	15
Total	11	11	22
Pottery			
Brown Ware	545	165	710
Paddle/Anvil	168	866	1,034

Note: Site totals determined by dominant ware types, i.e., those sites that include over 50% of either paddle/anvil or brown ware.

groups. To the extent that paddle and anvil wares are generally associated with Yuman-speaking groups of the lower Colorado River, it is likely that this occupation originated from the south. This southern center of gravity for Patayan settlement activity can be seen in the south-to-north distribution of Patayan versus brown ware sherds at Gold Butte. When we divide the study area into north and south zones (at the UTM 4020000 northing) where the greatest contrast exists, we find the distribution of Patayan-dominant sites and sherd frequencies that is shown in Table 8.5.

As can be seen in both site counts and total sherd frequencies, Patayan pottery is decidedly a southern manifestation, with 73 percent of all Patayan-dominated sites and 84 percent of all Patayan sherds identified in the southern zone. Conversely, brown ware is distributed in an almost inverse fashion, being dominant in the northern half.

Additional evidence for a late-dating Patayan occupation of Gold Butte is found in the obsidian source and hydration data sets. It is at this time when we see an influx of obsidian from sources to the southeast, from lands generally perceived as more traditional Yuman territory. Virtually all the hydration values associated with these Arizona glass sources cluster around 2.0 microns, indicating that this pattern is a Late Prehistoric phenomenon. The sample, however, is small, and most obsidian that dates to this time still emanates from the closer sources to the north and northwest (i.e., Kane Springs, Delamar Mountains, and Modena/Panaca Summit).

These data indicate an expansion of Patayan influence, if not territory, into Gold Butte sometime between AD 1000 and 1500. This influence appears to have emanated from settlements located to the south, along the Colorado River; but given the north-south gradient

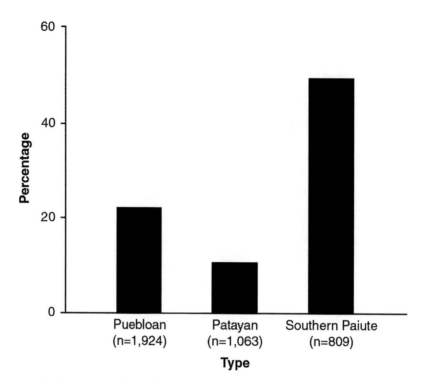

FIGURE 8.11. Percentage of total sherds from sites with only one pottery series represented.

of their pottery, not up the Virgin River corridor that bounds virtually the entire western and northern periphery of Gold Butte. Patayan control of Gold Butte appears to have been weakest to the north and strongest to the south.

The frequency distributions and co-occurrences of Puebloan, Patayan, and Southern Paiute ceramics within project site components may further explicate the temporal and cultural relationships between populations representing these three groups. Noteworthy in this regard are that brown ware sherds (Southern Paiute) tend to be in "stand-alone" contexts, that is, not associated with either Puebloan or Patayan wares. Figure 8.11 plots the frequency of sherds for each group recovered from sites with no "mixed" pottery assemblages. Fully half of all brown ware sherds recovered from the study area meet this criterion, whereas the Puebloan and Patayan sherds tend to occur in temporally mixed contexts.

On closer examination of this pattern, Patayan and Puebloan ceramics co-occur at 19 of the 33 systematically collected sites, and those 19 contexts yielded 88 percent of all Patayan sherds. Conversely, brown ware and Puebloan sherds co-occur at only 14 of the 33 sites, with 49 percent of the brown ware coming from these mixed contexts. Patayan and brown ware sherds seem to share the least affinity: they co-occur at only 12 sites (and always with Puebloan pottery present), with only

23 percent of brown ware coming from these contexts. In essence, Puebloan and Patayan pottery tend to co-occur at Gold Butte whereas brown ware is often found in separate contexts.

If our pottery chronologies are accurate, there was probably some temporal overlap associated with Puebloan and Patayan occupation of Gold Butte in the period from about AD 1000 to 1250. Patayan pottery, however, was not documented in middle Pueblo II contexts at Main Ridge (Lyneis 1992:77), although it appears in the very latest-dating Puebloan sites (Late Pueblo II to Pueblo III, i.e., about AD 1150–1250) in Moapa Valley (e.g., Mesa House).

The evidence at hand thus begs the issue as to the nature of Puebloan/Patayan interactions at Gold Butte—invaders, competitors, cooperators, trading partners? Here the strong spatial co-association of Patayan and Puebloan pottery discussed above may be significant. The high frequency at which these two pottery groups occur at the same sites implies a convergence of some combination of subsistence pursuits, settlement practices, social interactions, and/or exchange relationship. We know, for example, that they were both farming populations, and thus they needed to attend to the planting, harvesting, and storing of their crops along the major river corridors. Therefore, they did not permanently occupy Gold Butte and thus were probably not in direct and continuous competition for local resources. The resolution of the Gold Butte database probably prevents any further commentary or insight with regard to these possibilities. Suffice it to say that the overall pattern suggests some level of benign interaction between the two groups, as opposed to avoidance or open hostility.

The Southern Paiute

As we noted in Chapter 2, a dramatic population displacement is represented by the Southern Paiute expansion into southern Nevada, southern Utah, and northern Arizona, in areas formerly occupied by Puebloans. Although this intrusion probably postdated the collapse of the Puebloan occupation of the lower Virgin River Basin by as much as a century or more, it is now clear that Southern Paiute populations encountered an existing Patayan occupation at Gold Butte. Furthermore, the lack of Patayan III ceramics at Gold Butte strongly suggests that Southern Paiute had fully displaced Patayan populations by approximately AD 1500.

Under the same logic as above (i.e., a strong spatial co-association of the pottery groups infers a convergence of subsistence-settlement, social, or exchange relationships), the negative correlation between Patayan and brown ware strongly suggests a relatively low level of interaction, avoidance, or perhaps even conflict between the two groups. Indeed, it is hard to imagine how the abandonment of Gold Butte by the Patayan at approximately AD 1500 could have been accomplished without some level of conflict (Kelly and Fowler 1986:370).

The driving force behind this immigration appears to have been the Southern Paiute's unique "family band" foraging system, most famously described by Julian Steward (1938). Its adaptive resilience and competitive advantage over other cultural groups is described by Bettinger and Baumhoff (1982) as part of their Numic expansion hypothesis, in which, from a putative homeland in eastern California, the Numa expanded across the entire Great Basin and portions of the Southwest. At Gold Butte the Southern Paiute may well have been the first permanent residents in this hinterland. Unlike the Puebloans or the Patayan, they were not initially tied to agricultural plots along the Virgin, Muddy, or Colorado Rivers (or at least not until historic times [Kelly and Fowler 1986]).

Several aspects of Southern Paiute feature and assemblage structure at Gold Butte highlight this discontinuity in land-use practices. It should be reiterated at this point that our level of archaeological resolution was often not able to distinguish Southern Paiute from Patayan components, both of which fell into a more generic "Late Prehistoric" designation. However, we believe that many of the trends are so distinct as to identify the influence of the Southern Paiute in this final phase of prehistoric activity at Gold Butte.

As we saw in Figure 8.6, the lowest ratio of flaked stone tools to milling equipment at single-component survey sites occurred among Late Prehistoric components. Only in this interval does milling equipment actually outnumber flaked stone tools. Along these same lines, virtually all Desert Side-notched points—arguably a Numa marker (Delacorte 2008)—found during the survey are associated with milling equipment. The ubiquity of milling equipment at these late-dating sites, as well as the more even balance of hunting implements and processing tools, suggests occupation by a small, gender-balanced residential group analogous to a family band. Finally, Southern Paiute painted rock art, limited almost exclusively to the Red Rock zone, is both less abundant and more modest in scale than earlier-dating styles, focusing on simple abstract elements with little emphasis on representational forms.

The Southern Paiute land-use system documented at Gold Butte also appears to have been sustained by the addition and intensified use of a series of lower-ranked resources, most notably agave. Most of the 19 radiocarbon-dated agave ovens at Gold Butte date to the Late Prehistoric period (Figure 8.3), and 10 out of 11 dated Late Prehistoric period ovens are younger than AD 1440, suggesting that these features are primarily a Southern Paiute manifestation. Indexed against flaked stone tools, the frequency of agave ovens also spikes in the Late Prehistoric period (Figure 8.9). Not surprisingly, charred agave remains are most abundant in flotation samples dating to this period (Figure 8.7b). Agave may have served as a critical early-season resource for the Southern Paiute, as it is best harvested in spring before it sends up its stalk. With regard to animal resources, the Southern Paiute, along with the Basketmaker III and Puebloan groups, appear to have relied on tortoise, and somewhat less on artiodactyls and rabbits (Figure 8.7a).

9 Summary and Conclusion

The prehistory of Gold Butte reminds us how far we've come from Jennings's conception of a stable Desert Culture, or even from the variation observed in the archaeological record in more recent scholarship. In this area of the Desert West, especially over the last several millennia, dramatic developments took place. We see the sudden appearance of farmers in the Virgin River Valley and the eclipse of Archaic populations (but the latter continuing to thrive just beyond the bounds of this river corridor). Full village and agricultural life develops over the span of a few hundred years, along with increasing integration with core population centers in the Southwest, only to completely vanish after a series of droughts and other cultural disruptions. The Patayan then hold sway for several hundred years but don't advance much beyond the Colorado River corridor. Lastly, the Numa arrive, not only occupying the Virgin River Valley and Gold Butte but overwhelming much of the northwestern quadrant of the Southwest.

This is a strong brew of historical contingency, in-place development, and external relationships, one that should be expected in a boundary land where the Great Basin, Colorado Plateau, and Mojave Desert meet. The complexity of these prehistoric boundaries has been the subject of recent scholarly attention, with the conclusion that such areas can't be understood without a full exploration of the interactions between adjoining regions. As Rhode points out (2012:12), boundary lands are where the spread of ideas and innovations, the establishment of economic ties (including resource sharing and exchange systems), the maintenance of group identity and kin networks, and the processes of migration and assimilation all play out.

Our approach has been to address these issues, to the extent possible, by looking at hinterlands adjoining the prehistoric settlements that clustered along the Virgin River, Moapa Valley, and Colorado River before, during, and after the Puebloan period. The thought here is that changes in settlement-subsistence and lifeways at core settlements along the riverine corridor have corresponding effects on the character and intensity of hinterland land use. Our theoretical approach is grounded in human behavioral ecology, but it is also here that foraging models run in to the welter of game-changing historical events that characterize this region. These two explanatory frameworks are, however, not incompatible, and as we have argued elsewhere (Hildebrandt et al. 2010:686), major historical events serve to periodically "reshuffle the deck," creating new contexts on which the systematic processes of behavioral ecology continue to operate.

With this background and approach in mind, we briefly summarize the major findings of the Gold Butte project:

- Evidence for Paleo/Early Archaic occupation, as it is for all subsequent occupations, is concentrated in and near outcrops of Red Rock sandstone. In various locations this sandstone traps seasonal run-off in small basins (tenajas). Thus it is water, or lack thereof, that explains much of the prehistoric settlement history at Gold Butte.
- Late Archaic/BM-II assemblages contain the highest ratios of hunting gear (projectile points, bifaces) to milling equipment and the highest relative frequencies of artiodactyl remains. This emphasis on hunting, particularly of bighorn sheep, is reflected in

the rock art dating to this time and appears related to the late Holocene rise of logistical hunting observed throughout the Desert West.

- Dietary remains recovered from project area components suggest a transition from a pre-agriculture, seasonally restricted reliance on highly ranked resources (i.e., bighorn sheep and pinyon taken in the fall) to a reliance on a seasonally variable suite of small seeds, tortoise, and agave. The overall Puebloan profile of dietary remains suggests use of Gold Butte primarily during episodes of reduced or failed agricultural harvests.

- Using a variety of proxies for measuring land use, we find that settlement intensity appears to have ramped up during the Late Archaic, Basketmaker II–III, and Pueblo I periods; decreased during the Puebloan II, III, and immediate post-Puebloan period; and again increased during the middle and latter part of the Late Prehistoric period (post–AD 1400).

- Based on the seriation of Puebloan ceramic wares from dated site and room blocks located in the Virgin River Basin, the Gold Butte profile for these wares indicates a dominant Basketmaker III–Pueblo I occupation.

These last two findings together form the basis for our inference that Basketmaker III–Pueblo I times along the Virgin River corridor were characterized by Barlow's informal plant-and-harvest farming strategy, whereas the Pueblo II and III periods represent the more intensive typical agricultural pattern. The commitment to intensive agriculture during the latter periods necessarily limited foraging opportunities for wild foods at Gold Butte.

- Based on the project-wide distribution of Puebloan trade wares, the primary trade corridor from the Southwest core zones to major settlements located along the Virgin and Muddy rivers may have passed through the center of Gold Butte.

- Patayan occupation at Gold Butte probably occurred toward the very end of the Puebloan period and ended by AD 1500, mostly in the southern zone of the project area. Co-associations of Puebloan and Patayan ceramics in site components suggest that the interactions of these two groups before the collapse of the former may have been relatively benign.

- Although previous studies have identified a distinct "West Virgin" Puebloan rock art style, the current investigation suggests that this is simply the result of the admixture of Patayan motifs with Puebloan elements commonly observed to the east. These results speak to the cultural unity of Puebloan groups rather than intragroup differentiation.

- By AD 1500 the Southern Paiute had displaced the Patayan from Gold Butte. The infrequent co-association of Patayan and Southern Paiute ceramics at site components suggests that this displacement may not have been benign. The Numic family-band lifeway may have allowed the Southern Paiute to occupy Gold Butte year round, perhaps facilitated by an intensified spring agave harvest.

These results make up only an initial framework of working hypotheses and possible answers to some of the research questions raised in this book, as well as those applicable to any boundary land study. Much remains to be learned. Thus, for example, the Gold Butte record is largely silent as to why the Puebloans abandoned the Virgin River Basin at AD 1250, but perhaps we now have a fuller appreciation of the processes and changes wrought by this transition. Final answers to this question and others will no doubt require us to rethink many of the conclusions presented here. This is the way of archaeology.

References Cited

Adams, Karen R., and Suzanne K. Fish
2006   Southwest Plants. In *Environment, Origins, and Popu-lation*, edited by Bruce Smith, pp. 284–291. Hand-book of North American Indians, Vol. 3, William C. Sturtevant, general editor. Smithsonian Institution, Washington, D.C.

Ahlstrom, Richard V. N.
2005   *Desert Oasis: The Prehistory of Clark County Wetlands Park, Henderson, Nevada.* HRA Papers in Archae-ology No. 4. HRA Conservation Archaeology, Las Vegas.

Aikens, C. Melvin
1966   *Virgin-Kayenta Cultural Relationships.* University of Utah Anthropological Papers No. 79. University of Utah Press, Salt Lake City.

Allen, Mary
1998   Description of the Grand Canyon Polychrome Style. In *Travels with a River Guide.* http://www.xmission.com/~mkallen/gcpoly/gcpsynopsis.html.

Allison, James R.
1996   Comments on the Impacts of Climatic Variability and Population Growth on Virgin Anasazi Cultural Development. *American Antiquity* 61:414–418.
2000   Craft Specialization and Exchange in Small-Scale Societies: A Virgin Anasazi Case Study. Unpub-lished Ph.D. dissertation, Department of Anthro-pology, Arizona State University, Tempe.

Allison, James R., and Arlene Coleman
1998   Ceramic Analysis. In *Excavation/Mitigation Report of Three Sites near Hildale, Utah: 42WS2195, 42WS2196, and AZB:1:35 (BL) (the Reservoir Site),* compiled by Asa S. Neilson. Baseline Data Research Report No. 98-8. Orem, Utah.

Altschul, Jeffrey H., and Helen C. Fairley
1989   *Man, Models, and Management: An Overview of the Archaeology of the Arizona Strip and the Management of Its Cultural Resources.* Technical Report No. 93-19. Statistical Research, Tucson.

Ambler, J. Richard, and Mark Q. Sutton
1989   The Anasazi Abandonment of the San Juan Drain-age and the Numic Expansion. *North American Archaeologist* 10(1):39–54.

Amsden, Charles
1937   The Lake Mohave Artifacts. In *The Archaeology of Pleistocene Lake Mohave: A Symposium,* by Eliza-beth W. C. Campbell et al., pp. 51–98. Papers No. 11. Southwest Museum, Los Angeles.

Anderson, M. Kat
2005   *Tending the Wild: Native American Knowledge and the Management of California's Natural Resources.* University of California Press, Berkeley.

Barlow, K. Renee
2005   A Formal Model for Predicting Agriculture among the Fremont. In *Behavioral Ecology and the Tran-sition to Agriculture,* edited by Douglas J. Kennett and Bruce Winterhalder, pp. 87–102. University of California Press, Berkeley.

Basgall, Mark E.
1988   *Archaeology of the Komodo Site, an Early Holocene Occupation in Central-Eastern California.* Anthropo-logical Papers No. 21. Nevada State Museum, Carson City.
1990   Hydration Dating of Coso Obsidian: Problems and Prospects. Paper presented at the 24th Annual Meeting of the Society for California Archaeology, Foster City.
1993   Early Holocene Prehistory of the North-Central Mojave Desert. Unpublished Ph.D. dissertation, De-partment of Anthropology, University of California, Davis.
1996   *A Brief Cultural History of the National Training Center, Fort Irwin, San Bernardino County, California.* Department of Anthropology, California State Uni-versity, Sacramento. Submitted to the Department of Defense, National Training Center, Fort Irwin, California.
2000   The Structure of Archaeological Landscapes in the North-Central Mojave Desert. In *Archaeological Pas-sages: A Volume in Honor of Claude Nelson Warren,* edited by Joan S. Schneider, Robert M. Yohe II, and Jill K. Gardner, pp. 123–138. Publications in Archae-ology No. 1. Western Center for Archaeology and Paleontology, Hemet, California.

Basgall, Mark E., and Matthew C. Hall
1992   Fort Irwin Archaeology: Emerging Perspectives on Mojave Desert Prehistory. *Society for California Archaeology Newsletter* 26(5):1–7.
1994a   *Status Report on Cultural Resources Management at*

the *National Training Center, Fort Irwin, 1993–1994: An Addendum to the Fort Irwin Historic Preservation Plan.* Department of Anthropology, University of California, Davis, and Archaeological Research Unit, University of California. Submitted to the Department of Defense, National Training Center, Fort Irwin, California.

1994b *Archaeological Investigations at Goldstone (CA-SBR-2348): A Middle Holocene Occupation Complex in the North-Central Mojave Desert, California.* Department of Anthropology, University of California, Davis, and Archaeological Research Unit, University of California. Submitted to the Department of Defense, National Training Center, Fort Irwin, California.

2000 Morphological and Temporal Variation in Bifurcate-Stemmed Dart Points of the Western Great Basin. *Journal of California and Great Basin Anthropology* 22(2):237–276.

Basgall, Mark E., and Kelly R. McGuire

1988 *The Archaeology of CA-INY-30: Prehistoric Culture Change in the Owens Valley, California.* Far Western Anthropological Research Group, Davis, California. Submitted to California Department of Transportation, Sacramento.

Baumhoff, Martin A., and J. S. Byrne

1959 Desert Side-Notched Points as a Time Marker in California. *University of California Archaeological Survey Reports* 48:32–65. Berkeley.

Bean, Lowell John

1978 Cahuilla. In *California*, edited by Robert F. Heizer, pp. 575–587. Handbook of North American Indians, Vol. 8, William C. Sturtevant, general editor. Smithsonian Institution, Washington, D.C.

Bean, Lowell John, and Katherine Siva Saubel

1972 *Temalpakh (from the Earth): Cahuilla Indian Knowledge and Usage of Plants.* Malki Museum Press, Banning, California.

Beard, L. S.

1991 Preliminary Geologic Map of the Devils Throat Quadrangle, Clark County, Nevada. USGS Open-File Report 91-132.

1992 Preliminary Geologic Map of the St. Thomas 7.5-Minute Quadrangle, Clark County, Nevada. USGS Open-File Report 92-326.

1993 Preliminary Geologic Map of the Whitney Pocket 7.5-Minute Quadrangle, Clark County, Nevada. USGS Open-File Report 93-716.

Beck, Charlotte

1995 Functional Analysis and the Differential Persistence of Great Basin Dart Forms. *Journal of California and Great Basin Anthropology* 17(2):222–241.

Bedwell, Stephen F.

1973 *Fort Rock Basin: Prehistory and Environment.* University of Oregon Books, Eugene.

Bennyhoff, James A., and Richard E. Hughes

1987 *Shell Bead and Ornament Exchange Networks between California and the Western Great Basin.* Anthropological Papers Vol. 64, No. 2. American Museum of Natural History, New York.

Berry, Claudia F., and Michael S. Berry

1986 Chronological and Conceptual Models of the Southwestern Archaic. In *Anthropology of the Western Desert: Essays in Honor of Jesse D. Jennings*, edited by Carol J. Condie and Don D. Fowler, pp. 252–327. University of Utah Anthropological Papers No. 110. University of Utah Press, Salt Lake City.

Bettinger, Robert L.

1980 Explanatory/Predictive Models of Hunter/Gatherer Adaptation. *In Advances in Archaeological Method and Theory*, Vol. 3, edited by Michael B. Schiffer, pp. 189–255. Academic Press, New York.

1989 *The Archaeology of Pinyon House, Two Eagles, and Crater Middens: Three Residential Sites in Owens Valley, Eastern California.* Anthropological Papers No. 67. American Museum of Natural History, New York.

1999 From Traveler to Processor: Regional Trajectories of Hunter/Gatherer Sedentism in the Inyo-Mono Region, California. In *Fifty Years since Viru: Theoretical Advances and Contributions of Settlement Pattern Studies in the Americas*, edited by Brian R. Billman and Gary M. Feinman, pp. 39–55. Smithsonian Institution Press, Washington, D.C.

Bettinger, Robert L., and Martin A. Baumhoff

1982 The Numic Spread: Great Basin Cultures in Competition. *American Antiquity* 47:485–503.

Bettinger, Robert L., and Robert E. Taylor

1974 Suggested Revisions and Archaeological Sequences of the Great Basin and Interior Southern California. *Nevada Archaeological Survey Research Report* 5:1–26.

Billat, Lorna Beth, James D. Wilde, and Richard K. Talbot

1992 *Archaeological Testing and Excavation of Five Western Anasazi Sites along State Route 9, East of Virgin City, Utah.* Technical Series No. 90-20. Brigham Young University Museum of Peoples and Cultures, Provo, Utah.

Bird, Douglas W., Rebecca Bliege Bird, and Brian F. Codding

2009 In Pursuit of Mobile Prey: Martu Hunting Strategies and Archaeofaunal Interpretation. *American Antiquity* 74(1):3–29.

Blair, Lynda M.

2004 *Firebrand Cave: Scope of Work for Task Order FAA 990008.* Harry Reid Center for Environmental Studies, University of Nevada, Las Vegas. Prepared for Las Vegas Field Office, Bureau of Land Management.

2006 *Firebrand Cave: An Archaic Ceremonial Site in Southern Nevada.* BLM Report 5-2516. Harry Reid Center for Environmental Studies, University of Nevada,

Las Vegas, and Bureau of Land Management, Las Vegas District Office.

Bleed, Peter
1986 The Optimal Design of Hunting Weapons: Maintainability or Reliability? *American Antiquity* 51(4): 737–747.

Bradley, W. Glen, and James Everett Deacon
1967 The Biotic Communities of Southern Nevada. In *Quaternary History of Tule Springs, Nevada*, pp. 201–295. Nevada State Anthropological Papers No. 13.

Brenzel, Kathleen N. (editor)
1995 *Sunset Western Garden Book.* 6th ed. Sunset Publishing Corporation, Menlo Park, California.

Brooks, Richard H., D. O. Larson, K. Olson, J. King, G. King, R. Leavitt, and P. Anderson
1975 *Prehistoric and Historic Research along the Navajo-McCullough Transmission Line Right-of-Way.* Report No. 4-2-1. Nevada Archaeological Survey, University of Nevada, Las Vegas.

Broughton, Jack M., and Frank E. Bayham
2003 Showing Off, Foraging Models, and the Ascendance of Large-Game Hunting in the California Middle Archaic. *American Antiquity* 68(4):783–789.

Broughton, Jack M., David A. Byers, Reid A. Bryson, William Eckerle, and David B. Madsen
2008 Did Climatic Seasonality Control Late Quaternary Artiodactyl Densities in Western North America? *Quaternary Science Reviews* 27:1916–1937.

Buck, Paul E., and Anne DuBarton
1994 Archaeological Investigations at Pintwater Cave, Nevada, during the 1963–64 Field Season. *Journal of California and Great Basin Anthropology* 16(2):221–242.

Byers, David A., and Jack M. Broughton
2004 Holocene Environmental Change, Artiodactyl Abundances, and Human Hunting Strategies in the Great Basin. *American Antiquity* 69:235–256.

Byrd, Brian, D. Craig Young, Kelly McGuire, and William R. Hildebrandt
2005 *Archaeological and Geomorphic Investigations along the South Edge of the Avawatz Mountains: A 6,945 Acre Archaeological Survey and Evaluation of 58 Sites.* Far Western Anthropological Research Group, Davis, California. Submitted to Directorate of Public Works, U.S. Army National Training Center, Fort Irwin, California.

Campbell, Elizabeth W. C., and William H. Campbell
1935 *The Pinto Basin Site.* Papers No. 9. Southwest Museum, Los Angeles.

Carpenter, John P., Guadalupe Sanchez, and Maria Elisa Villalpando C.
2005 The Late Archaic/Early Agricultural Period in Sonora, Mexico. In *The Late Archaic across the Borderlands: From Foraging to Farming*, edited by Bradley J. Vierra, pp. 13–40. University of Texas Press, Austin.

Castleton, Kenneth B.
1987 *Petroglyphs and Pictographs of Utah: The South, Central, West and Northwest (Volume 2).* Utah Museum of Natural History, Salt Lake City.

Castleton, Kenneth B., and David B. Madsen
1981 The Distribution of Rock Art Elements and Styles in Utah. *Journal of California and Great Basin Anthropology* 3(2):163–175.

Christensen, Don D., and Jerry Dickey
2001 The Grapevine Style of the Eastern Mojave Desert of California and Nevada. In *American Indian Rock Art*, Vol. 27, edited by Alanah Woody and Steven M. Freers, pp. 185–200. American Rock Art Research Association, Tucson, AZ.

2004 The Esplanade Style: A Reappraisal of Polychrome Rock Art in the Grand Canyon Region, Arizona. In *American Indian Rock Art*, Vol. 30, edited by Joseph T. O'Connor and Reinaldo Morales, pp. 69–85. American Rock Art Research Association, Tucson, AZ.

Christenson, Andrew L.
1994 Test of Mean Ceramic Dating Using Well-Dated Kayenta Anasazi Sites. *Kiva* 59(3):297–317.

Clark, Jeanne Wilson
1984 *Prehistoric Settlement in the Moapa Valley.* Anthropological Papers No. 19. Nevada State Museum, Carson City.

Cole, Sally J.
1990 *Legacy on Stone: Rock Art of the Colorado Plateau and Four Corners Region.* Johnson Books, Boulder, Colorado.

2004 Origins, Continuities, and Meaning of Barrier Canyon Style Rock Art. In *New Dimensions in Rock Art Studies*, edited by Ray T. Matheny, pp. 7–78. Occasional Paper Series No. 9. Brigham Young University, Provo, Utah.

Colton, Harold S.
1952 *Pottery Types of the Arizona Strip and Adjacent Areas in Utah and Nevada.* Ceramic Series No. 1. Museum of Northern Arizona, Flagstaff.

Copeland, James M., and Richard E. Fike
1988 Fluted Projectile Points in Utah. *Utah Archaeology* 1:5–28.

Cordell, Linda S.
1997 *Archaeology of the Southwest.* Academic Press, San Diego.

Coulam, Nancy J., and Alan R. Schroedl
2004 Late Archaic Totemism in the Greater American Southwest. *American Antiquity* 69(1):41–62.

Cummings, Linda Scott
2008 Paleobotanical Analysis. In *Main Ridge 2006 Research Project: Condition Assessments, Test Excavations, and Data Analyses for the UNLV Fall 2006 Field School*, edited by Karen G. Harry, pp. 67–96. Submitted to the Lake Mead National Recreation Area

by the Department of Anthropology and Ethnic Studies and the Public Lands Institute, University of Nevada, Las Vegas.

Davis, C. Alan, and Gerald A. Smith

1981　*Newberry Cave.* San Bernardino County Museum Association, Redlands, California.

Dean, Rebecca

2001　Social Change and Hunting during the Pueblo III to Pueblo IV Transition, East-Central Arizona. *Journal of Field Archaeology* 28:271–285.

2007　Hunting Intensification and the Hohokam "Collapse." *Journal of Anthropological Archaeology* 26: 109–132.

Delacorte, Michael G.

1997　*Culture Change along the Eastern Sierra Nevada/ Cascade Front, Volume I: History of Investigations and Summary of Findings.* Far Western Anthropological Research Group, Davis, California. Submitted to the Tuscarora Gas Transmission Company, Reno, Nevada.

1999　*The Changing Role of Riverine Environments in the Prehistory of the Central-Western Great Basin: Data Recovery Excavations at Six Prehistoric Sites in Owens Valley, California.* Far Western Anthropological Research Group, Davis, California. Submitted to California Department of Transportation, District 9, Bishop.

2008　Desert Side-Notched Points as a Numic Population Marker in the Great Basin. In *Avocados to Millingstones: Papers in Honor of D. L. True,* edited by Georgie Waugh and Mark E. Basgall, pp. 111–136. Monographs in California and Great Basin Anthropology No. 5. Archaeological Research Center, California State University, Sacramento.

Desert Research Institute

1996　*Ethnographic and Ethnohistoric Overview of the Nellis Air Force Base and Range Complex, Nevada.* Prepared for the Native American Interaction Program, SAIC, Las Vegas, Nevada.

Dickey, Jerry, and Don D. Christensen

2009　A Preliminary Comparison of Colorado Plateau Rock Art: Barrier Canyon and the Esplanade Styles. In *American Indian Rock Art,* Vol. 35, edited by James D. Keyser, David Kaiser, George Poetschat, and Michael W. Taylor, pp. 101–120. American Rock Art Research Association, Tucson, Arizona.

Diehl, Michael W., and Jennifer A. Waters

2005　Aspects of Optimization and Risk during the Early Agricultural Period in Southeastern Arizona. In *Behavioral Ecology and the Transition to Agriculture,* edited by Douglas J. Kennett and Bruce Winterhalder, pp. 63–86. University of California Press, Berkeley.

Dobyns, Henry F., and Robert C. Euler

1976　*The Walapai People.* Indian Tribal Services, Phoenix.

Dougherty, Paul J.

2009　*Wound Ballistics: Minié Ball vs. Full Metal Jacketed Bullets—A Comparison of Civil War and Spanish American War Firearms.* Military Medicine, http://findarticles.com/p/articles/ mi_qa3912/is_200904 /ai_n31964160/. Accessed April 2010.

Duke, Daron, Amy Gilreath, and Jerome King

2004　*Cultural Resources Survey (Random and Non-random) of the Sloan NCA, Clark County, Nevada.* BLM Report No. 5-2480. Submitted to Bureau of Land Management, Las Vegas Field Office.

Ellis, Robert R., Richard H. Brooks, Eileen Green, and Teri Swearingen

1982　*A Cultural Resources Survey and Limited Test Excavations in the Vicinities of Quail Point, Bunkerville Ridge, and Hackberry Spring, Virgin and Mormon Mountains, Southern Nevada.* BLM Report No. 5-1107 (HRC 2-5-8). Submitted to Bureau of Land Management, Las Vegas Field Office.

Elston, Robert G., and Kenneth Juell

1987　*Archaeological Investigations at Panaca Summit.* Cultural Resource Series No. 10. Bureau of Land Management, Reno, Nevada.

Elston, Robert G., Susan Stornetta, Daniel P. Dugas, and Peter Mires

1994　*Beyond the Blue Roof: Archaeological Survey on Mt. Rose Fan and Northern Steamboat Hills.* Intermountain Research. Prepared for Toiyabe National Forest, Sparks, Nevada.

Emslie, Steven D., Jim I. Mead, and Larry Coats

2005　Split-Twig Figurines in Grand Canyon, Arizona: New Discoveries and Interpretations. *Kiva* 61(2): 145–173.

Euler, Robert C.

1964　Southern Paiute Archaeology. *American Antiquity* 29(3):379–381.

1978　Archaeological and Paleobiological Studies at Stanton's Cave, Grand Canyon National Park, Arizona— A Report of Progress. In *Abstracts and Reviews of Research and Exploration Authorized under Grants from the National Geographic Society during the Year 1969,* pp. 141–162. National Geographic Society Research Reports, Washington, D.C.

Euler, Robert C., George J. Gumerman, Thor V. N. Karlstrom, Jeffrey S. Dean, and Richard H. Hevly

1979　The Colorado Plateaus: Cultural Dynamics and Paleoenvironment. *Science* 205:1089–1101.

Fitzwater, Robert

1967　Localities 3 and 4A, Tule Springs, Nevada. In *Pleistocene Studies in Southern Nevada,* edited by H. M. Wormington and D. Ellis, pp. 353–364. Anthropological Papers No. 13. Nevada State Museum, Carson City.

Fowler, Catherine S.

1995 Some Notes on Ethnographic Subsistence Systems in Mojavean Environments in the Great Basin. *Journal of Ethnobiology* 15(1):99–117.

Fowler, Donald D.

1973 *S. M. Wheeler's The Archaeology of Etna Cave, Lincoln County, Nevada: A Reprint.* Publications in the Social Sciences No. 7. University of Nevada, Desert Research Institute, Reno.

Fowler, Donald D., Robert C. Euler, and Catherine S. Fowler

1969 *John Wesley Powell and the Anthropology of the Canyon Country.* U.S. Geological Survey Professional Paper No. 670. Department of the Interior, Washington, D.C.

Fowler, Catherine S., and Donald D. Fowler

1981 The Southern Paiute: AD 1400–1776. In *The Protohistoric Period in the North American Southwest, AD 1450–1700*, edited by D. R. Wilcox and B. Masse, pp. 12–162. Anthropological Research Papers No. 24. Arizona State University, Tempe.

Fowler, Donald D., and Jesse D. Jennings

1982 Great Basin Archaeology: A Historical Overview. In *Man and the Environment in the Great Basin*, edited by David B. Madsen and James F. O'Connell, pp. 105–120. SAA Papers No. 2. Society for American Archaeology, Washington, D.C.

Fowler, Don D., and David B. Madsen

1986 Prehistory of the Southeastern Area. In *Great Basin*, edited by Warren L. d'Azevedo, pp. 173–182. Handbook of North American Indians, Vol. 11, William C. Sturtevant, general editor. Smithsonian Institution, Washington, D.C.

Fowler, Donald D., David B. Madsen, and Eugene Hattori

1973 *Prehistory of Southeastern Nevada.* Publications in the Social Sciences No. 6. Desert Research Institute, Reno.

Geib, Phil R.

1996 *Glen Canyon Revisited.* University of Utah Anthropological Papers No. 119. University of Utah Press, Salt Lake City.

Geib, Phil R., and Kimberly Spurr

2000 The Basketmaker II–III Transition on the Rainbow Plateau. In *Foundations of Anasazi Culture: The Basketmaker-Pueblo Transition*, edited by Paul F. Reed, pp. 175–200. University of Utah Press, Salt Lake City.

Gilreath, Amy J.

1999 *Chronological Assessment of the Coso Rock Art Landmark—An Obsidian Hydration Analysis.* Far Western Anthropological Research Group, Davis, California. Submitted to the Environmental Project

Office, Naval Air Weapons Station, China Lake, California.

2003 Rock Art. In *Archaeological Testing of Fourteen Prehistoric Sites within the Coso Target Range at Naval Air Weapons Station, China Lake*, by William R. Hildebrandt and Allika Ruby. Far Western Anthropological Research Group, Davis, California. Submitted to Southwest Division, Naval Facilities Engineering Command, San Diego, California.

2009 *Gypsum Cave Revisited.* Far Western Anthropological Research Group, Davis, California. BLM Report No. CR5-2462-4(P). Submitted to Bureau of Land Management, Las Vegas Field Office.

Gilreath, Amy J., and William R. Hildebrandt

1997 *Prehistoric Use of the Coso Volcanic Field.* Contributions No. 56. University of California Archaeological Research Facility, Berkeley.

2008 Coso Rock Art within Its Archaeological Context. *Journal of California and Great Basin Anthropology* 28(1):1–22.

Gilreath, Amy J., William R. Hildebrandt, Kelly R. McGuire, Jerome King, D. Craig Young, Ron Reno, Charles Zeier, and Virginia Bengston

2006 *Research and Class II Sample Survey Design for the Gold Butte Study Area, Clark County, Nevada.* Far Western Anthropological Research Group, Davis, California, Zeier & Associates, and Bengston Consulting. BLM Report No. 5-2617. Submitted to Bureau of Land Management, Las Vegas Field Office.

Grant, Campbell, James W. Baird, and J. Kenneth Pringle

1968 *Rock Drawings of the Coso Range, Inyo County, California.* Publication No. 4. Maturango Museum, China Lake, California.

Haarklau, Lynn, Lynn Johnson, and David L. Wagner

2005 *Fingerprints in the Great Basin: The Nellis Air Force Base Regional Obsidian Sourcing Study.* Prepared for the U.S. Army Corps of Engineers, Fort Worth District, Fort Worth, Texas.

Hall, Matthew C.

1983 Late Holocene Hunter-Gatherers and Volcanism in the Long Valley–Mono Basin Region: Prehistoric Culture Change in the Eastern Sierra Nevada. Unpublished Ph.D. dissertation, Department of Anthropology, University of California, Riverside.

1992 *Final Report on the Archaeology of Tiefort Basin, Fort Irwin, San Bernardino County, California.* Far Western Anthropological Research Group, Davis, California. Report submitted to the U.S. Army Corps of Engineers, Los Angeles.

Hall, Matthew C., and Robert J. Jackson

1989 Obsidian Hydration Rates in California. In *Current Directions in California Obsidian Studies*, edited by

Richard E. Hughes. Contributions No. 48. University of California Archaeological Research Facility, Berkeley.

Harrington, Mark R.

1930 Introduction. In *Archaeological Explorations in Southern Nevada: Report of the First Sessions Expedition, 1929*, pp. 1–25. Papers No. 4. Southwest Museum, Los Angeles.

1933 *Gypsum Cave, Nevada: Report of the Second Sessions Expedition.* Papers No. 8. Southwest Museum, Los Angeles.

1937 Some Early Pit-Dwellings in Nevada. *Masterkey* 11:122–124. Southwest Museum, Los Angeles.

Harrington, Mark R., and Ruth D. Simpson

1961 *Tule Springs, Nevada, with Other Evidence of Pleistocene Man in North America.* Papers No. 18. Southwest Museum, Los Angeles.

Harry, Karen G.

2008 *Main Ridge 2006 Research Project: Condition Assessments, Test Excavations, and Data Analyses for the UNLV Fall 2006 Field School.* Submitted to the Lake Mead National Recreation Area by the Department of Anthropology and Ethnic Studies and the Public Lands Institute, University of Nevada, Las Vegas.

Haury, Emil M.

1965 Shell. In *Excavations at Snaketown: Material Culture,* edited by Harold S. Gladwin, Emil M. Haury, E. B. Sayles, and Nora Gladwin, pp. 135–151. University of Arizona Press, Tucson.

Hayden, Irwin

1930 Mesa House. In *Archaeological Explorations in Southern Nevada: Report of the First Sessions Expedition, 1929*, pp. 26–92. Papers No. 4. Southwest Museum, Los Angeles.

Hayes-Gilpin, Kelly

2001 *Virtual Ceramic Manual—Northern Arizona University.* http://www2.nau.edu/~sw-ptry.

Heaton, T. J., P. G. Blackwell, and C. E. Buck

2009 A Bayesian Approach to the Estimation of Radiocarbon Calibration Curves: The IntCal09 Methodology. *Radiocarbon* 51(4):1151–1164.

Hedges, Ken

1973 Rock Art in Southern California. *Pacific Coast Archaeological Society Quarterly* 9(40):1–28.

1982 Great Basin Rock Art Styles: A Revisionist View. In *American Indian Rock Art,* vols. 7 and 8, pp. 205–211. American Rock Art Research Association.

2002 Rock Art Styles in Southern California. In *American Indian Rock Art,* Vol. 25, edited by Steven M. Freers, pp. 25–40. American Rock Art Research Association.

2003 Rock Art Sites at Palo Verde Point. In *A View across the Cultural Landscape of the Lower Colorado Desert: Cultural Resource Investigations for the North Baja Pipeline Project,* by James H. Cleland and Rebecca M.

Apple, pp. 179–204. EDAW, San Diego, California. Prepared for TetraTech, Santa Ana, California, and North Baja Pipeline, Portland, Oregon.

Heizer, Robert F., and Martin A. Baumhoff

1961 The Archaeology of Two Sites at Eastgate, Churchill County, Nevada. *University of California Anthropological Records* 20(4):119–149.

1962 *Prehistoric Rock Art of Nevada and Eastern California.* University of California Press, Berkeley.

Heizer, Robert F., Martin A. Baumhoff, and C. William Clewlow Jr.

1968 Archaeology of South Fork Shelter (NV-El-11), Elko County, Nevada. *University of California Archaeological Survey Reports* 71:1–58.

Heizer, Robert F., and C. William Clewlow Jr.

1973 *Prehistoric Rock Art of California.* Ballena Press, Ramona, California.

Hildebrandt, William R., and Kelly R. McGuire

2002 The Ascendance of Hunting during the California Middle Archaic: An Evolutionary Perspective. *American Antiquity* 67(2):231–256.

Hildebrandt, William R., Kelly R. McGuire, and Jeffrey S. Rosenthal

2010 Human Behavioral Ecology and Historical Contingency: A Comment on the Diablo Canyon Archaeological Record. *American Antiquity* 75(3):686.

Hildebrandt, William R., and Allika Ruby

1999 *Archaeological Survey of the Coso Target Range: Evidence for Prehistoric and Early Historic Use of the Pinyon Zone at Naval Air Weapons Station, China Lake, Inyo County, California.* Far Western Anthropological Research Group, Davis, California. Submitted to Engineering Field Activity, West, Naval Facilities Engineering Command, San Bruno, California.

Hill, Jane H.

2003 The Uto-Aztecan Presence in the US Southwest: The Evidence from Language. In *Oral Tradition, Language, and Archaeology in Mutual Support—Southwestern USA and Northern Mexico,* co-chaired by L. S. Teague and H. Lomawaima, 5th World Archaeological Congress, Washington, D.C.

Hockett, Bryan S.

1995 Chronology of Elko Series and Split Stemmed Points from Northeastern Nevada. *Journal of California and Great Basin Anthropology* 17(1):41–53.

Holmer, Richard N.

1986 Common Projectile Points of the Intermountain West. In *Anthropology of the Desert West: Essays in Honor of Jesse D. Jennings,* edited by Carol J. Condie and Don D. Fowler, pp. 89–116. University of Utah Anthropological Papers No. 110. University of Utah Press, Salt Lake City.

Holmes, Elaine, and Anne Carter

2009 The Dynamic Duo: Superheroes of Pahranagat

Rock Art. *Utah Rock Art*, Vol. 28. Utah Rock Art Research Association, Salt Lake City.

Huckell, Bruce, Lisa Huckell, and Karl K. Benedict

2002 Maize Agriculture and the Rise of Mixed Farming-Foraging Economies during the Second Millennium BC. In *Traditions, Transitions, and Technologies: Themes in Southwestern Archaeology*, edited by Sarah H. Schlanger, pp. 136–159. University Press of Colorado, Boulder.

Huffman, Jim

1993 Between River and Rim: A Comparative View of Subsistence Systems in Grand Canyon, Arizona. Unpublished Master's thesis, Department of Anthropology, Northern Arizona University, Flagstaff.

Hughes, Richard E.

1986 *Diachronic Variability in Obsidian Procurement Patterns in Northeastern California and Southcentral Oregon*. University of California Publications in Anthropology Vol. 17. University of California Press, Berkeley.

Hughes, Richard E., and Randall Milliken

2007 Prehistoric Material Conveyance. In *California Prehistory: Colonization, Culture, and Complexity*, edited by Terry L. Jones and Kathryn Klar, pp. 259–271. Altamira Press, New York.

Hull, Kathleen

1994 Chapter 7: Obsidian Studies. In *Kern River Pipeline Cultural Resources Data Recovery Report: Utah, Volume III, Syntheses and Conclusions*, by Dames & Moore, Las Vegas, Nevada. Submitted to Federal Energy Regulatory Commission for Kern River Gas Transmission Company.

Janetski, Joel C.

1993 The Archaic to Formative Transition North of the Anasazi: A Basketmaker Perspective. In *Anasazi Basketmaker: Papers from the 1990 Wetherill–Grand Gulch Symposium*, edited by V. M. Atkins, pp. 223–241. Cultural Resource Series No. 24. Bureau of Land Management, Salt Lake City, Utah.

1994 Recent Transitions in Eastern Great Basin Prehistory. In *Across the West: Human Population Movement and the Expansion of the Numa*, edited by David B. Madsen and David R. Rhode, pp. 157–178. University of Utah Press, Salt Lake City.

2002 Trade in the Fremont Society: Contexts and Contrasts. *Journal of Anthropological Archaeology* 21(3): 344–370.

Janetski, Joel C., and James D. Wilde

1989 A Preliminary Report of Archaeological Excavations at Antelope Cave and Rock Canyon Shelter, Northwestern Arizona. *Utah Archaeology* 2(1): 88–106.

Jenkins, Dennis L.

1981 Cliff's Edge: A Pueblo I Site on the Lower Virgin River. Unpublished Master's thesis, Department of Anthropology, University of Nevada, Las Vegas.

Jennings, Jesse D.

1980 *Cowboy Cave*. University of Utah Anthropological Papers No. 104. University of Utah Press, Salt Lake City.

Jensen, Eva A.

2002 Exploring the Shivwits Production Zone. Unpublished Master's thesis, Department of Anthropology, University of Nevada, Las Vegas.

Jensen, Eva A., Gregory R. Seymour, and Laureen M. Perry

2006 "…From a Lump of Clay…": Replicating Prehistoric Pottery in the Moapa Valley. In *Beginnings: Proceedings of the 2005 Three Corners Conference*, edited by Mark C. Slaughter, Gregory R. Seymour, and Laureen M. Perry, pp. 275–299. Distributed by Nevada Archaeological Association, Las Vegas.

Jones, Robert C., and Susan R. Edwards

1994 A Clovis Point on the Nevada Test Site. *Nevada Archaeologist* 12:18–23.

Kelly, Isabel T.

1934 Southern Paiute Bands. *American Anthropologist* 36(4):548–560.

1936 Chemehuevi Shamanism. In *Essays in Anthropology Presented to A. L. Kroeber in Celebration of His Sixtieth Birthday, June 11, 1936*, edited by Robert Lowie, pp. 129–142. University of California Press, Berkeley.

1976 Southern Paiute Ethnography. In *Paiute Indians II*, compiled and edited by David Agee Horr, pp. 11–223. Garland Publishing, New York.

Kelly, Isabel T., and Catherine S. Fowler

1986 Southern Paiute. In *Great Basin*, edited by Warren L. d'Azevedo, pp. 368–397. Handbook of North American Indians, Vol. 11, William C. Sturtevant, general editor. Smithsonian Institution, Washington, D.C.

Kelly, Robert L.

1988 Three Sides of a Biface. *American Antiquity* 53:717–734.

2001 *Prehistory of the Carson Desert and Stillwater Mountains*. University of Utah Anthropological Papers No. 123. University of Utah Press, Salt Lake City.

Kennett, Douglas J., and Bruce Winterhalder

2005 Behavioral Ecology and the Transition from Hunting and Gathering to Agriculture. In *Behavioral Ecology and the Transition to Agriculture*, edited by Douglas J. Kennett and Bruce Winterhalder, pp. 1–21. University of California Press, Berkeley.

Kidd, Kenneth E., and Martha A. Kidd

1970 A Classification System for Glass Beads for the Use of Field Archaeologists. In *Canadian Historic Sites Occasional Papers in Archaeology and History* 1:45–89. Ottawa.

King, Chester D.

1990 *Evolution of Chumash Society: A Comparative Study of Artifacts Used for Social System Maintenance in*

the Santa Barbara Channel Region before AD 1804.
Garland Publishing, New York.

Kolvet, Renee Corona, Richard Deis, Susan Stornetta, and
Mary K. Rusco

2000   *A Stratified Archaeological Sample of Low Elevation
Areas on Nellis Air Force Range, Nevada.* Prepared
for the U.S. Army Corps of Engineers, Fort Worth
District, Fort Worth, Texas.

Kroeber, Alfred L.

1935   *Walapai Ethnography.* Memoirs No. 42. American
Anthropological Association, Menasha, Wisconsin.

Lanning, Edward P.

1963   The Archaeology of the Rose Spring Site (INY-372).
*University of California Publications in American
Archaeology and Ethnology* 49(3):327–336.

Larson, Daniel O.

1987   An Economic Analysis of the Differential Effects
of Population Growth and Climatic Variability
among Hunters and Gatherers and Food Producers.
Unpublished Ph.D. dissertation, Department of Anthropology, University of California, Santa Barbara.

Larson, Daniel O., and Joel Michaelsen

1990   Impacts of Climatic Variability and Population
Growth on Virgin Branch Anasazi Cultural Developments. *American Antiquity* 55(2):227–49.

LeBlanc, Steven A.

1999   *Prehistoric Warfare in the American Southwest.* University of Utah Press, Salt Lake City.

Lockwood, Daniel W.

1872   Appendix A: Report of Daniel W. Lockwood, First
Lieutenant of Engineers. In *Preliminary Report
Concerning Explorations and Surveys Principally in
Nevada and Arizona,* edited by George M. Wheeler,
pp. 62–76. Government Printing Office, Washing-
ton, D.C.

Longwell, C. R., E. H. Pampeyan, Ben Bowyer, and
R. J. Roberts

1965   *Geology and Mineral Deposits of Clark County, Nevada.* Nevada Bureau of Mines and Geology Bulletin
No. 62. University of Nevada, Reno.

Lowie, Robert H.

1924   *Notes on Shoshonean Ethnography.* Anthropological
Papers Vol. 20, Pt. 3. American Museum of Natural
History, New York.

Lyle, D. A.

1872   Appendix B: Report of Second Lieutenant D. A.
Lyle, Second United States Artillery. In *Preliminary
Report Concerning Explorations and Surveys Princi-
pally in Nevada and Arizona,* edited by George M.
Wheeler, pp. 76–90. Government Printing Office,
Washington, D.C.

Lyneis, Margaret M.

1982   Prehistory in the Southern Great Basin. In *Man and
the Environment in the Great Basin,* edited by David
B. Madsen and James F. O'Connell, pp. 172–185. SAA

Papers No. 2. Society for American Archaeology,
Washington, D.C.

1986   A Spatial Analysis of Anasazi Architecture, AD 950–
1150, Moapa Valley, Nevada. *Kiva* 52:53–74.

1988   Tizon Brown Ware and the Problems Raised by
Paddle-and-Anvil Pottery in the Mojave Desert.
Journal of California and Great Basin Anthropology
10(2):146–155.

1992   *The Main Ridge Community at Lost City: Virgin Ana-
sazi Architecture, Ceramics and Burials.* University of
Utah Anthropological Papers No. 117. University of
Utah Press, Salt Lake City.

1994   East and Onto the Plateaus? Archaeological Visibility of the Numic Spread in Southern Nevada, Northern Arizona, and Southern Utah. In *Across the West:
Human Population Movement and the Expansion of
the Numa,* edited by David B. Madsen and David R.
Rhode, pp. 141–149. University of Utah Press, Salt
Lake City.

1995   The Virgin Anasazi, Far Western Puebloans. *Journal
of World Prehistory* 9:199–241.

2000   Life at the Edge: Pueblo Settlements in Southern
Nevada. In *The Archaeology of Regional Interaction:
Religion, Warfare and Exchange across the American
Southwest; Proceedings of the 1996 Southwest Sym-
posium,* edited by Michelle Hegmon, pp. 257–274.
University Press of Colorado, Boulder.

2004   Ceramics from the Sloan NCA, Appendix E. In *Cultural Resources Survey (Random and Non-random)
of the Sloan NCA, Clark County, Nevada,* by Daron
Duke, Amy Gilreath, and Jerome King. BLM Report
No. 5-2480. Submitted to Bureau of Land Management, Las Vegas Field Office.

2007   Surprising Shifts: Changes in Middle Pueblo II
Pottery Frequencies at the Yamashita Sites. Paper
presented at the Three Corners Conference, Las
Vegas, Nevada.

Lyneis, Margaret M. (assembler)

2008   New and Revised Prehistoric Pueblo Pottery Wares
and Types from North and West of the Colorado
River: Gray Wares from the Western Area. *Pottery
Southwest* 27(1), pt. 2:3–20.

Lyneis, Margaret M., Mary K. Rusco, and Keith Myhrer

1989   *Investigations at Adam 2 (26CK2059): A Mesa House
Phase Site in the Moapa Valley, Nevada.* Anthro-
pological Papers No. 22. Nevada State Museum,
Carson City.

Mabry, Jonathan B.

1998   Archaic Complexes of the Late Holocene. In *Paleo-
indian and Archaic Sites in Arizona,* edited by J. B.
Mabry, pp. 73–88. Technical Report 97-7. Center for
Desert Archaeology, Tucson.

2005   Changing Knowledge and Ideas about the First
Farmers in Southeastern Arizona. In *The Late Archaic across the Borderlands: From Foraging to Farm-*

ing, edited by Bradley J. Vierra, pp. 41–83. University of Texas Press, Austin.

Madsen, David B., and David R. Rhode (editors)

1994 *Across the West: Human Population Movement and the Expansion of the Numa.* University of Utah Press, Salt Lake City.

Madsen, David B., and Steven R. Simms

1998 The Fremont Complex: A Behavioral Perspective. *Journal of World Prehistory* 12(3):255–336.

Madsen, Rex E.

1977 *Prehistoric Ceramics of the Fremont.* Ceramic Series No. 6. Museum of Northern Arizona, Flagstaff.

Marmaduke, William S.

1978 Prehistoric Culture in Trans Pecos, Texas: An Ecological Explanation. Unpublished Ph.D. dissertation, Department of Anthropology, University of Texas, Austin.

Matson, R. G.

2005 Many Perspectives but a Consistent Pattern: Comments on Contributions. In *The Late Archaic: Across the Borderlands from Foraging to Farming,* edited by Bradley J. Vierra, pp. 279–299. University of Texas Press, Austin.

McFadden, Douglas A.

1994 Virgin Anasazi Settlement on the Grand Staircase. Paper presented at the Western Anasazi Symposium, Utah Professional Archaeological Council, Cedar City, March 13, 1993 (revised).

McGuire, Kelly R.

1997 Fort Sage Uplands and Spanish Springs Valley. In *Culture Change along the Eastern Sierra Nevada/ Cascade Front,* Vol. 4. Coyote Press, Salinas, California.

2002 Obsidian Production in Northeastern California and the Northwestern Great Basin: Implications for Land Use. In *Boundary Lands: Archaeological Investigations along the California–Great Basin Interface,* by Kelly R. McGuire, pp. 85–104. Anthropological Papers No. 24. Nevada State Museum, Carson City.

McGuire, Kelly R., Michael G. Delacorte, and Kimberly Carpenter

2004 *Archaeological Excavations at Pie Creek and Tule Valley Shelters, Elko County, Nevada.* Anthropological Papers No. 25. Nevada State Museum, Carson City.

McGuire, Kelly R., and William R. Hildebrandt

2005 Re-thinking Great Basin Foragers: Prestige Hunting and Costly Signaling during the Middle Archaic Period. *American Antiquity* 70(4):695–712.

McGuire, Kelly R., William R. Hildebrandt, and Kimberly Carpenter

2007 Costly Signaling and the Ascendance of No-Can-Do Archaeology: A Reply to Codding and Jones. *American Antiquity* 72(2):358–365.

McGuire, Thomas R.

1983 Walapai. In *Southwest,* edited by Alfonso Ortiz,

pp. 25–37. Handbook of North American Indians, Vol. 10, William C. Sturtevant, general editor. Smithsonian Institution, Washington, D.C.

Menzies, M. A., J. R. Arculus, M. G. Best, S. C. Bergman, S. N. Ehrenberg, A. J. Irving, M. F. Roden, and D. J. Schulze

1987 A Record of Subduction Process and Within-Plate Volcanism in Lithospheric Xenoliths of the Southwestern USA. In *Mantle Xenoliths,* edited by P. H. Nixon, pp. 59–74. John Wiley and Sons, New York.

Miller, Wick R.

1986 Numic Languages. In *Great Basin,* edited by Warren L. d'Azevedo, pp. 98–106. Handbook of North American Indians, Vol. 11, William C. Sturtevant, general editor. Smithsonian Institution, Washington, D.C.

Milliken, Randall T., and James A. Bennyhoff

1993 Temporal Changes in Beads as Prehistoric California Grave Goods. In *There Grows a Green Tree: Essays in Honor of D. A. Fredrickson,* edited by Gregory White, Patricia Mikkelsen, William R. Hildebrandt, and Mark E. Basgall, pp. 381–395. Center for Archaeological Research at Davis No. 11. University of California, Davis.

Myhrer, Keith M., and Margaret M. Lyneis

1985 *The Bovine Bluff Site: An Early Puebloan Site in the Upper Moapa Valley.* Technical Report No. 15. Bureau of Land Management, Reno, Nevada.

Nussbaum, Jesse L.

1922 A Basket-Maker Cave in Kane County, Utah. In *Indian Notes and Monographs: A Series of Publications Relating to the American Aborigines,* edited by F. W. Hodge. Museum of the American Indian, Heye Foundation, New York.

Oeschger, H., U. Siegenthaler, U. Schotterer, and A. Gugelmann

1975 A Box Diffusion Model to Study the Carbon Dioxide Exchange in Nature. *Tellus* 27:168–192.

Ortiz, Alfonso

1979 Key to Tribal Territories. In *Southwest,* edited by Alfonso Ortiz, p. ix. Handbook of North American Indians, Vol. 9, William C. Sturtevant, general editor. Smithsonian Institution, Washington, D.C.

Pandolf, K. B., B. Givoni, and R. F. Goldman

1977 Predicting Energy Expenditure with Loads while Standing or Walking Very Slowly. *Journal of Applied Physiology* 43:577–581.

Perkins, R. F.

1967 Clovis-Like Points in Southern Nevada. *Nevada Archaeological Survey Reporter* 9:9–11.

1968 Folsom and Sandia Points from Clark County. *Nevada Archaeological Survey Reporter* 2(4):4–5.

Perry, Laureen M.

2003 Ceramic Analysis. In *The Coral Canyon Project Archaeological Investigations in the St. George Basin, Southwestern Utah,* edited by Heidi Roberts and

Richard V. N. Ahlstrom, pp. 201–212. HRA Papers in Archaeology No. 3. HRA Conservation Archaeology, Las Vegas, Nevada.

Pickrell, Jordan

2005   Diachronic Patterns in Faunal Exploitation. In *The Kern River 2003 Expansion Project, Vol. IV, Chapter 30*, by Alan D. Reed, Matthew Seddon, and Heather Stettler. SWCA Environmental Consultants, Salt Lake City, Utah, and Alpine Archaeological Consultants, Montrose, Colorado. Submitted to Federal Energy Regulatory Commission for Kern River Gas Transmission Company.

Plog, Stephen

1997   *Ancient Peoples of the American Southwest.* Thames and Hudson, London.

Plog, Stephen, and Jeffrey Hantman

1986   Multiple Regression Analysis as a Dating Method in the American Southwest. In *Spatial Organization and Exchange*, edited by S. Plog, pp. 87–113. Southern Illinois University Press, Carbondale.

Rafferty, Kevin A.

1984   *Cultural Resources Overview of the Las Vegas Valley.* Technical Report No. 13. Bureau of Land Management, Reno, Nevada.

Reed, Alan D., Matthew Seddon, and Heather Stettler

2005   Project Background and Approach. In *The Kern River 2003 Expansion Project, Vol. I.* SWCA Environmental Consultants, Salt Lake City, Utah, and Alpine Archaeological Consultants, Montrose, Colorado. Submitted to Federal Energy Regulatory Commission for Kern River Gas Transmission Company.

Reimer, P. J., M. G. L. Baillie, E. Bard, A. Bayliss, J. W. Beck, P. G. Blackwell, Ramsey C. Bronk, C. E. Buck, G. S. Burr, R. L. Edwards, M. Friedrich, P. M. Grootes, T. P. Guilderson, I. Hajdas, T. J. Heaton, A. G. Hogg, K. A. Hughen, K. F. Kaiser, B. Kromer, F. G. McCormac, S. W. Manning, R. W. Reimer, D. A. Richards, J. R. Southon, S. Talamo, C. S. M. Turney, J. van der Plicht, and C. E. Weyhenmeyer

2009   IntCal09 and Marine09 Radiocarbon Age Calibration Curves, 0–50,000 Years cal BP. *Radiocarbon* 51(4):1111–1150.

Rhode, David R.

1990   On Transportation Costs of Great Basin Resources: An Assessment of the Jones-Madsen Model. *Current Anthropology* 31:413–419.

2012   Intergroup and Interregional Interactions in and around the Intermountain West. In *Meetings at the Margins: Prehistoric Cultural Interactions in the Intermountain West*, edited by David Rhode. University of Utah Press, Salt Lake City.

Rhode, David R., and David B. Madsen

1994   Direct Dating of Brownware Ceramics Using Thermoluminescence and Its Relation to the Numic

Spread. In *Across the West: Human Population Movement and the Expansion of the Numa*, edited by David B. Madsen and David R. Rhode, pp. 124–131. University of Utah Press, Salt Lake City.

Riddell, Francis A.

1960   *Honey Lake Paiute Ethnography.* Anthropological Papers No. 4. Nevada State Museum, Carson City.

Roberts, Heidi R., and Richard V. N. Ahlstrom

2000   *Fragile Past: Archaeological Investigations in Clark County Wetlands Park, Nevada.* Report 00-03. HRA Conservation Archaeology. Report prepared for Southern Nevada Water Authority, Las Vegas, and Bureau of Reclamation, Boulder City, Nevada.

Rose, Martin R.

1989   Present and Past Environmental Conditions. In *Man, Models and Management: An Overview of the Archaeology of the Arizona Strip and the Management of Its Cultural Resources*, edited by Jeffrey H. Altschul and Helen C. Fairley. Technical Report No. 93-19. Statistical Research, Tucson.

Rowe, Susanne

2002a   Evidence for Virgin Anasazi Presence in the Las Vegas Valley and Adjacent Areas. Master's thesis, University of Nevada, Las Vegas.

2002b   A Design Analysis of Decorated Sherds from the Yamashita-5 Site in Moapa Valley, Nevada. Manuscript in possession of author.

Ruby, Allika, and Amy J. Gilreath

2006   *Class III Inventory of the Nevada Power Storage Yard and Ponds Expansion Project at Reid Gardner Facility, Clark County, Nevada.* Far Western Anthropological Research Group, Davis, California. Submitted to Bureau of Land Management, Las Vegas Field Office.

Ruby, Allika, Amy J. Gilreath, and Jerome King

2005   *Mitigation of Site 26CK4247 in Northern Las Vegas Valley, Clark County, Nevada.* Far Western Anthropological Research Group, Davis, California. Submitted to Bureau of Land Management, Las Vegas Field Office.

Sakai, Sachiko

2000   Explaining Changes in Subsistence Strategies and Settlement Patterns among the Virgin Branch Anasazi through Ceramic Provenance Study Using Inductively Coupled Plasma–Mass Spectrometry. Unpublished Master's thesis, Department of Anthropology, California State University, Long Beach.

Schaafsma, Polly

1971   *The Rock Art of Utah.* Peabody Museum of Archaeology and Ethnology, Harvard University, Cambridge. Reprinted 1994 by University of Utah Press, Salt Lake City.

1980   *Indian Rock Art of the Southwest.* School of American Research, Santa Fe, New Mexico.

Schroeder, Albert H.

1953a A Few Sites in Moapa Valley, Nevada. *Masterkey* 27(1):18–24. Southwest Museum, Los Angeles.

1953b A Few Sites in Moapa Valley, Nevada—II. *Masterkey* 27(2):62–68. Southwest Museum, Los Angeles.

1979 Prehistory: Hakataya. In *Southwest*, edited by Alfonso Ortiz, pp. 100–107. Handbook of North American Indians, Vol. 9, William C. Sturtevant, general editor. Smithsonian Institution, Washington, D.C.

Schroth, Adelia B.

1994 The Pinto Point Controversy in the Western United States. Unpublished Ph.D. dissertation, Department of Anthropology, University of California, Riverside.

Seddon, Matthew T.

2005 A Revised Relative Obsidian Hydration Chronology for Wild Horse Canyon, Black Rock Area, and Panaca Summit/Modena Obsidian: Interpreting Obsidian Hydration Results within the Framework of a Relative Chronology. In *The Kern River 2003 Expansion Project, Vol. IV, Chapters 24–25*, by Alan D. Reed, Matthew Seddon, and Heather Stettler. SWCA Environmental Consultants, Salt Lake City, Utah, and Alpine Archaeological Consultants, Montrose, Colorado. Submitted to Federal Energy Regulatory Commission for Kern River Gas Transmission Company.

Seymour, Gregory R.

1997 A Reevaluation of Lower Colorado Buff Ware Ceramics: Redefining the Patayan in Southern Nevada. Unpublished Master's thesis, Department of Anthropology and Ethnic Studies, University of Nevada, Las Vegas.

2001 *Cultural Resource Management Plan for the Las Vegas Springs Preserve, Clark County, Nevada.* Report prepared for the Las Vegas Springs Preserve, Las Vegas, Nevada.

Seymour, Gregory R., and Laureen Perry

1998 *A Guide to the Ceramic Type Collection at the Harry Reid Center for Environmental Studies, University of Nevada, Las Vegas, and the Bureau of Reclamation.* Report No. 1-3-31. Harry Reid Center, University of Nevada, Las Vegas.

Shutler, Richard, Jr.

1961 *Lost City: Pueblo Grande de Nevada.* Anthropological Papers No. 5. Nevada State Museum, Carson City.

1967 Cultural Chronology in Southern Nevada and Archaeology of Tule Springs. In *Pleistocene Studies in Southern Nevada*, edited by H. M. Wormington and D. Ellis, pp. 298–308. Anthropological Papers No. 13. Nevada State Museum, Carson City.

Spencer, William

2005 Various Essays and Editorials concerning Paiutes and the Washington Palm. http://www.xeri.com /Moapa/. Accessed August 2006.

Stein, Walter T.

1967 Locality 1 (C1-244), Tule Springs, Nevada. In *Pleistocene Studies in Southern Nevada*, edited by H. M. Wormington and D. Ellis, pp. 307–329. Anthropological Papers No. 13. Nevada State Museum, Carson City.

Steward, Julian H.

1938 *Basin-Plateau Aboriginal Sociopolitical Groups.* Smithsonian Institution Bureau of American Ethnology Bulletin No. 120. Government Printing Office, Washington, D.C. Reprinted 1997 by University of Utah Press, Salt Lake City.

Stoffle, Richard W., and Michael J. Evans

1976 Resource Competition and Population Change: A Kaibab Paiute Ethnohistorical Case. *Ethnohistory* 23(2):173–197.

Stoffle, Richard W., and M. Nieves Zedeño

2001 Historical Memory and Ethnographic Perspectives on the Southern Paiute Homeland. *Journal of California and Great Basin Anthropology* 23(1):229–248.

Stuiver, M., and T. F. Braziunas

1993 Modeling Atmospheric 14C Influences and 14C Ages of Marine Samples to 10,000 BC. *Radiocarbon* 35(1):137–189.

Sutton, Mark Q.

1987 A Consideration of the Numic Spread. Unpublished Ph.D. dissertation, Department of Anthropology, University of California, Riverside.

Szuter, Christine R., and Frank E. Bayham

1989 Sedentism and Animal Procurement among the Desert Horticulturalists of the North American Southwest. In *Farmers and Hunters: The Implications of Sedentism*, edited by Susan Kent, pp. 67–78. Cambridge University Press, Cambridge.

Talma, A. S., and J. C. Vogel

1993 A Simplified Approach to Calibrating C14 Dates. *Radiocarbon* 35(2):317–332.

Thomas, David Hurst

1981 How to Classify the Projectile Points from Monitor Valley, Nevada. *Journal of California and Great Basin Anthropology* 3:7–43.

1983 *The Archaeology of Monitor Valley 2: Gatecliff Shelter.* Anthropological Papers Vol. 59, Part 1. American Museum of Natural History, New York.

Tipps, Betsy L.

1995 *Holocene Archaeology near Squaw Butte, Canyonlands National Park, Utah.* Selections from the Division of Cultural Resources No. 7. Rocky Mountain Region, National Park Service, Denver, Colorado.

Tuohy, Donald R.

1986 Portable Art Objects. In *Great Basin*, edited by Warren L. d'Azevedo, pp. 227–237. Handbook of North

American Indians, Vol. 11, William C. Sturtevant, general editor. Smithsonian Institution, Washington, D.C.

Turner, Christy G., II
1963 *Petrographs of the Glen Canyon Region.* Bulletin No. 38. Glen Canyon Series No. 4. Museum of Northern Arizona, Flagstaff.
1971 Revised Dating for Early Rock Art of the Glen Canyon Region. *American Antiquity* 36(4):469–471.

Vaughan, Sheila J., and Claude N. Warren
1987 Toward a Definition of Pinto Points. *Journal of California and Great Basin Anthropology* 9:199–213.

Vierra, Bradley J.
2005 Late Archaic Stone Tool Technology from Across the Borderlands. In *The Late Archaic: Across the Borderlands from Foraging to Farming*, edited by Bradley J. Vierra, pp. 187–218. University of Texas Press, Austin.

Walling, Barbara A., Richard A. Thompson, Gardiner F. Dalley, and Dennis G. Weder
1986 *Excavations at Quail Creek.* Cultural Resources Series No. 20. Bureau of Land Management, Utah State Office, Salt Lake City.

Warren, Claude N.
1984 The Desert Region. In *California Archaeology*, edited by Michael J. Moratto, pp. 338–430. Academic Press, New York.
1986 Early Holocene Cultural Adaptations in the Mojave Desert, California. In *The Pleistocene Perspective*, Vol. 2, pp. 1–26. World Archaeological Conference, Southampton, U.K.

Warren, Claude N., and Robert H. Crabtree
1986 Prehistory of the Southwestern Area. In *Great Basin*, edited by Warren L. d'Azevedo, pp. 183–193. Handbook of North American Indians, Vol. 11, William C. Sturtevant, general editor. Smithsonian Institution, Washington, D.C.

Watkins, Chris
2006 Parowan Pottery and Fremont Complexity: Late Formative Ceramic Production and Exchange. Unpublished Master's thesis, Department of Anthropology, Brigham Young University, Provo. Available at http://contentdm.lib.byu.edu/cdm/ref/collection/ETD/id/603.

Watson, James
2008 Faunal Analysis. In *Main Ridge 2006 Research Project: Condition Assessments, Test Excavations, and Data Analyses for the UNLV Fall 2006 Field School*, edited

by Karen G. Harry, pp. 53–65. Submitted to the Lake Mead National Recreation Area by the Department of Anthropology and Ethnic Studies and the Public Lands Institute, University of Nevada, Las Vegas.

White, William G.
2002 *Cultural Resource Plan for the Protection and Management of Rock Art Resources, Clark County, Nevada.* BLM Report No. 5-2426. Submitted to Bureau of Land Management, Las Vegas Field Office.

Willig, Judith A., and C. Melvin Aikens
1988 The Clovis-Archaic Interface in Far Western North America. In *Early Human Occupation in Far Western North America: The Clovis-Archaic Interface*, edited by J. A. Willig, C. M. Aikens, and J. L. Fagan, pp. 1–40. Anthropological Papers No. 21. Nevada State Museum, Carson City.

Winslow, Diane L.
2004 Possibly One of the Earliest, and Not Necessarily One of the Poorest: Luminescence Dating of Logandale Gray Ceramics from Black Dog Mesa. Paper presented at the 29th Biennial Great Basin Anthropological Conference, Sparks, Nevada.
2006 Pithouses, Pithouses, Pithouses: Basketmaker II Architecture at Black Dog Mesa. In *Beginnings: Proceedings of the 2005 Three Corners Conference*, edited by Mark C. Slaughter, Gregory R. Seymour, and Laureen M. Perry, pp. 229–248. Three Corners Conference, Las Vegas.

Winslow, Diane L., Lynda M. Blair, L. S. Cummings, Kathryn Puseman, R. L. Orndorff, J. Watson, and S. M. Wheeler
2003a *Mitigation: Black Dog Mesa Archaeological Complex (26CK5686/BLM 53-7216); Volume I, History and Project Overview.* Prepared for Bureau of Land Management, Las Vegas Field Office, and Nevada Power Company.
2003b *Mitigation: Black Dog Mesa Archaeological Complex (26CK5686/BLM 53-7216); Volume II, Black Dog Cave.* Prepared for Bureau of Land Management, Las Vegas Field Office, and Nevada Power Company.

Wohlgemuth, Eric
2004 The Course of Plant Food Intensification in Native Central California. Unpublished Ph.D. dissertation, Department of Anthropology, University of California, Davis.

Zeanah, David W.
2004 Sexual Division of Labor and Central Place Foraging: A Model for the Carson Desert of Western Nevada. *Journal of Anthropological Archaeology* 23:1–32.

Index

abstract designs, in rock art, 165, *175*, *176*

active displacement hypothesis, and Southern Paiute, 25

aeolian deposits, 8

agave and agave ovens: and diet of Southern Paiute, 17, 19, 217; importance of as food source, 210–11; and Late Prehistoric period, 79, 217; and radiocarbon dates, *48*; and Sheep Shelter (26CK8179), 146, 149, 154; and site types, 31; and summary of site reports, 159

Agave Ovens (26CK1991), 74–79

agriculture: local importance of in Basketmaker II–III period, 12–13; "plant and harvest" versus "typical" strategy of, 208–12, 219; and Southern Paiute, 15, 17–18, 19; and use of hinterland areas as research issue, 23. *See also* maize

Ahlstrom, Richard V. N., 11

Allison, James R., 10, 22, 54, 57, 62, 63, 201, 212

Altschul, Jeffrey H., 10, 15

animals. *See* artiodactyls; bighorn sheep; birds; carnivores; cattle; desert tortoise; fauna and faunal remains; horses; lagomorphs; lizards; tracks

anthropomorphs. *See* human forms

Archaeometrics (California), 32, 64

Archaic period. *See* Early Archaic; Late Archaic

artifact inventory: for Cedar Basin Midden (26CK6078/6095), 105–7; for Collapsed Rock Shelter (26CK3201), 86–90; for Dart Shaft Shelter (26CK8047), 144–45; for Dune Field (26CK8013), 139–41; for Ian's Rock Shelter (26CK6080/6081), 116–20; for Riverside Pithouse Village (26CK4891), 100–101; for Sheep Shelter (26CK8179), 152–54; summary of results from sites excavated in study, 155–59; for 26CK7994, 129–30. *See also* diagnostic artifacts; flaked stone and debitage; ground and battered stone artifacts; historic artifacts; pottery; projectile points; shell and shell artifacts

artiodactyls, and faunal remains at excavated sites, 90, 122, 130, 159, 161, 162, *163*, 164, 206. *See also* bighorn sheep

Asteraceae (sunflower family), 96

atlatl and dart weaponry, 144, 168, 169

awls, and bone artifacts, 119, 153, 159

Aztec sandstone, 8, 176, 179, 203, 205, 212

Azure Ridge, 7

Barlow, K. Renee, 23, 208, 210, 219

Barrier Canyon rock art style, 166, *167*, 168

Basgall, Mark E., 10, 11

Basketmaker II: and Cedar Basin Midden (26CK6078/6095), 105; and Collapsed Rock Shelter (26CK3201), 86, 88, *89*, 90, 91; and Dart Shaft Shelter (26CK8047), 144, 145, 146; duration of overlap with Late Archaic, 206; and Ian's Rock Shelter (26CK6080/6081), 110, 116, *118*, *119*, 122; and overview of cultural history of Gold Butte, 12–13; and rock art, *167*, 169–71, 172, 174, *175*, *180*, 186, *191*, *192*, *193*; subsistence-settlement patterns and lifeways during, 205–8; and 26CK7994, 126, 129–30, 131, 134

Basketmaker III: land-use intensity during, 201–3; and overview of cultural history of Gold Butte, 12–13; and Riverside Pithouse Village (26CK4891), 100; subsistence-settlement patterns and lifeways during, 208–14; and 26CK7994, 126

battered cobble artifacts. *See* ground and battered stone artifacts

Baumhoff, Martin A., 24, 52, 54, 165, 168, 217

Bean, Lowell John, 130

Beck, Charlotte, 52

Bennyhoff, James A., 63, 153

BetaAnalytic (Florida), 31

Bettinger, Robert L., 217

bifaces, and flaked stone tool types, 155, *157*, *158*

bighorn sheep: and faunal remains at excavated sites, 90, 122, 141, 154, 206; representations of in rock art, 165, 168, 171, 174, *175*, 176, 186, 207–8

birds: and fauna of Gold Butte, 10; in rock art, 169, 171, 174

blackbrush vegetation community, 9

Black Dog Cave, 53, 210

Black Dog Mesa complex, 12, 13

Black Tank, as obsidian source, 70, 115, 128

Boaretto, Elisabetta, 31

bone artifacts: from Ian's Rock Shelter (26CK6080/6081), 119, 120–21; from Sheep Shelter (26CK8179), 153; and summary of site reports, *156*

Boulder Gray ceramics, 57

boundary lands, and prehistory of Gold Butte, 218

bow and arrow: and rock art, 168; and Rosegate points, 53, 54; and technological change in Basketmaker II–III period, 13

Bradley, W. Glen, 8

brown ware: and Collapsed Rock Shelter (26CK3201), 85; and Dune Field (26CK8013), 141; frequency of and time span for in Gold Butte region, 55, 62; as signature of Southern Paiute presence, 15, 216, 217